Development of Nonverbal Behavior in Children

Edited by
Robert S. Feldman

With 21 Figures

Springer-Verlag   New York   Heidelberg   Berlin

Robert S. Feldman
Department of Psychology
University of Massachusetts—Amherst
Amherst, Massachusetts 01003, U.S.A.

Library of Congress Cataloging in Publication Data
Main entry under title:
Development of nonverbal behavior in children.

Includes bibliographies and index.
1. Nonverbal communication in children. I. Feldman,
Robert S. (Robert Stephen), 1947–
BF723.C57D47 1982   155.4'13   82-10547

Typeset by Publishers' Service, Bozeman, Montana
Printed and bound by R.R. Donnelley and Sons, Harrisonburg, Virginia
Printed in the United States of America

9 8 7 6 5 4 3 2 1

ISBN 0-387-90716-5 Springer-Verlag New York Heidelberg Berlin
ISBN 3-540-90716-5 Springer-Verlag Berlin Heidelberg New York

Development of Nonverbal Behavior in Children

Preface

When I organized a symposium on the development of nonverbal behavior for the 1980 meeting of the American Psychological Association, I was faced with an embarrassment of riches. Thinking about the many people who were doing important and interesting research in this area, it was hard to narrow down the choice to just a few. Eventually, I put together a panel which at least was representative of this burgeoning area of research.

In planning this volume two years later, I was faced with much the same predicament, except to an even larger degree. For, during that short period, the area of children's nonverbal behavior came to grow even larger, with more perspectives being brought to bear on the question of the processes involved in the development of children's nonverbal behavior. The present volume attempts to capture these advances which have occurred as the field of children's nonverbal behavior has moved from its own infancy into middle childhood.

The book is organized into five major areas, representative of the most important approaches to the study of children's nonverbal behavior: 1) Psychobiological and ethological approaches, 2) social developmental approaches, 3) encoding and decoding skill approaches, 4) discrepant verbal-nonverbal communication approaches, and 5) personality and individual difference approaches. The discreteness of these categories should not be overemphasized, as there is a good deal of overlap between the various approaches. Nonetheless, they do represent the major areas of interest in the field of the development of nonverbal behavior in children.

In the section on psychobiological and ethological approaches, the three chapters provide a comprehensive review of the major issues in the area. Camras presents a broad overview of the ethological orientation and shows the utility of such an approach. Buck and Zivin each address the basic issue (which runs through a number of chapters) of tracing the development of spontaneous, voluntary, and symbolic nonverbal communication. Buck does this by referring to a fascinating literature on cerebral lateralization. Zivin shows how the results of her own research lead to the development of a clear taxonomy of nonverbal signals.

The chapters in the social development section focus on the question of how the nature of social factors affects children's use of nonverbal behavior. Shennum and Bugental discuss developmental changes in the management of affect in facial and vocal channels under conditions calling for differential norms for the appropriateness of nonverbal expressivity. Saarni integrates work on the social and affective functions of nonverbal behavior and how children learn nonverbal display rules that facilitate social interaction.

The section on encoding and decoding skill approaches presents two chapters that hold the view that nonverbal behavior should be looked at as a skill that develops with increasing age. Morency and Krauss examine the development and relationship between encoding and decoding skills. DePaulo and Jordan use children's abilities to be deceptive nonverbally and to identify the deception of others to show how nonverbal behavioral skills develop with age.

Two chapters address the issue of how children learn to resolve communications that present discrepancies between two or more channels. Blanck and Rosenthal delineate age-related changes in decoding discrepant communications, and they describe the development of a new measure of verbal and nonverbal sensitivity. In an interesting methodological innovation, Volkmar and Siegel show that children's responses to discrepant messages can be analyzed using psychometric scaling techniques.

The final section of the book presents chapters that take an individual difference approach to children's nonverbal behavior. Feldman, White, and Lobato discuss how children's social skill abilities relate to their use and control of nonverbal behavior. Finally, Field presents some fascinating research on individual differences in nonverbal behavior in a difficult population to study: neonates and young infants.

The chapters represent the best theory and research in the field of children's nonverbal behavior, and this volume should prove useful to theoreticians in the field of psychology, communication, ethology, and anthropology. In addition, practitioners in more applied areas should find the research instructive.

In editing this book, I was fortunate to have extremely good cooperation from the chapter authors and from the staff of Springer-Verlag. I am grateful for their intellectual integrity and efforts. I am also thankful to my two outstanding typists, Jean Glenowicz and Kathleen Cleary. The ever-present contribution of my parents, Leah R. Brochstein and the late Saul D. Feldman, is acknowledged with love and gratitude. Finally, Kathy Vorwerk and Jonathan and Joshua Feldman provided constant support, love, and a practical understanding of children's nonverbal behavior, and I am always grateful to them.

Amherst, Massachusetts   ROBERT S. FELDMAN

Contents

Contributors

Peter D. Blanck, Department of Psychology and Social Relations, Harvard University, Cambridge, Massachusetts 02138, U.S.A.

Ross Buck, Department of Communication Sciences, University of Connecticut, Storrs, Connecticut 06268, U.S.A.

Daphne B. Bugental, Department of Psychology, University of California—Santa Barbara, Santa Barbara, California 93106, U.S.A.

Linda A. Camras, Department of Psychology, DePaul University, Chicago, Illinois, 60614, U.S.A.

Bella M. DePaulo, Department of Psychology, University of Virginia, Charlottesville, Virginia 22901, U.S.A.

Robert S. Feldman, Department of Psychology, University of Massachusetts—Amherst, Amherst, Massachusetts 01003, U. S. A.

Tiffany Field, Mailman Center for Child Development, University of Miami, Miami, Florida 33101, U.S.A.

Audrey Jordan, Department of Psychology, University of Virginia, Charlottesville, Virginia 22901, U.S.A.

Robert M. Krauss, Department of Psychology, Columbia University, New York, New York 10027, U.S.A.

Debra Lobato, Department of Psychology, University of Vermont, Burlington, Vermont 05401, U.S.A.

Nancy Lee Morency, Department of Psychology, Columbia University, New York, New York 10027, U.S.A.

Robert Rosenthal, Department of Psychology and Social Relations, Harvard University, Cambridge, Massachusetts 02138, U.S.A.

Carolyn Saarni, Department of Counseling, Sonoma State University, Rohnert Park, California 94928, U.S.A.

William A. Shennum, Department of Psychology, University of California—Santa Barbara, Santa Barbara, California 93106, U.S.A.

Alberta E. Siegel, Department of Psychiatry and Behavioral Sciences, Stanford University Medical Center, Stanford, California 94305, U.S.A.

Fred R. Volkmar, Yale University School of Medicine, Child Study Center, New Haven, Connecticut 06520, U.S.A.

John B. White, Department of Psychology, University of Massachusetts—Amherst, Amherst, Massachusetts 01003, U.S.A.

Gail Zivin, Departments of Psychiatry and Human Behavior, and of Family Medicine, Jefferson Medical College of Thomas Jefferson University, Philadelphia, Pennsylvania 19107, U.S.A.

Part One
Psychobiological and Ethological Approaches to Nonverbal Behavior

CHAPTER ONE

Ethological Approaches to Nonverbal Communication

Linda A. Camras

> *"He who admits . . . that the . . . habits of all animals have gradually evolved will look at the whole subject of Expression in a new and interesting light."*
>
> —Darwin (1872/1965)

Ethology is a branch of evolutionary biology which focuses on the behavioral, rather than the morphological, characteristics of animal species. Since ethologists originally restricted themselves to investigating nonhuman organisms, of necessity they developed a methodology particularly appropriate to the study of nonverbal behaviors. In recent years, researchers have begun to apply the concepts and methods of ethology to the study of humans, and especially human children. In this chapter, I will explore the contribution which an ethological approach can make to our understanding of children's facial expressions, one important form of nonverbal communication. I will begin by describing characteristics of the ethological approach, and contrasting it with the methods often used by psychologists. Following this, I will review selected ethological studies of children which have examined facial behavior. Lastly, I will describe my own work, focusing on the relationship between primate threat displays and children's use of facial expressions in a conflict situation.

General Characteristics of the Ethological Approach

Perhaps the most important characteristic of the ethological approach is its reliance on direct observation and careful description of behavior. Ethologists identify specific nonverbal actions or action patterns which then are subjected to further analysis. Such analysis may involve addressing a number of questions about the behavior (What is its phylogenetic origin? How is it interpreted by the observer?). However, what is important is that such questions are tied to identifiable nonverbal acts, not to nonverbal behavior as a global construct or an undescribed "black box" of behavior.

This emphasis on the identification and description of behavioral units stands in sharp contrast to the approach often used by psychologists studying nonverbal communication. Much work in psychology has proceeded without an attempt to specify precisely the elements of behavior which are the presumed target of analysis. For example, early investigators of emotional expression (e.g., Feleky, 1924; Woodworth, 1938) had subjects make judgments about photographs of actors attempting to express particular emotions. However, virtually no attempt was made to describe what the actors actually were producing or to identify those elements of the photograph which were responsible for the subjects' judgments. Similarly, many recent studies also have involved judgments of unspecified stimulus features of photographs or videotapes. Thus, in a study of emotion communication (Buck, 1975), adults viewed videotapes of children and were able to judge with significant accuracy the category of slide (e.g., familiar persons, strangers) which the children themselves were watching. However, no information was given about the children's behavior, and one can not determine whether adult judgments were based on the child's production of specific emotional expressions or on some behavior less uniquely affective, such as visual attention to the slide.

Ethology's concern with description of behavior reflects its close relationship to biology which has long emphasized careful description of morphological structure of organisms. Once specific behaviors have been identified, ethologists may seek explanations for those behaviors. Traditionally, explanations have been sought at four different levels of analysis: immediate causation, ontogeny, evolution (phylogeny), and survival value. Studies of immediate causation concentrate on identifying internal and external factors which induce the performance of a particular act. Motivational states such as fear or aggression are typically considered as internal causes, while environmental "sign stimuli" may be identified as external causes. Studies of ontogeny examine factors which determine the emergence of an act in the behavioral repertoire of an individual. Frequently such studies attempt to analyze the roles of innate and environmental influences on development. Investigations of evolution are concerned with the phylogenetic roots of behavior. Using the comparative method (comparing the behaviors of a number of related species), hypotheses are generated regarding the evolutionary origins and history of a behavior. Studies of survival value are directed toward elucidating a behavior's adaptive function. In the case of some acts, such as signals, the immediate function or effect also must be determined.

A Representative Review of Facial Expression Studies

Description and Causal Basis

Many of the early ethological studies of human nonverbal behavior focused on identification and description of behavior units. Thus, Blurton Jones (1971, 1972), Brannigan and Humphries (1972), Grant (1969), McGrew (1972), Smith and Connolly (1972), and Young and Decarie (1977) all published checklists of nonverbal actions they viewed in the course of naturalistic observation. In addition to describing nonverbal acts, these studies often provided information regarding temporal and situational relationships among nonverbal behaviors. For example, Blurton Jones (1972) reported that hitting and lowering of the brows are temporally related among nursery school children. Ethologists usually consider temporal relationships among behaviors to be evidence for a common causal basis (Hinde, 1974). Thus if one admits hitting to be an aggressive act for children, one might interpret Blurton Jones' finding as indicating that brow lowering also has aggression as its immediate cause. Although these early ethological studies should be interpreted cautiously due to the limited number of behavioral contexts which were observed, their data are considered useful for generating hypotheses about the immediate causation of the facial expressions they describe.

While most descriptive studies of children have focused on normal individuals, some investigators (Currie & Brannigan, 1970; Greenbaum, 1970; Hutt & Hutt, 1970; Hutt & Ounsted, 1970) have examined special populations, such as autistic children. In some cases, these investigators have adopted hypotheses regarding the causation of particular nonverbal acts based on findings from studies of normals. Assuming that the same factors cause the behavior when it is seen in their special population, the investigators formulate hypotheses about the motivations of their subjects. In the best known example of this strategy, Tinbergen (1974) proposed that the gaze aversion typically shown by autistic children is caused by and also signals their fear of social contact.

A few ethological studies have used experimental manipulation to investigate the causation of facial actions previously seen in the context of naturalistic observation. In these studies, the experimenter typically introduces various stimuli to the subject in a systematic fashion and observes the facial behavior which the subject produces. For example, using this strategy, Blurton Jones and Konner (1971) and Wheldall and Mittler (1976) conducted interesting, though inconclusive, experiments on the causes of eyebrow raising by children. A number of other investigators (Sroufe & Waters, 1976; Sroufe & Wunsch, 1972; Wolff, 1963) have attempted to determine the features of a stimulus configuration which are most effective in eliciting smiling in infants.

Ontogeny

Human ethologists have focused much of their effort on examining the roles of biological and environmental influences on the development of facial expressions. Extending earlier work by Goodenough (1932) and Thompson (1941), Freedman (1964), Charlesworth (1970), and Eibl-Eibesfeldt (1973) addressed the issue of innate vs. acquired facial behaviors by studying the expressions of congenitally blind children. These individuals are considered to be naturally deprived of the opportunity to learn to produce facial expressions and particularly to produce them appropriately in response to various stimulus situations. Both Freedman and Charlesworth compared the facial responses of blind and sighted children to stimulus events systematically introduced by the experimenter. Eibl-Eibesfeldt, on the other hand, preferred a more naturalistic approach. He studied facial expressions produced spontaneously by blind-deaf children in the course of their daily activities. Although some differences were observed in the behavior of blind vs. sighted children, in most respects their facial expressions appeared to be essentially the same. These studies are considered evidence for the role of innate influences on the development of facial behavior.

The development of facial expressions in normal sighted infants has also been investigated by several researchers. Using Ekman and Friesen's precise anatomically-based system for coding facial movement, Oster (1978) has determined that young infants can produce all the individual facial muscle movements produced by adults. Furthermore, a number of investigators (Hiatt, Campos, & Emde, 1979; Izard, Huebner, Risser, McGinnes, & Doughterty, 1980; Stenberg, Campos, & Emde, in press; Haviland, Note 4) have observed that infants produce emotional expressions similar to those described for older persons. The early appearance of expressions of emotions again argues for innate influence on the development of facial expressions, although the precise nature of this influence remains to be clarified.

Developmental studies of facial expression in older children generally have involved documentation of age changes in facial behavior. Abramovitch and Marvin (Note 1) studied two- to five-year-olds and found the older children to use a wider range of distinct facial expressions. Cheyne (1976) reported that use of social smiles increases from two-and-one-half to four-and-one-half years of age. Zivin (1977a, 1977b) has described complex developmental changes in the use of facial expressions which she reports to be associated with the successful or unsuccessful meeting of a "challenge" by nursery school children. Studies which elucidate the mechanisms underlying these observed changes remain to be carried out. However, Zivin believes that the age differences she found are due to learned modification of facial behavior by older children. Saarni's (1979) work on children's understanding of cultural display rules provides some initial, indirect evidence in support of this hypothesis.

Crosscultural studies can provide another source of data relevant to the question of innate vs. acquired facial expressions. That is, similarities in facial behavior by members of very diverse cultures would suggest that innate factors play an important (though not necessarily exclusive) role in development. Unfortunately, few systematic observational studies of facial expression in non-Western cultures have been conducted. Eibl-Eibesfeldt (1970, 1972) has studied some selected expressions (brow raises) in several diverse societies. However, more work is needed before we understand the extent and limits of crosscultural similarities in the development of facial communication.

Evolution

Few investigators since Darwin have speculated on the phylogeny of facial behavior. A notable exception to this is the work of van Hooff (1972) on the origins of smiling and laughter. By comparing the form and usage of smiling and laughter in humans with the expressive behaviors of other primates, van Hooff has constructed a hypothetical evolutionary history for these behaviors. Although van Hooff's argument rests on questionable assumptions regarding the evolution of facial musculature (Ekman, Note 3), his hypothesis has motivated several interesting studies on situational use of smiles and laughter (Kraut & Johnson, 1979; Lockard, Fahrenbruch, Smith, & Morgan, 1977).

Chevalier-Skolnikov (1973) has compared a wider range of human facial expressions of emotion to the expressions of other primate species. While not tracing detailed evolutionary histories, her work suggests phylogenetic bases for a number of human emotional expressions. A third investigator who has discussed the evolution of facial expression is Andrew (1963, 1972). Andrew's approach differs from that of van Hooff and Chevalier-Skolnikov in one important respect. He rejects an analysis of facial expression that assumes exclusive causal associations between facial expressions and underlying motivational or emotional states such as fear or aggression. Instead, he sees facial expressions as being related to self-regulative functions such as protection of one's facial structures by movements which shield them (pressing the lips together to cover the teeth). However, like van Hooff and Chevalier-Skolnikov, Andrew believes that human facial expressions evolved from the expressions of prehuman primates.

Survival Value

Direct investigation of facial behavior's survival value for humans would be a virtually impossible task. However, reasonable speculations regarding the adaptive value of facial expressions may be made based on studies of their direct functions. Facial expressions may function by means of their effects on individuals who observe them and also by means of the direct alterations they create in the physiognomy or perhaps even internal state of the expresser.

The effects of facial expressions on the individuals who perceive them can be indirectly assessed in studies that require observers to interpret or make judgments about expressions. The assumption, of course, is that one's interpretation of the facial expression will affect one's behavior or attitude toward the expresser. Such indirect methods for assessing the effects of facial expressions generally have been eschewed by ethologists who favor direct observation rather than verbal reports. However, recently it has been argued that verbal reports should be admissible as useful evidence by ethologists interested in human behavior (Marvin & Mossler, 1976; Omark & Marvin, Note 7). On the basis of such data, for example, Marvin and Mossler (1976) speculated that children's coy expressions serve to draw attention to the expresser and also to elicit protective feelings and inhibit aggressive responses in the adults who observe them. Keating and her colleagues (Keating, Mazur, & Segall, 1977; Keating, Mazur, Segall, Cysneiros, Divale, Kilbride, Komin, Leahy, Thurman, & Wirsing, 1981) conducted judgment studies which suggest that in many cultures (though not all cultures) lowered eyebrows is perceived to be associated with dominance, while smiling is not. In a study using schematic faces, Sternglanz, Gray, and Murakami (1977) found adult preferences for infantile features described by Lorenz as releasing positive responses in adults.

Direct assessments of recipient responses to facial expressions have been attempted in only a few cases. Most of these studies examine responses to smiling individuals. Kendon (1975) reported differential responses to two forms of smiles in his analysis of the facial behavior of two individuals whom he videotaped unobserved as they engaged in a "kissing round." In a seminaturalistic field study, Mackey (1976) found that greetings which included smiles elicited more smiling in recipients than greetings which did not include smiles. He interprets this finding as support for the hypothesis that smiling serves an appeasement function similar to the submissive displays of primates. Connolly and Smith (1972) studied the reactions of nursery school children to unfamiliar observers (experimenters recording children's behavior in a naturalistic setting). They found that children also tended to respond differently to observers who smiled or did not smile at them. Other studies have shown that staring with or without smiling differentially affects the walking speed of stare recipients (Ellsworth, 1975; Elman, Schulte, & Bukoff, 1977). These data can be interpreted as supporting hypotheses regarding the function of stares and smiles which have been proposed by ethologists (threat and appeasement, respectively).

Regarding infants, a number of recent seminaturalistic studies (Brazelten, Kozlowski, & Main, 1974; DeBoer & Boxer, 1979; Fogel,

1977; Kaye & Fogel, 1980; Stern, Beebe, Jaffe, & Bennett, 1977) have examined mothers' and infants' responses to each other's behavior, including both facial expressions and vocalizations. Although the facial behavior seen in these studies often is imprecisely described, the research has produced some interesting results. The findings indicate that "young" infants (around 4 months old) attend longer and are more expressive when their mothers are facially active rather than relaxed (Kaye & Fogel, 1980). Young infants also appear to respond to bizarre deviations from normal facial behavior, such as a lengthy "deadpan" expression (Cohn & Tronick, 1982; Tronick, Als, & Adamson, 1979; Cohn, Note 2). However, they are not as sensitive as their mothers to variation in facial and vocal expressiveness (Gottman & Ringland, 1981). In contrast, "older" infants (6 months or older) may be sensitive to vocal and facial expressions of emotion (Kreutzer & Charlesworth, Note 6). In particular, one-year-olds appear to use mothers' facial expressions as a source of information when they are placed in a position of uncertainty (Klinnert, Note 5; Sorce, Emde, & Klinnert, Note 8). For example, when confronted with a moderately deep visual cliff, one-year-olds tend to cross more often when their mothers smile than when their mothers show a fearful facial expression.

The above studies all discuss functions of facial expressions involving effects on recipients (communicative functions). Regarding noncommunicative functions, speculations have been made by Darwin (1872/1965), Andrew (1963, 1972), and Sroufe and Waters (1976). For example, Andrew has proposed that lowering the brows aides in the scrutiny of an object by aiding optical convergence. Sroufe and Waters propose that laughter functions as a tension-release mechanism for the laughing individual. An interesting discussion and evaluation of several of these hypotheses can be found in Ekman (1979). Ekman has criticized some of these proposals but feels that others can be verified by simple demonstration (e.g., raising the eyebrows and observing the increase in the vertical dimension of the visual field).

Facial Expressions Used by Children in Conflict Situations

While communication by means of facial signals is probably ubiquitous in human social interaction, ethological work with nonhuman animals suggests that it may be of particular interest to study facial behavior in selected social situations. Studies of primate communication (see Redican, 1975) indicate that many species use facial threat displays in the process of conflict resolution. Threat displays generally are defined as specialized acts which signal the displayer's likelihood of attacking another individual and reflect an increase in the displayer's underlying attack tendency. Such displays are thought to be tied to aggression as their underlying cause and to produce an increase in fear in the recipient (Moynihan, 1955). When two individuals are in conflict, threat displays may be produced and followed by submission or withdrawal by one of the participants. These displays are considered adaptive because they enable individuals to resolve conflicts without recourse to physical altercations.

Some previous studies of children's nonverbal behavior produced data suggesting that certain facial expressions used by children might function as threat displays. Blurton Jones (1972) reported that two expression components, *frown* (i.e., lowered eyebrows) and *fixate* (i.e., an abrupt, unsmiling look of about two seconds), were associated with hitting and pushing by the expresser. In addition, Grant (1969) described a set of "aggressive" expression components which he reported to predict an increasing probability of subsequent attack by nursery school children. Grant's report included no quantified data in support of his claim. However, the facial expression components which he and Blurton Jones described might indeed tend to precede physical attacks and thus in conflict situations could serve as signals indicating the probability that aggression will occur. If so, these expressions could play a role in conflict encounters which would be analogous to the role played by threat displays of primate species.

In the studies to be described, I explored children's use and understanding of the facial expressions considered aggressive by Grant and Blurton Jones (see Figure 1-1 and Table 1-1). Since I later will reopen the question of whether the expressions are truly aggressive, on Table 1-1 I refer to them as the target expressions rather than the aggressive expressions. Several features of Table 1-1 deserve comment. First, the reader should note that most of the target expressions technically are *components* of facial expressions rather than complete expressions (i.e., descriptions of the appearance of the entire face). These components may be produced in isolation (e.g., *lowered brows* alone) or in conjunction with other facial movements (e.g., *lowered brows* with *smile*). Second, the reader will note that some of the items (e.g., *face thrust*) actually involve no facial muscle movements but rather are head movements or are defined by gaze duration (e.g., *stare*). They were included because Grant or Blurton Jones described them as aggressive signals along with the other facial expressions. Third, I have taken the liberty of grouping some of Grant's items (e.g., *sneer* and *wrinkle*) into a single category (e.g., *nose wrinkle*), since they share the same defining feature. Lastly, I have provided a verbal description of each expression and indicated where possible its anatomical basis and its Facial Action Coding System (FACS) code numbers (Ekman & Friesen, 1978). This represents an attempt to translate Grant and Blurton Jones' verbal descriptions into terms that would allow their expressions to be coded using an accurate and reliable scoring system. FACS is an improvement over previous systems which have relied solely on sometimes ambiguous verbal descriptions of facial expressions. Facial expressions defined in terms of FACS action units can be recognized more easily across minor variations in appearance produced by individual differences in facial structure.

To study the possible function of the target expressions in children's conflicts, I videotaped kindergarteners in a seminaturalistic play situation during which a certain number of conflicts tended to arise (Camras, 1977). My goal was to determine whether there were relationships between a child's use of these expressions and the subsequent behavior of both himself and his interactional partner. The first relationship would indicate that the target expressions are informative, that is, observing the expressions enables one to make a prediction about the expresser. The second relationship would suggest that children use these expressions as a source of information about the expresser and the expressions influence the observing child's behavior. I was particularly interested in expression-behavior relationships that would indicate that

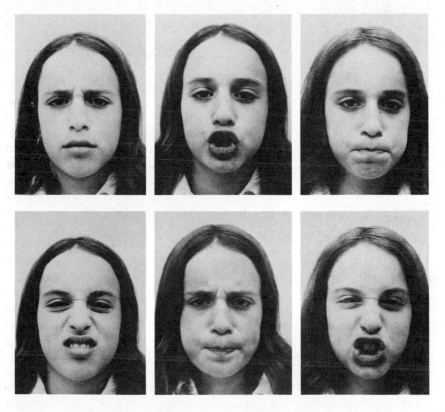

Figure 1-1. Some facial expressions used by children during conflict. *Top row, left to right*: lowered brows, both lips thrust forward, lips pressed together. *Bottom row, left to right*: nose wrinkled, lowered brows with lips pressed together and small mouth, nose wrinkled with both lips thrust forward.

Table 1-1. Some Facial Expressions Used by Children During Conflicts.

Target Expression	Verbal Description	Equivalent Expression Described by Other Authors	Verbal Description	FACS Action Unit Coding and Muscular Basis of Facial Movements
Lowered brows	Eyebrows drawn down or together and down	Aggressive frown (Grant, 1969)	"The eyebrows are drawn together and drawn down in the center" (Grant, 1969, p. 527)	AU4 m. depressor glabellae; m. depressor supercilli; m. corrugator
		Low frown (Blurton Jones, 1972)	"Brows lowered with no obvious vertical furrowing of forehead . . . plus any record of frown . . . where not also called pucker or oblique" (Blurton Jones, 1972, p. 105)	
Both lips thrust forward	Lips apart and thrust forward	Lips forward (Grant, 1969)	"The lips are apart and pushed forward" (Grant, 1969, p. 529)	AU22 m. obicularis oris
Small mouth	Corners of mouth drawn in to center so mouth appears small	Small mouth (Grant, 1969)	"The corners of the mouth are drawn in towards the center . . . little or no pushing forward of the lips" (Grant, 1969, p. 529)	AU18 m. incisivii labii superioris; m. incisivii labii inferioris
Lips pressed together	Lips pressed together, may be slightly rolled under	Tight lips (Grant, 1969)	"The lips are pressed tightly together" (Grant, 1969, p. 529)	A variety of AUs and AU combinations, including AU24 with or without

				AU14 or AU23 m. obicularis oris with or without m. buccinator
Lower lip drop	Jaw thrust forward and lower lip dropped exposing teeth	Intention bite (Grant, 1969)	"The lower jaw is pushed forward and the lower lip dropped to expose the lower teeth" (Grant, 1969, p. 529)	AU16 with AU29 m. depressor labii
Nose wrinkle	Skin on bridge and sides of nose is wrinkled	Sneer (Grant, 1969)	"The centre of the upper lip is drawn up to expose the teeth . . . results in the wrinkling on the bridge of the nose" (Grant, 1969, p. 529)	AU9 m. levator labii superioris; m. alaeque nasi
		Wrinkle (Grant, 1969)	"The skin on the bridge of the nose is wrinkled . . . however, the teeth are not exposed" (Grant, 1969, p. 530)	
Stare	An abrupt unsmiling look at other's face for 1.5 seconds or longer	Fixate (Blurton Jones, 1972)	"Looking directly at eyes of other child for more than about two seconds, with rapid onset of this position and with no smile" (Blurton Jones, 1972, p. 105)	

Table 1-1. (*Continued*)

Target Expression	Verbal Description	Equivalent Expression Described by Other Authors	Verbal Description	FACS Action Unit Coding and Muscular Basis of Facial Movements
Face thrust	Face is thrust forward by extending the neck	Head forward (Grant, 1969)	"The head is brought forward towards the other person . . . a distinctly slower movement than . . . threat . . . likely to be held for some considerable time" (Grant, 1969, p. 530)	
		Threat (Grant, 1969)	"A sharp movement of the head towards the other person" (Grant, 1969, p. 530)	
		Chin out (Grant, 1969)	"The chin is pushed forward, tilting the head back and stretching the neck" (Grant, 1969, p. 530)	

the facial expressions were serving as threat displays. Do these expressions predict aggression by the expresser? If so, Grant and Blurton Jones' hypothesis about their causal basis would receive additional support. Are these expressions followed by submission or withdrawal on the part of the recipient? If so, they might have the immediate effect and adaptive advantage of reducing the number of physical injuries which could be sustained if physical attack, rather than aggressive signaling, always occurred.

In the study (Camras, 1977), 72 pairs of unacquainted kindergarten children each were given a brief play session involving an object with which only one child could play at a time. The children were seated opposite each other at a table bisected by a transparent vertical divider. On the table was a box which could be pulled back and forth through an opening in the divider. The box contained a pair of gerbils which a child could see and play with only if he pulled the box over to his own side. Several play activities were possible: the children could feed the gerbils, dangle a string into their box, or give them a ride on a merry-go-round which was built into the floor of the box. Subjects were allowed to play with the gerbils for twelve minutes while the experimenter was out of the room. No instructions were given about sharing or competing for the gerbil box. However, the children were asked to remain in their seats and pull the box over to their own side of the table when they wanted to play. Each play session was videorecorded by a hidden camera.

Conflicts between the children arose when the child who was playing with the gerbil box (called the *player*) resisted an attempt by his partner (called the *nonplayer*) to obtain it. Nonplayers attempted to obtain the box by pulling on the rope handle and/or producing a verbal statement such as "My turn" or "Let me play." Players resisted these attempts by holding onto the box and/or verbally indicating the desire to retain it by saying, for example, "I'm not done yet" or simply "no." Target expressions were used by the player as he defended his possession of the gerbil box in about 25% of the conflict episodes.

Expresser's Subsequent Behavior

Data analysis revealed that there was a relationship between the facial expression used by the player during conflict and his own subsequent behavior. When players used target expressions, they were more persistent in their effort to retain the gerbil box, tending to resist the nonplayer's subsequent attempt to get it. However, players did not follow their target expressions with behaviors which could readily be termed aggressive. No physical attacks ever occurred during this study—not even when the nonplayer appeared to ignore the player's target expression and persist in his attempt to get the gerbil box.

This finding suggested that the original hypothesis regarding the motivational underpinnings of the target expressions (aggression) be reconsidered—though not rejected outright. Although the target expressions were never followed by attack in this study, possibly they still reflected an increase in aggressive tendency. Among nonhuman animals, aggressive displays are not always followed by overt attack. However, ethologists will consider a display to be "aggressive" if it sometimes accompanies attack and if one reasonably could assume the presence of an attack tendency whenever the display is produced (Hinde, 1974). Grant (1969) and Blurton Jones (1972) observed the target expressions to be associated with attack in their studies. In my own study, perhaps a tendency to attack was present but no fights occurred because the children had been asked to remain in their seats. If the target expressions do not appear in other situations where aggression would be unlikely, we still might reasonably retain the hypothesis that these expressions are causally related to an increase in the expresser's underlying aggressive tendency.

With respect to this possibility, relevant observations regarding these expressions have been made by both myself and others. For example, in the context of another study, I observed *lowered brows* to occur quite often during cooperative play sessions involving mothers and children. During one session, a two-year-old boy lowered his brow as he attempted to balance one object on top of another, a task which obviously required his fullest concentration. In another session, a five-year-old girl lowered her brows as she pointed to an unfamiliar toy and asked her mother, "What's this?" Nose wrinkling also has often been seen in nonconflict situations. For example, I observed a five-year-old boy wrinkle his nose when told about "a girl who ate a rotten apple." Among investigators of emotional expression (Darwin, 1872/1965; Ekman and Friesen, 1975; Izard, 1971, 1977; Tomkins, 1963), *nose wrinkle* generally is thought to characterize the emotion of disgust. According to Darwin, *lowered brows* may occur when "something difficult or displeasing [is] encountered in a train of thought or action" (Darwin, 1872/1965, p. 222). Thus, *lowered brows* may be associated with perplexity of thought, determination, or anger (Darwin, 1872/1965; Ekman & Friesen, 1975).

Given these observations, it appears untenable to maintain that the target expressions are all directly and causally related to an underlying aggressive tendency. A more reasonable hypothesis is that the different target expressions reflect different feeling states in the expresser (e.g., disgust, determination, anger) and that these feeling states all have features which lead them to be associated with player persistence in the player-nonplayer conflict study. Thus a player who was angered by his partner's attempt to get the gerbil box would be expected to make a greater effort to retain it than a player who was not angry. A player who was disgusted by his partner's attempt would be expected to act in a similar manner.

This hypothesis regarding the target expressions could account for Blurton Jones's and Grant's reports of an association between the expressions and physical attack in their studies. In the natural peer interactions observed by Grant and Blurton Jones, anger, disgust, and determination frequently may have occurred in the context of aggressive interactions. However, the additional observations reported above indicate that use of the target expressions is not limited to aggressive contexts and the expressions are not invariant signals of attack.

Nonplayer's Subsequent Behavior

Turning to the second expression-behavior relationship which was explored, data analysis showed a relationship between the facial expressions used by players during conflict and the post-conflict behavior of nonplayers. Players tended to win conflict episodes (i.e., keep the gerbil box) irrespective of their facial expressions. However, after conflict the nonplayers usually waited for some period of time and then made a new attempt to get the gerbil box. Nonplayers tended to wait longer after observing the player use one of the target expressions than after observing only other types of facial expressions. One nontarget expression, *oblique brows*, also was associated with nonplayer hesitancy in renewing his attempt to take the gerbil box. *Oblique brows* (which involves lifting the inner corner of the eyebrows) usually is considered to characterize the expression of sadness (Darwin, 1872/1965; Ekman & Friesen, 1975; Izard, 1971, 1977; Tomkins, 1963).

The data thus suggest that target expressions influenced their recipients, increasing nonplayers' hesitancy to take the gerbil box. However, it is possible that these facial expressions were associated with some other aspect of player behavior which was actually the critical factor affecting the nonplayer response. For example, the target expressions may have been associated with particularly angry verbal statements, aggressive body postures, uneven turn-time distributions, or any of an infinite number of other factors. Nonplayers may have been responding only to these other factors and may have been unaffected by the facial expressions they observed.

Several approaches might be adopted in order to produce further evidence that the nonplayers indeed were responding to the facial expressions. For example, one might simultaneously examine a number of likely influences on nonplayer behavior, including both facial expressions and nonfacial player behaviors. Using a multiple regression approach, one might attempt to determine the percent of variance accounted for by facial expressions as opposed to other factors. While very informative, this approach would rely on the experimenter's ability to identify all nonfacial factors operating in the situation in order to be certain no crucial factor associated with facial expressions was overlooked. A second approach may be taken for adducing further evidence that facial expressions have an influence on recipient behavior. This approach would involve training selected children to be experimental "confederates" who would produce the target expressions during a predetermined subset of conflict episodes. Target expressions thus could be presented independent of aggressive posture, intonation, verbal statements, etc. Such use of artificially produced stimuli occurs in both social psychological and ethological research (Tinbergen, 1969). However, children's limited abilities to produce voluntary facial expressions (Ekman, Roper, & Hager, 1980; Odom & Lemond, 1972) would make it difficult to obtain spontaneous and natural-looking behavior from child confederates. A third approach to the problem would involve questioning children about the facial expressions of interest and obtaining verbal responses that suggest whether or not the children would be influenced by these expressions when they occurred in conflict encounters. Of course this approach has important limitations, but it is a simple means of obtaining data which could converge with other evidence to support the hypothesis that facial expressions serve an important communicative function in conflict situations.

In accord with this third approach, a judgment study was conducted with kindergarten children (Camras, 1980b). In this study, subjects were told a story designed to represent the type of conflicts that occurred during the play sessions: "One day my friend was playing with a toy. Another child tried to take it. My friend held onto the toy and wouldn't let the other child have it. My friend wanted to keep that toy very much." For each of five trials, subjects were shown three pictures of facial expressions: one target expression and two other expressions which also had been observed in the player-nonplayer conflict study (e.g., *smile, open mouth, raised brows, lower lip bite*). In each trial, the subject was asked to choose the expression which would be used by the child in the story. In a sixth trial, subjects were shown a picture of *oblique brows*, the expression that unexpectedly was found to be associated with recipient hesitancy in the earlier study. Along with this expression, two other expressions were presented and the same question was asked.

Results showed that children generally chose the target expressions and *oblique brows* significantly more often than the nontarget expressions. However, one target expression, *both lips thrust forward*, was chosen less frequently than any of the others and in fact was not selected more often than would be expected by chance. In general, the findings are consistent with the hypothesis that the target expressions were influencing children's behavior during the conflicts observed in the previous study. During these conflicts, nonplayers may have perceived the players using target expressions to be very unwilling to relinquish the box. Consequently, nonplayers may have been hesitant about renewing their attempts to take it.

Beyond their perception of player unwillingness, nonplayers also may have made other inferences and/or predictions about the player who used a target expression. For example, the nonplayer may have inferred that the player who was very unwilling to give up the object might become physically aggressive if pressed too hard. Perhaps this inference caused the nonplayer's hesitancy which was observed. Alternatively (or in addition), nonplayers may have perceived players to be experiencing the feeling states proposed to be associated with the target expressions (e.g., disgust, anger, determination). Perhaps nonplayers inferred that a player who was angry, disgusted, or determined would become aggressive in behavior if further provoked. In either case, if the nonplayer inferred that the player might become aggressive, one could hypothesize that the target expressions were functioning as threat displays in the conflict interactions observed. That is, they may have produced some (probably slight) degree of fear or intimidation in the recipient and consequently recipient hesitancy in taking the box.

It is important to note, however, that the target expressions could not be considered threat displays as traditionally conceived. As indicated above, the expressions themselves do not appear to be specific signals of attack. Furthermore, it is unlikely that they invariably produce an increase in fear in the recipient. For example, when a child lowers her brows as she asks her mother, "What's this?", fear is not very likely as a maternal response. However, *lowered brows* observed in a situation where expresser attack is a real possibility might indeed produce an increase in fear in the recipient.

The line of reasoning developed here points to a context-dependent model of communication via facial expression. According to this model, the function of an expression (its effect on the recipient) depends in part on its context of occurrence. Thus not all expressions which function as threat displays need be unique signals of attack. Rather they sometimes may be used by the recipient to make inferences about attack probabilities but only when they occur in contexts where such an inference would be appropriate. This context-dependent model of communication differs from traditional ethological models which conceive of signals as releasing invariant stereotyped responses in the recipient. Here facial expressions are not considered releasers but are one source of information which the recipient may use when he wishes to make some prediction or inference about the expresser. The recipient's response to the facial signal will depend upon the judgment that he is trying to make, and this itself will vary with the situational context in which the signal is produced.

In a departure from the traditional ethological approach, a context-dependent model of communication has been presented by Smith (1965, 1977) in the nonhuman ethological literature (see also Camras,

1980a, for an extended discussion). Furthermore, recent primate studies have provided examples of signals which fit the context-dependent model for threat displays suggested above. Several investigators (Bernstein cited in Rowell, 1972; Van Lawick-Goodall, 1968) have found that expressions that occur in hostile situations also are associated with activities such as infant retrieval and/or copulation. These expressions appear to function as threats when they are used in hostile interactions but serve other functions in other situations.

Further Inferences Based on the Target Expressions

In an earlier section, I proposed that the aggressive expressions of Grant and Blurton Jones actually indicate a variety of expresser feeling states (e.g., anger, disgust, determination) which may or may not be associated with aggressive behavior, depending on the situation. In terms of a context-dependent model of recipient response, children who observe these expressions during object disputes might infer that the expresser is experiencing these feelings and that such an expresser might become physically aggressive if further opposed. In order for this proposed line of inference to be plausible, however, one must determine whether children do indeed perceive the target expressions to be associated with emotions or feelings.

To examine this possibility, a second part to the judgment study described above was conducted. The purpose of the second part was to assess kindergarten children's ability to associate at least some of the target expressions with the specific emotions to which they are related. In particular, children's ability to associate *lowered brows* with anger and *nose wrinkle* with disgust was examined. In addition, children's ability to associate *oblique brows* with sadness was examined since *oblique brows* also had been found to be related to nonplayer hesitancy in the previous observational study.

Subjects were told stories portraying children's emotional responses to both conflict and nonconflict situations. Specifically, these stories were:

1. *Anger story* "One day my friend came outside and saw someone beating on his/her car and smashing the windows. My friend was very angry and went over to fight them."
2. *Sadness story* "My friend's puppy died and he/she felt sad."
3. *Disgust story* "My friend was sitting on a bus and the child sitting next to him/her threw up. My friend felt yechy because it got all over him/her. He/she was disgusted."
4. *Conflict-anger story* "One day my friend was playing with a toy. Another child tried to take it. My friend said, 'Don't take my toy. I'll be angry and hit you if you do.'"

5. *Conflict-sadness story* "One day my friend was playing with a toy. Another child tried to take it. My friend said, ' "Don't take my toy. I'll be sad and cry if you do.' "

A conflict-disgust story was not presented because many kindergarten children do not understand the word *disgust* and because an action which would characterize disgust as opposed to anger in a conflict situation could not be described.

With each story, the subject was shown a triad of facial expression photographs. For some subjects, the triad showed the target expressions *lowered brows* (related to anger), *nose wrinkle* (related to disgust), and also *oblique brows* (related to sadness). For other subjects, the triad showed complete facial expressions of these three emotions. Complete expressions were included in this study to allow a comparison of children's responses to full vs. partial emotional expressions. For the complete expression photos, the pictures of anger and sadness showed *lowered brows* and *oblique brows* respectively, but also showed mouth configurations characteristic of the complete emotional expressions (Ekman & Friesen, 1975). For the emotion disgust, the photograph showed only *nose wrinkle* since this single muscle movement comprises the complete facial expression of disgust. After being told each story and shown a triad of photographs, the subject was asked to choose the expression which would be used by the child in the story.

Results showed that children associated both the complete expressions and the partial expressions with their related emotions. For both the conflict-anger and the conflict-sadness story, subjects chose the appropriate expression significantly more often than would be expected by chance. In the stories which presented nonconflict emotion situations, children associated *lowered brows* with anger, *oblique brows* with sadness, and *nose wrinkle* with disgust as well as associating the complete facial expressions of sadness, disgust, and anger with the appropriate emotion stories. When children's responses to partial vs. complete emotional expressions were compared, results showed that children chose *oblique brows* to correspond with the sadness stories just as frequently as they chose the complete facial expression of sadness. In contrast, however, children were less likely to identify *lowered brows* with anger than they were to identify the complete facial expression of anger with anger.

In summary, with regard to the target expressions, children do not appear to indiscriminately associate all of these expressions with anger or aggression but can use them to make differentiated emotion-related inferences about the expressers. Regarding children's interpretation of target expressions in a real-life situation, the judgment studies described here do not enable us to determine with certainty the spontaneous inferences which children made upon seeing these expressions in the conflict encounters of the player-nonplayer conflict study. Possibly, nonplayers perceived the players to be angry, disgusted, or sad. Perhaps they feared a subsequent attack by the angry or disgusted child (although this would be less reasonable to assume for nonplayers observing the sad expression). However, it also is possible that nonplayers made no specific emotion inferences when observing the emotion-related expressions in the context of the conflict interactions. Possibly they merely perceived the players to be unwilling to relinquish the toy and hesitated to take it only for this reason. The purpose of the judgment studies described here was not to definitively determine children's spontaneous interpretations of the target expressions. Instead, its purpose was to show that children can make inferences about the expressions that are consistent with the expression-behavior relationships which were previously observed. Further, consistent with the context-dependent model discussed above, children do not invariably perceive all these target expressions to be signals of attack. However, in some situations they may indeed be associated with attack and children may recognize this fact and respond accordingly.

Phylogeny and Ontogeny

Regarding the issue of phylogenetic origin, comparison of the target expressions to facial displays of other primates suggests that threat displays of primate ancestors are a possible evolutionary basis for the target expressions. However, in the course of evolution, changes in the motivational underpinnings of some target expressions may have occurred to make them differentially related to different emotions (see Camras, 1980a, for further discussion of phylogeny and possible ritualization of the target expressions).

Regarding ontogeny, some of the target expressions are seen early in infancy in response to appropriate emotional stimuli (Izard, Huebner, Risser, McGinnes, & Dougherty, 1980; Oster, 1978). This suggests that their production may be in part innately determined. However, use of the target expressions, like other facial expressions, may be subjected to learned modification. For example, cultural "display rules" (Ekman, 1972, 1977; Saarni, 1979) may dictate their suppression in situations where expression of anger or disgust are considered inappropriate.

Conclusion

In this chapter I have attempted to demonstrate the utility of taking an ethological approach to the study of children's facial behavior. Ethological studies have provided valuable information regarding the causes, functions, ontogeny, and phylogeny of facial expressions. Furthermore, animal models and ethological concepts such as the threat display have served as useful heuristic devices for generating research on humans. The results of such research (including my own) often indicate that these concepts can not be applied to humans in their original unaltered form. However, enough similarity between human and nonhuman nonverbal communication has been found to warrant continued exploration from an ethological point of view.

Regarding directions for future research, some important aspects of facial behavior heretofore have been disregarded by ethologically oriented investigators. Particularly notable has been the lack of studies on the relationship between verbal and facial communication. Such studies probably have been neglected for historical reasons: ethology originated in the investigation of nonverbal organisms. However, studies of verbal communication are not inherently incompatible with an ethological viewpoint. For example, one might profitably examine relationships between the affective facial expressions previously studied by ethologists and affective features of language (e.g., verbal politeness).

Other aspects of facial behavior might seem harder to fit into an ethological framework. For example, cultural variation and learned modification of facial expressions appear to some to be antithetical to notions of species-characteristic behavior. However, as ethologists frequently protest, environmental influences on behavior are not denied within their discipline. Studies of the processes by which biologically based expressive patterns may be systematically modified during the course of development (e.g., via cultural display rules) make a valuable contribution to our understanding of relationships between biological and environmental influences on nonverbal communication. Furthermore, these studies would be directly relevant to the question of ontogeny, one of the four major issues of concern to ethologists.

Assertions of compatibility between ethology and studies of language or cultural variation should not be regarded as ethological imperialism. No exclusive claim to the study of communication is being made. However, ethology's concern with identifying and describing nonverbal actions can provide important direction to the study of children's nonverbal behavior. Furthermore, it is not inherently in conflict with the theoretical perspectives of most nonethologically oriented investigators.

Reference Notes

1. Abramovich, L. & Marvin, R. *Facial expression in preschool children.* Paper presented at the meeting of the Society for Research in Child Development, Denver, CO, April 1975.
2. Cohn, J. *Three-month old infants' reaction to simulated maternal depression.* Paper presented at the meeting of the Society for Research in Child Development, Boston, MA, April 1981.
3. Ekman, P. Personal communication, October 1977.

4. Haviland, J. *Individual differences in affect*. Paper presented at the meeting of the Society for Research in Child Development, Denver, CO, April 1975.
5. Klinnert, M. *Infants' use of mothers' facial expressions for regulating their own behavior*. Paper presented at the meeting of the Society for Research in Child Development, Boston, MA, April 1981.
6. Kreutzer, M. & Charlesworth, W. *Infants' reactions to different expressions of emotions*. Paper presented at the meeting of the Society for Research in Child Development, Philadelphia, PA, March 1973.
7. Omark, D. & Marvin, R. *Problems in human ethology*. Paper presented at the meeting of the Animal Behavior Society, University of Illinois, Urbana, IL, May 1974.
8. Sorce, J., Emde, R., & Klinnert, M. *Maternal emotional signaling: Its effect on the visual cliff behavior of one-year-olds*. Paper presented at the meeting of the Society for Research in Child Development, Boston, MA, April 1981.

References

Andrew, R. J. The displays of the primates. In J. Buethner-Janusch (Ed.), *Genetic and evolutionary biology of the primates*. New York: Academic Press, 1963.

Andrew, R. J. The information potentially available in mammalian displays. In R. Hinde (Ed.), *Nonverbal communication*. London: Cambridge University Press, 1972.

Blurton Jones, N. Criteria for use in describing facial expressions of children. *Human Biology*, 1971, *43*(3), 365-413.

Blurton Jones, N. Categories of child-child interaction. In N. G. Blurton Jones (Ed.), *Ethological studies of child behavior*. London: Cambridge University Press, 1972.

Blurton Jones, N. & Konner, M. An experiment on eyebrow-raising and visual searching in children. *Journal of Child Psychology and Psychiatry*, 1971, *11*, 233-240.

Brannigan, C. & Humphries, D. Human non-verbal behavior, a means of communication. In N. G. Blurton Jones (Ed.), *Ethological studies of child behavior*. London: Cambridge University Press, 1972.

Brazelton, T., Koslowski, B., & Main, M. The origins of reciprocity: The early mother-infant interaction. In M. Lewis and L. Rosenblum (Eds.), *The effect of the infant on its caregiver*. New York: Wiley, 1974.

Buck, R. Nonverbal communication of affect in children. *Journal of Personality and Social Psychology*, 1975, *31*(4), 644-653.

Camras, L. Facial expressions used by children in a conflict situation. *Child Development*, 1977, *48*, 1431-1435.

Camras, L. Animal threat displays and children's facial expressions: A comparison. In D. Omark, F. Strayer, and D. Freedman (Eds.), *Dominance relations: An ethological view of human conflict and social interaction*. New York: Garland STPM Press, 1980. (a)

Camras, L. Children's understanding of facial expressions used during conflict encounters. *Child Development*, 1980, *51*, 879-885. (b)

Charlesworth, W. R. *Surprise reactions in congenitally blind and sighted children*. National Institute of Mental Health Progress Report, 1970.

Chevalier-Skolnikov, S. Facial expression of emotion in nonhuman primates. In P. Ekman (Ed.), *Darwin and facial expression*. New York: Academic Press, 1973.

Cheyne, J. Development of forms and functions of smiling in preschoolers. *Child Development*, 1976, *47*, 820-823.

Cohn, J. & Tronick, E. Communicative rules and the sequential structure of infant behavior during normal and depressed interaction. In E. Tronick (Ed.), *Social interchange in infancy: Affect, cognition, and communication*. Baltimore: University Park Press, 1982.

Connolly, K. & Smith, P. Reactions of preschool children to a strange observer. In N. Blurton Jones (Ed.), *Ethological studies of child behavior*. London: Cambridge University Press, 1972.

Currie, K. & Brannigan, C. Behavioral analysis and modification with an autistic child. In S. Hutt and C. Hutt (Eds.), *Behavior studies in psychiatry*. Oxford, England: Pergamon Press, 1970.

Darwin, C. *The expression of the emotions in man and animals*. London: John Murray, 1872. Reprinted, Chicago: University of Chicago Press, 1965.

DeBoer, M. & Boxer, A. Signal functions of infant facial expressions and gaze direction during mother-infant face-to-face play. *Child Development*, 1979, *50*, 1215-1218.

Eibl-Eibesfeldt, I. *Ethology, the biology of behavior*. New York: Holt, Rinehart and Winston, 1970.

Eibl-Eibesfeldt, I. Similarities and differences between cultures in expressive movements. In R. A. Hinde (Ed.), *Non-verbal communication*. London: Cambridge University Press, 1972.

Eibl-Eibesfeldt, I. The expressive behavior of the deaf-and-blind born. In M. von Cranach and I. Vine (Eds.), *Social communication and movement*. London: Academic Press, 1973.

Ekman, P. Universals and cultural differences in facial expressions of emotion. In J. Cole (Ed.), *Nebraska symposium on motivation, 1971*. Lincoln, NB: University of Nebraska Press, 1972.

Ekman, P. Biological and cultural contributions to body and facial movement. In J. Blacking (Ed.), *Anthropology of the body*. London: Academic Press, 1977.

Ekman, P. About brows: Emotional and conversational signals. In M. von Cranach, K. Foppa, W. Lepenies, and D. Ploog (Eds.), *Human ethology*. London: Cambridge University Press, 1979.

Ekman, P. & Friesen, W. V. *Unmasking the face*. Englewood Cliffs, NJ: Prentice-Hall, 1975.

Ekman, P. & Friesen, W. V. *Facial action coding system: A technique for the measurement of facial movement*. Palo Alto, CA: Consulting Psychologists Press, 1978.

Ekman, P., Roper, G., & Hager, J. Deliberate facial movement. *Child Development*, 1980, *51*, 886-891.

Ellsworth, P. Direct gaze as a social stimulus: The example of aggression. In P. Pliner, L. Krames, and T. Alloway (Eds.), *Nonverbal communication of aggression*. New York: Plenum Press, 1975.

Elman, D., Schulte, D., & Bukoff, A. Effects of facial expression and stare duration on walking speed: Two field experiments. *Environmental Psychology and Nonverbal Behavior*, 1977, *2*(2), 93-99.

Feleky, A. *Feelings and emotions*. New York: Pioneer Publishing Company, 1924.

Fogel, A. Temporal organization in mother-infant face-to-face interaction. In H. Schaffer (Ed.), *Studies in mother-infant interaction*. New York: Academic Press, 1977.

Freedman, D. G. Smiling in blind infants and the issue of innate versus acquired. *Journal of Child Psychology and Psychiatry*, 1964, *5*, 171-184.

Goodenough, F. L. Expression of the emotions in a blind-deaf child. *Journal of Abnormal and Social Psychology*, 1932, *27*, 328-333.

Gottman, J. & Ringland, J. The analysis of dominance and bidirectionality in social development. *Child Development*, 1981, *52*(2), 393-412.

Grant, E. C. Human facial expression. *Man*, 1969, *4*, 525-536.

Greenbaum, G. Regularity and consistency in the behavior of autistic children. In S. Hutt and C. Hutt (Eds.), *Behavior studies in psychiatry*. Oxford, England: Pergamon Press, 1970.

Hiatt, S., Campos, J., & Emde, R. Facial patterning and infant emotional expression: Happiness, surprise, and fear. *Child Development*, 1979, *50*, 1020-1035.

Hinde, R. A. *Biological basis of human social behavior*. New York: McGraw-Hill, 1974.

Hutt, S. J. & Hutt, C. *Direct observation and measurement of behavior*. Springfield, IL: Charles C. Thomas, 1970.

Hutt, C. & Ounsted, C. Gaze aversion and its significance in childhood autism. In S. Hutt and C. Hutt (Eds.), *Behavior studies in psychiatry*. Oxford, England: Pergamon Press, 1970.

Izard, C. E. *The face of emotion*. New York: Appleton-Century-Crofts, 1971.

Izard, C. E. *Human emotions*. New York: Plenum Press, 1977.

Izard, C., Huebner, R., Risser, D., McGinnes, G., & Dougherty, L. The young infants' ability to produce discrete emotion expressions. *Developmental Psychology*, 1980, *16*, 132-140.

Kaye, K. & Fogel, A. The temporal structure of face-to-face communication between mothers and infants. *Developmental Psychology*, 1980, *16*(5), 454-464.

Keating, C., Mazur, A., & Segall, M. Facial gestures which influence the perception of status. *Sociometry*, 1977, *40*(4), 374-378.

Keating, C., Mazur, A., Segall, M., Cysneiros, P., Divale, W., Kilbride, J., Komin, S., Leahy, P., Thurman, B., & Wirsing, R. Culture and the perception of social dominance from facial expression. *Journal of Personality and Social Psychology*, 1981, *40*(4), 615-626.

Kendon, A. Some functions of the face in a kissing round. *Semiotica*, 1975, *15*(4), 299-334.

Kraut, R. & Johnson, R. Social and emotional messages of smiling: An ethological approach. *Journal of Personality and Social Psychology*, 1979, *37*(9), 1539-1553.

Lockard, J., Fahrenbruch, C., Smith, J., & Morgan, C. Smiling and laughter: Different phyletic origins? *Bulletin of the Psychonomic Society*, 1977, *10*, 183-186.

Mackey, W. Parameters of the smile as a social signal. *The Journal of Genetic Psychology*, 1976, *129*, 125-130.

Marvin, R. & Mossler, D. A methodological paradigm for describing and analyzing complex non-verbal expressions: Coy expressions in preschool children. *Representative Research in Social Psychology*, 1976, *7*, 133-139.

McGrew, W. C. *An ethological study of children's behavior*. New York: Academic Press, 1972.

Moynihan, M. Types of hostile displays. *Auk*, 1955, *72*, 247-259.

Odom, K. & Lemond, C. Developmental differences in the perception and production of facial expressions. *Child Development*, 1972, *43*, 359-369.

Oster, H. Facial expression and affect development. In M. Lewis and L. Rosenblum (Eds.), *The development of affect.* New York: Plenum Press, 1978.

Redican, W. K. Facial expressions in nonhuman primates. In L. A. Rosenblum (ed.), *Primate behavior: Developments in field and laboratory research* (Vol. 4). New York: Academic Press, 1975.

Rowell, T. *The social behavior of monkeys.* Harmondsworth, England: Penguin Books, Ltd., 1972.

Saarni, C. Children's understanding of display rules for expressive behavior. *Developmental Psychology,* 1979, *15*(4), 424-429.

Smith, P. & Connolly, K. Patterns of play and social interaction in preschool children. In N. G. Blurton Jones (Ed.), *Ethological studies of child behavior.* London: Cambridge University Press, 1972.

Smith, W. J. Message, meaning, and context in ethology. *The American Naturalist,* 1965, *99*(908), 405-409.

Smith, W. J. *The behavior of communicating.* Cambridge, MA: Harvard University Press, 1977.

Sroufe, L. A. & Waters, E. The ontogenesis of smiling and laughter: A perspective on the organization of development in infancy. *Psychological Review,* 1976, *83* (3), 173-189.

Sroufe, L. A. & Wunsch, J. The development of laughter in the first year of life. *Child Development,* 1972, *43*, 1326-1344.

Stenberg, C., Campos, J., & Emde, R. The facial expression of anger in seven-month-old infants. *Child Development,* in press.

Stern, D., Beebe, B., Jaffe, J., & Bennett, S. L. The infants' stimulus world during social interaction. In H. Schaffer (Ed.), *Studies in mother-infant interaction.* New York: Academic Press, 1977.

Sternglanz, S., Gray, J., & Murakami, M. Adult preferences for infantile facial features: An ethological approach. *Animal Behavior,* 1977, *25*, 108-115.

Thompson, J. Development of facial expression in blind and seeing children. *Archives of Psychology,* 1941, *264*, 1-47.

Tinbergen, N. *The study of instinct* (2nd Ed.). New York: Oxford University Press, 1969.

Tinbergen, N. Ethology and stress diseases. *Science,* 1974, *185*, 20-27.

Tomkins, S. S. *Affect, imagery and consciousness, Vol. 2. The negative affects.* New York: Springer, 1963.

Tronick, E., Als, H., & Adamson, L. Structure of early face-to-face communicative interactions. In M. Bullowa (Ed.), *Before speech: The beginnings of human communication.* London: Cambridge University Press, 1979.

van Hooff, J. A. R. A. M. A comparative approach to the phylogeny of laughter and smiling. In R. Hinde (Ed.), *Non-verbal communication.* London: Cambridge University Press, 1972.

Van Lawick-Goodall, J. The behavior of free-living chimpanzees in the Gombe Stream reserve. *Animal Behavior Monographs,* 1968, *1*(3), 161-311.

Wheldall, K. & Mittler, P. Eyebrow raising, eye-widening and visual search in nursery school children. *Journal of Child Psychology and Psychiatry,* 1976, *17*(1), 57-62.

Wolff, P. Observations on the early development of smiling. In B. Foss (Ed.), *Determinants of infant behavior, II.* New York: Wiley, 1963.

Woodworth, R. *Experimental psychology.* New York: Henry Holt, 1938.

Young, G. & Decarie, T. An ethology-based catalogue of facial/vocal behavior in infancy. *Animal Behavior,* 1977, *25*, 95-107.

Zivin, G. Facial gestures predict preschoolers' encounter outcomes. *Social Science Information*, 1977, *16*(8), 715-730. (a)

Zivin, G. On becoming subtle: Age and social rank changes in the use of a facial gesture. *Child Development*, 1977, *48*, 1314-1321. (b)

CHAPTER TWO

Spontaneous and Symbolic Nonverbal Behavior and the Ontogeny of Communication

Ross Buck

Historically, one of the central issues in the study of nonverbal communication has involved the question of whether nonverbal behavior should be regarded as innate or as learned and culturally patterned. Most now recognize that nonverbal behavior involves both innate and learned aspects, with the individual essentially learning how to use a system of communication that has deep evolutionary roots: it is simultaneously a biological phenomenon involving the expression of emotion, and a learned phenomenon analogous to, and interacting with, language.

A consideration of the biological foundations of emotion, on one hand, and of language, on the other, allows a useful perspective on this problem. It is clear from both human and animal studies that activation in the neural systems underlying emotion is associated with expressive nonverbal behavior. It is also clear that human language is based upon biological mechanisms, the destruction of which can result in extremely severe language disorders: the aphasias. At the same time, it is clear that many aspects of both emotional expression and language are learned. All of this suggests that the study of the biological foundations of nonverbal communication may yield a coherent view of both its innate aspects and the nature and extent of learned influences.

The purpose of this chapter is threefold: (a) to distinguish between "spontaneous" nonverbal behavior, which is expressive of emotion, and "symbolic" nonverbal behavior, which is organized to support language; (b) to relate this distinction to the biological bases of emotion and language and, particularly, to recent developments in the literature on right hemisphere versus left hemisphere brain functioning; and (c) to discuss the implications of this view that are relevant to the analysis of the ontogeny of nonverbal communication. This chapter first will discuss the problems involved in distinguishing voluntary and nonvolun-

tary nonverbal behavior. It shall then define and contrast the characteristics of spontaneous and symbolic communication, discussing evidence
which suggests that spontaneous communication is particularly related
to right hemisphere brain functioning, while symbolic communication
is particularly related to left hemisphere functioning. Based on studies
of the neural bases of vocalization and communication in animals and
humans, it shall suggest that there are several kinds of voluntary bases
of symbolic communication, and shall outline their possible neural
bases, as well as the possible neural bases of spontaneous communication. Finally, the chapter will turn to studies on the development of
nonverbal communication, discussing the implications of the present
point of view for the analysis of the interactions between emotional,
cognitive, and social development, and the development of language.
The goal of this chapter is to show how the analysis of the biological
bases of nonverbal behavior may provide an integrative view of how
constitutional and social learning variables interact in the development
of spontaneous and symbolic nonverbal expression.

The Problem of Intention

One of the central assumptions of the present approach is that it is
possible and useful and, indeed, necessary to distinguish between voluntary and nonvoluntary nonverbal behavior. At the outset, we should perhaps consider whether this is the case, given the long-standing debates
regarding the problems of dealing with voluntary and involuntary
processes. The importance of the distinction between voluntary and
nonvoluntary nonverbal behavior has long been recognized (e.g., Ekman
& Friesen, 1969), but the distinction has been difficult to make because
of the difficult empirical and conceptual problems presented by the
concept of intention. However, this assumption is warranted for two
reasons. First, the increasing knowledge of the neural bases of communication has made distinguishing between voluntary and nonvoluntary
nonverbal behavior virtually unavoidable. The neural systems underlying facial expression and other skeletal muscle activity clearly vary in
what neurologists have long recognized to be the degree of their voluntary control. For example, it is clear that spontaneous facial expressions
and automatic movements associated with emotional expression are
under the control of the nonpyramidal motor system, while voluntary
skilled movements are controlled by motor systems in the precentral
gyrus via the pyramidal motor system. Thus, neurologists have long
recognized that lesions in the former system cause deficits in spontaneous expression while leaving voluntary expression intact, while lesions
in the latter system have the opposite pattern of effects (cf. Geschwind,
1975).

A second reason why the distinction between spontaneous and voluntary communication is useful is that there are ways in which these behaviors can be empirically distinguished. Unfortunately, we do not know how to determine the extent to which a given expression is voluntary. However, Ekman (1979) has suggested a number of characteristics which might differentiate spontaneous and voluntary expression in his distinction between emotional and conversational facial expression, stating, for example, that emotional expressions should occur earlier in the development of the individual and should be universal to the human species.

Eliciting Voluntary Expressions

Even though it may be difficult or impossible to determine the degree of voluntary control in a given expression, it is possible to structure an experimental situation so that one might expect that expressions should generally be spontaneous, or generally voluntary. To study voluntary expression, one may simply ask the subject to pose different expressions. This might be done in different ways; for example, one might ask the subject to attempt to "feel" the emotion in question, as in Stanislaviski acting (Ekman, Hagar, & Friesen, 1981). Alternatively, one might ask subjects to show what their faces looks like when they feel angry, happy, and so forth, or to show what they think are strong facial expressions for various emotions. This may be done with or without a "model" expression, such as a photograph or film of another person performing the relevant expression. Still another way to study voluntary facial expression is to ask the subject to perform the relevant muscle manipulations, without providing an emotional label; for example, ask the subject to "move the corners of your mouth towards your eyes" (Koff, Borod, & White, 1981), as opposed to saying "smile." Such muscle manipulations may or may not be relevant to emotional expression. Table 2-1 summarizes the various ways in which voluntary expressions may be evoked.

Eliciting Spontaneous Expressions

Defining Conditions

When attempting to elicit spontaneous expression, at least three conditions must be met. First, the subject must be made to experience a real emotion of some kind. This has been done by showing emotionally loaded color slides or films, by conducting interviews with specific emotional content, and by observing behavior in natural situations in which it is expected that subjects should be experiencing emotion (cf.

Table 2-1. Different Ways of Evoking Voluntary Expressive Behavior.[a]

Emotional expressions (either facial or postural-gestural responses could be assessed).
  Experiential—"Feel happy."
  Verbal cue—"Look happy."
  Vignette cue—"Look as if you found money."

Purposeful actions (praxis) (can be done with or without the relevant object).
  Nonemotional context—"Blow out a match." "Reach for something with your
    right hand."
  Emotional context—"Blow a kiss." "Shake hands."

General movements
  Relevant to emotion—"Draw the corners of your mouth up toward your eyes."
    "Hold out your right hand."
  Not relevant to emotion—"Put your mouth out to the side." "Hold up three
    fingers."

---

[a]All of these behaviors can be performed with or without a relevant model, using
drawings, photographs, films, or real-life situations.

Buck, in press (b)). Second, the subjects must be observed as unobtru-
sively as possible, so that they do not realize that their expressions are
being studied. Such knowledge would insure that nonspontaneous factors associated with display rules would intervene to influence the
expression. Third, it is preferable that the subjects not be in a social situation and that if they are in a social situation they should not be engaged
in conversation. Conversation insures that many facial movements will
occur to support the verbal flow, functioning as emblems, illustrators,
and/or regulators (Ekman & Friesen, 1969). Thus it has been observed
that talking influences everything that a person does (Dittman, 1972),
and indeed it appears that even the act of solitary conversation causes
facial expressions and gestures to be organized to support that conversation (Buck, Baron, & Barrette, 1982).

The Miller Paradigm

One experimental paradigm which satisfies these conditions is derived
from R. E. Miller's cooperative conditioning paradigm, in which two
rhesus monkeys are taught to press a bar when a light comes on to avoid
shock or gain food reward. The punishment and reward consitute the
source of the emotion. They are then paired so that the sending animal,
alone in a room, can see the light but has no access to the bar, while the
receiver has the bar but cannot see the light. The receiver, however, is
provided with the video image of the facial region of the sender. Miller
and his colleagues have shown that the sender makes emotion-related
facial expressions when the emotionally loaded light is activated, and
that the receivers can apparently perceive and interpret these expressions,
for they quickly learn to press the bar which gains the reward or avoids

the punishment for both animals (Miller, 1967, 1971, 1974). A number of investigators, including Buck, Ekman, Harper, Lanzetta, and Zuckerman, have applied Miller's pardigm to humans, using shock, color slides, or films to generate emotion in solitary subjects who do not know that they are being filmed, and demonstrating that receiver subjects watching the sender's facial/gestural responses can make correct judgments about the nature of the emotional stimuli (Buck, 1979a, 1979b, in press (b)).

It thus can be argued on procedural grounds that the Miller paradigm should uniquely reflect spontaneous, as opposed to voluntary, express-iveness. There is also empirical evidence of this, including Miller's own demonstrations that the procedure can be used to study affect communication in nonhuman primates, and recent demonstrations that facial expression, as measured by the slide-viewing technique developed from Miller's paradigm, shows relationships between brain damage and communication ability that are very different from the relationships demonstrated between brain damage and voluntary expression (Buck & Duffy, 1980). As we shall see, there is much evidence that left-hemisphere brain damage but not right-hemisphere damage leads to deficits in voluntary communication, both verbal and nonverbal in nature. Buck and Duffy (1980) showed that patients with left hemisphere damage did *not* show deficits in spontaneous communication, but patients with right hemisphere damage did. The implications of this finding are discussed below.

Defining Spontaneous and Symbolic Communication

Defining Communication

The distinction between spontaneous and symbolic communication necessarily involves the definition of communication itself. *Communication* is broadly defined as occurring whenever the behavior of one interactant (the sender) influences the behavior of another (the receiver). Many definitions of communication would exclude influences transmitted via spontaneous behavior. Weiner, Devoe, Rubinow, and Geller (1972), for example, define communication as necessarily involving a symbolic code which is socially learned and shared. Such definitions are unduly restrictive in that they do not consider the possibility of a *biologically* based system of influence—a biologically based as opposed to a socially based signal system.

Socially vs. Biologically Shared Signal Systems

A biologically shared signal system is implicit in Darwin's (1872) analysis in *Expression of the Emotions in Man and Animals* (Buck,

1981a). Darwin argued that displays of emotion have adaptive value in social animals in that they reveal something about certain inner states of the responder--those inner states that have social relevance in that they are necessary for social coordination, which is relevant to survival in that particular species. This analysis implies (a) that the inner state of the responder must be expressed in a display, which may involve facial expressions, body movements, vocalizations, coloration changes, olfactory cues, or whatever; (b) that the receiver must be able to receive the expressive display via sensory cues; and (c) that the receiver must be able to respond appropriately to the display. In other words, Darwin's thesis requires that both sending and receiving mechanisms must have evolved in order for the adaptive value of the emotional expression system to be realized.

There are many examples of such communication mechanisms. In one interesting observation, Koenig (1951) reported that he had difficulty in raising titmice because the parent birds kept removing their young from the nest, even though the latter were healthy and well fed. Koenig found that the nestlings were apparently *too* well fed. Because they had been fed artificially, their hunger was satisfied, and they failed to make the gaping response that has evolved in hungry titmouse nestlings. Apparently, the parent birds required this gaping display to respond with appropriate caregiving since the failure to gape in nature is presumably associated with a sick or dead nestling, and they responded as they had evolved to respond despite the fact that the nestlings were neither sick nor dead. Koenig reported that he cut back on the artificial feeding of the nestlings, the gaping response was restored, and he was able to raise healthy titmice.

Sending Mechanisms

There are suggestions that a complex facial musculature has evolved in primates, including humans, largely to support the communicative demands in these highly social animals. Andrew (1963, 1965) has analyzed the facial and vocal displays of primates in detail, suggesting, for example, that grunts evolved in baboons because "the nature of their societies was such as to greatly favor any change making the transfer of information by display more explicit and less ambiguous" (1963, p. 91), and noting that the displays of the highly social plains-dwelling baboon are more complex than are those of the more solitary drill baboon, or mandrill, which lives in the forest (1965).

The argument that these sending mechanisms are innate is supported by the observation that squirrel monkeys deafened at birth, and/or raised with muted mothers in isolation from species-specific vocalization, produce vocalizations that are virtually identical to those of monkeys raised under normal conditions (Riggs, Winter, Ploog, &

Mayer, 1972; Winter, Handley, Ploog, & Schott, 1973). This implies a genetically determined, prewired model for call production.

Receiving Mechanisms

In essence, the reasoning behind the evolution of sending mechanisms is that, given that the communication of a certain motivational-emotional state is adaptive to a species, individuals who show evidence of that internal state in their external behavior will tend to be favored, so that over the generations these behaviors will become "ritualized" into displays (cf. Buck, 1981a). The same reasoning applies to the evolution of receiving mechanisms: individuals who attend to, and respond appropriately to, these displays would tend to be favored, so that the perceptual systems of species members would eventually become "pre-attuned" to these displays. The latter is consistent with Gibson's (1966, 1977) ecological theory of perception, which argues that perception must be determined by the nature of the ecological niche in which the species has evolved, and with Sackett's (1966) demonstration that infant monkeys who have been isolated since birth, and have never seen another monkey, react appropriately to photographs of monkeys making a threat display.

Signs Versus Symbols

In summary, biologically based systems of communication, involving both sending and receiving mechanisms, have evolved in species in which the coordination of social behavior is necessary for survival. George Herbert Mead (1934) argued that this constitutes the system from which human verbal communication arose. In doing so, Mead distinguished between the spontaneous displays analyzed by Darwin, which Mead called *gestures* and *significant symbols*.

Symbols

Symbols involve communicative behaviors that have arbitrary, socially-defined relationships with their referent, knowledge of which is shared by the sender and receiver. Thus, the word *rain* in English and the sign for rain in American Sign Language (ASL) are both examples of symbols in that both the sender and the receiver must have learned the relationship between the symbol and the referent in order for communication to occur. Note that the symbol in ASL may be more *iconic* in that it may have a resemblance to the referent, while the word *rain* does not, but we shall consider it to be a symbol nevertheless.

Signs

In contrast, the gesture is not symbolic because its relationship to its referent is not at all arbitrary, and it does not have to be learned. The gesture is a *sign* that bears a natural relationship to the referent, and in fact the sign is an externally visible or otherwise accessible aspect of the referent. For example, dark clouds are a sign of rain because the darkness of the clouds is an externally accessible aspect of the rain—the high water content of the clouds is associated with low light transmission and, therefore, darkness. In exactly the same way, spontaneous gestures and facial expressions are signs of an animal's motivational-emotional state in that the occurrence of activity in the neural systems' underlying motivation and emotion have evolved to be associated with tendencies toward bodily-facial response. In other words, the facial-gestural responses are externally accessible aspects of the motivational-emotional state.

Accessibility

The notion that visibility, or, more broadly, accessibility, is an important aspect of responding has implications both for the analysis of the ritualization process in evolution and emotional development in children (Buck, 1971, 1981a, 1981b). In brief, it can be shown that the degree of accessibility of a response—the degree to which it is apparent to the responder and to others via sensory cues—will influence the role that that response may play in the processes of ritualization and emotional development (Buck, 1981a, 1982, in press (b)). Thus, responses that are relatively inaccessible, such as most physiological responses, will tend to undergo a very different process of social learning than will responses that are relatively accessible such as goal-directed overt behaviors (Buck, 1981b).

Spontaneous vs. Voluntary Responding

In summary, we are suggesting that certain responses have evolved as externally accessible signs of the occurrence of internal motivational-emotional states. There are several implications of this analysis. One is that the expression of internal motivational-emotional states by gestures that have evolved to be signs for those states must be nonvoluntary, or spontaneous. Mead's (1934) example of a conversation of gestures was a dog fight, in which the antagonists circle each other, responding instantly to signs of attack or retreat on the part of the other. The gestures on which this conversation is based are not voluntary, but are implicit and spontaneous signs of the momentary feelings and intentions—emotions and motives—of the other. Mead states: "It is quite impossible to assume that animals do undertake to express their emotions. They certainly do not undertake to express them for the benefit of other animals" (1934, p. 16).

On the other hand, the use of symbols in communication must be voluntary on some level, although this need not be a conscious level. Many aspects of language are learned so thoroughly that they operate virtually without the sender's or receiver's awareness. Also, there are a wide variety of nonverbal behaviors—emblems, illustrators, and regulators—which are analogous to or directly related to language and which are not directly related to the expression of motivational emotional states (Ekman & Friesen, 1969). We noted above that Ekman (1979) has distinguished between conversational and emotional facial expressions, suggesting that the former include facial actions that are related to the process of speaking or listening, or facial emblems which occur without speech. Such behaviors have been emphasized in the work of Birdwhistell (1970), Scheflen (1973), and their colleagues, who have demonstrated the close relationships of body movements and language behaviors (cf. Key, 1980). Like many aspects of language, these behaviors appear to operate virtually automatically and outside conscious awareness, but they are not signs of an existing motivational-emotional state and are therefore not spontaneous behaviors, in our definition. However, it is apparent that these behaviors differ in the degree to which they are consciously voluntary, implying that there must be a number of mechanisms underlying what we are calling symbolic communication. We shall discuss this in more detail below.

Propositional vs. Non-propositional Communication

Another implication of the present analysis is that spontaneous communication must be nonpropositional. Bertrand Russell (1903) restricted the term *proposition* to refer to a statement that is capable of logical analysis, i.e., a test of truth or falsity. Since in our definition spontaneous communication occurs via signs which are externally accessible aspects of the referent, the presence of the sign by definition implies the presence of the referent. Therefore, spontaneous communication cannot be falsified and is thus nonpropositional. Its content consists of the expression of motivational-emotional states, rather than propositions. In contrast, the content of symbolic communication consists of propositions.

It might be argued that a person who experiences some emotion but alters its expression in some way is falsifying spontaneous communication. Ekman and Friesen (1975) have described a number of ways in which learned "display rules" can alter spontaneous expression. This, it may be suggested, involves suppression of the spontaneous display rather than falsification, and the resulting "false" expression is actually an example of symbolic communication.

A Model of Spontaneous vs. Symbolic Communication

The Model

The model of spontaneous and symbolic communication that we have suggested is summarized in Table 2-2. We have defined spontaneous communication as having the following major qualities: it is based upon a biologically shared signal system; the elements of the message are signs that bear a natural relationship to the referent; it is nonvoluntary, or spontaneous; it is nonpropositional in that it is not falsifiable; and, its content involves motivational-emotional states. In contrast, symbolic communication is based upon a socially defined system of symbols, which have arbitrary relationships with their referents. It involves a transmission of falsifiable propositions which, on some level, are intentional or voluntary. In addition, as we shall see, there is evidence that spontaneous communication is particularly associated with right-hemisphere brain functioning, while symbolic communication is based on left-hemisphere functioning.

It should be emphasized that spontaneous and symbolic communication are conceived of as occurring simultaneously; that is, human communication is seen as occurring in two simultaneous and interacting streams. These two streams involve different sorts of behavior, with the spontaneous stream being popularly associated with "nonverbal communication" or "body language." However, we have seen that nonverbal behavior is not necessarily spontaneous and that indeed much of it occurs in the direct service of the symbolic stream of communication.

Each of these two streams also has both sending and receiving aspects. Thus, in principle one could analyze the communication behavior of the sender into those behaviors that spontaneously reflect the sender's motivational-emotional state, and those that reflect and support the

Table 2-2. Summary of the Characteristics of Spontaneous and Symbolic Communication.

Characteristics	Spontaneous Communication	Symbolic Communication
Basis of signal system	Biologically shared	Socially shared
Elements	Signs: Natural externally visible aspects of referent	Symbols: Arbitrary relationship with referent
Intentionality	Spontaneous: Communicative behavior is an automatic or a reflex response	Voluntary: Sender intends to send a specific message
Content	Nonpropositional motivational/ emotional states	Propositions: Expressions capable of logical analysis (test of truth or falsity)
Cerebral processing	Related to right hemisphere	Related to left hemisphere

message that the sender is voluntarily trying to send. Also, one could analyze the processes by which the receiver perceives and interprets the spontaneous as opposed to the symbolic behaviors of the sender.

The Relationship Between Spontaneous and Symbolic Communication

One of the difficult aspects of the present analysis is the question of the relationship between spontaneous and symbolic communication: Are they two ends of a continuum, or are they dichotomous types? In what sense is there mixed spontaneous-symbolic communication? These questions are difficult to answer because symbolic and spontaneous communication are not logically related to one another but rather are *biologically* related, and the answers thus must be based upon the nature of the biological relationship, which is incompletely understood.

The general outlines of this relationship may, however, be suggested by an analogy. Let us compare the evolving brain to an evolving city in which new buildings are constructed, new roadways are built, and new centers of learning and commerce emerge, but in which *nothing is ever torn down.* The old buildings remain, the old transportation centers are still in use, and the old centers of learning and commerce still function. The old functions continue, hidden yet constantly present.

So it is with spontaneous and symbolic communication. The emotional states upon which spontaneous communication is based are phylogenetically ancient and yet always present. The reader can recognize them easily, informing constantly about the state of the body. However, like the appearance of the color red or the taste of a pear, one's personal knowledge of emotion resists easy description. Pure spontaneous communication represents our innate tendencies to express this state via sending mechanisms that have evolved specifically for this purpose. Thus, pure spontaneous communication is logically possible.

Pure symbolic communication, conversely, is not possible because spontaneous expressive tendencies are always present. Like the functioning of the new aspects of the city, they are always accompanied by the functioning of the old. Symbolic communication may become progressively complex as one moves up the phylogenetic scale, and also as a child develops. It is free from the strict biological determinism of spontaneous communication—symbolic communication involves a general information processing system that is sensitive to the structure of the external world. As Piaget (1971) has suggested, the general purpose cognitive system that underlies symbolic communication "constructs its own structure" in the course of experiencing the external world, and that structure thus comes to reflect the nature of that world as physical reality interacts with the cognitive system by way of experience.

Symbolic communication thus reflects learning and experience, and it develops with the course of cognitive development in the child. Spontaneous communication, in contrast, strictly reflects the functioning of neurochemical systems involved in motivation and emotion. These may change with maturation as new systems come "on line" as the child develops, go "off line" with aging, and so forth (Buck, 1981a). Spontaneous expression may also be altered (usually inhibited) via conditioning (Buck, 1979a), but it is not influenced by instrumental learning.

Thus the relationship between spontaneous and symbolic communication may be similar to that represented in Figure 2-1. There can be pure spontaneous communication but not pure symbolic communication, except perhaps between computers. With biological organisms, the factors underlying spontaneous communication are always present, and therefore symbolic communication is always mixed with the spontaneous. It may well be that symbolic communication originates from spontaneous communication, either phylogenetically in the evolution of the species, ontogenetically during the development of the individual, or both.

This analysis, of course, still does not answer the question of how spontaneous and symbolic communication are related in any given instance, or explain the detailed nature of their interaction. Instead, it suggests that the answers to these questions lie in our gaining a greater understanding of the nature of the relationships and interactions between the biological systems upon which spontaneous and symbolic

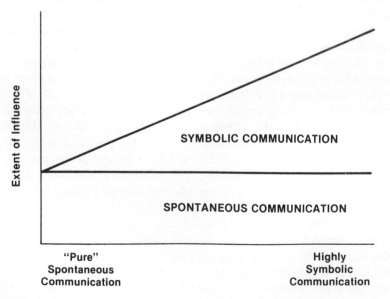

Figure 2-1. Hypothesized Relationship Between Spontaneous and Symbolic Communication.

communication are based. There is intriguing evidence that the relationship between spontaneous and symbolic communication involves the interactions between the right and left hemispheres of the brain.

Cerebral Lateralization and Communication

Spontaneous vs. Symbolic Communication and Cerebral Lateralization

We noted above that Buck and Duffy (1980) found that patients with left hemisphere brain damage showed no deficit in spontaneous communication, while right hemisphere-damaged patients did show significant deficits. The implications of this finding are considerable, for previous research on brain-damaged patients uniformly found left hemisphere-damaged patients to show deficits in communication via nonverbal behavior which seem closely related to the verbal impairment (aphasia) seen in these patients. For example, persons who suffer left hemisphere damage are likely to lose the ability to communicate via nonvocal means: they lose abilities at such skills as telegraphy, semaphore, sign language, and finger spelling (Kimura, 1979). Also, many studies have demonstrated deficits of gestural and pantomime recognition and expression in left hemisphere-damaged patients (Goodglass & Kaplan, 1963; Pickett, 1974; Duffy, Duffy, & Pearson, 1975; Gainotti, & Lemmo, 1976; Varney, 1978; Seron, van der Kaa, Remitz, & van den Linden, 1979; Duffy & Duffy, 1981). Moreover, the degree of gestural-pantomime impairment has been found to be closely related to the degree of aphasic verbal impairment in these patients. Six studies of the relationship between gestural-pantomime recognition impairment and verbal impairment found an average r of .73 ($p < .001$), and two studies of the relationship between gestural-pantomime expression impairment and verbal impairment found an average r of .82 ($p < .001$; Buck, Note 2). In contrast, Buck and Duffy (1980) found that, while pantomime recognition and expression were strongly related to verbal ability in left hemisphere-damaged aphasic patients ($r = .90$ and .99 respectively), spontaneous expressiveness as measured by the slide-viewing technique showed no evidence of a relationship with verbal ability ($r = .00$).

These findings suggest the following interpretation: The pantomime-gestural recognition and expression tests used in previous research involve symbolic communication, albeit via "nonverbal" channels. Since these abilities are adversely affected by left hemisphere brain damage, and since these deficits are closely associated with the aphasic verbal deficits that have long been related to left hemisphere brain damage, this interpretation suggests the hypothesis that symbolic communication in general is associated with left hemisphere processing, and is consistent with Finkelnberg's (1870) characterization of aphasia as "asymbolia" (Duffy and Liles, 1979). On the other hand, since spontaneous communication is not affected by left hemisphere brain damage, and since it is unrelated to verbal deficits, these findings suggest that spontaneous communication is relatively independent of left hemisphere brain processing. Instead, since spontaneous communication is adversely affected by right hemisphere brain damage, the data suggest the hypothesis that spontaneous communication is associated with right hemisphere processing (cf. Buck & Duffy, 1980; Buck, in press (b); Note 2).

Based partly on evidence from an internal analysis, Buck and Duffy (1980) suggested that the left hemisphere may normally exert an inhibitory influence over the emotionality of the right hemisphere. This suggestion is quite consistent with recent evidence regarding the important emotional functions of the right hemisphere, as opposed to the verbal processing of the left hemisphere. For example, in a recent review of this literature, Tucker (1981) has suggested that the left hemisphere is associated with anxiety and the verbally mediated inhibition of the emotional functions of the right hemisphere. Tucker and his colleagues have found evidence that subjects asked to either facilitate or inhibit their emotional response to color slides spontaneously report using an imagal and holistic strategy reminiscent of right hemisphere processing to facilitate their response, while they report using an analytic and verbal strategy reminiscent of left hemisphere processing to inhibit their response (Shearer and Tucker, 1981). Also, Tucker and Newman (1981) instructed subjects to inhibit their response to the slides using either an imagal or analytic strategy, and found that the latter strategy was more effective.

In summary, we are suggesting that spontaneous communication is related to right hemisphere brain processing, symbolic communication is related to left hemisphere brain processing, and the left hemisphere normally exerts an inhibitory influence upon the spontaneous expressive tendencies mediated by the right hemisphere. These suggestions are based in great part on the application of data on brain-damaged patients to normal subjects, but as we shall presently see there is considerable corroborative evidence from normal subjects as well. We shall now consider other evidence relating cerebral lateralization to spontaneous and symbolic communication.

Sending Aspects

Symbolic Communication

Left hemisphere damage results in deficits of both verbal comprehension and expression, and these deficits are associated with damage near the auditory sensory area and the precentral motor area, respectively. In general, lesions in Wernicke's area in the left temporal lobe near the auditory sensory area result in what has been termed receptive aphasia, with severe comprehension deficits, while lesions in Broca's area near the left precentral motor cortex produces expressive aphasia involving disorders of spoken and written expression without a loss of comprehension. Lesions of the arcuate fasciculus connecting Wernicke's and Broca's areas produce conduction aphasia, in which comprehension is essentially normal but which differs in other ways from Broca's aphasia.

We saw above that, in addition to language deficits, left hemisphere damage is associated with deficits in a variety of nonverbal communicative behaviors, including gestural and pantomime recognition and expression. It is also the case that left hemisphere damage is often associated with deficits in more general, noncommunicative pyramidal movements which are termed apraxias. Geschwind (1975) defines apraxias as disorders of learned movement which cannot be ascribed to weakness, incoordination, sensory loss, inattention, or a lack of comprehension of commands. For example, a patient may be unable to pretend to blow out a match but may perform correctly when an actual match is provided. Apraxias are typically less severe with axial movements which involve midline structures (other than the lips, tongue and larynx), such as the eyes, trunk, shoulders, hips, etc. Geschwind cites a case in which a patient could correctly assume the stance of a boxer but could not respond to the commands to punch, jab, or uppercut: "he simply looked with great perplexity at his fists, without making any response" (1975, p. 192). He suggests that the relative preservation of axial movements depends on the presence of nonpyramidal motor systems which remain intact following brain damage.

Although apraxic disorders are often associated with left hemisphere brain damage, there is evidence that the language functions underlying aphasia and the motor functions underlying apraxia can reside in different hemispheres. Thus Geschwind (1975) notes that Heilman, Coyle, Gonyea, and Geschwind (1973) found that a left-handed patient with a right hemisphere lesion demonstrated apraxia with his unparalyzed right arm without manifesting any language disorder. This observation suggested that the programs for motor action in this case had been based in the right hemisphere, while language was based in the left hemisphere.

This brings us to the question of whether the deficits in gesture and pantomime in patients with left hemisphere damage are due to a general disorder of symbolic communication, as suggested above, or whether they are aspects of an apraxic disorder (cf. Goodglass & Kaplan, 1963; Kimura, 1979). To the extent that the deficits involve pyramidal motor movements, one would expect that they would be disrupted in apraxia, while on the other hand since they are involved so intimately with language, one might expect that they would be disrupted in aphasia. Perhaps deficits in gesture and pantomime occur in both aphasia and apraxia. This question is of considerable theoretical and practical interest, but final resolution will require more research. For example, Duffy, Watt, and Duffy (1981) have recently completed a path analysis of pantomime recognition and expression, aphasic verbal impairmant, intelligence deficits, and limb apraxia, and report that the parsimonious models are those that treat the aphasic impairment as the primary determinant of the other measures, which suggests that apraxia is of relatively lesser importance.

Spontaneous Communication

We have seen that left hemisphere damage leads to deficits of symbolic communication but not spontaneous communication, while right hemisphere damage has the opposite pattern of effects. Other studies, using normal subjects, have shown that right hemisphere-dominant persons (as measured by a preponderance of left-sided conjugate lateral eye movements) are more accurate senders in the slide-viewing task (Graves & Natale, 1979). Also, a number of studies have shown that facial asymmetery or "facedness" is significantly left sided (suggesting relative right hemisphere activation or left hemisphere inhibition) during the posing of emotional expressions (Borod & Caron, 1980; Borod, Caron, & Koff, in press; Campbell, 1978; Sackheim, Gur, and Saucy, 1978).

The question of whether this is true of spontaneous expression as well is unresolved. Moscovitch and Olds (1982, Note 5) report left facedness in the expressions associated with relating emotional experiences, and in my own studies I have noted, but not yet systematically investigated, pronounced asymmetrical smiles to sexual slides. Ekman, Hagar, and Friesen (1981) have found evidence that deliberate smiles are often one-sided (24% in a study employing children), and that 89% of these are more pronounced on the left side. However, spontaneous smiles were rarely one-sided (6% in the sample of children; 4% in a sample of women viewing films), and these were evenly divided between left and right asymmetries. Ekman et al. (1981) also report that posed negative expressions were asymmetrical and left-sided in children. Unfortunately, few spontaneous negative expressions occurred in the women, and although they were often asymmetrical (25%), they were evenly divided between right and left. Ekman et al. (1981) also cite unpublished observations suggesting that nonemotional facial actions involving the punctuation of speech and the concealment of felt expression are asymmetrical and left-sided. Ekman et al. (1981) conclude that there is evidence for "left facedness" in deliberate, but not spontaneous, emotional expressions.

Clearly, much remains to be explored in the area of facial assymetry. But existing research supplies additional evidence of the special importance of cerebral lateralization in emotional expression, and it suggests that the distinction between spontaneous and symbolic expression is particularly important (cf. Buck, in press (b)).

The right hemisphere has also been implicated in more general emotional processes. In normal right-handed subjects, left-sided conjugate lateral eye movements suggestive of right hemisphere activation occur during stress (Tucker, Roth, Arneson, & Buckingham, 1977) and when the subjects are answering emotion-related questions (Schwartz, Davidson, & Maer, 1975). Also, in cases of hysteria, conversion symptoms appear to occur more frequently on the left side (Galin, Diamond, & Braff, 1977; Stern, 1977). In brain-damaged patients, left hemisphere damage has been associated with a "catastrophic reaction" of depression, hostility, and fear, while right hemisphere damage has been associated with an "indifference reaction" characterized by indifference, denial of illness, disinhibition, and euphoria (Gainotti, 1972; Geschwind, Note 4). Terzian (1964; Terzian and Ceccotto, 1959) observed similar symptoms in patients whose left or right hemisphere had been temporarily inactivated. Also, Lishman (1971) has observed that, in patients whose hemispheres are disconnected through commissurotomy, the right hemisphere may be capable of an integrated emotional response without the disconnected left hemisphere knowing the reason. Thus one patient was observed to smile and appear amused when a photograph of a nude was presented to the right hemisphere via tachistoscope, but was unable to explain the reason for the amused reaction (Sperry & Gazzaniga, 1967). Finally, there is evidence that right hemisphere brain damage reduces skin conductance responding to pain (Heilman, Schwartz, and Watson, 1978) and emotionally-loaded slides (Morrow, Virtunski, Kim, and Boller, 1981).

Receiving Aspects

The spontaneous and symbolic communication streams also involve different kinds of processing by the receiver. Tucker (1981) has pointed out that the right and left hemispheres are associated with different ways of processing and representing information that amount to different sorts of cognition, with the right hemisphere being associated with wholistic, imagal, "syncretic" cognition and the left hemisphere being associated with a sequential, linear, "analytic" cognition. Thus it is possible that the right hemisphere is more involved in responding to the wholistic spontaneous "message" in another's behavior, while the left hemisphere is involved with decoding the symbolic message.

Symbolic Communication

There is much evidence that the left hemisphere is associated with the processing of sequential verbal stimuli (cf. Tucker, 1981). We saw above that damage in Wernicke's area produces severe comprehension deficits, with an ability to speak fluently. It is noteworthy that Wernicke's and Broca's aphasia have been associated with patterns of gesture that fit their different patterns of verbalization (Cicone, Wapner, Foldi, Zurif, & Gardner, 1979).

Spontaneous Communication

There is plentiful evidence that the right hemisphere is associated with a "syncretic" cognition which is sensitive to simultaneous wholistic stimuli, as opposed to sequential verbal stimuli. Also, there is evidence that the right hemisphere is specifically involved in emotion recognition. This evidence comes from studies of both right-handed normal subjects and brain damaged patients. For example, several studies have shown that in dichotic listening tasks the left ear (i.e., the right hemisphere) better recognizes emotional expression in speech—*how* the statement is expressed; while the right ear better recognizes the content of the statements *what* is expressed (Carmon & Nachson, 1973; Haggard & Parkinson, 1971; Safer & Leventhal, 1977). Also, a considerable number of studies have demonstrated that there is a left visual field (right hemisphere) superiority for the processing of faces, particularly faces expressing emotion (Buchtel, Campari, DeRisio, & Rota, 1978; Campbell, 1978; Heller & Levy, 1981; Landis, Assal, & Perret, 1979; Ley & Bryden, 1979; Safer, 1981; Subri & McKeever, 1977). "Right hemisphere-damaged" patients (a) have particular difficulties with affective speech as opposed to propositional speech (Heilman, Scholes, & Watson, 1975; Tucker, Watson, & Heilman, 1977); (b) have particular difficulties with the recognition and discrimination of emotional faces and pictures (Cicone, Wapner, & Gardner, 1980; DeKosky, Heilman, Bowers, and Valenstein, 1980; Katz, 1980); and (c) do poorly on the Profile of Nonverbal Sensitivity (PONS) test of nonverbal sensitivity (Benowitz, Bear, Rosenthal, & Mesulam, Note 1).

It should be noted that these results do not imply that the right hemisphere is associated only with the processing of spontaneous communication. We have seen that much nonverbal behavior is organized in the service of language, and it seems probable that this behavior in the sender would be processed via the right hemisphere of the receiver, as are certain aspects of language. However, our analysis does imply that that any spontaneous behavior that does occur will be preferentially processed in the right hemisphere.

A Typology of Voluntary Communication

We have seen that there is considerable evidence that spontaneous expression is associated with right hemisphere processing and that symbolic expression is associated with left hemisphere processing. Before discussing the implications of this evidence on the analysis of the onto-geny of communication, we shall consider some of the complexities of voluntary expression. We noted above (Table 2-1) that there are a number of ways in which one might evoke voluntary expressions from subjects and that there is evidence that symbolic expressions may be under more or less conscious control. It is possible that the different ways of evoking expressions cited in Table 2-1 are associated with different types of voluntary control.

The Voluntary Control of Vocalization

Jurgens (1979) has presented a neurological model of the control of spontaneous and voluntary vocalization based upon an extensive review of the literature on the neural control of expressive vocalization in primates. Jurgens suggests that this control is organized hierarchically, with the lowest level involving the facial and respiratory nuclei in the brainstem reticular formation at the level of the pons and medulla. The level coordinates the specific motor responses necessary for phonation but does not contain the "programs" underlying specific calls. The second level involves midbrain mechanisms which contain these innate prewired programs which control specific calls.

These midbrain mechanisms may be activated, or disinhibited, in several ways. First, they may be activated by motivational-emotional systems in the hypothalamus and limbic system. This, in our terms, would constitute spontaneous expression. Secondly, they may be activated voluntarily, in at least two ways: the responder may call forth the expression by voluntarily experiencing the emotion, or the responder may learn how to directly activate the midbrain mechanism through voluntary means. This kind of voluntary response, in which the expression organized in the midbrain is activated or disinhibited voluntarily, is termed "voluntary expression initiation" by Jurgens, and he suggests that the area of the cingulate gyrus, comprising the anterior limbic cortex in monkeys and the supplementary motor area in humans, is associated with this kind of voluntary expression. This constitutes his third hierarchical level of control.

The fourth level of control involves the voluntary "formation" of calls, in which the midbrain program is not used. Here, the influences upon the facial and respiratory centers come not from the midbrain but from the precentral gyrus via the pyramidal motor system. As we have seen, these influences are lateralized in the left hemisphere in humans. This system gains increasing importance in the control of vocalization as one moves from lower mammals, to monkeys, to humans—it is dispensible to the extent that the vocal repertoire of a species in innate and voluntary call formation is not necessary, but damage to this system in humans causes severe disorders, as we have seen. It might be noted that highly stereotyped verbalizations, and emotional utterances such as expletives, often survive left hemisphere damage in humans, possibly because voluntary call formation is relatively unimportant for such vocalizations (Jurgens, 1979).

Voluntary Nonverbal Behavior

I have presented a model of the neural bases of facial expression, based largely upon Jurgens' model of vocalization (Buck, in press (a), (b)). The model assumes that the mechanisms underlying facial expression and vocalization are similar in general ways, with the justification that (a) facial expression and vocalization serve similar functions via similar peripheral mechanisms—the expression of emotion via the facial musculature; and (b) the literature on the neural bases of facial expression is generally consistent with this assumption, suggesting that some facial expressions are prewired in midbrain mechanisms, that apparently analogous voluntary and nonvoluntary systems have been identified underlying facial expression, etc. (Buck, in press (b)). In essence, this model assumes that voluntary vocalization, like voluntary facial expression, involves both a nonpyramidal "expression initiation" system and a pyramidal "expression formation" system. In other words, the different methods of calling forth facial expressions summarized in Table 2-1 may be based on different voluntary mechanisms with different physiological bases.

This suggests that the detailed analysis of different types of voluntary as well as spontaneous expression in the same individuals may shed light on the nature of these physiological bases. This analysis should be done with normal subjects, but it may be particularly informative when done with brain-damaged patients. Studies of this nature are presently being conducted by Drs. Joan Borod and Elissa Koff at the Aphasia Research Center of the Boston Veterans Administration Hospital, and the initial results suggest that different methods of eliciting voluntary and spontaneous facial expressions may produce vastly different results.

Implications for the Ontogeny of Emotion Expression

The Ontogeny of Spontaneous and Symbolic Communication

In this chapter I have developed the notion that human communication occurs in two simultaneous streams: a spontaneous stream reflective of emotion and associated particularly with right hemisphere processing, and a symbolic stream reflective of intentional propositions and based on left hemisphere processing. Nonverbal behavior is influenced by both streams: there is no clearly defined way to determine which aspects of behavior truly reflect spontaneous communication, although we saw that the situation can be structured to make such behavior more or less likely. The implications of this point of view in the analysis of the ontogeny of communication are considerable. One obvious implication is that the communication of the newborn infant must be spontaneous and that symbolic communication will increase in relationship to language learning. However, this increase in symbolic communication does not lessen the importance of spontaneous communication. Studies in the nonverbal communication literature have demonstrated again and again that spontaneous behavior exerts a profound albeit largely unrecognized influence upon behavior, and this fact is responsible for much of the present interest in this field.

A Model of Ontogeny

In previous work, I developed a model of the ontogeny of emotional expression that attempted to take into account the influence of innate species-specific factors, temperament, social learning, and cognitive development (Buck, 1979a; 1981a; 1982). This model may be summarized as follows.

The Animal Model of Emotion Ontogeny

An animal model of emotion ontogeny, stemming largely from Harlow's studies of social development in monkeys, has proved extremely useful and accounts for much of our present understanding of emotion ontogeny in humans. In brief, this model suggests that motivational-emotional systems relevant to social relations, spontaneous communication mechanisms, and normal social experience have evolved to develop hand-in-hand in the individual (Buck, 1981a; 1982a). For example, there is evidence that the rhesus monkey is born with the capacity for affection but without the capacity to experience fear or anger, and that early in life it transfers these positive feelings to the other animals in its group (Deets & Harlow, Note 3). The capacity to experience fear and anger does not develop until the infant has had much social experience and has come to trust and perhaps "love" its fellow monkey. These observations are quite compatible with the results of studies by Izard and his collegues on the facial expressions of human infants to the process of receiving a painful injection, which found that the classic facial expressions of fear and anger appear only in older infants (Izard, Huebner, Risser, McGinnes, & Dougherty, 1980).

The Role of Temperament

Although there appear to be species-specific patterns to the normal ontogeny of emotion and emotion expression, there are individual differences as well. Preschool children show great variation in their spontaneous facial expressiveness to color slides, and this expressiveness is related both to teachers' ratings of the child's affiliativeness and assertiveness in the preschool, and (negatively) to the child's skin conductance response to the slides (Buck, 1975; 1977). Field and Walden (1981) have demonstrated individual differences in facial expressiveness in newborn infants, which is negatively related to their acceleratory heart rate response to affective stimuli. These observations suggest the operation of a biologically based source of individual differences, analogous to Jones's (1935; 1950; 1960) notion of externalizing vs. internalizing modes of response, and Eysenck's (1967) extraversion-introversion, which may involve biological mechanisms of inhibition (Buck, 1979a; in press (a), (b)).

The Role of Social Learning

At the same time, there is evidence that social learning causes situationally-specific changes in emotional expression. Adult males are less spontaneously facially expressive than adult females (Buck, Savin, Miller, & Caul, 1972; Buck, Miller, & Caul, 1974; Buck, in press (b)), and preschool-aged boys (but not girls) show a negative relationship between spontaneous expressiveness and age (Buck, 1975). Boys also have been shown to become less adept at posing expressions as they grow older (Zuckerman & Przewuzman, 1979). On the other hand, there is evidence that girls in our culture learn to inhibit their spontaneous expression of aggression and achievement-oriented behaviors (Buck, 1979a; 1981a; 1981b).

The Role of Cognitive Development

All of the foregoing findings can be accomodated within an animal model of emotion ontogeny, and in fact they could be accounted for by the action of subcortical and paleocortical reward and punishment systems in which biologically based tendencies toward internalizing or externalizing modes of response are present at birth, which can be modified in situationally specific ways by social learning (cf. Buck, 1979a, pp. 156-160; in press (b)). However, this model does not account for the great extent to which human behavior, including emotional behavior, comes under the control of cognitive factors in general and language in particular. In fact, emotion ontogeny in humans involves emotion education—the acquisition of knowledge about emotion in oneself and others—as surely as intellectual development involves the acquisition of knowledge about the external world (Buck, 1982).

It is in this context that the present analysis becomes most relevant, for the functioning of the left and right hemispheres clearly involves cognition, and in fact the hemispheres involve different types of cognition: the wholistic, analogic and imagal syncretic cognition associated with the right hemisphere, and the linear, sequential, and verbal analytic cognition associated with the left hemisphere (Tucker, 1981). The process of cognitive development, then, cannot be separated from the process of emotion development. The processes occur simultaneously and interactively, just as they are manifested simultaneously and interactively in spontaneous and symbolic behavior.

The question of the relationship between cognition and cognitive development on the one hand, and emotion and emotional development on the other, can thus be seen to involve the following considerations: (a) there are emotional processes (the animal model) which can be seen to involve both innate factors and social learning, but which appear to be independent of higher-order verbal and analytic cognitive processes; (b) in humans these "basic" emotional processes interact with verbal and analytic cognitive processes; (c) these processes are expressed via spontaneous and symbolic behavior, respectively; and (d) there are two sorts of cognition associated with the two cerebral hemispheres—the syncretic cognition associated with the right hemisphere and the analytic cognition associated with the left. In the concluding sections, I shall relate these considerations to one another and discuss some of the implications of this analysis.

Syncretic and Analytic Cognitive Development

The above discussion implies that any comprehensive consideration of the ontogeny of emotion in humans must begin with the animal model but must go beyond that model to show the interactive influence of higher-order analytic cognitive processes. It also suggests that there are in effect two simultaneous processes of cognitive development: the development of syncretic cognition and the development of analytic cognition.

Syncretic Cognition

Syncretic cognition involves a direct process of "knowledge by acquaintance": it is completely given by the nature of the stimulus with no intervening rules of information processing or organization. It is "direct perception" in the Gibsonian sense (Gibson, 1966; 1977). However, different stimuli are by nature differentially "visible" or "accessible" to the individual via syncretic cognition. We suggested above that an "accessibility dimension" has important implications for the analysis of emotional development. Some responses (particularly goal-directed overt behaviors) are readily accessible both to the responder and to others; other responses (particularly subjective experiences) are accessible to the responder but not to others; and still other responses (particularly physiological responses) are normally not accessible without special equipment. Expressive nonverbal behaviors are interesting

in this regard in that they are potentially accessible both to the responder and to others, but they are often not attended to. Ekman and Friesen
(1969) have suggested that expressive behaviors that are normally
ignored may often "leak" the true feelings of the responder.

This brings up another important consideration regarding the ontogeny of syncretic cognition: the *education of attention*. There are a
variety of ways in which one might direct one's attention, resulting in
widely different experiences via syncretic cognition. Wenger for example has suggested that persons from India may often learn to attend to
internal physiological events that remain "unaccessed" by most Western-
ers (Wenger and Bagchi, 1961; Wenger, Bagchi, and Anand, 1961). The
education of attention is Gibson's (1966) phrase for the process that
determines the perceptual selection of information, and thus determines
the organization or perceptual experience: the raw material which the
perceiver draws on in making the judgments and inferences involved in
analytic cognition.

A third consideration in the analysis of the development of syncretic
cognition involves the maturation and cycling of motivational and
emotional systems which affect such cognition. We noted above that
different systems go "on line" and "off line" at different times. For
example, the very young infant may be incapable of experiencing fear
or anger, the adolescent may experience the world differently in certain
ways following puberty, etc.

Emotion Education

In contrast to the development of syncretic cognition, the development of an analytic cognition takes place via the processes familiar from
conventional analyses of "cognitive development:" via assimilation and
accommodation (Piaget, 1971), cognitive growth cycles (Elkind, 1971),
and the like. As noted above, the general information processors underlying analytic cognition in effect construct their own structure in the
course of interaction with and adaptation to physical reality.

A similar process must take place with regard to emotional reality,
where the relevant phenomena involve not only experience with physical processes, but subjective emotional experience as well, mediated
by syncretic cognition. This process may be aptly termed *emotion education* (Buck, 1982).

The Role of Cerebral Lateralization

If the foregoing is correct, one would expect that the course of emotion ontogeny would be closely related to the course of cognitive
development, the development of language, and the development of
specialization of function in the two cerebral hemispheres. This last

concept stems from the identification of syncretic and analytic cognition with right hemisphere and left hemisphere processing, respectively. Unfortunately, very few studies have explicitly considered the relationships between these "cognitive" phenomena and emotion development. In fact, cognitive theories of emotion are often presented as competing against rather than being complementary to more biologically based approaches (Sommers, 1981). Thus, this area remains extraordinarily fertile and unexplored and holds great potential importance for the analysis of both cognitive and emotional development.

Cognitive Understanding of Emotion

One area in which some study has been done concerns the child's (analytic) cognitive understanding of emotion and the situations in which emotion is evoked. Barden, Zelko, Duncan, and Masters (1980) asked children of various ages (4 to 5, 9 to 10, and 12 to 13 years) about the probable emotional reaction to events described in brief vignettes ("If a classmate walked up to you and hit you in the stomach, would you feel...?"). The children chose among the following emotions: happiness, sadness, fear, anger, and neutral affect. The vignettes were categorized in terms of eight types of experience: success, failure, nurturance, aggression, justified punishment, unjustified punishment, dishonesty-caught, and dishonesty-not caught. The results indicated that there was a high degree of consensus across ages about some vignettes, e.g., being happy at success and sad and angry about aggression and unjustified punishment. However, other vignettes showed age changes suggestive of developmental changes in the children's understanding of emotion: younger children expected a happy response to dishonest-not caught, while older cildren predicted fear; older children moved toward a neutral rather than a happy response to nurturance.

Discrepant Messages

Another example, which particularly illustrates the potential application of the cerebral lateralization literature to emotion development, involves the effects of messages in which verbal and nonverbal cues are discrepant from one another. A number of studies have investigated how such messages are resolved and have studied developmental sequences by which such resolution occurs (Bugental, 1974; Bugental, Kaswan, & Love, 1970; Bugental, Kaswan, Love, & Fox, 1970 Mehrabian & Ferris, 1967; Mehrabian & Weiner, 1967; Volkmar, Hoder, & Siegel, 1980). In general, such resolution has been defined in terms of the subjects' overt understanding of the message. For example, Volkmar and Siegel (this volume) studied the responses of young (1- to 3-year-old) children to messages asking them to approach or stay away, with systematic variation of discrepancies between channels. They found that the messages could be considered to form a unidimensional cumulative hierarchy—a Guttman scale—in terms of the child's approach tendencies.

By focusing exclusively on the overt understanding, however, sucn studies may miss other, more hidden, effects of discrepant communications. In effect, they focus exclusively on the symbolic communication process, ignoring the spontaneous. In contrast, Galin (1974) has analysed a double-bind situation in which a parent gives a child a voluntary message verbally, "I love you," and a contradictory negative spontaneous message via tone of voice and facial-bodily expression. Because of their different cognitive skills, the left hemisphere and right hemisphere extract different information from the experience: "the left will attend to the verbal cues because it cannot extract information from the facial gestalt effectively; the right will attend to the nonverbal cues because it cannot easily understand the words" (Galin, 1974, p. 576). Because of the different information, the response tendencies of the two hemispheres would be different—the left hemisphere would tend to approach, the right hemisphere to flee. Typically, the response tendencies of the left hemisphere seem to dominate those of the right hemisphere, so that the apparent resolution of the message would reflect analytic cognition. However, if the left hemisphere is unable to inhibit the response tendencies of the right hemisphere completely, Galin suggests that the transfer of conflicting information from the other side may somehow become blocked. In effect, the information contained in the right hemisphere would be "repressed" and become "unconscious."

It is possible that studies of discrepant messages might be able to demonstrate these more covert effects, for example by ratings of the message source. It may be that such effects will be demonstrated only when the discrepant message is highly important to the recipient.

Sex Differences

Another area in which the cerebral lateralization literature may have significant impact is in the analysis of sex differences in the ontogeny of emotion. Substantial sex differences have been demonstrated in spontaneous communication, in both sending accuracy and receiving ability (Buck, Miller, & Caul, 1974; Buck, Savin, Miller, & Caul, 1972; Hall, 1978). In recent studies employing a segmentation technique to analyze the events in the temporal stream of spontaneous expression, we have found evidence of fundamental differences in the spontaneous communication process in females and males. Females show evidence of more spontaneous behavior, and particularly more facial expression, than do males while viewing affective slides, but not while discussing their responses to them. Observers showed a greater consensus about the location of meaningful events in the expressions of females than males; the meaningful events in the expressions of females were more closely related to the females' sending accuracy than was the relationship between meaningful events and sending accuracy in males (Buck, Baron, & Barrette, 1982; Buck, Baron, Goodman, & Shapiro, 1980).

In regard to receiving ability, accurate female receivers were found to indicate fewer meaningful points while viewing adults, and they were more accurate in the location of the points in the behavior stream— accurate female receivers had more "hits" and fewer "misses" on the points consensually identified as "meaningful" by the group as a whole. There was no significant relationship between receiving ability and segmentation accuracy for males (Buck et al., 1980; in press (b)).

In other words, these findings indicate that spontaneous communication is more related to segmentation measures in females than males. This suggests the possibility that the spontaneous communication may involve a more direct perception-based syncretic-cognitive processing in females but a more mediated, analytic-cognitive processing in males. It may be relevant in this regard that there are known albeit little understood sex differences in cerebral lateralization (cf. Moore & Haynes, 1980; Trotman & Hammond, 1979) and, as we have seen, that cerebral lateralization has been implicated in both emotion expression and perception. Thus, although there is no direct evidence that the sex differences in spontaneous communication are based on differences in cerebral lateralization, the evidence suggests that the links between gender, spontaneous communication, and cerebral lateralization should be actively investigated.

Conclusions

The analysis of cerebral lateralization is relevant to the understanding of how, in the life of the individual, symbolic communication grows out of spontaneous communication, and how symbolic and spontaneous communication continue to interact throughout life. This analysis encourages, and indeed necessitates, a broad view of human behavior in which emotional and cognitive factors cannot be fully understood in isolation. It provides a physiological base with which to view the nature of the ontogeny of spontaneous and symbolic communication, emotion and cognition, and the relationships between them. It also shows us that an animal model of emotion ontongeny must fall short in explaining human emotion, and alerts us to the importance of the realm of emotion education, where phylogenetically ancient systems of motivation and emotion come into contact with cognition and language, making the human animal the creative, unpredictable, adventurous, and extremely dangerous species that it is.

Summary

In this chapter the argument has been made that a consideration of the biological foundations of nonverbal behavior provides a coherent basis for understanding the role of nonverbal behavior in the ontogeny of communication. We have suggested that it is necessary to distinguish between voluntary and nonvoluntary nonverbal behavior and have contrasted the characteristics of spontaneous communication, which is nonvoluntary, and symbolic communication, which is voluntary on some level but not necessarily a conscious level. Spontaneous communication involves the expression of motivational-emotional states. It is based on a biologically shared signal system and is nonpropositional; information is transferred via signs. Symbolic communication involves the encoding of propositions within a socially shared signal system, with information being transferred via symbols. Adult human communication is seen as being composed of simultaneous and interacting streams of spontaneous and symbolic communication.

This chapter reviewed evidence that spontaneous communication is based upon right hemisphere processing and is associated with a wholistic, imagal, syncretic cognition; while symbolic communication is based upon left hemisphere processing and associated with a sequential, verbal, analytic cognition. If this is the case, the study of cerebral lateralization may provide the basis for a biological model highly relevant to the analysis of the ontogeny of communication and, specifically, to the analysis of how emotion and cognitive factors interact in the development of human communication. Hence, an understanding of cerebral lateralization provides a new perspective on the long-standing issue of the role of innate vs. learned factors in nonverbal behavior.

This chapter also reviewed a model which suggested that different kinds of voluntary expression are based on different physiological mechanisms. Finally, the chapter reviewed studies of the development of nonverbal behavior, suggesting that an animal model of emotion ontogeny—encompassing the roles of species-specific communication patterns, temperament, and social learning—cannot deal with the complexity of human emotion ontogeny, and that cognitive development and emotion education must be accounted for as well. It is suggested that the analysis of cerebral lateralization may provide evidence particularly relevant to the latter problem: the ontogeny and interaction of phylogenetically ancient motivational-emotional systems with their associated syncretic cognition on one hand, and of language and analytic cognition on the other. This all suggests that two of the most active and vital areas within psychology at the present time—the study of the role of nonverbal behavior in emotional expression and communication, and the study of cerebral lateralization—have much to contribute to one another.

Reference Notes

1. Benowitz, L. I., Bear, D. M., Rosenthal, R., & Mesulam, M. Sensitivity to non-verbal communication after unilateral brain damage. Unpublished manuscript, Harvard University, 1980.
2. Buck, R. Symbolic vs. spontaneous communication processes and left vs. right hemisphere brain functions. Unpublished paper, University of Connecticut, November 1980.
3. Deets, A., & Harlow, H. F. Early experience and the maturation of agonistic behavior. Paper presented at the convention of the American Association for the Advancement of Science, New York, Dec 1971.
4. Geschwind, N. Neurological denial syndromes. Paper presented at the University of Connecticut, October 1979.
5. Moscovitch, M. & Olds, J. Right-hemisphere superiority in controlling the pro-duction of spontaneous facial expressions. Presented at the meeting of the International Neuropsychology Society, Holland, June 1979.

References

Andrew, R. J. The origin and evolution of the calls and facial expressions of the pri-mates. *Behavior*, 1963, *20*, 1-109.

Andrew, R. J. The origins of facial expressions. *Scientific American*, 1965, *213*, 88-94.

Barden, R. C., Zelko, F. A., Duncan, S. W., & Masters, J. C. Children's consensual knowledge about the experiential determinants of emotion. *Journal of Person-ality and Social Psychology*, 1980, *39*, 968-976.

Birdwhistell, R. L. *Kinesics and context.* Philadelphia: University of Pennsylvania Press, 1970.

Borod, J., & Caron, H. Facedness and emotion related to lateral dominance, sex and expression type. *Neuropsychologia*, 1980, *18*, 237-241.

Borod, J. C., Caron, H. S., & Koff, E. Facial asymmetry related to quantitative measures of handedness, footedness, and eyedness. *Cortex*, in press.

Buchtel, H., Campari, F., DeRisio, C., & Rota, R., Hemispheric differences in the discrimination reaction time to facial expressions. *Italian Journal of Psychology*, 1978, *5*, 159-169.

Buck, R. Differences in social learning underlying overt-behavioral, self-report, and physiological responses to emotion. *Research in Education*, 1971, *6*, 19. (abstract)

Buck, R. *Human motivation and emotion.* New York: John Wiley & Sons, Inc., 1976.

Buck, R. Individual differences in nonverbal sending accuracy and electrodermal responding: The externalizing-internalizing dimension. In R. Rosenthal (Ed.), *Skill in nonverbal communication: Individual differences.* Cambridge, MA: Oelgeschlager, Gunn & Hain, 1979. (a)

Buck, R. Measuring individual differences in the nonverbal communication of affect: The slide-viewing paradigm. *Human Communication Research*, 1979, *6*, 47-57. (b)

Buck, R. Nonverbal behavior and the theory of emotion. The facial feedback hy-pothesis. *Journal of Personality and Social Psychology*, 1980, *38*, 811-824.

Buck, R. The evolution and development of emotion expression and communication. In S. Brehm, S. Kassin, and R. Gibbons (Eds.), *Developmental social psychology*. New York: Oxford University Press, 1981. (a)

Buck, R. Sex differences in psychophysiological responding and subjective experience: A comment. *Psychophysiology*, 1981, *18*, 349-350. (b)

Buck, R. Emotion development and emotion education. In R. Plutchik and H. Kellerman (Eds.), *Emotions in early development*. New York: Academic Press, 1982. (a)

Buck, R. The physiological bases of nonverbal communication. In W. Waid (Ed.), *Sociophysiology*. New York: Springer-Verlag, in press. (a)

Buck, R. *Emotion and nonverbal behavior: The communication of affect*. New York: Guilford Press, in press. (b)

Buck, R. W. Nonverbal communication of affect in children. *Journal of Personality and Social Psychology*, 1975, *31*, 644-654.

Buck, R. W. Nonverbal communication of affect in preschool children: Relationships with personality and skin conductance. *Journal of Personality and Social Psychology*, 1977, *35*, 225-236.

Buck, R., Baron, R., & Barrette, D. The temporal organization of spontaneous nonverbal expression: A segmentation analysis. *Journal of Personality and Social Psychology*, 1982, *42*, 506-517.

Buck, R., Baron, R., Goodman, N., and Shapiro, B. The unitization of spontaneous nonverbal behavior in the study of emotion communication. *Journal of Personality and Social Psychology*, 1980, *39*, 522-529.

Buck, R., & Duffy, R. Nonverbal communication of affect in brain-damaged patients. *Cortex*, 1980, *16*, 351-362.

Buck, R. W., Miller, R. E., & Caul, W. F. Sex personality and physiological variables in the communication of emotion via facial expression. *Journal of Personality and Social Psychology*, 1974, *30*, 587-596.

Buck, R. Savin, V., Miller, R. E., & Caul, W. F. Nonverbal communication of affect in humans. *Journal of Personality and Social Psychology*, 1972, *23*, 362-371.

Bugental, D. E. Interpretations of naturally occurring discrepancies between words and intonation: Modes of inconsistency resolution. *Journal of Personality and Social Psychology*, 1974, *30*, 125-133.

Bugental, D. E., Kaswan, J. W., & Love, L. R. Perception of contradictory meanings conveyed by verbal and nonverbal channels. *Journal of Personality and Social Psychology*, 1970, *16*, 647-655.

Bugental, D. E., Kaswan, J. W., Love, L. R., & Fox, M. N. Child versus adult perception of evaluative messages in verbal, vocal, and visual channels. *Developmental Psychology*, 1970, *2*, 367-375.

Campbell, R. Asymmetries in interpreting and expressing a posed facial expression. *Cortex*, 1978, *14*, 327-342.

Carmon, A., & Nachshon, I. Ear asymmetry in perception of emotional and nonverbal stimuli. *Acta Physiologica*, 1973, *37*, 351-357.

Cicone, M., Wapner, W., Foldi, N., Zurif, E., & Gardner, H. The relation between gesture and language in aphasic communication. *Brain and Language*, 1979, *8* 324-349.

Cicone, M., Wapner, W., & Gardner, H. Sensitivity to emotional expressions and situations in organic patients. *Cortex*, 1980, *16*, 145-147.

Darwin, C. Expressions of the emotions in man and animals. London: John Murray, 1872.

DeKosky, S. T., Heilman, K. M., Bowers, D., & Valenstein, E. Recognition and discrimination of emotional faces and pictures. *Brain and Language*, 1980, *9*, 206-214.

Dittman, A. The body movement-speech rhythm relationship as a cue to speech encoding. In A. W. Siegmen and B. Pope (Eds.), *Studies in dyadic communication*. New York: Pergamon Press, 1972.

Duffy, J. R., Watt, J., Duffy, R. J. Path analysis: A strategy for investigating multiple causal relationships in communication disorders. *Journal of Speech and Hearing Research*, 1981, *24*, 474-490.

Duffy, R. J., & Duffy, J. R. Three studies of deficits in pantomimic expression and pantomimic recognition in aphasia. *Journal of Speech and Hearing Research*, 1981, *24*, 70-84.

Duffy, R. J., & Liles, B. Z. A translation of Finkelnburg's (1870) lecture on aphasia as "asymbolia" with commentary. *Journal of Speech and Hearing Disorders*. 1979, *44*, 156-168.

Ekman, P. About brows: Emotional and conversational signals. In M. von Cranach, K. Foppa, W. Lepenies, Y. D. Ploog (Eds.), *Human Ethology*. London: Cambridge University Press, 1979.

Ekman, P. & Friesen, W. V. The repertoire of nonverbal behavior: Categories, origins, usage and coding. *Semiotica*, 1969, *1*, 49-98.

Ekman, P. & Friesen, W. V. Detecting deception from the body or face. *Journal of Personality and Social Psychology*, 1974, *29*, 288-298.

Ekman, P. & Friesen, W. V. *Unmasking the face*. Englewood Cliffs, NJ.: Prentice Hall, 1975.

Ekman, P., Hagar, J., & Friesen, W. The symmetry of emotional and deliberate facial action. *Psychophysiology*, 1981, *18*, 101-106.

Elkind, D. Cognitive growth cycles in mental development. In J. K. Cole (Ed.), *Nebraska Symposium on Motivation*. Lincoln: University of Nebraska Press, 1971.

Eysenck, H. J. *The biological basis of personality*. Springfield, IL.: Charles C. Thomas, 1967.

Field, T. M. & Walden, T. A. Perception and production of facial expressions in infancy and early childhood. In H. Reese & L. Lipsett (Eds.), *Advances in child development and behavior*, Vol. 16. New York: Academic Press, 1981.

Finkelnburg, F. Niederrheinische Gesellschaft, Sitzung vom 21. Marz 1870 in Bonn. Berl. Klin, Wschr. 7:449-450, 460-462.

Gainotti, G. Emotional behavior and hemispheric side of the lesion. *Cortex*, 1972, *8*, 41-55.

Gainotti, G. & Lemmo, M. Comprehension of symbolic gestures in aphasia. *Brain Lang.*, 1976, *3*, 451-460.

Galin, D. Implications for psychiatry of left and right cerebral specialization: A neurophysiological context for unconscious processes. *Archives of General Psychiatry*, 1974, *31*, 572.

Galin, D., Diamond, R., & Braff, D. Lateralization of conversion symptoms: More frequent on the left. *American Journal of Psychiatry*, 1977, *134*, 578-580.

Geschwind, N. The apraxias: Neural mechanisms of disorders of learned movement. *American Scientist*, 1975, *63*, 188-195.

Gibson, J. J. *The senses considered as perceptual systems*. Boston: Houghton-Mifflin, 1966.

Gibson, J. J. The theory of affordances. In R. E. Shaw and J. Bransford (Eds.), *Perceiving, acting and knowing: Toward an ecological psychology*. Hillsdale, NJ: Lawrence Erlbaum Assoc., 1977.

Goodglass, H. & Kaplan, E. Disturbances of gesture and pantomime in aphasia. *Brain*, 1963, *86*, 703-720.

Graves, C. A. & Natale, M. The relationship of hemispheric preference, as measured by conjugate lateral eye movements, to accuracy of emotional facial expression. *Motivation and Emotion*, 1979, *3*, 219-234.

Haggard, M. P. & Parkinson, A. M. Stimulus and task factors as determinants of ear advantages. *Quarterly Journal of Experimental Psychology*, 1971, *23*, 168-177.

Hall, J. A. Gender effects in decoding nonverbal cues. *Psychological Bulletin*, 1978, *85*, 845-857.

Heilman, K. M., Coyle, J. M., Gonyea, E. G., & Geschwind, N. Apraxia and agraphia in a left-hander. *Brain*, 1973, *99*, 21-28.

Heilman, K. M., Scholes, R., & Watson, R. T. Auditory affective agnosia. *Journal of Neurology, Neurosurgery and Psychiatry*, 1975, *38*, 69-72.

Heilman, K. M., Schwartz, H. D., & Watson, R. T. Hypoarousal in patients with the neglect syndrome and emotional indifference. *Neurology*, 1978, *28*, 229-232.

Heller, W. & Levy, J. Perception and expression of emotion in right-handers and left-handers. *Neuropsychologia*, 1981, *19*, 263-272.

Izard, C. E., Huebner, R. R. Risser, D., McGinnes, G. C., & Dougherty, L. M. The young infant's ability to produce discrete emotion expressions. *Developmental Psychology*, 1980, *16*, 132-140.

Jones, H. E. The galvanic skin response as related to overt emotional expression. *American Journal of Psychology*, 1935, *47*, 241-251.

Jones, H. E. The study of patterns of emotional expression. In M. Reymert (Ed.), *Feelings and emotions*. New York: McGraw-Hill, 1950.

Jones, H. E. The longitudinal method in the study of personality. In I. Iscoe & H. W. Stevenson (Eds.), *Personality development in children*. Chicago: University of Chicago Press, 1960.

Jurgens, Uwe. Neural control of vocalization in nonhuman primates. In H. D. Steklis & M. J. Raleigh (Eds.), *Neurobiology of social communication in primates*. New York: Academic Press, 1979.

Katz, R. C. Perception of facial affect in aphasia. In R. H. Brookshire (Ed.), *Clinical aphasiology: Conference proceedings 1980*. Minneapolis: BRK Publishers, 1980.

Key, M. R. *The relationship of verbal and nonverbal communication*. New York: Mouton, 1980.

Kimura, D. Neuromotor mechanisms in the evolution of human communication. In H. D. Steklis & M. J. Raleigh (Eds.), *Neurobiology of social communication in primates*. New York: Academic Press, 1979.

Koenig, O. Das aktionssystem der Bartmeise (Panurus biarmicus L). *Oesterr. Zool. Z.*, 1951, *3*, 247-325.

Koff, E., Borod, J., & White, B. Asymmetries for hemiface size and mobility. *Neuropsychologia*, 1981, *19*, 825-930.

Landis, T., Assal, G., & Perret, E. Opposite cerebral hemisphere superiorities for visual associative processing of emotional facial expressions and objects. *Nature*, 1979, *278*, 739-740.

Ley, R. G. & Bryden, M. P. Hemispheric differences in processing emotions and faces. *Brain and Language*, 1979, *1*, 127-138.

Lishman, W. A. Emotion, consciousness, and will after brain bisection in man. *Cortex*, 1971, *7*, 181-192.

Mead, G. H. *Mind, self, and society*. Chicago: University of Chicago Press, 1934.

Mehrabian, A. & Ferris, S. R. Inference of attitudes from nonverbal communication. *Journal of Consulting Psychology*, 1967, *31*, 248-252.

Mehrabian, A. & Wiener, M. Decoding of inconsistent communications. *Journal of Personality and Social Psychology*, 1967, *6*, 109-114.

Miller, R. E. Experimental approaches to the autonomic and behavioral aspects of affective communication in rhesus monkeys. In S. Altmann (Ed.), *Social communication among primates*. Chicago: University of Chicago Press, 1967.

Miller, R. E. Experimental studies of communication in the monkey. In L. Rosenblum (Ed.), *Primate behavior developments in field and laboratory research*, Vol. 2. New York: Academic Press, 1971.

Miller, R. E. Social and pharmacological influences on nonverbal communication in monkeys and man. In L. Krames, T. Alloway, & P. Pliner (Eds.), *Nonverbal communication*. New York: Plenum Press, 1974.

Moore, W. H. & Haynes, W. O. A study of alpha hemispheric asymmetries for verbal and nonverbal stimuli in males and females. *Brain and Language*, 1980, *9*, 338-349.

Morrow, L., Virtunski, P. B., Kin, Y., & Boller, F. Arousal responses to emotional stimuli and laterality of lesion. *Neuropsychologia*, 1981, *19*, 65-71.

Moscovitch, M. & Olds, J. Asymmetries in spontaneous facial expressions and their possible relation to hemispheric specialization. *Neuropsychologia*, 1982, *20*, 71-82.

Piaget, J. Piaget's theory. In P. Mussen (Ed.), *Handbook of child development*, Vol. 1. New York: Wiley, 1971.

Pickett, L. W. An assessment of gestural and pantomimic deficit in aphasic patients. *Acta Symbolica*, 1974, *5*, 69-86.

Riggs, G., Winter, P., Ploog, D., & Mayer, W. Effects of deafening on the vocal behavior of the squirrel monkey. *Folia primat*, 1972, *17*, 404-420.

Russell, B. *The principles of mathematics*. London: Allen & Unwin, 1903.

Sackeim, H. A., Gur, R. C., & Saucy, M. C. Emotions are expressed more intensely on the left side of the face. *Science*, 1978, *202*, 434-435.

Sackett, G. P. Monkeys reared in isolation with pictures as visual input: Evidence for an innate releasing mechanism. *Science*, 1966, *154*, 1468-1473.

Safer, M. A. Sex and hemisphere differences in access to codes for processing emotional expressions and faces. *Journal of Experimental Psychology: General*, 1981, *110*, 86-100.

Safer, M. A. & Leventhal, H. Ear differences in evaluating emotional tones of voice and verbal content. *Journal of Experimental Psychology: Human Perception and Performance*, 1977, *3*, 75-82.

Scheflen, A. *Communicational structure*. Bloomington, IN: Indiana University Press, 1973.

Schwartz, G. E., Davidson, R. J., & Maer, F. Right hemisphere lateralization for emotion in the human brain: Interactions with cognition. *Science*, 1975, *190*, 286-288.

Seron, X., van der Kaa, M. A., Remitz, A., & van den Linden, M. Pantomime interpretation and aphasia. *Neuropsychologia*. 1979, *17*, 661-667.

Shearer, S. L. & Tucker, D. M. Differential cognitive contributions of the cerebral hemispheres in the modulation of emotional arousal. *Cognitive Therapy and Research*, 1981, *5*, 85-93.

Sommers, S. Emotionality reconsidered: The role of cognition in emotional responsiveness. *Journal of Personality and Social Psychology*, 1981, *41*, 553-561.

Sperry, R. W. & Gazzaniga, M. S. Language following surgical disconnection of the
commissures. In F. L. Darley (Ed.), *Brain mechanisms underlying speech and
language*. New York: Grune & Stratton, 1967.

Stern, D. B. Handedness and the lateral distribution of conversion reactions. *Journal
of Nervous and Mental Disease*, 1977, *164*, 122-128.

Suberi, M. & McKeever, W. F. Differential right hemispheric memory of emotional
and non-emotional faces. *Neuropsychologia*, 1977, *15*, 757-768.

Terzian, H. Behavioural and EEG effects of intracarotid sodium amytal infections.
Acta Neurochirurgica (Wien), 1964, *12*, 230-239.

Terzian, H. & Ceccotto, C. Su un nuova metodo per la determinazione e lo studio
della dominanaza emisferica. *Giorn. Psichiat. Neuropat.*, 1959, *87*, 889-924.

Trotman, S. C. A. & Hammond, G. R. Sex differences in task-dependent EEG
asymmetries. *Psychophysiology*, 1979, *16*, 429-431.

Tucker, D. M. Lateral brain function, emotion, and conceptualization. *Psychological
Bulletin*, 1981, *89*, 19-46.

Tucker, D. M. & Newman, J. P. Lateral brain function and the cognitive inhibition
of emotional arousal. *Cognitive Therapy and Research*, 1981, *5*, 197-202.

Tucker, D. M., Roth, R. S., Arneson, B. A., & Buckingham, V. Right hemisphere
activation during stress. *Neuropsychologia*, 1977, *15*, 697-700.

Tucker, D. M., Watson, R. T., & Heilman, K. M. Discrimination and evocation of
affectively intoned speech in patients with right parietal disease. *Neurology*,
1977, *27*, 947-950.

Varney, N. R. Linguistic correlates of pantomime recognition in aphasic patients.
Journal of Neurology, Neurosurgery and Psychiatry, 1978, *41*, 564-568.

Volkmar, F. R., Hoder, L., & Siegel, A. E. Discrepant social communications.
Developmental Psychology, 1980, *16*, 495-505.

Weiner, M., Devoe, S., Rubinow, S., & Geller, J. Nonverbal behavior and nonverbal
communication. *Psychological Review*, 1972, *79*, 185-214.

Wenger, M. A. & Bagchi, B. K. Studies of autonomic functions in practitioners of
yoga in India. *Behavioral Science*, 1961, *6*, 312-323.

Wenger, M. A., Bagchi, B. K., & Anand, B. K. Experiments in India on "voluntary"
control of the heart and pulse. *Circulation*, 1961, *24*, 1319-1325.

Winter, P., Handley, P., Ploog, E., & Schott, D. Ontogeny of squirrel monkey calls
under normal conditions and under acoustic isolation. *Behaviour*, 1973, *47*, 230-
239.

Zuckerman, M. & Przewuzman, S. Decoding and encoding facial expressions in preschool-age children. *Environmental Psychology and Nonverbal Behavior*, 1979,
3, 147-163.

CHAPTER THREE

Watching the Sands Shift: Conceptualizing Development of Nonverbal Mastery

Gail Zivin

How does mastery over nonverbal signal use develop with age? The answer likely differs with the conditions of a signal's initial production, maintenance, and usefulness. Studies of nonverbal communication in humans have tended to ignore differences in these conditions, treating all signals studied as instances of one signal type assumed by the researcher. The present chapter recruits these differences in a taxonomy of signals and shows how two facial patterns, traced from preschool through adulthood, initially appeared to be of the most biologically basic type in the taxonomy but were eventually seen to be—or to have developed into—another type. Tracking these type differences made comprehensible conflicting findings across different ages.

The conflicting findings are developmental discontinuities in signal form, use and context. They are troublesome for the developmental researcher who assumes, as we once did for those facial patterns, that the signal is of a type that stays constant on these dimensions. When such discontinuities co-occur, they create havoc for the developmental researcher. In relating the course of our research project, this chapter illustrates one case in which taking into account increased symbolic functioning made sense of apparent discontinuities, provided specific hypotheses on the course of mastery, and inspired a more comprehensive, multi-leveled, and interactive coding scheme for conceptualizing and studying signal behavior. This approach, by encompassing transformations of biologically based signals into symbol-dominated use, contrasts with prevalent approaches to developmental study of signal mastery.

Developmental study of the mastery of signal use, whether comprehension or production, has generally taken one of three approaches. The oldest is the test under laboratory conditions for production and comprehension as in tests for differing age's *proficiency* in recognizing and/or emitting gestures that indicate an emotional state (Blanck &

Rosenthal, this volume). Very new is the study, also usually under test conditions, of conceptions of the *culture's rules* as display rules for one's conducting gestures indicative of emotional state (Saarni, this volume), of social category (Mayo & Henley, 1981), or for deception (De Paulo & Jordan, this volume). The third approach is to trace, in natural and quasinatural settings, the actual *interactive use* of specific gestures as they become well integrated with age as social signals in appropriate settings. This started with early observations of infant smiles (e.g., Spitz & Wolf, 1946; Ambrose, 1959; Freedman, 1964; Polak, Emde, & Spitz, 1964). This approach has now blossomed into rigorous, fine-grained analyses of caregiver-child (e.g., Stern, 1974; Condon, 1980; Brazelton, Tronick, Adamson, Als, & Wise, 1975; Brazelton, Als, & Lester, 1981) and peer-peer (e.g., Blurton Jones, 1967; McGrew, 1972; Lamb, 1978; Strayer & Strayer, 1976; Note 15) interactions in which the focus is not specifically on the mastery of use of particular signals, but on the pattern of interaction, with recognition of caregiver or peer contribution. These studies do not focus on masteries of particular signals' use but on the broad characteristics of communicative or social competence. Perhaps also included under this last type is the growing work of developmental pragmatics on how nonverbal acts contribute to the acquisition of verbal language (Ochs & Schieffelin, 1979) and of developmental sociolinguistics on the acquisition of conversational patterns and appropriate social cues (Ervin-Tripp & Mitchell-Kernan, 1977).

Most work on social signalling assumes stabilities among the state of the signal-maker, the conditions of the signal's emission, and the signal's form (Friedman, 1979; Izard et al., 1980). New work, noted in this chapter's section on hard and soft signals, is beginning to reject these assumptions of stability and to formulate descriptions including more of the complexity of human development. Those assumptions fit the classic conception of animal signals, or "displays," and they are usually held by developmentalists.

The concept of display is the one well-developed and easily available model of nonverbal social signals. It is a scientifically sound concept that captures Western intuitions about expression of inner state (cf. Darwin, 1872/1965; Freud, 1924). The classic conception of display seems helpful to developmental researchers because it allows one to assume stabilities among several variables in the face of the many discontinuities across development.

For these reasons it is unsurprising that the classic conceptions of display guided the early work in our project. Eventually, the gradual uncovering of results, as age increased, that did not fit this model required our reconceptualization of the signal faces. We saw them as having originated early in life with some biological stabilities similar as displays and as having been transformed through learning into cues that convey quite different messages which are out of focal awareness but under control of symbolic social inference.

The Concept of Display

A display is "any behavior specially adapted in physical form or frequency to subserve social signal functions" (Smith, 1977, p. 7). The classic conception of display intended in this chapter refers to the conception of display before W. J. Smith broadened the notion of "adapted" in his important 1977 book, *The Behavior of Communicating.* Classically, adaptation was considered to occur only over phylogenetic time. Over this time, some genetically inherited feature (e.g., behavior pattern, coloration, structure, sound or chemical emission) acquired through natural selection communication functions as a survival benefit to the group. The feature likely lost its original noncommunication function while it became specialized as a display. This process of specialization of the feature was termed "ritualization" by Huxley (1923) to refer to the rigidity and stereotype of the early studied signal behavior patterns. The term's unintended connotation of culturally transmitted ritual is unfortunate.

Ontonogenetically, displays do rely on experience and learning, but only to the small degree that these may aid an individual to put together components (Marler & Tamura, 1964) or perfect the form (e.g., through "interlocking," Lorenz, 1935/1957) of the prefigured behavior. The general format of the behavior and the impulse to execute it are provided by genetic programs and not learning processes. The context, or efficient stimulus for the display, is also provided by genetic program. In some well-known cases, one highly specific stimulus acts as a "releaser" for the behavior, but much more frequently, as Smith has demonstrated even for classic displays (1977), the condition of emission is a complex interaction of internal stimuli and an external context assessed by the individual through experience as approximating an evocative stimulus. Classic displays are always, at least partially, an immediate product of an internal state, whether they are elaborate action patterns of minutes' duration, or a brief physiological spinoff, such as a blush.

In addition to other sophistications Smith brought to the concept of display, several of which are mentioned below, he suggested that adaptation could also occur experientially, in the life of the community, and thus be selected and transmitted culturally. He termed this specialization "conventionalism," and classified it with "ritualization" as two forms of the more general signal-specializing process of "formalization" (1977, p. 10). Smith seems to leave open the question of the relation between state and signal in conventionalized displays. Since the relation

of state to signal behavior is of central interest to the taxonomy presented in this chapter, *display* will be employed to refer only to the
classic notion which uses genetically based ritualization, not culturally
predominant conventionalization, to explain the adaptive origin of communicative behaviors. Thus *display* here refers to signals whose emission
and interpretation by conspecifics depend greatly, but not exclusively,
on genetic prewiring.[1]

Displays are always about the signal-maker (Sebeok, 1967; Smith,
1977). Smith (1969, 1977) has specified this basic semiotic postulate
by classifying vertebrate display messages into four categories of information about the signal-maker: identity (sex, age, and other crucial
social classification information), location, what behavior the signaller
is likely to show, and how the signaller will show it (degrees of vigor,
decisiveness or probability, and completeness of behavior pattern). For
nonhuman as well as human recipients, the meaning of a "message,"
that which finally influences a recipient's response, comes from the
recipient's experience-based evaluation of the display in its full context
(Smith, 1977). That is, seeing a particular signal in a particular setting
leads the viewer to expect, within a range of probability, a particular
course of action by the signal-maker. Experience allows the evaluation
of the setting, recognition of this variant of the signal, and a sense of
the probabilities. Humans, it seems, go beyond sensing a probable next
action by the signal-maker. They make attributional inferences from
displays and other behaviors (Jones, Kanouse, Kelly, Nisbitt, Valins,
& Weiner, 1972; Hastie, Ostrom, Ebbeson, Wyer, Hamilton, & Carlston,
1980). These inferences, or attributions, help them predict others'
actions or help them understand motivations for others' actions: these
inferences attribute internal states and action tendencies to others as
causes of their behaviors. The culture teaches the inferential links
between the signals (which are often "expressive" behaviors that may
be based on displays), the inner state or tendency that allows the signal to "leak" out, and the subsequent behavior that is supposedly motivated by that state or tendency.

Smith's broadening of display and display message serves a similar
goal to that of this chapter's taxonomy of signals. Both attempt to provide for the complexity of biological and experiential interaction in
communication, even at the more biological pole of communication
types. Whereas Smith's approach is more broadly aimed at cross-species
comparisons, and does not examine shifts of signal use within the devel-

---

[1] Accepting for classical displays Smith's (1977) analysis that the message of a display results from an animal evaluating both the display itself and the full extra-
display information of the context, it would be inaccurate to say that interpretation
of classic displays depends *entirely* on prewiring. Similarly, accepting Smith's interactional perspective of display functions, it is appropriate to consider the displayer
affected by experiential knowledge of contextual information while predominantly
motivated to display by prewired stimulus-display connections.

opment of single individuals, this taxonomy creates more specific distinctions to aid understanding of the development of signal mastery. Before examining that taxonomy, it will be useful to have some details about the two facial patterns to which the taxonomy will be applied in this chapter. A description of those facial signals studied by our project thus follows.

The Plus and Minus Faces: Basic Data and Early Assumptions

The two signals whose course our project studied are two facial patterns which, when made at the outset of a conflict interaction, respectively correlate with the face-maker winning or losing the conflict. The course of our inquiry into the functions and mechanisms underlying the two faces is presented as a case study of coming to understand the development of specific social signals. The faces came to my attention as distinct social signals while I was developing behavioral repertoire lists, or ethograms,[2] of preschoolers. The faces are particularly interesting in that they appear to have elements of signals of several traditional categories: emotional expression, interactional negotiation, social role signal, and even (Saarni, Note 12) self-regulatory manipulation of one's own emotional state. To what degree they are exemplars of these more simple and classic categories of social signals has not been directly studied. The course of inquiry presented here illustrates ways in which their characteristics have been hypothesized, studied, and reformulated.

The win-predicting face, the plus face, has the three major features of medially raised brows (not the brows characteristic of surprise or fear), direct eye contact, and slightly raised chin. The loss-predicting face has the morphological inverses of the plus face: brows are pinched (not heavily lowered as in rage), eye contact is broken by downward gaze, and chin is lowered and retracted. These facial patterns were located by employing a component code which, while developed independently, resembled Kendon's (1975) and which, like his, was employed in real-time field settings by trained observers (Zivin, 1977a, Note 13). That the two faces were correlated with conflict outcome was established in a set of systematic studies that initially found that preschool age boys showed a significantly nonrandom patterning of components into these two facial expressions at the beginning of naturally occurring conflicts (Zivin, 1977a, Study I). Other studies extended this finding of nonrandom patterning of components to school age children of both sexes (Zivin, 1977a, Study II) and through middle school age, adolescence,

---

[2] Ethograms are exhaustive lists, sometimes recording sequence and frequency, derived by naturalistic observation, of all the behaviors, especially of a social nature, that are shown by a species. When applied to human observation, the exhaustiveness is bounded by age, relations, and/or contexts of observation.

Figure 3-1. Preschooler's full plus face.

and adulthood (Hottenstein, Note 7). The correlation between face occurrence and conflict outcome was rigorously established against chance outcomes and random facial components for the preschoolers (Zivin, 1977a): plus faces rather than any other facial pattern appeared at the outset of 66% to 67% of the win situations ($p < .008$); and minus

Figure 3-2. Preschooler's full minus face.

Figure 3-3. Adult's full plus face.

faces, rather than any other facial pattern, appeared at the outset of 51% to 52% loss situations ($p < .008$).

The project then systematically collected over one semester random focal samples of natural interactions among peers of five ages in natural settings that were as equivalent as possible across the different life

Figure 3-4. Adult's full minus face.

involvements of such different age groups: each group was video-taped in middle class, age-appropriate unstructured school settings in urban Philadelphia. These settings included a progressive preschool of 16, 3- to 4-year-olds, and 23, 4- to 5-year-olds; a private open classroom, mixed grade elementary school class of 26, 7- to 10-year-olds; a private, very loosely structured social science discussion group of 11, 16- to 17-year-olds; and a spontaneous group process training group for graduate students at a private university with 17 students aged 21 to 45. These observations, edited for technical quality and criteria of visibility relevant to each hypothesis, as described below, comprised the basic data of the project. The criteria for tape editing, definitions of situations, and codings of wins and losses are detailed in Zivin, 1977a,b, Note 15. All five age groups replicated the first studies' (Zivin, 1977a, Note 15) findings on the faces' relations to win and loss outcomes. The same subjects also participated by describing their peers and by observing videotapes of others and of peers. Secondary studies, with different subjects and techniques, were also conducted and are described in this chapter's section on motivation, perception, and inference.

At the outset of the research, it seemed quite likely that the faces were evolutionary analogues, if not homologues,[3] of nonhuman primate facial gestures of threat and submission. We surmised this on the

Table 3-1. Prevalence of Plus and Minus Faces in Conflict and Relations of Faces to Conflict Outcomes.

	Plus Faces		Minus Faces	
	Percentage in Wins	r with Wins	Percentage in Losses	r with Losses
Adults $n = 17$	96*	.94**	33*	.49*
Adolescents $n = 11$	96**	.96**	75**	.94**
School Agers $n = 26$	98**	.89**	67**	.82**
Old preschoolers $n = 23$	94**	.95**	58**	.85**
Young preschoolers $n = 16$	96**	.97**	59**	.72**

Note. Significance tests on percentage done by χ^2 and on correlations by t-test.
* $p < .05$.
**$p < .001$.

---

[3] In evolutionary theory, "homologue" and "analogue" respectively differentiate between similarities across species that come from shared genetic ancestry and those that come from independent but similar adaptations without common ancestry (e.g., to similar survival problems through natural selection).

basis of several factors: (1) The appearance of these faces in the context of the start of conflict situations seemed parallel to the appearance of facial threat and submission gestures that occur at the start of conflicts among apes and monkeys (Jay, 1965; Hall & DeVore, 1965). These gestures are considered genetically prefigured displays in these non-human primates; such rigidly repeatable facial gestures in humans seemed likely also to have biological roots. (2) Some components of these faces appear morphologically similar to those of nonhuman primates, notably the eye contact stare and the forward raised and the retracted chin angles. The morphological similarity to nonhuman primates of these whole facial gestures is, however, much less than that of the selected threat components indicated by Camras (see Camras, this volume; 1977). (3) The nonrandom appearances of the faces in a child as young as 2½ years, in children of different socioeconomic-ethnic subcultures, and in a child newly arrived from Iran who as yet spoke no English (Zivin, 1977a) all weakly suggest a species-wide gesture. (4) That the faces relate to such a biologically basic social setting as conflict suggests that the gestures might be important enough in adaptation to have been selected by natural selection processes as displays. (5) That the faces appear to be morphological-motoric inverses of each other fits Darwin's Principle of Antithesis (1872/1965), which states that opposite internal states (such as emotional states) are expressed by opposing directions of muscle movement. This suggests that the faces somehow express opposite inner states, perhaps confidence and lack of it or openness and closedness to struggle. Based on these five points, we initially assumed the two faces to be instances of displays, classically conceived.

Types of Hard and Soft Signals

Some few developmental researchers are beginning to ask whether young humans' seemingly innate early signal repertoire becomes transformed into more masterfully controlled social cues and, if so, by what mechanisms. They are searching beyond the model of displays, on the one hand, and beyond wholly learned gestures, on the other, to discover processes whereby biological propensities are modified by experience to fit social communication. For the study of emotionally expressive behaviors, these researchers tend to start with display-like reflexivity of expressive components in early infancy and, as subjects increase in age, change their focus toward modification of the movements, their eliciting conditions, and cognitive and social control over their appropriate presence. Ekman and Oster (Ekman, 1979; Oster & Ekman, 1978) and Sroufe and Waters (1976) point out elements in cognitive appraisal that moderate emotional expression. Saarni (1978 and this volume) focuses on the acquisition of one of these elements, display rules.

Malatesta and Izard (in press) and Sroufe (1978) suggest stages in the transformation of infants' expressive reflexes into cognitively controlled communicative signals. The latter work focuses on the cognitive and interpersonal conditions necessary for these steps over the infants' first year and a half, and the former work outlines the interactional steps that stabilize and teach voluntary control of emotional expression over the first year of life. Emde (Emde, Kligman, Reich, & Wade, 1978) notes basic dimensions of emotional signalling as they emerge through interaction. Oster (1978) and Malatesta (Note 8) both note processes by which infant facial components shed their lability and come under organized social and cognitive control. A specific process in learning to perceive facial signals of emotion, "social referencing," is noted by Sorce, Emde, and Klinnert (Note 13) and by Campos (Note 3).

For nonverbal behaviors which are not emotionally expressive, but rather contribute to the flow of conversations and interactions, almost no early developmental work has been done. Classical developmental psycholinguists' examination of verbal signals and symbols (Bloom, Lightbown, & Hood, 1975), developmental sociolinguists' study of verbal moves in interactions (Ervin-Tripp & Mitchell-Kernan, 1977), and the semantic focus on early action-meaning by developmental pragmatists (Ochs & Schieffelin, 1979), are so tied to verbal symbolism that their relevance to the development of the general structure of social signaling is not yet clear. Only Ekman (1979), to my knowledge, has published some general conclusions on young childrens' nonemotional "conversational actions." His conversational actions include both movements that aid or stand for spoken meaning and those that negotiate conversational moves and roles. While some pragmatists (Bates, Camioni, & Volterra, 1979; Greenfield, 1979) see the developmental trend of symbols and conversational rule as one that proceeds through learning from physically fixed constraints on action and demonstration, Ekman eschews any universal base of converational actions.

Ekman (1979) proposed a two division taxonomy of all nonverbal behaviors based on the functional distinction between emotional expression and conversational action.[4] By contrast, the taxonomy proposed

----

[4] A brief summary of Ekman's 1979 taxonomy, which is a recasting and expansion of his 1969 categories (Ekman & Friesen, 1969), might be helpful. The 1979 paper indicates two major divisions of social signals: emotional expressions and conversational actions. In this work Ekman does not divide emotional expression into distinct categories, but he points out that emotional expressions may vary in the degree of voluntary control over their emission, have many but not total universal bases, and have much cultural and individual learning contributing to their variability in form and contexts of emission. Chief among the influences of cultural learning are display rules that indicate the type, intensity, and contexts of emotional expression considered appropriate in one's culture. Ekman does not see behaviors conducted in accord with display rules as affecting the genuine emotional state of the expressor; this is in contrast to Saarni (this volume).

here bases its distinctions on the degree of stability of the relation of a signal behavior to an internal state. At one end of the continuum fall classic displays, and at the other fall conversational actions that are wholly culturally derived and are not seen by the culture as conveying information about the inner state of the signaller. The signals of Ekman's two divisions (and their several categories) are encompassed in the present taxonomy, sorted across its five categories. The category criterion here is where a signal behavior falls in the possible range from display-like fixity to learned negotiation of interactional moves. While Ekman points out that many emotional expressions and conversational actions have voluntary and involuntary features and that emotional expression has elements of biological base as well as of cultural and individual learning, the present taxonomy specifically sorts the acts from both of these broad divisions on the basis of stability. This stability is a compound dimension which, among other features, reflects the degree of tie to biological base and to involuntary emission.

It is only incidental that the five categories of stability reflect amounts of biological base and volition. The categories are framed to capture the varying mechanisms by which signal acts are acquired and transformed. Each category is distinguished by the mechanisms that link each type of signal behavior with an inner state, if any, and with the voluntary use, if any, of the behavior *as* a (intentional) signal rather than as a spontaneous expression of state. The five stability categories of this taxonomy are designed to aid research on all social signals in at least three ways: they should refocus work from the controversies over whether all signals of a functional class are biologically based or learned; they can focus attention on the biological, psychological, and interactional mechanisms by which any one signal is acquired, possibly transformed, and maintained; and they are available as a developmental grid in which to trace the transformation of a signal as it is perhaps transformed from one set of mechanisms at one degree of stability to another set at another degree.

The taxonomy presentation in Table 3-2 is based on the following

---

Ekman divides conversational actions, or conversational signals, into three types. (1) "Speaker conversational signals" are further broken down into "baton" and "underliner" which mark intonational stress, "punctuation" and "question mark" which help indicate sentence boundaries and types, "word search" which helps the speaker hold the floor while pausing, and "other speaker conversational signals" which include the many remaining signals that help speakers negotiate their roles in conversations. (2) "Listener's responses" are not subcategorized but are exemplified by "agreement responses" such as head nods and um-hms; these generally are signals that show how the listener is playing the role of listener and that he or she wants to speak, break off the conversation, etc. (3) "Conversational signals without speech (emblems)" are movements that stand for discrete concepts such as that which is conveyed by a wink, a signal for OK, or a greeting, etc. Ekman does not present categories of emblems.

Table 3-2. Taxonomy of Nonverbal Signals.

Category Type (Example)	State	Link	Behavior	Link	Emission as Signal
Hard					
Fixed (displays,[a] e.g., gasp)	Present	Prewired	Present	Prewired[b]	Optional
Firm (displaylike behaviors, e.g., gaze avert)	Present	Prewired to one state plus classically conditioned to other state	Present	Possible conditioning as signal	Optional
Soft					
Forced (display rule behavior, e.g., hold back tears)	Present	Prewired and social learning of modification	Present	Conditioning as signal	Modified form
Flexible (conventional expressions,[c] e.g., pout)	Optional	Social learning (and perhaps varying conditioning to state)	Present	Conditioning as signal	Modified form
Fluid (conversational/interactional gestures, e.g., head nod)	None	Social learning	Present	Conditioning as signal	Present

[a] Displays, classically conceived: excluding Smith's conventionalized displays (1977).
[b] See the "Forced" type for display rule learning that may modify emission by prewiring.
[c] Including Smith's conventionalized displays (1977).

three-part division of a nonverbal signal: the signal *behavior*, the *state* (if any) of which the signal indicates the presence, and the *emission* of the behavior *as a signal* indicating the state. Three major mechanisms can account for the *link between a state (if any) and a signal behavior*: (1) genetic prewiring, whose advantage may be only the long-term advantage of increased fitness, or (2) delayed social imitation, whose benefits lie in the complex consequences of behaving in the manner of one's immediate social group (as would be the primary mechanism reinforcing conversational gestures), or (3) instrumental reinforcement by interactants of the behavior *as* a signal. Crying, for example, can be potently reinforced as a signal (of state) by responses that attempt to assuage the assumed discomfort. These three mechanisms link the behavior to its emission (which may overlap with spontaneous emission) as a signal. In Table 3-2, these mechanisms appear in the right-hand slot for links between behavior and emission as a signal.

The *link between state and the spontaneous presence of behavior* (which may be read as a signal of the state) can be achieved by three plausible mechanisms: (1) prewiring of state and correlated behavior, or (2) prewiring of one relation plus conditioning of a simultaneous relation. Oster (Note 10) has suggested such a mechanism that would work in the following way: The behavior that becomes the signal is originally prewired to a nonemotional internal state (e.g., information processing). That state and the behavior to which it is prewired frequently co-occur with another, socially recognized state, such as an emotion. The co-occurrence is sufficiently frequent for the internal stimuli that accompany the socially recognized state to come to elicit the behavior. The behavior thus becomes an index of the secondary socially recognized state. Finally, (3) state and behavior may be linked by classical conditioning of social learning such that the internal stimuli for the wholly voluntary expression of state becomes conditioned to the presence of the state. Thus an originally learned expression becomes a spontaneous expression of that state. An example might be calling out "Ah ha!", although alone, upon solving a problem. These are three mechanisms that cause a signal to be emitted spontaneously. Lack of intentional inhibition of these behaviors is not here considered a separate mechanism. In Table 3-2, these three mechanisms appear in the left-hand slot for links between state and behavior. Notice that mechanisms for wholly voluntary, nonspontaneous signals of state have already been mentioned and appear in the right-hand slot for links to emission as a signal.

The names for these signal types have been selected to emphasize the degree to which inner state is stably indexed by the signal behavior. There are two broad categories of each signal type, hard and soft. Hard contains two types: *fixed* and *firm*. Soft has three: *forced*, *flexible*, and *fluid*.

The *hard* category is composed of signal types that have deep roots in biological organization. The feature that divides hard from soft signals is that for hard signals there is a reliable link between the appearance of a signal and the presence of the internal state that it is thought to index. There is no reliable link for the soft signals, and one never knows, in a particular instance, if there is a link by learning of the signal to a state that it may be thought to index. This unreliability is what makes it soft. No specific attention is given in this taxonomy to learning to transfer inner state reactions to new stimuli and contexts. It is assumed that ubiquitous processes can attach state or behavior to any new stimuli, whether by generalization, conditioning, observational learning, or rule learning. These added flexibilities would not usefully differentiate between the five signal types.

Note that the taxonomy separates signal types without indicating possible hybrids between them. Hybrid behavior types, particularly those wherein cognitive control mechanisms are laminated upon biologically given predispositions, are most likely forms of human social behavior (Zivin, in press). Some forms of such lamination are, in obvious ways, built into the taxonomy's firm and forced types. But more complex and yet likely hybridization could arise when several mechanisms in this taxonomy underlie a single signal behavior.

The first type of hard signal, the *fixed* signal, is simply the classically conceived, genetically prewired display. (If a display is modified in its expression by a culture's display rules, the new modified behavior is here considered a signal of the soft forced type.) Fixed signals need not be reinforced as signals in order to function in a display-maker's repertoire as an index of inner state. Prewiring controls emission and also, presumably, the perceiver's interpretation. Thus it is optional whether the fixed signal may be emitted voluntarily as a signal. If this occurs, we assume that the state is present.

The second type, the *firm* signal, is hypothesized to explain a troublesome observation. The observation begins with a number of expressive behaviors that, through their frequency in nonsystematically sampled cross-cultural data, appear to be universal (e.g., Eibl-Eibesfeldt, 1972). The observation continues, however, that most human genetic programming appears to be at the more general level of programming for acquiring adaptive behavior options rather than at the more specific level of prewiring for specific behavioral configurations. If this is true, the observation raises the question of how it might be that so many behaviors appear to be prewired expressions, particularly as signals of interest or intention. For example, gaze direction is taken in most cultures as an indication of attitude, but the many visual functions also served by gaze suggest that a specific behavior such as gaze aversion was not likely ritualized in evolution to serve primarily as an attitude signal. Oster (Note 10), as mentioned above, specified a mechanism which had been generally suggested by Allport (1924) and Pieper (1961/1963) and that could help explain such seemingly universal signals: basic biological processes, particularly those for information processing, can include overt behaviors such as eye movements that have instrumental functions. These processing states and their behaviors often co-occur with other states, such as emotions. By a classical conditioning process, which is generally suggested by the first part of Darwin's Principle of Serviceable Associated Habits (1872/1965), the behavior comes to be elicited by the previously co-occurring emotion and can function as an index of it. Because such biologically-ecologically rooted behaviors would function well as signals across the generations, social learning could teach that the behavior can be read as signals of state. The culture could thus transmit the interpretation of the behavior, while pre-wiring plus conditioning would transmit the connection to state within each individual's development.

The broad category of *soft* signals holds the signals that arise in the course of social learning. As the learning may or may not condition the behavior to the state, the reliability of the behavior as index to state is statistically variable across and within individuals. Yet, besides including behaviors that are wholly conversational/interactional (e.g., throat clearing to gain the floor), this category includes the many behaviors that culture has taught to be taken as indicators of state. Humans' tendency to attribute state to others is so strong (Jones & Nesbitt, 1972) and cultural learning of state indicators so pervasive (e.g., Kraut, 1978) that attributions of state continue to be made in the absence of clear evidence that the attribution is correct (Ross, 1977).

Forced is the first type of soft signal. Its signals of inner state do not accurately reflect that state because they have been modified in accord with display rules or other motives to dissimulate. This type is a modification of the fixed signal; it modifies by conscious control the form of fixed behavior when the state occurs, in accord with the display rules for each context. Originally put forth by Ekman (1972), and newly researched in psychology (see Saarni, this volume), display rules are culturally taught rules about what expressions are appropriate in which cultural settings. People use display rules to modify their natural, spontaneous emotional expressions. The modifications may be to intensify or deintensify a spontaneous expression or to substitute a different one. An expression that follows a display rule may not always be voluntary, as when it becomes so habitual that its emission becomes automatic (Ekman, 1979). Saarni (this volume) further suggests that one can voluntarily modify one's expression along the lines of display rules and thereby change what one truly feels. If this change were to occur, the behavior would not be of this category, but of the firm category in which a state is paired by circumstance with a reliable indicator of its presence.

Flexible signals of state are derived from social learning. Their origin rests on imitation, perhaps aided by instrumental learning. An example might be a pout when not getting what one wants. One particularly striking process that might contribute to such learning is described by Sorce, Emde, and Klinnert (Note 13) and Campos (Note 3) as "social referencing" wherein an infant checks its mother's face or voice when in situations of uncertainty. While these researchers suggest that this teaches the infant how to evaluate the situation, Malatesta (Note 9) extends the function of this social referencing to the infant's learning how to feel and/or display in specific contexts. Some classical conditioning might link the expressive behaviors to the slowly differentiated state. It is clear, however, that learning to make such expressive gestures may occur as instrumental learning to perform a signal in a context rather than as learning to have the state in a context. Such learned expressive behaviors are responded to as signals of state because social learning has taught perceivers that they are signals of state.

Fluid signals provide no knowledge of state, although cultural teaching of perception and social inference may be that they do. These behaviors are acquired through their reinforcement by others who read them as signals of state or of social appropriateness and comprehensibility. One may experience states in conjunction with these behaviors, but no mechanism binds repetition of the state to repetition of the behavior. This type of signal behavior includes most paralinguistic conversational behaviors (excepting, e.g., those suggested as indexing the state of information processes [Druckman, Rozelle, & Baxter, 1982]), interaction management routines, and idiosyncratic nonverbal mannerisms.

The taxonomy predicts some developmental time courses and distributions in light of the stabilities suggested by the mechanisms for each signal type. These predictions should be of practical use to the developmental researcher in tracking the course of signal mastery. (1) Form: It is clear that the two hard signals are likely to undergo relatively little modification in signal form with age: the form is given by biological structure and is not importantly shaped by effective outside agents of learning. The soft signals, by contrast, should not appear until late infancy or early preschool and would be subject to progressive form change over age with increased skill in signal use. (2) Context: As mentioned earlier, any of the signals could, in principle, increase their contexts of occurrence by generalization. However, a context shift, wherein old contexts are abandoned when new contexts are acquired would be likely only in the event of a new communication rule, and such rule learning would characterize only soft signals. For these soft signals, there would be little reason to believe that the state has sharply shifted its context along with the rule-bound signal behavior. (3) Expression in isolation: Appearance of a signal when one has no reason to believe that there is an audience has been interpreted as evidence of true expression of inner state (e.g., Ekman, 1971). (This logic ignores the over-learned nature of some gestures, e.g. in cases of emblematic gestures when one is alone or of conversational gestures on the telephone.) Allowing this logic for most gestures, soft signals should not appear when signallers experience themselves as being without an audience, while hard signals should appear whether one is alone or not. (4) Time course: One might, in general, expect that the hard signals would appear earlier in development than the soft ones. The soft ones would be expected to first appear during the time of overall conversational mastery in toddler and early preschool years. Thereafter, their form would likely be refined through middle childhood.

These expectations help make sense of the distributional data that characterize the use of the plus and minus faces. A description of the course of collection and interpretation of those data follows.

The Plus and Minus Faces: Uncovering Signal Complexity and Developmental Discontinuities

Keeping in mind this taxonomy, its mechanisms, characteristics, and predicted variations in signal distributions, we can return to the course of research on the development of the use of plus and minus faces. The first studies reported here focus on face-making. Through them it will be seen how the faces differ from and yet retain characteristics of pure fixed signals. These studies also suggest the types (or hybrid type) that the faces exemplify. At the end of this section studies on responses to the faces are reported. Those studies point to considerations of better methods for studying the developmental discontinuities in face use that have been found during the course of the research.

Faces as Biologically Fixed Signals: Dominance and Group Differences

The plus and minus faces, as discussed earlier, had appeared to be human displays of a sort analogous or homologous to threat and sub-mission gestures found in nonhuman primates. Because these nonhuman primate gestures had been found to characterize higher and lower rank-ing individuals in dominance challenges (Jay, 1965), we looked for relations between plus faces and high dominance rank. We excluded our youngest group of 3- to 4-year-olds, and used our four oldest groups. The technique used to measure dominance rank was the toughness ranking developed by Edelman and Omark (1973). Our use of this now controversial technique (Sluckin & Smith, 1977; Zivin, in press) derived a linear order from the average of each subject's paired comparisons of all peers. For the two younger groups, this ranking was on the attribute of "is tough," and for the two older groups it was on the attribute of "gets own way a lot." (See Zivin, 1977b for details of the procedure and analysis.) Analyses of the two younger groups were done first and were encouraging. When divided into quartiles of the linear ranks, both the 4- to 5-year-olds and the 7- to 10-year-olds showed clear decrease in number of plus faces made per unit time as rank quartile decreased. Furthermore, correlations of quartile rank and number of plus faces made were in the expected direction for both groups, and $r = .36$ was significant at $p < .05$ for the 7- to 10-year-olds. However, further analyses did not find this trend continued in the two older groups (Hottenstein, Note 7).

This was the first of several occasions on which the findings supported a simple model of the signals at one end of our age spectrum and not at the other. In this case, the younger subjects' data supported predictions based on the model that the plus face was a particular known kind of fixed signal, but the results indicated that, by adolescence, either the signal or the measured dominance phenomenon, or both, no longer seem to characterize humans. Such discontinuities had to accumulate in our findings over several years before they led to a reconsideration of the models for the signal and for the social structure (Zivin, in press).

While the plus face was still being thought of as a primate display, the question had to be asked whether such a biologically based behavior was distributed differently along the lines of traditionally studied genetic subgroups, sex and race. Inspection of the full set of our collected observations informed us about distributions of the faces with sex. A separate secondary study looked at face distributions along race and class lines.

The first two samples to locate the faces in preschool children had used only boys (Zivin, 1977a). Our early expectation that the faces were primarily involved with biologically based negotiation of overt physical conflict led us to seek samples of boys as more efficient in yielding high face frequencies. However, in our full sample of both sexes at five ages, no sex differences in general face frequencies were found. Even among adults, the main variations in face frequencies appear to be due to individual differences, and not to sex differences (Acosta, Woodman, & Zivin, Note 1).

Dancey, Moore and Zivin (Note 5) examined the effects of race, social class, cultural setting, and age on frequency of plus faces. This was done in naturalistic observations of two sets of samples: (1) middle class black and white 5- and 8-year-olds in an urban school and (2) lower and middle class black 5- and 8-year-olds in a rural community center for play activities. The findings were, after controlling for context, that at the younger, but not at the older age, black urban children make significantly more plus faces than white urban children, and at the older age but not the younger, black lower class children make significantly more plus faces than do black middle class children: the two classes had similar high rates at age 5, but the middle class dropped significantly more by age 8. However, both middle and lower class rural black children significantly decrease their plus face-making with age. In just the opposite pattern, black urban children start out at age 5 with significantly more plus faces than white urban 5-year-olds, but by age 8 the black children are socialized to the lower rate and do not differ from whites. Both rural and urban samples thus show socialization effects on rate with age. These age differences, particularly the urban school rates, appear to show context-sensitive modulations. The most interesting finding for our present purposes, however, is not in statistically significant differences when both groups show notably large frequencies. It is in the finding that both younger black and white groups do show face frequencies at similar absolute levels (1.2 vs. .81 in 10 min.) in the same contexts. While 5 years of age is far from a sample point before early socialization, at this preschool age, both groups have the same capacity and use for plus faces. By these crude estimates of group differences, there appear no distributional differences by sex or race that one might want to attribute to a biological base.

Facial Mastery via Subtlety: Context
Camouflage and Abbreviation

Even within the early report that focused exclusively on 4- to 5-year-olds and 7- to 10-year-olds (Zivin, 1977b), there emerged a powerful contrast between age groups. It became a key to understanding the seemingly discontinuous developmental trend that eventually took shape. The contrast concerned the context in which the bulk of the plus faces occurred. The higher ranking younger children and the lower ranking (perhaps less mature or less socially skilled) older children placed the majority of their plus faces just where one would expect to find primate threat faces: in conflict situations. However, the higher ranking 7- to 10-year-olds made the majority of their plus faces quite casually during nonconflictful situations that merely called for the use of a skill such as reading.[5] Thus, whether or not they were excelling in the skill, the higher ranking older children gestured in a manner that conveyed an impression of winningness or competence.

This phenomenon deserves some attention in its own right. This distribution of faces appears to indicate an early and sophisticated

---

[5] By strict observational criteria (Zivin, 1977a,b), interactions and their outcomes were coded as being in one of four situations. The first three are overt conflicts or "agonistic" situations. The fourth is a "competence win" in which there is a test of skill against oneself or against a standard or a goal. In it there is no conflict with another person.

form of "impression management" (Goffman, 1959), a phenomenon that has not been studied in children except as display rule use and deception. (See Saarni, and DePaulo and Jordan, this volume.) Impression management, however, includes far more than managing others' impressions of what one is feeling. For instance, one phenomenon is the management of others' impressions of the type of person one is. The emission of plus faces in nonconflict situations seems to carry an impression of winningness into neutral situations. It impresses this observer as creating an air of self-confidence or competence about the face-maker. The high ranking children as young as 7 years old appear to be creating this impression for others by the nonconflict distribution of their plus faces. The faces are emitted very smoothly in integration with other movements and speech and do not seem to be in the awareness of the face-maker. The management may well be out of focal awareness and under the control of social reinforcement. There are several reasons why the plus faces do not stand out to the observer as unfitting or as challenging in nonconflict settings: the observer is not prepared to interpret gestures in these settings as conflictful; the discomfort of being aware of conflict in nonconflict settings would facilitate overlooking dissonant gestures; the faces flow well with the other movements and do not stand out. Thus the plus faces are likely to be "culturally invisible" (Zivin, Note 19) yet subliminally perceived in an impression of winningness. Data that appear later in this section support this guess about the plus faces' effect.

What type of signal is likely to show such a dramatic shift in its context of occurrence with age and sophistication? In the implication about context at the end of the previous section, it was noted that only soft and not hard signals would show a sharp shift in context due to environmental stimuli or rule learning. This present case appears to be such a shift. On this count, the plus face of the older child seems likely to be a soft rather than a hard signal.[6]

Hottenstein (1977) found a different type of subtlety with age. She found that both faces, plus and minus, became abbreviated in form with increased age. Using all five of the groups described earlier, Hottenstein analyzed their videotapes for presence of "full faces," i.e., faces having the brow, eye, and chin components, and for "partial faces," i.e., faces having combinations of one or two of the three components. She counted frequencies of full and partial faces per age and related them to the categories of interaction outcomes. She found that, from age three through adult years, across all contexts, full plus faces decrease in frequency by about 400% and full minus faces by 1300%.

---

[6] It is possible that if these older, more sophisticated children took part in more overt conflicts, in which they now appear less often, they would also show more plus faces in them. Under those circumstances, this apparent shift of context would only be a case of generalization and would not necessarily invite special attention as a sharp shift in the context of signal occurrence.

Meanwhile, partial plus and minus faces increase by 300% and 400% respectively. Unsurprisingly, one-way F-tests over age for these four trends were highly significant. Scheffé tests at the .05 level indicated that the major break in these linear trends was between the 7- to 10-year-olds and the adolescents. Despite the greater break at the beginning of adolescence, there is a roughly linear decrease in the more noticeable use of full faces and a concurrent increase in the use of less emphatic partial faces.

By far the most frequent partial faces were those including the chin. Partial faces continued to predict outcome at $p < .001$, as the full faces do, with correlations averaging across all ages about $r = .50$ for plus face chin clusters. For the 7- to 10-year-olds and the adolescents, the minus chin clusters predicted loss at an average of $r = .80$. It is not clear how the minus chin clusters do predict at the two younger ages and at the oldest age, because there were few chin clusters in the former and few losses in the latter. Thus for the plus faces, and apparently for the minus faces, older persons increasingly use partial faces, and these transformed faces have the same effect on outcomes as full ones. As noted in the previous section's implication about form, a significant change in form is not expected for hard signals. Once again, the maturing faces appear more soft than hard.

There is still another feature of this abbreviation with age that seems to classify the maturing faces with soft signals. Words, as conventionalizations whose semantic functions develop ontogenetically out of the young child's actions, could be classified in the fluid category of the soft division of our taxonomy. Bates et al. (1979) describe the transformation of young children's actions into meaningful protolinguistic objects. This transformation of actions has two features clearly shown by the transformation of the full faces: abbreviation of form and stabilization of structure around key elements. (Other features of protolinguistic transformations are less obviously seen in these faces' development but may generally characterize the developmental course of hard signals being transformed into soft ones through conventionalization. These features are the disconnection of the signal behavior from original practical action and the signal behavior's coming less to resemble its original practical action [Bates et al., 1979].) As hard signals would be unlikely to undergo much change of form, they would be unlikely to show abbreviation and stabilization of transformed features. By resembling the development of soft protolinguistic signals in the abbreviated faces stabilizing around the chin, the development of the faces again seems to follow a soft signal course.

Faces and Internal State

A primary focus of the taxonomy and of much research in nonverbal communication is on whether a signal behavior is a reliable index of an internal state. When one contemplates why the plus and minus faces might affect outcome, an immediate wonder is whether some state such as feeling confident is the "cause" of the facial expression and perhaps also of the outcome. That is, the faces may not be instrumental behaviors, but expresives ones.

Early in the project we had the opportunity to look at whether the faces were made voluntarily-instrumentally or more spontaneously-expressively. We reasoned that if the faces were made instrumentally, when a face-maker knows he cannot be seen by a competitor, their frequency should approach zero. If made expressively, they should remain as frequent in situations contrived to block mutual view as they are in natural conflicts. An excellent situation for this test was made available by Linda Camras who gave us access to her video tapes of 23 pilot pairings of 4- to 6½-year-olds in her gerbil box test. See her detailed descriptions of apparatus (Camras, 1975, 1977 or this volume), and see Zivin (1977a) for this procedure and analysis. The task placed paired children on either side of a table in reach of a box with a gerbil in it; if the box were pulled (on rails) over to the child's edge of the table, he or she could look or poke at it. The box would be tugged back and forth between paired children. Crucially, the children's view of each other could be blocked by a removable board perpendicular to the surface of the table. (A hole in the board allowed the box to be pulled through.) Each pair member, matched for age, could either see or not see each other.

The results showed that the plus faces followed our hypothesized directions but the minus faces did not: the plus faces in the See condition appear in a similar percentage of win situations for this age range as they do in the natural field, 60% vs. 66.67%, and they drop to 28% when vision is blocked. The minus faces did not approach their field-derived percentage for natural loss situations in this laboratory setting of the See condition: 26% in the laboratory vs. 51% to 52% in the field. The percentage of the minus faces stayed roughly the same in the Blocked as in the See condition at 29%. It appears that minus face use was sufficiently affected by the laboratory treatment that nothing useful can be inferred about it from this manipulation. The plus face, on the other hand, appears robust to the transplantation and is significantly (χ^2 (1)=3.85, $p < .05$) but not completely affected by blocking vision. Thus, the plus face appears already at the preschool age to be significantly voluntary and instrumental. The remaining Blocked 28% plus faces seem likely to represent a residual component of expressiveness within instrumental face use. Without further data, however, experimental artifact, residual behavioral habit, or the imperfect fine-tuning of preschoolers' communicative adaptations must also be considered as possible explanations of that 28%. It remains striking that the plus face may be neither a simple instrumental signal behavior nor a simple display behavior. It may have a large expressive component characteristic of hard signals amid development and function characteristic of soft ones.

In summarizing what we have learned about who makes these faces and why, it seems that both faces appear in equivalent proportions with the same effects in both sexes at all five ages and in reasonably equivalent proportions for blacks and whites at age 5 regardless of social class. Everyone shows modulation of plus face frequency in response to cultural settings by age 8. Further, it appears that the plus face is predominantly made for its instrumental signal function and that this function follows evident lines of socialization. This socialization learning achieves mastery by decreasing overall amount, making amount sensitive to setting, and increasing subtlety of form and non-abrasiveness of context. The plus and minus faces are sufficiently subject to modification of form that they are clear candidates for being soft signals. Whether the mature plus face is built on an originally display-like fixed expressive core is open for investigation, but apparent expression of state in a proportion of faces made without an audience suggests that the mature plus face is partially expressive of inner state.

Responses to Faces: Motivation, Perception, and Inference

We have so far focused on why the faces are emitted, not on how they have their apparent effect on conflict outcome or on impression once they are emitted. Indeed the signal taxonomy is only in terms of mechanisms that occasion a signal to be emitted; it does not deal with effects of signals. Studies discussed below examine how the faces seem to work to influence outcomes and impressions. As Smith (1977) carefully elaborates, an approach to communication should consider the *interaction* of signal sender and perceiver as the central unit to be explained in order to be conceptually adequate and biologically complete. While the following is not a full interactional approach (such would look at the joint product of moves of each participant), it does ask what the perceiver contributes to the face-maker's seeming influence over the outcome.

The first point at which the perceiver can contribute to the outcome is his/her immediate reaction to the face. Seeing one of the two faces could cause an immediate emotional motivational change in the perceiver that would lead to a change in the perceiver's vigor. This had been suggested by a notion that the faces could act as preprogrammed releasers (Zivin, Note 18), but a motivational change in the perceiver could also be due to a learned emotional reaction to the faces as social signals. Either mechanism of change could produce a change in vigor of response after seeing a face.

One study (Zivin, Note 18) contrasted behavioral indications of vigor in the perceiver after seeing the plus or minus faces in natural settings.

The study used specially selected observations from our pool of natural interaction videotapes for the three youngest age groups. In the two oldest age groups, wholly analogous interactions could not be found. Interactions were selected from overt conflicts over material possessions in which the profile of both participants could be seen and in which plus face-makers won and minus face-makers lost. The measure of vigor was the reaction time of the perceiver from the onset of the face to the perceiver's making any movement or sound. Reactions were further classified into those that specifically appeared to retaliate in the conflict.

The results were stunning. Averaging across the three age groups (which did not differ importantly from each other in results), the reaction times after seeing a plus face, in contrast to a minus, was twice as long for any response and three times as long for retaliations (1.26 vs. .64 and 1.86 vs. .54 sec, $t(14)=2.10$ and 3.06, both $p < .05$). Clearly, seeing a plus face has a different effect on a perceiver than seeing a minus face, regardless of the mechanisms by which the perceiver acquired that reaction tendency. It seems that the perceivers of plus faces contribute to their loss by a diminution of response vigor. This diminution may occur upon seeing a neutral face as well as upon seeing a minus face, but from these comparisons that lack a neutral condition, we cannot tell. Neither can we tell whether the winner perceivers of minus faces increase their vigor over a neutral level after seeing a minus face, or whether their vigor is unchanged but still greater than that of perceivers of plus faces. Also it is possible that emission of the faces and the immediate reaction times are mere selections from two basically different interaction patterns, one having a plus face and the other a minus. This more interactionistic possibility is brought under study at the end of this section in a more comprehensive, interactional approach to studying signals.

This study pointed up discontinuity important for the study of communication development. The impossibility of matching behaviorally equivalent conflict situations between older and younger groups reminds one that children and adults have very different ways and contexts of interacting, perhaps particularly so around conflict (Zivin, in press; Notes 1 and 2). Thus as the form and specific meaning of signals change with age, so do the settings in which the transformed signals are employed. The researcher of signal development therefore needs a way of recognizing developmentally equivalent but seemingly different settings across age groups through which to trace transformed signals. Our project attempted to find indications of a similar underlying state by which to recognize equivalent conflict settings, as is described below. The wiser course may well be for developmental researchers to learn from sociologists and anthropologists of settings (e.g., Goffman, 1974) how to recognize equivalent settings which show little behavioral similarity.

A separate study took on the question of whether perception of one of the faces influences an observer's impression that the face-maker will win or lose. It also examined how aware the perceiver is of using the face as a cue to impression or outcome prediction. The study looked for developmental differences on these points.

Our subjects in the four oldest age groups were shown natural inter-action videotapes of strangers in conflict. The tape segments ended early in the interactions, just after a face was made. After seeing each segment, each subject was probed on "What do you think will happen?" and "What did you see that made you think that?" The two younger groups saw a plus and a minus segment, each done by preschoolers. The two older groups saw these tapes and also saw the more subtle plus and minus segments of adults.

Table 3-3 summarizes some of the results of this study. It should be noted that, for the first column of the table, subjects have much less than a 50% chance of guessing the "correct" predictions (i.e., predictions that plus face-makers win and minus face-maker lose), because the possible predictions are open-ended: many other predictions than that an interactant wins or loses could be made. Therefore, even for pre-schoolers, a solid percentage of the predictions are what one would expect if they were based on seeing the faces as indicators of winning-ness. And this percentage increases with age. The last column tells the percentage of explanations of predictions in which the actual presence of the plus and minus faces was indicated. Few of these explanations explicitly mentioned the correct plus or minus face. Rather, they mentioned a feeling about seeing a face or they imitated some aspect of the plus or minus face. Preschoolers are poor on this, but specific face indications increase through adulthood. The middle column counts any

Table 3-3. Percentages of Persons Per Age Group Showing Correct Outcome Predictions and Attention to Facial Cues on Videotaped Observations of Strangers' Conflict.

	50% Correct Predictions	Any Facial Area Explanation	Precise[a] Face Type Explanation
Adults n = 16	56	81	50
Adolescents n = 10	67	56	22
School Agers n = 12	58	9	5
Old Preschoolers n = 10	33	16	0

[a] Any of three types of specific reference to plus or minus faces (imitation, relevant emotion "seen" in face, or description of face components) in explanation of correct prediction for the segment's face-maker.

reference to either interactant's face anywhere in an explanation. From this it appears that faces in general are mentioned with increasing prevalence with age in people's explanations of their predictions and attributions. As faces are always important in getting one's situational bearings, it seems likely that part of what is increasing is the metacognitive knowledge that faces should count in explanations of social judgments. It is also likely that this increased attention to faces for purposes of social inference is increasingly differentiated. Such increasing differentation is suggested by the last column's increasing indications that the plus and minus faces, specifically, are perceived. In summary, then, Table 3-3 suggests an increase in attribution to facial cues over age and increased differentiation that observers do seem to use perception of the faces to predict who will win and who will lose, and that this use, as well as self-awareness of this use, increases with age.

This last point bears on the hypothesis of subliminal impression formation mentioned earlier. Since a large percentage of predictions per group appears to be in accord with what would be expected if the faces were used for forming an impression, and since only a small percentage (but a percentage large enough to indicate some recognition) reports recognizing plus or minus faces as a cue used in forming an impression, it seems possible that the faces have a large impact on impression-making cues without the perceivers' being aware of what is causing the impression. As suggested earlier, this is to be expected even more extremely in contexts where cultural invisibility would make one less prepared for or comfortable with perceiving the face as a cue. One would be quite unaware of the impression being formed.

In answer to this section's question of how recipients of faces participate in creating the faces' predictions of outcomes, three points are clear. First, perception of the plus face appears to have an effect on the motivation of the perceiver, at least in the studied situations of overt conflict among children ages 4 through 10. It is not known whether this inhibiting effect lasts longer than the first few seconds after seeing the face, whether this is the same effect in situations of nonovert struggle for older persons, or whether this apparent drop in vigor is due to an arbitrary selection out of a larger interaction pattern. There is no direct evidence on how the minus face works. Second, by whatever mechanisms the faces have effect, one third of late preschoolers appear to use view of the faces to predict outcomes for strangers, and this percentage increases regularly with age. Third, self-aware report of the plus and minus faces as cues is not prevalent until adulthood, yet there is evidence that even preschoolers have metacognitive knowledge that the face area is relevant to reports of impressions.

Symbol-Using Creatures and How to Study Them

Critical considerations for methodology and theory are raised by the developmental discontinuities encountered in these studies. In each case, the discontinuities turn on the younger child functioning closer to biological and immediate stimulus dictates and the older individual functioning by more symbolically toned transformations of earlier behavior. Several shifts found by the studies reported here, such as the plus face becoming used more subtly, are more comprehensible through developmental theories that emphasize the individual's increasing freedom with age from physical stimuli and his or her increasing flexibility through symbols (Inhelder & Piaget, 1958; Bruner, 1966).

More challenging than comprehending discontinuity *post hoc* is the problem of how such discontinuities are to be studied by designs that cannot predict where discontinuities are to be found. This project has unearthed formidable instabilities: not only do the definitions of contexts change with age such that researchers cannot select behaviorally similar contexts across age groups, but the morphology of the signals themselves may alter greatly. How can developmental researchers objectively trace the mastery in use of behaviors whose forms and whose reliable occasions for appearances both shift with age—in the current absence of any theory that suggests where to find stable frames for studying their development?

This chapter has no suggestion of theory that might point out stable frames. The taxonomy simply separated several relations between signal and state which should be taken into account in a theory of the development of signal mastery. Such a theory would also have to take into account perceivers' contributions to signal acquisition, modification, and maintenance; and this would require a truly interactive interpretation of signal-using events, evidence for which is not presented in this chapter. That approach is rare in psychology, but might in the future be best modelled after ethologists inspired by W. J. Smith's work, interaction analytic anthropologists such as Kendon (1975) and McDermott (McDermott & Roth, 1978), developmental pragmatists who keep their eye on the interactive function of a communicative behavior, as do Bates, Greenfield, and others collected by Ervin-Tripp and Mitchell-Kernan (1977), and developmental sociolinguists who focus on the rules and patterns that coordinate all interactants in an event, as do those in Ochs and Scheiffelin (1979). Such a comprehensive approach need not give up a strong basis in biology, whether in recognizing genetically prefigured contributions to signal emission and reception or in emphasizing the functional fit of signal use to social adaptation. Hinde's (1976) ethologically informed, multi-level scheme for including discrete interactive behaviors through relationships and larger social structures would accommodate such an interactive analysis and still provide for biological bases.

In the absence of such a theory, our project has attempted two methodological end runs around the problem of discontinuities in observables due to symbolic reinterpretations and social rules. The first was an unsuccessful attempt to locate stable and observable contexts for adults' subtle conflicts. This sampling problem had arisen, as noted above, when it was found impossible to locate conflict interactions in natural settings that were equivalent for young children and for adolescents or adults. The study was a localized attempt to solve only a sampling problem for one set of hypotheses, but it reflected the general problem that contexts change with age in form and meaning. The second attempt is much more ambitious, and is still in its early stages. This latter effort reflects a shift in our definition of units, away from the signal maker and perceiver as separately functioning entities who merely exchange information by turns, and toward seeing both interactants as participating in context-dependent patterns of behavior. Within such a focus, individual variables of biology, individual motivation, and elementary learning can be conceptualized to contribute on some levels while social rules and cultural interpretations of settings and behaviors contribute on other levels to a full explanation of signal use and mastery.

The first attempt (Acosta, Woodman, & Zivin, Note 1) tried to locate a pattern of nonverbal cues that would be a high probability index of the presence of *sub rosa* conflicts in polite adults. In this we ignored the conventionalized symbolic nature of the interactions and attempted to find the constant nonverbal cue indicators of physiological tension that should be independent of conventions. Our statistical strategy was inspired by van Hooff's success with chimpanzees in locating behavior contexts. Van Hooff did not interview his chimps to learn what composed different action contexts for them. He relied on the stability of behaviors and behavior sequences per context, and used factor analysis of typical behaviors to define contexts on the basis of behavior clusters that loaded together on factors (van Hooff, 1973). Our factor analyses did not adequately follow his model in having a fairly large number of subjects and in using transition probabilities rather than frequencies as input data. Although our factor structures did discriminate conflict from nonconflict situations,[7] there was sufficient overlap of behavior clusters between situation types to prevent practical differentiation in sampling situations. Single cue t-tests also differentiated situations, but not with sufficient practical lack of overlap.[8]

The second, broader effort attempts to capture the several levels of action and interaction that are simultaneously relevant to signal use. It is an approach to coding videotapes of interactions that represents

---

[7] The validity of the discrimination of conflict from nonconflict situations was initially established by having two hypothesis-naive informants from that subculture and age group sort segments of videotapes into two types of conflict and two nonconflict situations. They showed a coefficient of concordance with each other of .87 (Acosta, Woodman, & Zivin, Note 1).

[8] The cues that were seen significantly more in conflict than in non-conflict were: speech hesitancies, nervous laughter, excessive gesticulation, interruptions, voice pitch extremes, prolonged stare, and plus face.

what is going on at three levels of behavior analysis plus verbal transcription. It also codes who is attending to whom (Zivin, 1978, Note 21). The level of the temporally smallest units is the microanalytic level that codes small movements as possible cues; it includes the plus and minus faces. The next level is of goal-oriented acts which seem objective to Western observers; this includes the usual units of human ethograms and other common behavioral records such as "run" and "say." The highest level captures the interactants' interpretive label for the event, such as "having a fight" or "doing the reading lesson." To create this third level, we independently ask three members of each group, as anthropological informants, to tell us "what was going on." Newtson (1976) has demonstrated the feasibility of children indicating where events start and stop on videotapes of their action, and we have found agreement among young or old interactants' labels for situations (Zivin, 1978, Notes 20 and 21). The (so far) synonymous labels are placed on the observation record to bracket the action of the other two levels. This coding is done manually on paper and has not been programmed for a computer medium.

Two problems mentioned earlier as nested in human symbolic transformations are approached through this coding system. One, the question of interactants having symbolic interactions of indistinct identity to outside observers, is handled by having the interactants apply their own labels to interpret the interactions. The observer can then judiciously use these labels' symbolic equivalences to compare across age groups and across other variables. The other problem, the question of whether a signal is itself having an effect or whether it is the larger pattern already underway that carries through to an end, is approached by capturing attention stream and a complete record of action at three levels, before and after signals, from all interactants. With these data, one can search for larger-than-signal coordinating patterns.

Methods for such search will probably need to go outside the linear organization yielded by sequential analyses (e.g., Sackett, 1978). Discussion of some of the limiting problems of current interactional analyses and suggestions beyond them appear in Lamb, Suomi, and Stephenson (1979) and have been squarely addressed in a symposium for the purpose by Brazelton, Als, and Lester (Note 2), Hinde (Note 6), Rosenblum (Note 11), Stettner (Note 14), and Zivin (Note 21). A wholly fitting nonlinear analysis for multiple levels has yet to be devised.

Our study of the development of mastery of the plus and minus face pauses with this construction of a multi-leveled interactive approach to the flow of signal use and mastery. Having seen that simple models of fixed signaling behavior would force us to lose track of increased sophistication in the use of these signals and would deprive us of our interest in watching the development of skill in self-presentation through subtlety, we have turned to conceptualizations of signal types and simultaneous signaling levels in order to better understand signal function patterns. These patterns may allow us to watch developmental transformations in signal use.

Conclusion

This chapter has emphasized limitations: limitations on continuities of form, function, and context in signal use that were found by the studies reported here, limitations in the common models of signal use which assume simple stabilities between state and signal behavior across development, and limitations of methodologies for studying communication development that capture only one level of analysis and no interaction patterns.

The discontinuities and less dramatic developmental shifts found in these cross-sectional studies of ages 2½ through 45 are: (1) The plus and minus faces seem to start life by display-like mechanisms but become transformed to a soft type of signal by social learning and reinforcement; (2) The frequency of plus faces straightforwardly correlates with dominance rank only through about 10 years of age (dominance hierarchies themselves appear to shift their bases from observable physical features to symbolic ones [Zivin, in press, Note 22]; (3) The context of the plus face shifts for socially competent individuals over age 7, away from overt physical conflicts and into nonconflictful exhibitions of competence; (4) Full plus and minus faces decrease with age and become replaced by abbreviated forms that usually include and formally stabilize around the chin; (5) The faces seem to begin to function in generalized impression management and formation, rather than in controlling discrete isolated conflicts, by middle school years; and (6) Adults hardly ever have the overt physical forms of conflict that are isomorphic to or as easily recognized as those of preschool and school aged children. Their conflicts are much more symbolic and covert. The interpretation to which all these findings point is that these faces, perhaps like other powerful social signals, start as display-like behaviors but are transformed through social learning and the growing child's greater symbol use into more general, subtle, and socially controlled movements that contribute to others' social inferences about the signal-maker.

A model of developing signal mastery, for signals that originate with display-like biological bases, would thus have to include a view of display-like signals and their underlying states becoming less fixedly linked and the contexts of their emission coming under greater symbolic control. Although this is a trend one could understand from general developmental principles and is a view being adopted by some researchers of nonverbal development (e.g., Campos, Note 3; Ekman, 1979; Emde et al., 1978; Malatesta & Izard, in press; Oster, 1978; Saarni, 1978 and this volume; Sorce, Emde, & Klinnert, Note 13), such a model has yet to be clearly put forth. The taxonomy presented here is an attempt to specify some of the transformable relations between state and signal behavior and the mechanisms that mediate these relations. The taxonomy might thus contribute to the creation of a more comprehensible model for the development of signal mastery.

The limitations of narrowly focused methodologies might also be loosened by the approach to interaction observation to which these studies led. In an awareness that signal use is likely multi-determined, we sought the larger patterns of joint action that occasion signal presence and function, and devised a multi-leveled descriptive coding system. The orientation of the coding system, rather than the specific system, may be useful to others. It interprets signal use as being simultaneously composed of minute, physically responsive components, goal-oriented voluntary acts, and socially defined context-specific meanings. This orientation preserves the biological core of expressive signals (and perhaps also a core of conventional signals), while allowing a theoretical place for their symbolic transformation with increased mastery.

Noting the limitations has therefore been useful. The discontinuities that had accumulated in our project's findings eventually indicated that plus and minus face mastery required a more complex model and a richer methodology than any easily available. It may be that this is also true for other signals—not only those that originate in display-like behaviors, such as emotional expressions and signals of receptiveness to contact—but also for those which are based on social learning from their start.

Acknowledgment. The research reported in this chapter was suggested by the Harry Frank Guggenheim Foundation.

Reference Notes

1. Acosta, P., Woodman, L., & Zivin. G. When is a fight a fight? Paper presented at the Annual Meeting of the Animal Behavior Society, New Orleans, 1979.
2. Brazelton, T. B., Als, H., & Lester, B. M. The important complexity of parent-infant interaction. In G. Zivin & L. Stettner (Co-Chairs), *Capturing the quality of a relationship.* Symposium presented at the Biennial Meeting of the Society for Research in Child Development, Boston, April 1981.
3. Campos, J. Social referencing in infants. In P. Read (Chair), *Measurement of emotions.* Symposium presented at the Biennial Meeting of the International Society for the Study of Behavioral Development, Toronto, August 1981.
4. Camras, L. *The role of children's facial expression in a conflict situation.* Unpublished doctoral dissertation, University of Pennsylvania, 1975.

5. Dancy, D. A., Moore, C. L., & Zivin, G. *The faces of success. Race, class and environmental effects on win-predicting faces.* Paper presented at the Annual Meeting of the Animal Behavior Society, New Orleans, June 1979.
6. Hinde, R. A. Discussion. In G. Zivin & L. J. Stettner (Co-Chairs), *Capturing the quality of a relationship: Progress in the observational analysis of social interaction.* A symposium presented at the Biennial Meeting of the Society for Research in Child Development, Boston, April 1981.
7. Hottenstein, M. P. *An exploration of the relationship between age, social status, and facial gesturing.* Unpublished doctoral dissertation, University Pennsylvania, 1977.
8. Malatesta, C. Z. Infant emotional lability and measurement by the MAX Method. In P. Read (Chair), *Measurement of emotions.* Symposium presented at the Biennial Meeting of the International Society for the Study of Behavioral Development, Toronto, August 1981.
9. Malatesta, C. A. Personal communication, August 1981.
10. Oster, H. Personal communication, July 1981.
11. Rosenblum, L. A. Behavioral allometry: Food for thought. In G. Zivin & L. J. Stettner (Co-chairs), *Capturing the quality of a relationship: Progress in the observational analysis of social interaction.* A symposium presented at the Biennial Meeting of the Society for Research in Child Development, Boston, April 1981.
12. Saarni, C. Personal communication, October 1981.
13. Sorce, J. F., Emde, R. N., & Klinnert, M. *Maternal emotional signalling: Its Effect on the visual cliff behavior of one-year-olds.* Paper presented at the Biennial Meeting of the Society for Research in Child Development, Boston, April 1981.
14. Stettner, L. J. Introductory remarks. In G. Zivin & L. J. Stettner (Co-Chairs), *Capturing the quality of a relationship: Progress in the observational analysis of social interaction.* A symposium presented at the Biennial Meeting of the Society for Research in Child Development, Boston, April 1981.
15. Strayer, F. F. Investigating the nature of social learning: An ethological approach to peer socialization. In W. Charlesworth (Chair), *Back to nature, changing paradigms and child ethology ten years later.* Symposium presented at the Biennial Meeting of the Society for Research in Child Development Boston, April 1981.
16. Zivin, G. *Preschoolers' facial-postural status messages.* Paper presented at the Third International Workshop on Human Ethology, Sheffield, England, July 1975.
17. Zivin, G. *Avoiding the "phenotypic fallacy" while tracing morphological change.* Paper presented at the Meeting of the Animal Behavior Society, University Park, June 1977.
18. Zivin, G. *Sight of two facial gestures differentially affects childrens' latencies in reaction.* Paper presented at the Annual Meeting of the Animal Behavior Society, Seattle, WA, June 1978.
19. Zivin, G. *The relation of facial gestures to conflict outcomes.* Paper presented at the First Annual Meeting of the International Society of Political Psychology, New York, September 1978.
20. Zivin, G. *Making sense in multi-level behavioral analyses.* Paper presented at the Annual Meeting of the Animal Behavior Society, Ft. Collins, CO, June 1980.

21. Zivin, G. Making a multi-level behavioral record for several interactants. In G. Zivin & L. J. Stettner (Co-chairs), *Capturing the quality of a relationship: Progress in the observational analysis of social interaction.* Symposium presented at the Biennial Meeting of the Society for Research in Child Development. Boston, April 1981.
22. Zivin, G. *Comparative issues illustrated by the application of primate models to human social behavior.* Paper presented at the Annual Meeting of the Animal Behavior Society, Knoxville, TN, June 1981.
23. Zivin, G. & Caruthers, B. *Do children see what we think they see on video screens?* Paper presented at Eastern Psychological Association, Washington, D.C., March 1978.
24. Zivin, G., Caruthers, B., & Glasser, D. *Developmental differences in social perception of body cues on video and in life.* Paper presented at Southeastern Conference on Human Development. Atlanta, April 1978.
25. Zivin, G., Caruthers, B., & Glasser, I. K. *Preschoolers perceive social cues differently in life and on video.* Paper presented at the Biennial Meeting of the Society for Research on Child Development, San Francisco, March 1979.

References

Allport, F. H. *Social psychology.* Boston: Houghton Mifflin, 1924.

Ambrose, J. A. The development of the smiling response in early infancy. In B. M. Foss (Ed.), *Determinants of infant behavior, Vol. I.* London: Metheun, 1959, 179-201.

Bates, E., Camioni, L., & Volterra, V. The acquisition of performatives prior to speech. In E. Ochs & B. B. Schieffelin (Eds.), *Developmental pragmantics.* New York: Academic Press, 1979, 111-130.

Bloom, L., Lightbown, P., & Hood, L. Structure and variation in child language. *Monographs of the Society for Research in Child Development,* 1975, *40*, whole no. 160.

Blurton Jones, N. G. An ethological study of some aspects of social behaviour of children in nursery school. In D. Morris (Ed.), *Primate ethology,* London: Weidenfeld & Nicolson, 1967.

Brazelton, T. B., Tronick, E., Adamson, L., Als, H., & Wise, S. Early mother-infant reciprocity. In M. A. Hofer (Ed.), *Parent-infant relationship,* Ciba Foundation Symposium 33, New York: Elsevier, Excerpta Medica, North Holland, 1975, 137-154.

Bruner, J. S. On cognitive growth, I & II. In Bruner, J. S., Olver, R. R., Greenfield, P. M., Hornsby, J. R., Kenney, H. J., Maccoby, M., Modiano, N., Mosher, F. A., Olson, D. R., Potter, M. C., Reich, L. C., & Sonstroem, A. M. *Studies in cognitive growth.* New York: Wiley, 1966.

Camras, L. Facial expression used by children in a conflict situation. *Child Development,* 1977, *48*, 1431-1435.

Condon, W. S. The relation of interactional synchrony to cognitive and emotional processes. In M. R. Key (Ed.), *The relationship of verbal and nonverbal communication.* New York: Mouton, 1980, 19-65.

Darwin, C. *The expression of the emotions in man and animals.* Chicago: University of Chicago Press, 1965. (Originally published, 1872.)

Druckman, D., Rozelle, R. M., & Baxter, J. C. *Nonverbal communication: Survey, theory, and research*. Beverly Hills, CA: Sage, 1982.

Edelman, M. S. & Omark, D. R. Dominance hierarchies in young children. *Social Science Information*, 1973, *12*, 103-110.

Eibl-Eibesfeldt, I. Similarities and differences between cultures in expressive movements. In R. A. Hinde (Ed.), *Non-verbal communication*. Cambridge, England: Cambridge University Press, 1972, 297-311.

Ekman, P. Universals and cultural differences in facial expressions of emotions. *Nebraska Symposium on Motivation*, 1971, 207-283.

Ekman, P. About brows: Emotional and conversational signals. In M. von Cranach, K. Foppa, W. Lepeniew, & D. Ploog (Eds.), *Human ethology*. London: Cambridge University Press, 1979, 169-249.

Ekman, P. & Friesen, W. V. The repertoire of nonverbal behavior: Categories, origins, usage, and coding. *Semiotica*, 1969, *1*(1), 49-98.

Emde, R. N., Kligman, D. H., Reich, J. H., & Wade, T. D. Emotional expression in infancy, I: Initial studies of social signaling and an emergent model. In M. Lewis & L. Rosenblum (Eds.), *The development of affect*. New York: Plenum, 1978.

Ervin-Tripp, S. & Mitchell-Kernan, C. (Eds.), *Child discourse*. New York: Academic Press, 1977.

Freedman, D. G. Smiling in blind infants and the issue of innate vs. acquired. *Journal of Child Psychology and Psychiatry*, 1964, *5*, 171-184.

Freidman, H. S. The concept of skill in nonverbal communication: Implications for understanding social interaction. In R. Rosenthal (Ed.), *Skill in nonverbal communication*. Cambridge, MA: Oelgeschlager, Gunn & Hain, 1979.

Freud, S. The psychology of errors. In *A general introduction to psychoanalysis*. New York: Washington Square Books, 1924, 29-83.

Goffman, E. *The presentation of self in everyday life*. New York: Doubleday, 1959.

Goffman, E. *Frame analysis*. New York: Harper & Row, 1974.

Greenfield, P. M. Informativeness, presupposition, and semantic choice in single word utterances. In E. Ochs & B. B. Schieffelin (Eds.), *Developmental pragmatics*. New York: Academic Press, 1979, 159-166.

Hall, K. R. L. & DeVore, I. Baboon social behavior. In I. DeVore (Ed.), *Primate behavior*. New York: Holt, Rinehart & Winston, 1965, 53-110.

Hastie, R., Ostrom, T. M., Ebbeson, E. B., Wyer, R. S., Hamilton, D. L., & Carlston, D. E. *Person memory: The cognitive basis of social perception*. Hillsdale, N.J.: Lawrence Erlbaum, 1980.

Hinde, R. A. Interactions, relationships, and social structure. *Man*, 1976, *11*, 1-17.

Huxley, J. Courtship activities in the red-throated diver (*Colymbus stellatus* Pontopp.); together with a discussion of the evolution of courtship in birds. *Journal of the Linnean Society of London, Zoology*, 1923, *53*, 253-292.

Inhelder, B. & Piaget, J. *The growth of logical thinking*. New York: Basic Books, 1958.

Izard, C. E., Huebner, R. R., Risser, D., McGinnes, G. C., & Dougherty, L. M. The young infant's ability to produce discrete emotional expressions. *Developmental Psychology*, 1980, *16*, 132-140.

Jay, P. C. The common langur in North America. In I. DeVore (Ed.), *Primate behavior*. New York: Holt, Rinehart & Winston, 1965, 197-249.

Jones, E. E., Kanouse, D. E., Kelly, H. H., Nisbitt, R. E., Valins, S., & Weiner, B. (Eds.), *Attribution: Perceiving the causes of behavior*. Morristown, NJ: General Learning Press, 1972.

Jones, E. E., & Nisbett, R. E. The actor and the observer. In E. E. Jones et al. (Eds.), *Attribution: Perceiving the causes of behavior*. Morristown, NJ: General Learning Press, 1972.

Kendon, A. Some functions of the face in a kissing round. *Semiotica*, 1975, *15*, 299-334.

Kraut, R. E. Verbal and nonverbal cues in the perception of lying. *Journal of Personality and Social Psychology*, 1978, *36*, 380-391.

Lamb, M. E. Interactions between eighteen-month-olds and their preschool-aged siblings. *Child Development*, 1978, *49*, 51-59.

Lamb, M. E., Suomi, S. J., & Stephenson, G. R. *Social interaction analysis: Methodological issues*. Madison: University of Wisconsin Press, 1979.

Lorenz, K. Companionship in bird life. In C. S. Schiller (Ed. & Trans.), *Instinctive behavior*. New York: International Universities Press, 1957, 83-128. (Originally published, 1935.)

McDermott, R. P. & Roth, D. R. Social organization of behavior: Interactional approaches. *Annual Review of Anthropology*, 1978, 7, 321-345.

McGrew, W. C. *An ethological study of children's behaviour*. New York: Academic Press, 1972.

Malatesta, C. Z. & Izard, C. E. The ontogenesis of human social signals: From biological imperative to symbol utilization. In N. Fox & J. Davidson (Eds.), *Affective development: A psychobiological perspective*. Hillsdale, NJ: Erlbaum, in press.

Marler, P. & Tamura, M. Culturally transmitted patterns of vocal behavior in sparrows. *Science*, 1964, *146*, 1483-1486.

Newtson, D. Foundations of attribution: The perception of ongoing behavior. In J. Harvey, W. Ickes, & R. Kidd (Eds.), *New directions in attribution research*. Hillsdale, NJ: Erlbaum, 1976.

Ochs, E. & Schieffelin, B. B. (Eds.), *Developmental pragmatics*. New York: Academic Press, 1979.

Oster, H. Facial expression and affect development. In M. Lewis & L. A. Rosenblum (Eds.), *Affect development*. New York: Plenum, 1978.

Oster, H. & Ekman, P. Facial behavior in child development. In A. Collins (Ed.), *Minnesota Symposium on Child Psychology*, *Vol. II*. Hillsdale, NJ: Erlbaum, 1978, 231-276.

Pieper, A. *Cerebral function in infancy and childhood*. B. & H. Nagler (Trans.), New York: Consultants Bureau, 1963. (Originally published, 1961.)

Polak, P. R., Emde, R. A., & Spitz, R. A. The smiling response to the human face, I: Methodology, quantification and natural history. *Journal of Nervous & Mental Disease*, 1964, *139*, 103-109.

Ross, L. The intuitive psychologist and his shortcomings: Distortions in the attribution process. In L. Berkowitz (Ed.), *Advances in experimental social psychology*, *Vol. 10*. New York: Academic Press, 1977.

Saarni, C. Cognitive and communicative features of emotional experience or do you show what you think you feel. In M. Lewis & L. Rosenblum (Eds.), *The development of affect*. New York: Plenum, 1978.

Sackett, G. P. The lag sequential analysis of contingency and cyclicity in behavioral interaction research. In J. Osofsky (Ed.), *Handbook of infant development*. New York: Wiley, 1978.

Sebeok, T. A. The word "zoosemiotics." *American Speech*, 1967.

Sluckin, A. M., & Smith, P. K. Two approaches to the concept of dominance in children. *Child Development*, 1977, *48*, 917-923.

Smith, W. J. Messages of vertebrate communication. *Science*, 1969, *165*, 145-150.

Smith, W. J. *The behavior of communicating: An ethological approach*. Cambridge, MA: Harvard University Press, 1977.

Spitz, R. & Wolf, K. M. The smiling response: A contribution to the ontogenesis of social relations. *Genetic Psychology Monographs*, 1946, *34*, 57-125.

Sroufe, L. A. Socioemotional development. In J. Osofsky (Ed.), *Handbook of infancy*. New York: Wiley, 1978.

Sroufe, L. A. & Waters, E. The ontogenesis of smiling and laughter: A perspective on the organization of development in infancy. *Psychological Review*, 1976, *83*, 173-189.

Stern, D. N. Mother and infant at play: The dyadic interaction involving facial, vocal, and gaze behaviors. In M. Lewis & L. A. Rosenblum (Eds.), *The effect of the infant on its caregiver*. New York: Wiley, 1974.

Strayer, F. F. & Strayer, J. An ethological analysis of social agonism and dominance relations among preschool children. *Child Development*, 1976, *47*, 980-989.

van Hooff, J. A. R. A. M. *Aspects of the social behavior and communication in human and higher nonhuman primates*. Rotterdam: Bronder-Offset, 1971.

van Hooff, J. A. R. A. M. A structural analysis of the social behavior of a semi-captive group of chimpanzees. In M. von Cranach & I. Vine (Eds.), *Social communication and movement*. New York: Academic Press, 1973, 75-162.

Zivin, G. Preschool children's facial gestures predict conflict outcomes. *Social Science Information*, 1977, *16*(6), 715-730. (a)

Zivin, G. On becoming subtle: Age and social rank changes in the use of a facial gesture. *Child Development*, 1977, *48*(4), 1314-1321. (b)

Zivin, G. Layers of description for studying contextual relations of facial gestures. *Sociolinguistic Newsletter*, Summer 1978.

Zivin, G. Hybrid models: Modifications in models of social behavior that are borrowed across species and up evolutionary grades. In D. W. Rajecki (Ed.), *Comparing behavior*. Hillsdale, NJ: Erlbaum, in press.

Part Two
Social Developmental Approaches to Nonverbal Behavior

CHAPTER FOUR

The Development of Control over Affective Expression in Nonverbal Behavior

William A. Shennum and Daphne B. Bugental

As adults in a Western culture, most of us have come to learn to control the extent to which, and the ways in which, we nonverbally display our emotions and attitudes. We may hide our feelings of disgust. Our anger may be partially concealed with a fixed smile. There are even situations in which we may wish to conceal our positive attitudes; for instance, in a bargaining exchange.

The notion of "display rules" for expressive behavior was first proposed by Ekman and Friesen (1969). In resolving historical disputes between those who maintained that nonverbal communication was innate and those who held that it was learned, they held that both notions were, in fact, true. Ekman (1971) proposed a "neuro-cultural" theory of facial expression of affect which postulated the existence of innate neural links between emotional states and specific facial muscles. The theory also included a social learning component, which suggested that an overlay of cultural/social learning can intervene between a felt and an expressed emotion. The individual comes to learn a set of display rules (personal, situational, and cultural norms) that govern the presence and form of facial expressions. The use of display rules not only involves *knowledge* about the do's and don'ts of expressing particular feelings in particular social contexts (e.g., Saarni, 1979), but also requires the *motivation* and the *ability* to control one's own behavior in accordance with that knowledge (e.g., Snyder, 1974). Three of the major types of display rules (Ekman, 1978) are:

1. *Simulation*: showing feelings when you have none.
2. *Inhibition*: giving the appearance of having no feeling when you in fact do.
3. *Masking*: covering a feeling with the expression of one you are not experiencing.

A question which has begun to attract some research attention is the course of development in the management of nonverbal communication of affect. Nonverbal expressions of emotion appear quite early in life, major identifiable affects being discernible while the child is still in infancy (Charlesworth & Kreutzer, 1973). It has been postulated, however, that emotional expressiveness in humans is under two forms of control. Early expressions of emotion in infancy are originally under autonomic control, and with learning come under the voluntary control of the child (Murray, 1979). The latter type of control provides a necessary but not sufficient basis for self-management of expressive behavior in interpersonal settings. The child must not only have the capability of controlling his or her own behavior; it is also necessary for the child to have the social experiences that teach the rules of interpersonal interaction and the cognitive capacity to understand how one is seen (and heard) by others.

Adult Self-Management of Affective Expression

Before we know what we should expect in the development of expressive management, it is necessary to consider related findings from adult research. In Ekman and Friesen's (1969) early studies, observations were made of the extent to which underlying unexpressed (verbally) affect may be "leaked" through nonverbal channels over which the communicator has differential degrees of control. They maintained that the controllability of a particular expressive channel (and, thus, the possibility that it may not accurately reveal underlying feelings) is a function of three characteristics: *sending capacity* of the channel (its range of expression and its salience to observers), *external feedback* (the extent to which others react to it), and *internal feedback* (the degree of self-awareness of the channel). They argued that the face is the most controllable channel, by virtue of the large number of messages it can send, its high salience to observers and resulting external feedback, and its relatively high self-awareness. Other channels, such as body behavior and voice quality, were presumed to be less controllable. In a study involving student nurses' deception abilities, Ekman and Friesen (1974) found that body cues revealed or leaked true affect during deception, whereas facial cues did not. Subsequently, others have analyzed tone of voice during deceptive and non-deceptive interactions and found that deception was also associated with increased pitch (Ekman, Friesen, & Scherer, 1976; Streeter, Krauss, Geller, Olson, & Apple, 1977).

In general, the deception accuracy of a particular channel (i.e., the extent to which one can use it to successfully present a false impression) has been found to be directly related to the channel's controllability (Zuckerman, DePaulo, & Rosenthal, 1981). In agreement with Ekman and Friesen's leakage formulations, research has generally found

that facial expressions provide little leakage of true affect during deception. Facial expressions can in fact be quite directly misleading. Before
the facial channel is dismissed entirely, however, it should be noted that
there are circumstances under which it can provide leakage/deception
cues. Morris (1977) discusses several interesting examples of potential
facial cues to deception. These generally involve overreactions and
underreactions and indicate failure of the communicator in judging the
right strength of a false facial expression. For instance, "overkill" reactions (sometimes referred to as "hamming") are stronger and more
exaggerated than natural affective expressions, thus reducing their cred-
ibility. Facial underreactions can also act as cues to deception. For
example, the "on-off" smile is too short; the "decaying smile" fizzles
out over time. Thus, facial expressions that are either "too much" or
"too little" compared to normal baseline expressions may be excellent
sources of leakage/deception.

Voice quality (tone of voice) is often considered to be one of the
least controllable of the nonverbal channels and is generally found to be
a significant source of leakage/deception (Zuckerman et al., 1981).
Studies by Weitz (1972) and by Bugental, Caporael, and Shennum
(1980) indicate that interpersonal attitudes and feelings of control can
leak through the affective and assertive qualities of voice tone, even
when they are not expressed verbally. Studies by Zuckerman and his
associates show that, during conscious attempts to deceive, the voice is
far less controllable than is facial behavior (Zuckerman, Larrance,
Spiegel, & Klorman, 1981). Thus, the adult literature might be taken to
suggest that developmental trends in expressive control may differ in
the various nonverbal channels. Greater age increases would be expected
in high vs. low controllability behaviors.

The adult literature also provides a point of reference in predicting a
differential course of communication development among boys vs. girls.
As a whole, females have been found to be more accurate encoders of
nonverbal affect than are males (Hall, 1980). But there is no evidence
that females are better able to self-manage their nonverbal behavior.
Zuckerman et al. (1981), in reviewing the deception literature, concluded that females are slightly (but not reliably) more detectable than
are males. Little distinction is made in the literature between deception, or self-management that involves inhibition of affect, and that
which involves masking (substituting one expressed affect for another).
It is reasonable to expect that males would have greater skills in inhibiting emotional expression, whereas females would excel in masking ability. If males are discouraged from engaging in affective displays, as is
suggested by the overall finding of lower expressiveness in males, they
are likely to become practiced in affective inhibition. Females, on the
other hand, with their greater experience in expressiveness, may be
more successful in deception tactics that involve masking. Currently,

there is insufficient evidence on sex differences in deception to make this distinction.

Child Self-Management of Affective Expression

Research on developmental trends in children's self-management of expressive behavior is just beginning. Saarni (1979) demonstrated that younger children (six- and eight-year olds) do not understand or use display rules as well as do older children (ten-year olds). She maintained that display rules are social conventions that must be learned. In her measurement of the understanding of display rules, Saarni focused her attention on children's knowledge of the socially appropriate facial expression that one would demonstrate in connection with a series of negative occurrences, e.g., receiving a disappointing birthday present. She followed up this judgment study with an investigation (Note 1) in which she measured the extent to which children behaviorally expressed or withheld expression of negative affect after receiving a disappointing present. The results provided a behavioral parallel to the previous research and indicated that older children did appear to make greater use of display rules than did younger children. No sex differences were found in either study.

Feldman and White (1980) examined children's ability to manage nonverbal expressions of preference. They studied face and body cues in two types of deception: pretending to like something that was actually disliked, and pretending to dislike something that was truly liked. Children (aged 5 to 12 years) tasted two drinks—sweetened and unsweetened. Half the children pretended to like both during a mock interview, and half pretended to dislike both. Thus, all children had both a lie and a truth condition. Behavior sequences were taped and later rated for deceptiveness, separately for face and body. Difference scores (deceptiveness during the deception sequence minus deceptiveness during the truth condition) were analyzed. High scores were taken to indicate unsuccessful deception. The primary finding was a significant interaction of age, sex, and communication channel. The interaction indicated little, if any, age differences in body cues to deception. For facial expressions, however, boys and girls showed opposite age trends. Girls became less revealing of deception (i.e., were better liars) with age, while boys became more revealing of deception. Additionally, there were sex differences in deception success associated with "faking like" (boys excelled) and "faking dislike" (girls excelled). These results do not completely agree with earlier research by Feldman, Jenkins, and Popoola (1979). In that study, overall age increases in facial expressive control (in pretending to like an unpleasant drink) were found for both sexes. It is important to note, however, that the earlier study measured *leakage* of underlying attitudes, whereas the later study was concerned with the presence of *deception* cues. The discrepancy in findings suggests the potential importance of the distinction between leakage and cues to deception.

Finally, Ekman, Roper, and Hager (1980) have found that children improve with age in ability to deliberately produce component actions involved in facial expression. They studied 5-, 9-, and 13-year-olds' ability to produce twelve elemental facial actions which were components of more complex emotional expressions (happiness, surprise, anger, disgust, fear and sadness). Performance improved with age, although actions associated with the expressions of fear, sadness, and anger were difficult even for the oldest children. This is reminiscent of the finding by Odom and Lemond (1972) that children are relatively unsuccessful in producing negative facial expressions.

Considering the child and adult literature together, it would appear fruitful for future research on children's expressive control to consider the following comparisons: (a) control of positive vs. negative expressions, (b) deception success in highly controllable vs. less controllable communication channels, (c) inhibition of affect as opposed to masking of affect, and (d) cues to leakage of underlying affect vs. cues to the presence of an attempted deception.

The Present Study

In order to further examine and refine our understanding of the developmental aspects of expressive control, the present study was designed to assess developmental shifts during childhood in the management of positive and negative affect both in facial and vocal channels, both under masking and under inhibition display rule conditions. Although there is evidence that young children do make successful use of tone of voice in expressing affect (Bugental & Moore, 1979), we know nothing of the extent to which children learn to manage their vocal expressions. Clearly, tone of voice is low in self-awareness (Holzman & Rousey, 1966), and to the extent that it is effectively uncontrollable, no developmental trends should be found. If this is the case, findings should parallel those of Feldman and White (1980) for face versus body, i.e., developmental trends should be stronger for facial self-management than for vocal self-management. Parents and teachers often act as though children do, in fact, have control over their own vocal intonations, however. Think of the adult injunction, "Don't take that tone with me, young man!" It will be important, correspondingly, to discover whether children have the capacity for expressive control over vocal intonation.

The facial-vocal comparisons were made in connection with both positive and negative effect. Although a few researchers have introduced this comparison, most studies are concerned only with the communicator's ability to inhibit or mask *negative* affects or attitudes. The rationale typically provided for this limitation is that there are more cultural display rules directed towards the inhibition and masking of negative affect than positive affect. Nonetheless, it is important to consider the developing capability of the child to manage both affects. One can think of instances (e.g., concealing positive interests in a bargaining situation, concealing interest in a member of the opposite sex when reciprocity is not assured) in which it is socially adaptive to inhibit or mask positive as well as negative affect.

This study also provided for separate judgments of the extent to which children leak underlying affect and the extent to which they provide cues to deception. It is obvious from the literature that there is no one-to-one correspondence between these two processes.

Two specific predictions regarding developmental trends were made. First, it was expected that expressive control would increase during childhood (age range 6 to 12 years). Greater increases were expected in the facial channel than in the vocal channel, owing to its greater potential controllability. Secondly, it was predicted that sex differences in developmental patterns would be found. Specifically, boys were expected to increase in deception skills involving inhibition, and girls were expected to improve in deception skills involving masking. Further, to the extent that expressive control represents a generalized ability, these two predictions would be expected to hold true for both positive and negative affect. If, on the other hand, control is more affect-specific, one would expect the predictions to hold primarily with respect to the concealment of negative underlying affect (because most display rules appear to involve the covering of negative affect).

Additional predictions were made with respect to several potential causal factors underlying developmental trends. A set of developmental predictor variables was selected to represent theoretical explanations from social learning theory and cognitive-developmental theory, and was examined in relationship to expressive control development. From the standpoint of social learning theory, it was expected that children with greater amounts of experience with other children (as measured by parent ratings and number of siblings) would show a higher capability of expressive control. Emotional expression during social interaction is subject to monitoring and feedback both by peers and adults. Social experience also exposes the child to models who exercise control over their expressive behavior. The sheer amount of social experience a person has may be a causal factor in expressive control. Shennum (Note 2), for instance, found that high affiliation was associated with high expressive control.

It was also predicted from a cognitive development point of view that expressive control has cognitive as well as social prerequisites. In order to successfully manage one's own appearance (or voice), it may be necessary to decenter—to step outside oneself and view the environ-ment from alternate perspectives. For example, in order to manage one's facial display of affect, a child may need to have a concept of how his or her face appears to observers. Correspondingly, measures were taken of children's general cognitive level and their perspective-taking ability.

Method

Sixty children (30 boys, 30 girls), ranging in age from 6 to 12 years, were brought to the lab by a parent or guardian. The parent was given a set of consent forms and child rating scales to fill out while the child and the experimenter went to a test cubicle. The child's behavior was videotaped throughout the 20-minute session through an unobtrusive two-way mirror (consent had been obtained in advance). The session began with an open-ended interview about the child's likes and dislikes. The child was encouraged to talk about and become involved in his or her reports about liked and disliked activities, places to go, foods, movies, television shows, etc. These responses were used as baselines for the child's spontaneous positive and negative affective expression. The specific likes and dislikes reported by the child were referred to later during the expressive control conditions. Neutral baseline expressions were obtained during responses to questions about the child's age, place of residence, etc.

An acting/role-playing format was used to assess the children's ability to control their expressions of like and dislike. The format of the acting tasks was a talk show. Each child played the role of a guest. The child was told to pretend she or he was a television movie actress or actor being interviewed about her or his likes and dislikes. However, rather than answering as they normally would, the children were told their job was to show how well they could act, as they were to answer the interviewer's questions in a preset way ("like a script"). As a warm-up for the acting tasks, the children first were shown a brief segment of a television talk show (*Kids Are People Too*) in which a child actress was being interviewed. It was emphasized that individuals of all ages are actors and actresses, and that acting is a lot like pretending. The subjects then were told that for the next few minutes the experimenter wanted to pretend that he and the child were on a talk show. The experimenter said, "Let's pretend that you're a famous actor (actress). I want you to show me how well you can act." The experimenter went on to say that he would ask about likes and dislikes again, but when he did so the sub-ject should pretend to feel differently about them than he or she really does. Four expressive control conditions were then administered:

1. *Masking of negative affect*: pretending to like something that is dis-liked.

2. *Inhibition of negative affect*: pretending to be neutral about something that is disliked.
3. *Masking of positive affect*: pretending to dislike something that is liked.
4. *Inhibition of positive affect*: pretending to be neutral about something that is liked.

Separate instructions were given prior to each condition, after which the experimenter played the role of the talk show host and asked, "Tell me, (child's name), how do you feel about _____ (reported like or dislike)?" In masking negative affect, for example, children were told that they would be asked about one of the things they earlier had reported as a dislike. However, since they were acting, each child was instructed to pretend to really like the item and to be as convincing as possible (no specific behaviors were suggested). On inhibition trials, children were instructed to act as if they neither liked nor disliked the item (i.e., indifferently), as if they didn't care about it, or they didn't have any feelings about it one way or the other. Children generally had little difficulty understanding the instructions, although the concept of "inhibition" tended to require more explanation than did "masking." If the child's verbal content during any condition suggested that the instructions had not been understood, the instructions were explained again and the condition was repeated.

The testing session also included several cognitive tasks. Cognitive measures included observing the child's conservation of liquid and solid quantity and conservation of volume, as well as a visual perspective taking task. The child's social experience was assessed by the number of siblings the child had and the parental rating of the overall amount of the child's social activity, using items from Buck's Affect Expression Rating Scale—Children's Form (Buck, 1977). The cognitive and social variables were examined for their relationship to age differences in expressive control.

Edited videotapes and audiotapes were prepared for rating by two separate groups of five trained adult raters. The tapes included, in random order, each child's complete response in the four expressive control conditions, as well as samples (usually two each) of positive, neutral, and negative affective baseline responses. Each sample for each child was rated, first, on a nine-point affect (positive-negative) scale. The tape was then replayed and each sample was rated on a nine-point deceptiveness (low-high) scale. Prior to each rating session, raters were trained and calibrated in using the scale via practice ratings, feedback, and discussion of the dimension being rated. One group of raters rated facial[1] behavior (videotape samples with no sound). The second group

---

[1] The term "facial" is used throughout, although both the face and the upper body were visible on the tapes.

rated voice quality based on content-filtered speech samples. The edited audiotape was played through a speech filtering device, which eliminated frequencies below 100 and above 600 cycles per second. This effectively eliminated the intelligibility of voice samples, while retaining voice quality information, thus insuring that ratings were uninfluenced by verbal content. The ratings of individual raters then were averaged, yielding measures of the mean facial and vocal affect and deceptiveness of each expressive control and baseline sample.

Results and Discussion

Nonverbal behavior was analyzed by using a within-subjects comparison strategy. That is, a child's behavior in an expressive control condition was always compared with his or her behavior during baseline conditions. The analysis of each type of expressive control condition (e.g., inhibition of positive affect, masking of negative affect, etc.) required two separate comparisons. First, it was important to examine a child's deviation from his or her baseline affect. For example, if the child truly liked an activity and "pretended" not to (i.e., masking of positive) we were concerned with the deviation between the nonverbal affect in acted performance and in expressed affect during baseline description of the liked activity. If there was little deviation from baseline, we would say that the true affect "leaked" nonverbally during the expressive control attempt. A relatively large deviation would suggest successful control. However, a second, equally important comparison concerned the approximation of the acted to the appropriate *target* (baseline) expression. That is, how similar to baseline negative was the attempt to mask true positive affect? To be an effective deception, a masked expression should not only deviate from the true expression but should also approximate the natural target expression. In similar fashion, an inhibited expression not only should deviate from the true affect, it also should approximate the baseline *neutral* expression. The first aspect relates to the leakage of true feelings; the second refers to the naturalness of the enactment. Thus, comparisons of controlled expressions both with baseline and target were made separately for each condition.

Expressive Control of Negative Affect

Age trends in the expressive control of negative affect in the facial channel and the vocal channel are shown in Figures 4-1 and 4-2. Trends were examined for the extent to which children deviated from underlying negative affect and the extent to which they approximated (or deviated from) the target behavior.

Facial Channel

In Figure 4-1, it can be seen that children deviated significantly from their true facially expressed affect (negative baseline) when attempting either to inhibit or mask their feelings. In other words, they did not leak underlying negative affect through their facial expression. Quite the opposite, they significantly overshot target behavior. That is, they looked very positive, approximating the level of naturally expressed positive feeling, when attempting to inhibit negative feelings. And, when attempting to mask negative feelings (i.e., feign positive feelings), they were significantly more positive than was the case during their baseline expression of positive affect. Additionally, as a possible example of naturally occurring inhibition, it should be noted that children's baseline expression of negative affect did not differ significantly from their baseline expression of neutral affect in the facial channel. The

Figure 4-1. Controlling the Expression of Negative Affect in the Facial Channel.

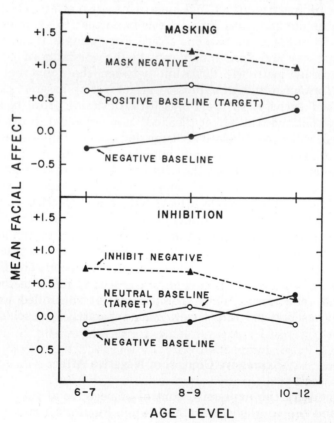

Note. Masking > Negative Baseline, $p < .001$; Inhibition > Negative Baseline, $p < .001$; Masking > Positive Baseline, $p < .001$; Inhibition > Neutral Baseline, $p < .001$.

Figure 4-2. Controlling the Expression of Negative Affect in the Vocal Channel.

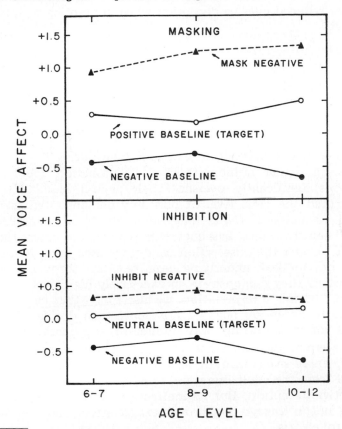

Note. Masking > Negative Baseline, $p < .001$; Inhibition > Negative Baseline, $p < .001$; Masking > Positive Baseline, $p < .002$; Inhibition > Neutral Baseline, $p < .05$.

negative baseline, nevertheless, does represent the standard of comparison in the test situation.

Most important for our consideration here, however, is the fact that there were significant developmental trends[2] in the direction of increased accuracy in approximating target behavior: older children showed reduced overshooting in their expressive enactments. Although the oldest age group still tended to overcorrect, they had by this age (10 to 12) learned to modulate their behavior so as to more closely approximate their intended expression than was true for the youngest age group (6- and 7-year olds).

As a secondary indication of "improved" (more accurate deception) facial performance, deception ratings also steadily decreased with age

---

[2] Significant for both sexes in the masking condition; significant only for boys in the inhibition condition.

during the inhibition condition. It appears that older children give somewhat reduced cues to deception when attempting to inhibit negative affect.

Vocal Channel

The pattern shown by children (Figure 4-2) in their tone of voice reveals a rather consistent level of overshooting. Children at every age group showed exaggerated positive voice quality when attempting to mask negative affect; their voice intonation was significantly and sizeably higher under masking instructions than during baseline positive messages. In similar fashion, their voice intonation under inhibition instructions significantly overshot their neutral baseline voices and approximated the same level of positivity demonstrated during baseline positive messages. (Note that, unlike the facial channel, the positive and negative voice baselines were equidistant from the neutral midpoint.) Under the observation conditions used here, it appears that children do not leak underlying negative affect through voice intonation; instead they demonstrate an excessively high level of positivity. In support of this interpretation, we also found that children showed high cues to deception (significantly more than during baseline messages) at all ages, during both inhibition and masking conditions.

There were no developmental changes (or even supportive trends) in children's expressive control of negative affect in their tone of voice. As predicted from the adult literature, tone of voice is not a good channel for effective deception. But its ineffectiveness in this observation setting rests not in leakage but through exaggeration produced by ineffective control efforts.

Comparison of Channels

In line with our hypotheses, children improve with age in their expressive control of negative affect—but only in terms of their facial expression. They do produce changes in their tone of voice when attempting to mask or inhibit negative affect, but these efforts are exaggerated and unconvincing both in terms of affective level and apparent deceptiveness. At age 6 or 7, they show an exaggerated, unbelievable, happy face when concealing negative affect; but by the time they reach an older age, they are beginning to scale down the level of exaggeration and are more closely approximating an expressed level of target affect that would provide a convincing deception.

These findings support previous research on the superiority of high control channels over low control channels as successful vehicles of deception. In the same way that tone of voice provides more cues to deception than does facial expression in adult efforts at deception (e.g., Zuckerman, DeFrank, Hall, Larrance, & Rosenthal, 1979), children do not convincingly regulate their tone of voice in concealing negative feelings. We did not, however, find evidence for leakage of underlying attitudes, as has been found in the adult literature (e.g., Weitz, 1972; Bugental et al., 1980). It may be speculated that communicators (adult or children), under directions to dissimulate, are more likely to make ineffective efforts to correct their tone of voice than they are to simply express their true affect. Leakage of true underlying feelings may be more probable under more natural communication conditions, whereas the exaggerated overshooting we witnessed here may be more typical when the speaker is making a very conscious effort to be deceptive.

Our results also parallel some of the child research on the development of control over the expression of negative affect. They agree with research by Feldman et al. (1979) in which they found that seventh graders and college students were more successfully deceptive in concealing negative affect than were first graders (but they do not agree with the findings of Feldman, Devin-Sheehan, & Allen, 1978, in which no difference in deception ability was found between third and sixth graders). Our results also agree with the findings of Morency and Krauss (this volume) who found that fifth graders were more effective in masking unpleasant feelings than were first graders.

Expressive Control of Positive Affect

Age trends in the expressive control of positive underlying affect are shown in Figures 4-3 and 4-4. The results for each channel are reported separately.

Facial Channel

No evidence was found for successful inhibition or masking of positive affect in the facial channel—at any age. Children were significantly more positive in their deception efforts than they were in their neutral baseline behavior. In neither inhibition nor masking were children significantly distinguishable from their positive baseline behavior. In other words, there was very high leakage of their actual feelings. Additionally, acted performances were judged to be significantly more deceptive than were both baseline and target behavior at all ages. In short, attempts to conceal positive affect were completely unsuccessful in the facial channel. With respect to liked things, children had difficulty acting more negatively than they really felt.

Vocal Channel

A child's tone of voice during efforts to inhibit or mask positive affect was significantly more negative than was baseline positive voice tone and did not differ significantly from target behavior. Inhibition of positivity produced messages did not differ significantly from baseline neutral messages. Masking of positivity produced messages did not differ significantly from baseline negative messages. Messages of all types, and at all age levels, however, were judged to be significantly more deceptive than baseline messages. No developmental trends were obtained. As can be seen from Figure 4-4, the affect expressed by children was quite variable in this condition. It is probably safest to conclude that instructions to conceal positivity acted to alter children's vocal intonation in a negative direction, but in an unconvincing way (i.e., they were deceptive sounding).

Comparison of Channels

Children were relatively unsuccessful in concealing positive affect either in their facial expression or in their tone of voice. Additionally, there were no age trends in the success of their enactments. The most

Figure 4-3. Controlling the Expression of Positive Affect in the Facial Channel.

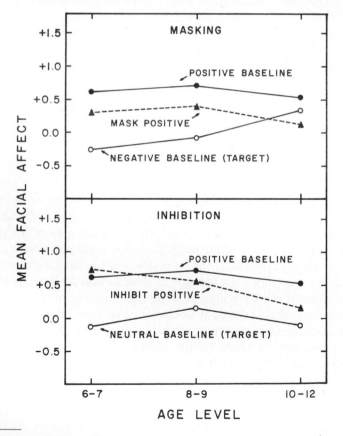

Note. Masking vs. Positive Baseline, *ns*; Inhibition vs. Positive Baseline, *ns*; Masking vs. Negative Baseline, *ns*; Inhibition > Neutral Baseline, $p < .002$.

Figure 4-4. Controlling the Expression of Positive Affect in the Vocal Channel.

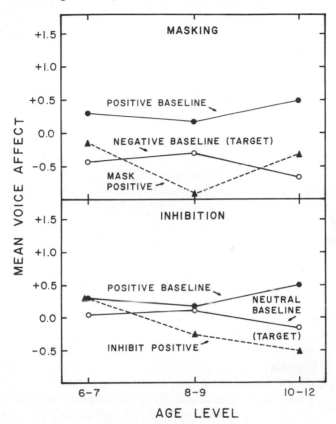

Note. Masking < Positive Baseline, $p <$ .001; Inhibition < Positive Baseline, $p <$ .07; Masking vs. Negative Baseline, *ns*; Inhibition vs. Neutral Baseline, *ns*.

defensible interpretation of these findings would involve a questioning of the validity of the "positive affect concealment" conditions. Perhaps there are so few display rules against displaying positive affect (in particular for children) that children either have not been exposed to any such norms or have little or no experience in inhibiting or masking positive feelings. Or, more specifically, they may have had no experience with the type of concealment required of them in this study, i.e., pretending to dislike or be neutral about a thing or activity that they actually like. Presumably children could be expected to have more experience with display rules governing expression of negative affect. If this were the case, it would explain the consistently high deception cues children showed during the positive manipulations, as well as the leakage (facial channel) or erraticism of behavior (vocal channel) demonstrated. In support of our findings, Morency and Krauss (this volume) found no difference between first graders and fifth graders in their ability to mask pleasant (as opposed to unpleasant) stimuli.

Sex Differences in Expressive Control

Significant sex differences in expressive behavior were only obtained in the facial inhibition of negative affect. There was a significant difference between boys and girls in the developmental progression of their ability to inhibit negativity (see Figure 4-5). In line with our predictions, girls consistently and significantly overshot the target behavior in attempting to inhibit negative effect. Boys, on the other hand, showed successive improvement in their ability to "neutralize" their negative affect. By ages 10 to 12, boys' acted behavior (inhibited negativity) provided a very close fit to their baseline neutral behavior. This agrees with views of Maccoby and Jacklin (1974) and Buck (1977), among others, that boys may learn to inhibit affective expression with age to a greater extent than do girls, by virtue of learned sex-role expectations.

Mediators of Expressive Control Development

A multivariate regression analysis was performed to examine the relationship, above and beyond age and sex, between cognitive and social predictor variables (overall cognitive level, perspective-taking ability, amount of social interaction experience, and number of siblings) and accuracy of expressive control in inhibiting and masking negative affect in the facial channel (the conditions which produced consistent age effects). Accuracy of expressive control was measured by composite scores which combined the deviation from original baseline affect with the degree of approximation to target baseline affect. This analysis revealed that when age, sex, and the other predictors were held constant, only visual perspective-taking ability was a significant factor in expressive control development. Of the four potential mediating variables (over and above the effects of sex and age), only perspective-taking ability was found to be related to accuracy of expressive control. The standardized regression coefficients were .29 ($p < .05$) and .23 ($p < .10$) between perspective-taking ability and inhibition success and masking success, respectively. Although visual perspective-taking (recognition that a given scene would appear different to persons who see it from a different physical location than the child does) is perhaps the least social of all perspective-taking measures of decentration, it does share a common basis with social perspective-taking (awareness that others may have different knowledge, motives, and attitudes than the child does). Moore and Underwood (1981), for instance, have recently shown that visual and social perspective-taking are both adequate predictors of prosocial development. The present study found that, above and beyond age and general cognitive level, high perspective-taking ability was generally associated with high expressive control. The ability to view the environment (including self, presumably) from perspec-

Figure 4-5. Sex Differences in Inhibiting the Expression of Negative Affect in the Facial Channel.

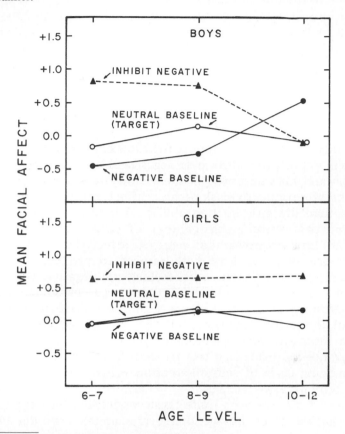

Note. Age Level × Sex × Inhibition Interaction, $p < .05$.

tives other than one's own appears to facilitate the successful enactment of self-presentation related behaviors. Perhaps it also may be suggested that individual differences in adult expressive control skills may be linked to differences in levels of perspective-taking ability. Role-taking is never complete; it represents an ongoing process of social development rather than something that is attained in any absolute sense by adulthood.

What might be the link between perspective-taking and expressive control? Perhaps it is simply that, to the extent role-taking abilities allow a person to "see" himself as others see him, the person knows how his or her behavior will appear to others, and can use this knowledge to construct nonverbal self-presentations suitable for various interpersonal purposes.

The failure of amount of social experience to emerge as a significant predictor of expressive control does not mean that such experience is unimportant in expressive development. The lack of a relationship may well be due to the unsuitability of the measures employed. It is possible that variations in social interaction quality, rather than quantity, would have been more strongly related to expressive control development. It is also possible that children in the present study did not have sufficient variation in amount of social interaction experience for relationships with expressive behavior to emerge.

Summary and Conclusions

This study has provided support for the existence of developmental processes in expressive control over negative affect in the facial channel. Both boys and girls improved in their ability to manage facial expressions when attempting to mask negative affect, but boys improved with age more than did girls in their ability to inhibit negative affect. We know from past research that children of both sexes learn the social norms that limit expression of negative affect, but boys appear to become more adept—at least with respect to producing realistically neutral behavior when their actual feelings are negative. Girls, in turn, alter their behavior in an effort to inhibit negativity, but they consistently overshoot the mark. Both sexes can be seen, then, to know how to control their facial behavior; but the strategy acquired by boys is the more successful one in negative affective contexts which call for an appearance of neutrality (no feeling). This pattern is reminiscent of an emerging style of self-presentation in which the person appears unaffected by negative feelings.

Children of all ages were quite unsuccessful in their expressive control of *negative* affect through the vocal channel. They did alter their voice intonation but in the direction of incredibly exaggerated, fake positive voice quality. While children succeeded at facial self-management, they failed in managing their tone of voice. As is true for adults, it appears that the facial channel is a better vehicle for successful management of negative affect than is the less controllable (or at least less successfully controllable) voice channel.

No developmental trends were found for the acquisition of control over *positive* affect. It was suggested that there may be few display rules for the concealment of positive feelings. Children of all ages were obviously able to alter their behavior (in an attempt to mask or inhibit positivity) on instruction, but they were not very successful in producing realistic communication patterns in the process.

Role-taking ability (perspective-taking) was found to be a significant mediator of expressive control. To the extent that children are sensitive to the perspective of others, they are better able to produce facial behaviors that will be interpreted in intended ways by observers. Cognitive development does, then, appear to be an important factor in the child's increasing ability to manage his or her own expressive behavior. Children's successful use of display rules requires a sufficiently high level of development that the child can be thought of as seeing him or herself as others do. Future research would do well to explore such links between the child's social and cognitive functioning. Although we were unable to find evidence in this study of the effect of different social experiences on children's expressive control, they undoubtedly contribute to this process—as evidenced by the presence of emerging sex differences. More research on causal factors in expressive control is needed.

Does the fact that aspects of expressive control are developmental in nature mean that social development is directed toward increased strategic interaction and impression management? Research shows that development brings an increased *capability* for expressive control, but it tells us little about how frequently people do, in fact, self-manage their expressive behavior across the course of development. That is, with development, we may become increasingly able to manage our expressive behavior, but do we actually manage it more often? It is not too farfetched to suggest that development brings increased flexibility for display rule usage. Once expressive control capabilities are established, further development may bring increased freedom to self-manage or not self-manage, as the situation requires. Effective social/interpersonal adaptation throughout the life span no doubt calls for complex mixtures of controlled and spontaneous nonverbal expression, which vary in relative proportion in different social domains. Of particular importance in future research will be to study children's and adults' expressive control in natural settings, and to relate this aspect of social behavior to the person's overall social adaptation success. Laboratory studies are excellent for providing profitable leads in a new area such as children's nonverbal communication, but ultimately the ecological validity of our findings must be tested in field settings.

Acknowledgment. This chapter is based on a dissertation by the first author in partial fulfillment of the requirements for the Ph.D. degree at the Department of Psychology, University of California, Santa Barbara. The research was partially supported by a University of California Chancellor's Patend Fund Grant.

Reference Notes

1. Saarni, C. *Observing children's use of display rules: Age and sex differences.* Paper presented at the meeting of the American Psychological Association, Montreal, Canada, 1980.
2. Shennum, W. A. *Being alone in a public place: The role of expressive management.* Paper presented at the meetings of the Western Psychological Association, Honolulu, Hawaii, 1980.

References

Buck, R. Nonverbal communication of affect in preschool children: Relationships with personality and skin conductance. *Journal of Personality and Social Psychology*, 1977, *35*, 225-236.

Bugental, D. B., Caporael, L., & Shennum, W. A. Experimentally produced child uncontrollability: Effects on the potency of adult communication patterns. *Child Development*, 1980, *51*, 520-528.

Bugental, D. B., Henker, B., & Whalen, C. K. Attributional antecedents of verbal and vocal assertiveness. *Journal of Personality and Social Psychology*, 1976, *34*, 405-411.

Bugental, D. B. & Love, L. R. Nonassertive expression of parental approval and disapproval and its relationship to child disturbance. *Child Development*, 1975, *46*, 747-752.

Bugental, D. B. & Moore, B. S. Effects of induced moods on voice affect. *Developmental Psychology*, 1979, *15*, 664-665.

Charlesworth, W. R. & Kreutzer, M. A. Facial expressions of infants and children. In P. Ekman (Ed.), *Darwin and facial expression*. New York: Academic Press, 1973.

Ekman, P. Universals and cultural differences in facial expressions of emotion. In J. K. Cole (Ed.), *Nebraska symposium on motivation*. Lincoln, NB: University of Nebraska Press, 1971.

Ekman, P. Facial expression. In A. W. Siegman & S. Feldstein (Eds.), *Nonverbal behavior and communication*. New York: Erlbaum, 1978.

Ekman, P. & Friesen, W. V. Nonverbal leakage and clues to deception. *Psychiatry*, 1969, *32*, 83-105.

Ekman, P. & Friesen, W. V. Detecting deception from the body or face. *Journal of Personality and Social Psychology*, 1974, *29*, 288-298.

Ekman, P., Friesen, W. V., & Scherer, K. R. Body movement and voice pitch in deceptive interaction. *Semiotica*, 1976, *16*, 23-27.

Ekman, P., Roper, G., & Hager, J. C. Deliberate facial movement. *Child Development*, 1980, *51*, 886-891.

Feldman, R. S., Devin-Sheehan, L., & Allen, V. L. Nonverbal cues as indicators of verbal dissembling. *American Educational Research Journal*, 1978, *15*, 217-231.

Feldman, R. S., Jenkins, L., & Popoola, O. Detection of deception in adults and children via facial expressions. *Child Development*, 1979, *50*, 350-355.

Feldman, R. S. & White, J. B. Detecting deception in children. *Journal of Communication*, 1980, *30*, 121-128.

Hall, J. A. Gender differences in nonverbal communication skills. In R. Rosenthal (Ed.), *Quantitative assessment of research domains*. San Franscisco: Jossey-Bass, 1980.

Holzman, P. S. & Rousey, C. The voice as a percept. *Journal of Personality and Social Psychology*, 1966, *4*, 78-86.

Maccoby, E. E. & Jacklin, C. N. *The psychology of sex differences*. Stanford, CA: Stanford University Press, 1974.

Moore, B. S. & Underwood, B. The development of prosocial behavior. In S. S. Brehm, S. M. Kassin, & B. F. X. Gibbons (Eds.), *Developmental social psychology*. New York: Oxford University Press, 1981.

Morris, D. *Manwatching: A field guide to human behavior*. New York: H. N. Abrams, 1977.

Murray, A. D. Infant crying as an elicitor of parental behavior: An examination of two models. *Psychological Bulletin*, 1979, *86*, 191-215.

Odom, R. D. & Lemond, C. M. Developmental differences in the perception and production of facial expressions. *Child Development*, 1972, *43*, 359-369.

Saarni, C. Children's understanding of display rules for expressive behavior. *Developmental Psychology*, 1979, *15*, 424-429.

Snyder, M. Self-monitoring of expressive behavior. *Journal of Personality and Social Psychology*, 1974, *30*, 526-537.

Streeter, L. A., Krauss, R. M., Geller, V., Olson, C., & Apple, W. Pitch changes during attempted deception. *Journal of Personality and Social Psychology*, 1977, *35*, 345-350.

Weitz, S. Attitude, voice, and behavior: A repressed affect model of interracial interaction. *Journal of Personality and Social Psychology*, 1972, *24*, 14-21.

Zuckerman, M., DeFrank, R. S., Hall, J. A., Larrance, D. T., & Rosenthal, R. Facial and vocal cues of deception and honesty. *Journal of Experimental Social Psychology*, 1979, *15*, 378-396.

Zuckerman, M., DePaulo, B. M., & Rosenthal, R. Verbal and nonverbal communication of deception. In L. Berkowitz (Ed.), *Advances in experimental social psychology* (Vol. 14). New York: Academic Press, 1981.

Zuckerman, M., Larrance, D. T., Spiegel, N. H., & Klorman, R. Controlling nonverbal cues: Facial expressions and tone of voice. *Journal of Experimental Social Psychology*, 1981, *17*, 506-524.

CHAPTER FIVE

Social and Affective Functions of Nonverbal Behavior: Developmental Concerns

Carolyn Saarni

Introduction

The significance of nonverbal behavior for psychological inquiry lies in two functions that nonverbal behavior plays. The first is the communicative or *social* function of nonverbal behavior, and the second is the expressive or *affective* function. These will be discussed in turn.

Social Function

In any given social transaction the nonverbal behavior of the interactants may be viewed as a continuous context accompanying the verbal messages that are exchanged. This accompanying context of nonverbal behavior qualifies the verbal (lexical) content. Ekman and Friesen (1969) have suggested that there are five ways in which nonverbal behavior qualifies the meaning of the verbal content: (a) repetition, (b) contradiction, (c) complementary function (e.g., praise may be accompanied by a smile or anger with a clenched fist), (d) accentuation, and (e) regulation (e.g., eye contact influences conversational turn-taking).

Family Systems Theory

A somewhat different perspective on the communicative or social impact of nonverbal behavior may be found in family systems theory (e.g., Bateson, 1972; Grinder & Bandler, 1976; Watzlawick, Beavin, & Jackson, 1967). This approach emphasizes the metacommunicative function that nonverbal behavior fulfills in interpersonal interaction. Metacommunication may be thought of as a message about a message. In this sense Ekman and Friesen's (1969) five nonverbal qualifiers also provide the receiver with metacommunicative information about the verbal message. However, in the systems theory approach the relationship between the interactants receives greater emphasis. Satir (1967), for example, states that metacommunication conveys three features about an interaction: (a) the sender's attitude about the verbal message itself (e.g., "The message I sent was a caring one."), (b) the sender's feelings and attitude about himself or herself (e.g., "I am an empathic person."), and (c) the sender's feelings, attitudes, and intentions toward the receiver (e.g., "I see you as someone that I want to be responsive toward.").

A fourth metacommunicative feature may be found in Haley's work (1963), which might be loosely phrased as the sender's perceptions about the structure of the interactants' relationship per se. Haley specifies that a relationship structure may be symmetrical (mutual and equal influence on one another) or complementary (differential influence exists between the two interactants as in superordinate and subordinate relations). For example, a complementary relationship would normally exist between parent and young child whereas a symmetrical relationship might more frequently be found among work colleagues, spouses, adult offspring and their older parents, and so forth. Thus, the fourth type of metacommunicative information seems to be about the distribution of power in a relationship (see also Mehrabian's work on nonverbal indicators of dominance or social control, 1970, 1972).

Family systems theorists contend that if one is in an interaction one cannot *not* metacommunicate (i.e., even silence and holding one's body still has metacommunicative impact on the receiver). They conclude that nonverbal (and verbal) behavior *must* shape and influence the relationship between the interactants. This conclusion is premised on the interactants' trying to decipher the meaning of one another's metacommunications and attempting to dovetail their own respective metacommunications to those inferred meanings. This may lead to incongruent messages, which can be discrepancies between what one says and does or inconsistencies between two (or more) nonverbal channels (e.g., the vocal channel expresses anxious hesitancy while the facial channel expresses unambiguous pleasure). Whereas Bateson (1972) suggested that one of these incongruent messages was the "real" or valid one, Grinder and Bandler (1976) contend that incongruities among the various channels or messages simply reflect different aspects of the person's representational system and can be viewed as flexible coping resources. Using the example above, the unambiguous pleasure expressed in the face may stem from the person's genuine affection for the receiver; the anxious, hesitant voice may stem from the sender's concern that his or her affection will not be reciprocated. The former nonverbal message derives from the sender's cognitions (representations) about the target person whereas the latter message derives from the sender's cognitions about the anticipated evaluation of self in the eyes of the other. This rather convoluted perspective-taking does provide considerable coping potential even as it makes for greater interpersonal complexity.

Report and command features. Finally, family systems theorists posit that any communication (verbal and nonverbal) has both report and command features. The report feature has typically been viewed as the verbal or lexical content while the command feature is a metacommunicative comment about the relationship between the interactants. Systems theorists have more often considered the command feature to be conveyed via nonverbal behavior. Satir (1967) describes the command aspect of a message as a way that the sender tries to influence the receiver to give him or her what he or she wants. She also contends that the essential aspect of all command features, embedded within any communication, can be characterized as a request for self-validation. Such self-validation "commands" are often in the implicit form of "agree with me," "be on my side," "validate me by showing your sympathy," or "validate me by showing you value my ideas" (Satir, 1967, p. 81). Such command features need not be consciously intended.

If systems theorists and experimental social psychologists such as Mehrabian have a valid perspective, then nonverbal behavior may well have a greater impact on social exchange than verbal transactions do. This would be largely due to the metacommunicative information about the interactants' relationship carried by the nonverbal channels. For the developmental psychologist many research questions emerge: How do children learn to "read" others' metacommunications? How are incongruencies acquired by children in their own nonverbal behavior? How do children respond to report and command features in others' communications as well as send out such features themselves? How does the development of self affect the complexity of metacommunication in light of Satir's contentions? To explore such issues may well first require a better taxonomy of infants' and children's nonverbal behavioral repertoire than we currently have. As we turn now to consider the second function of nonverbal behavior—the affective or expressive function—the picture takes on additional complexity for developmental inquiry.

Affective Function

Emotions appear to function as a system in which three major components are distinguishable: (a) physiological processes, (b) conscious definition or attribution of emotion, and (c) behavioral expressiveness. The last, behavioral expressiveness, is the focus here. Tomkins (1962, 1963) and Izard (1977), among others, postulate a primary neural connection between facial muscle activity and the cortex for specific definition of an emotion. Even when facial expression appears to be completely inhibited, electromyographic techniques have indicated that nonobservable muscle contractions occur, which correspond in pattern to the emotion-related facial expression (Schwartz, Fair, Greenberg, Freedman, & Klerman, 1974). Ethologists such as Blurton Jones (1972) and Eibl-Eibesfeldt (1974) endorse Darwin's early theorizing that expressive behaviors, notably in the face, have survival value and have most likely been selected in a fashion similar to that of other somatic features. Thus, from several different perspectives one particular channel of nonverbal behavior, namely, facial behavior, and affect seem inextricably linked.

This link between facial behavior and emotional experience has received some attention from a developmental perspective, notably from infancy researchers (cf. Lewis & Rosenblum, 1978). What has emerged from these infancy studies is that the development of affective nonverbal behavior cannot be readily separated from *interpersonal contexts*. In other words, affective nonverbal behavior and social-communicative nonverbal behavior appear to coincide or to co-occur in such a fashion that the two functions of nonverbal behavior discussed so far are really integrated together.

Integration of Social and Affective Functions of Nonverbal Behavior

When these two functions of nonverbal behavior—the social-communicative and the affective—are combined, three interdependent processes emerge: (a) the communicative impact of emotional displays (e.g., we might feel empathy at someone's visible distress), (b) the regulation of social transactions (e.g., we respond in predictable ways, or we might test out others' reactions by behaving unpredictably), and (c) the regulation of individual internal processes (e.g., we protect our basic patterns of intrapsychic adjustment through manipulation of our expressive behavior). These three complex processes normally have emerged as interdependent functions by the end of the first 18 months, if not earlier (cf. Lewis & Rosenblum, 1978), and continue to differentiate throughout childhood and adolescence (cf. Breger, 1974).

The differentiation of these three processes is clearly based on *interpersonal interaction*, leading to both cultural commonality as well as individual idiosyncracy. While the first two social-affective processes seem clearly interpersonally oriented, it may not be as evident that the last one is also. Yet our desire (or need) to protect our intrapsychic adjustment develops within an affectively loaded, interpersonal nexus. This is not to say that genetically influenced temperament or style (e.g., extraversion-introversion, degree of reactivity, etc.) are excluded from leaving their impact on our social-affective nonverbal behavior; rather our transactions with others and our biological endowment are viewed holistically here.

For the purposes of this chapter I shall restrict my discussion of these three social-affective processes in nonverbal behavior to the developmental considerations involving the "sending" or encoding process. However, it should be emphasized that, given my preceding perspective, what is encoded expressively is usually in the context of someone else's decoding, and the decoder's response to the sender's behavior exerts a reciprocal influence (cf. Cappella, 1981). An additional restriction in the current discussion will be that I shall focus on facial behavior as the primary (but not the only) nonverbal channel for carrying information which is both affective and interpersonal (cf. Ekman & Friesen, 1975; Izard, 1977).

The general outline of the remainder of this chapter will be first to discuss report and command features more extensively in so far as systems theory seems especially suitable as an organizational framework for examining the developmental relations between the affective and social domains of nonverbal behavior. Following this discussion will be a more specific consideration of how incongruence between affective state and nonverbal expressive behavior further illustrates the three social-affective processes described above. Children's dissimulations of affective state, as reflected in display rule use, may represent at this time the most immediate avenue for researching the acquisition of metacommunicative competence. Finally, my own developmental research on managed facial expressions will be described in some detail and used to elaborate the three social-affective processes of nonverbal behavior.

Report and Command in Nonverbal Behavior

As mentioned earlier, the terms *report* and *command* are used by Satir (1967), Watzlawick, et al. (1967), among others, to describe the content and communicative features, respectively, of interpersonal transactions. However, systems theorists do not appear to attribute report or content features to nonverbal behavior. Instead, command features are typically attributed to nonverbal behavior. My elaboration of report features in the present context is that the content which is reported by any particular nonverbal action may be either its phenomenological description (raised brows, for example) or its simple affective message (e.g., smiling with pleasure). The command feature of any nonverbal action communicates typically to observers the context in which the encoder wants his or her nonverbal report to be understood. The command feature is often then a comment on the relationship between the encoder and the decoder. The nonverbal action can also be viewed as a metacommunicative statement: a communication about a communication is produced. Thus, the raised brows could signal the beginning of a positive display, or they could be raised in mock surprise, perhaps indicating veiled sarcasm. Other expressive actions (including their sequence, duration, and intensity), the interpersonal situation, verbal communication, and the physical context also provide additional qualifying conditions in which command features are communicated. In the raised brows example, a smile or at the very least a relaxed lower face would probably accompany the positive display. The brows raised in mock suprise (whereby a sarcastic judgment is suggested) would be less likely accompanied by a genuine smile and in fact might coincide with pursed or puckered lips. The actual position of the brows might differ as well (the sarcastic raised brows might be exaggeratedly arched). Obviously the nature of the relationship between the encoder and the decoder is central to understanding many of the nuances of command features in nonverbal behaviour. Finally, it should be noted that antici- pated command features can also lead to direct modification in what is to be reported by the encoder. Furthermore, the encoder may produce command features which "counter-command" misattributed command features on the decoder's part (e.g., "Don't get me wrong, I really mean this!").

Social-Affective Processes

Report and command features seem to be central to understanding the three social-affective processes of nonverbal behavior. The com- municative impact of emotional displays obviously relies on the affective content of the expressive behavior, and yet the affected individual usu- ally produces command features that are intended to communicate to the the observer how to understand or respond to the expressive display (e.g., accompanying verbal and nonverbal behavioral cues may encourage or discourage one's sympathetic assistance upon seeing some- one trip when stepping off a curb).

The regulation of social transactions, in terms of predictable patterns of interpersonal interaction, is also premised on report and command features. Goffman's analyses (cf. 1959, 1967, 1974) are particularly insightful into the ritualistic character of some of our more common culturally sanctioned interactions in which behavior is carefully and conventionally managed. While the report or content features can range from "gender advertisements" (Goffman, 1976) to grief and mourning, the command feature, for social regulation purposes, *is* the convention- ality, predictability, or normativeness of one's nonverbal transactions, carefully dovetailed with those of the interactant. To respond unpre- dictably is to produce a very different communicative context in that the command feature then stresses *uniqueness*, or unpredictability. How one's interactant will decide to respond is perhaps then equally unpredictable (although there is a good likelihood that one's unpre- dicted behavior will be ignored, and the interactant will reassert the command feature of regulated and predictable exchange).

The third process, the regulation of internal processes, reveals report features or content in that we develop awareness of what our faces look like when experiencing various emotions. That awareness stems from feedback from others, from proprioceptive feedback, and from visual recognition (e.g., mirror images, others' facial expressions). (See Harris, Olthof, and Terwogt, in press, for a developmental model for how awareness of state develops.) Command features, on the other hand, operate more subtly. They can become internalized as communications with oneself; that is, one can command oneself to respond to a particular feeling by altering its impact on oneself, either through cognitive "self-talk" (cf. Mahoney, 1977; Meichenbaum & Turk, 1976; Lazarus, 1975), thus changing the appraisal process itself, or by modifying one's expressive nonverbal behavior.

This latter alternative corresponds to the third social-affective process of nonverbal behavior: to protect our intrapsychic adjustment. It is also a perspective which receives some theoretical support from Tomkins (1980) and Izard (1977), among others, that our *conscious* emotional experiences may rely heavily on the proprioceptive feedback from our facial muscle activity. Simplistically stated, this viewpoint would seem to be claiming that "how you look determines how you feel." However, considered within an extended socializing process, this theoretical viewpoint takes on greater meaning: children are often met with responses from their decoders (e.g., parents, peers, etc.) that serve to invalidate, reproach, or ignore the child's expressive behavior. For example, in our culture children's angry expressive behavior frequently provides the occasion for reproach and punishment. Children's fear and distress are also frequently invalidated through ridicule, misattribution, or avoidance (e.g., crying in anticipation of a medical appointment, fear of the dark, etc.). Children learn that certain feelings are "unacceptable," and that if they do not show them, they gain approval (or at least avoid disapproval). They may also take the additional intrapsychic leap of viewing themselves as "acceptable" when they neither experience nor express such unacceptable feelings. Thus, to modify one's facial expression, initially in accordance with approval from others and eventually in accordance with self-acceptance, can ultimately also modify one's conscious emotional experience.

It is in this sense that we make metacommunicative or command statements to ourselves: we have feelings about feelings. Those feelings (and their expressive behaviors which would betray us to others as well as confirm to ourselves through proprioceptive feedback that we were indeed experiencing these particular emotions) become the object of secondary appraisal, which results in a second emotional response. This second emotional response may be revealed expressively, whereas the first emotion will have been more or less inhibited in its expression. From a developmental perspective, we would expect that young children do not inhibit the expression of feelings, but increasingly as they enter the preschool years, we see the minimization or "miniaturization" of expressive behavior for fear, sadness, and anger, under certain conditions. I will return to this topic of minimization of nonverbal expressive behavior in the discussion of display rules.

Developmental Considerations

Increasing evidence suggests that infants possess at a very early age (perhaps as young as four weeks) a basic repertoire of facial behavior which appears linked to affective states. This suggests that the content or report features of our nonverbal behavior have genetic foundations and do not derive simply from imitative learning. This research evidence also indicates that simple affects may already be "wired" biologically to particular expressions. Examples of research in this area include work by Oster (1978) who noted that the rapid sequence of knit brows followed by smiling was related to the young infant's (4 to 10 weeks old) perception of contingencies. The brow knitting was associated with intense concentrated attention (not distress!) and the smile with recognition or successful assimilation of the contingency. Other evidence comes from Eibl-Eibesfeldt's (1974) observations that children blind and deaf from birth revealed many of the same expressive behaviors as children not so handicapped. Finally, Emde, Kligman, Reich, and Wade (1978) contend that maternal ratings of infants at 2.5 months consistently showed two dimensions in their affective interpretations of infants' facial expressions. The first dimension in their work was "hedonic tone" (pleasure-distress continuum), and the second was "activation" or state (low to high or intense activity level). By 3.5 months a third dimension appeared in the mothers' ratings, the internal-external continuum, e.g., contented (internal)-curious (external), and by 4.5 months most expression interpretations involved all three dimensions. However, the hedonic tone dimension accounted for at least half of the variance in all interpretations of infant facial expressions. Thus, facial behavior appears to provide infants with readily available schemes for exhibiting internal states or conditions, and their caregivers respond to their expressive behavior as having meaningful report features.

By the end of the first year, infants appear to make simple appraisals of a variety of situations and respond with appropriate expressive behavior (e.g., Lewis & Rosenblum, 1978), such that they reveal the seven basic and universal emotions postulated by Ekman, Friesen, and Ellsworth (1972): happiness, surprise, fear, anger, sadness, disgust, and interest. Obviously, compared to those of adults, the eliciting situations are very concrete, and the infant's appraisal process is characterized by sensorimotor cognition (cf. Décarie, 1978).

Mutual Influence

While infants seem readily capable of both demonstrating considerable variety in the content of their social-affective nonverbal behavior
and engaging in expressive cycles of mutual influence (see Cappella's
review, 1981), their control over command features, or metacommunicative messages, is more difficult to assess. It would appear that use of
command features by the encoder requires that he or she understand
others as having perspectives of their own. This understanding need not
be especially differentiated but would minimally encompass an infant's
or toddler's realization that others are independent sources of action—
but who can be influenced. An example of an early command feature
that parents can readily identify is that an infant progresses from crying *in such a manner as to gain* attention to crying *in order to get*
attention.

Another example that comes to mind is coy behavior, which may
emerge toward the end of the first year and often appears throughout
the second. Coy behavior, as analyzed in terms of nonverbal report
features, typically includes smiling, alternating eye contact and gaze
aversion, and alternating postural shifts toward and away from the target person (often an affable stranger). The command feature appears
to be "I think I might want to interact with you, but keep your distance and let me regulate my approach-avoidance ambivalence." While
I am not imputing such a complex cognition or intention to babies, the
above commanding message is often "felt" by the affable adult stranger.
Interestingly, coy behavior is rarely shown to other young children,
implying a distinctive communicative feature used by young children
toward certain friendly strangers. Anecdotal evidence for such a distinctive communicative feature may be gleaned from parents. For
example, the author's daughter (2.3 years) referred to her frequent coy
behavior displayed toward her uncle as, "I play game with Uncle Karl."
As she made the verbal reference, she turned her head away while raising her shoulder to touch the side of her chin.

Attributions of Command Features

Command features appear to be attributed more frequently by adult
observers to infant expressive behavior than the infants may actually
intend or are even able to communicate. Supporting evidence comes
from research by Condry and Condry (1976), among others, who found
that if adult observers thought a particular infant was a boy, they more
frequently labeled an ambiguously distressed facial expression as anger.
If they were led to believe that the infant was a girl, they labeled the

same expression as fear. Such attributions imply a set of expections which may, over time, in fact shape the expressive behavior of the young child in a sex-typed fashion.

Another commonly attributed command feature of infant expressive behavior is the infant's cognitive developmental level itself. Haviland (1976) has noted that Piaget used affective-expressive behavior to infer cognitive processes and that an expressive response is central to many aspects of developmental evaluation in the Bayley Scales of Mental and Motor Development. The issue of inseparability of affect and cognition is not disputed here; rather it is the use of expressive behavior by observers to elaborate a report (some instance of expressive behavior) into a metacommunicative transaction whereby the adult is influenced to believe an infant is more (or less) cognitively advanced, depending on the expressive behavior revealed in response to a particular situation. (It would appear that infants who are at temperamental extremes, e.g., high vs. low reactivity, might be evaluated disadvantageously in such cognitive assessments.)

Dissociation of Affect and Expressive Behavior

Older children obviously take into account how others might respond to their expressive behavior (cf. Saarni, 1979). In so doing they often dissociate internal emotional experience from external expressive behavior, although as mentioned previously, electromyographic techniques have indicated that nonobservable muscle contractions do occur, which correspond in pattern to the emotion-related facial expression (Schwartz et al., 1974). When such a dissociation or outright dissimulation of expressive behavior occurs, as is the case with display rule usage, the encoder manipulates both report and command features of his/her nonverbal communication. Thus, the content of what is communicated expressively is changed (e.g., a youngster may smile despite feeling quite disappointed upon receiving an undesirable gift). Command features provide the message for how the content is to be understood or responded to by the decoder. In the above example, the youngster may smile but then subsequently abruptly stop smiling, avert his or her eyes from the gift-giver, and mumble his or her thanks (see Saarni's observational research, Note 4). These accompanying behaviors inform the decoder that while the child is fulfilling his or her obligations to be expressively polite, they also communicate ambivalence. In some situations, command features paradoxically may take on content or report features about the real emotion felt by the encoder, although the expressive behavior also reports a dissimulation of internal emotional experience. The behaviors described above would generally suggest to the observer that the child is indeed less than enthusiastic about the gift.

As children mature, the practice of dissociating emotion from expressive behavior becomes well rehearsed; casual observers may be unable to read the expressive behavior for clues as to the nature of the internal emotional experience. Supporting evidence is to be found in research on children's and adolescents' ability to encode and decode deceptive nonverbal behavior (e.g., Feldman, Jenkins, & Popoola, 1979; DePaulo, Irvine, Jordan, & Laser, Note 1; Morency & Krauss, this volume). This research is discussed elsewhere in this volume and will not be reviewed here. However, additional supporting research may be found in Harris, Olthof, and Terwogt (in press), who studied Dutch children's (6 to 15 years old) verbalized knowledge about affect and display behavior. Their approach was to interview the children, and in one series of questions to ask the children if and how they could pretend to be *not* angry and *not* afraid. Approximately 50% of the six-year olds and 70% of the older children were able to justify how they could pretend to be not angry and unafraid. The most common suggestion for how to pretend otherwise, across all age groups, was to substitute other expressive displays. Older children were also able to suggest redirecting their thoughts as a way of changing the emotional experience itself, which is similar to the secondary appraisal notion suggested earlier.

Feeling Rules

One implication of such research findings is that the dissociation of emotion from expressive behavior may take on a *rule* or prescriptive character as children mature. To dissimulate the external expression of one's real internal state becomes condoned and "appropriate," depending on culture and context. Going one step further, Hochschild (1979), from a sociological perspective, has suggested that we actually create some of our emotional responses (internally and expressively) through the use of *feeling rules*. She discusses the moment of discrepancy between one's current feeling and what one believes one ought to feel. She uses the term "emotion work" to refer to assorted strategies for modifying feelings, which can be cognitive (e.g., secondary appraisal), physiological (e.g., alter breathing rate), or expressive interventions (e.g., display rule use). The concept of "feeling rules" becomes equivalent in her model to cultural (or subcultural) expectations for normative emotional responses in various situations. In contrast to most other codes or systems of rules, feeling rules refer to the precursors of action rather than to action itself. Yet in a communication context such feeling rules ultimately produce nonverbal actions, namely, expressive behavior, as well as verbal responses, which together provide report and command features to the interpersonal transaction.

The notion of feeling rules is similar to Ekman's et al. (1972) concept of *display rules*. *Display* refers to the expressive behavior revealed, and *rule* refers to the prescriptive or regulatory character that determines the expressive behavior actually shown. In a sense, Hochschild's feeling rules precede display rules; the former refers to modification of state and the latter to the modification of expressive behavior (viz., what state is observable and communicated to others). Display rules and their relationship to the social-affective processes of nonverbal behavior will be discussed in the next section.

Display Rules and Dissimulation in Expressive Behavior

The monitoring and modifying of our expressive behavior constitute aspects of both self-regulation and interpersonal regulation. Such capability is probably gradually acquired as children refine their social-cognitive capabilities (including role-taking skills, recursive thinking, and impression management) and their voluntary muscle control (especially those in the face). By the time we reach adulthood we have learned to regulate habitually our expressive behavior so that we are able to produce for others' observation and for our own coping needs expressive transformations of our otherwise direct emotional experience (cf. Ekman & Friesen, 1975).

There appear to be four basic categories of dissimulation or modification of expressive behavior: (1) the regulation created by adoption of cultural display rules; (2) the dissemblance created by personal or idiosyncratic display rules; (3) direct deception; and (4) theatrical or dramatic pretense. Each of these categories will be discussed in turn, with the exception of the last, theatrical pretense, which may be more appropriately examined within the context of children's play rather than under the rubric of impression management in nonverbal behavior.

Cultural display rules. Dissociation of emotional experience and expressive behavior is most obvious in cultural display rule usage. Display rules govern the appropriateness of expressive behavior: they are essentially social conventions that prescribe how one should look, even if one does not feel the emotion which would correspond to the acceptable facial expression (Ekman et al., 1972). For example, one does not normally show one's displeasure at receiving an unwanted gift if the gift-giver expects one to like it (Saarni, Note 3).

Cultural display rules illustrate particularly well the second social-affective function of nonverbal behavior: the acceptable or normative expressive display is produced in a given situation, and the interpersonal exchange is reliably regulated in that the interactants dovetail their nonverbal responses to one another in a predictable fashion. The affective content is predictably reported via appropriate expressive behavior e.g., one does not laugh aloud at funerals despite one's sense of irony or humor about the deceased, the funeral procedures, or whatever. The communicative command is that one is behaving conventionally (i.e., politely, predictably).

Cultural display rules may also illustrate the first social-affective function by mediating the communicative impact of emotional displays. For example, it is often culturally acceptable for the surviving spouse to weep openly at the deceased spouse's funeral. But what if the surviving spouse has chronically over the years inhibited displays of sadness and vulnerability? Now the spouse "must" reveal such behavior in order to be culturally appropriate. If the spouse's sad expressive behavior is inhibited, the impact on others may lead to negative attributions ("she seems glad he's gone"). Assuming the surviving spouse is indeed sad about the death, cultural display rules can "give permission" to reveal expressively one's affective experience, which otherwise might have been inhibited in order to protect one's basic pattern of intrapsychic adjustment. In this sense cultural display rules can break through personal display rules and mediate one's emotional experience to others.

Personal display rules. Personal display rules exemplify the second social-affective function of nonverbal behavior. They serve as coping strategies and allow the individual to regulate internal processes by protecting one's pattern of intrapsychic adjustment. Intrapsychic adjustment refers here to a dynamic condition of self-perceived equilibrium, akin to such concepts as self-acceptance or self-worth. Personal display rules seem to be motivated by the need to relieve the discomfort of negative feelings by transforming their behavioral expression. From a clinical perspective the perceived need to transform negative feelings varies considerably both across individuals and within an individual, depending on the affect in question and the situation. The primary criterion seems to be an intrapsychic barometer or tolerance level of vulnerability of the self. It is this "vulnerability barometer" that I contend signals the need to protect one's intrapsychic adjustment.

While personal display rules appear to reveal the operation of an individual vulnerability barometer, they are also influenced by one's cultural experience as mediated by socialization. As a result, people reveal a certain degree of commonality in their personal display rule use within a given culture or subculture, (Of course, there are also completely idiosyncratic personal display rules as well as those shared within a family.) For example, personal display rules which are frequently encountered in middle class American culture include appearing calm when feeling upset, smiling or even laughing when feeling anxious, revealing an angry expression when really feeling hurt, and so forth. Some personal display rules which appear to be highly prevalent may in fact function as cultural display rules; they have taken on a ritualistic and predictable character and function, in part, to regulate social exchange. There is no systematic research on personal display rules, despite the claims of such affect theorists as Tomkins (1980), Izard (1977), and Ekman and Friesen (1975) that adults rarely show affective facial expressions which are not regulated in some way. However, some of my work with children's display rule usage is directly related and will be discussed later.

Direct deception. A third category of dissimulation which produces a dissociation of affect and expressive behavior is outright deception. Deceptive facial expressions imply a deliberate attempt to mislead another about one's emotional experience in order to gain some advantage over the other or to avoid some distinct disadvantage. For example, an employee may mask an angry facial expression with a poker face while the boss rebukes her or him; revealing genuine feelings might aggravate the employee's situation to a disadvantage. A youngster who has set off a false fire alarm may suppress her or his gleeful expression while looking at the commotion she or he has caused. To reveal delight could make the youngster a suspect, a disadvantage presumably to be avoided. Directly deceptive dissimulation of expressive behavior is the area in which the most developmental research has been carried out, and is reviewed elsewhere in this volume (e.g., De Paulo & Jordan).

Directly deceptive dissimulation of expressive behavior could certainly subsume both cultural and personal display rule usage in that gaining advantages (or comfort) and avoiding disadvantages (or discomfort) are relevant to both types of display rule usage as well. However, the intent here is to highlight the sometimes subtle psychological distinctions among the categories of dissociation of affect and expression. The two categories of display rule usage have a presecriptive *rule* character to their application whereas direct deception is much more dependent on a win-loss distinction *within a particular and immediate situation.* From an experiential perspective these three categories of affect and expression dissociation need not be mutually exclusive, although they seem to have clearly distinguishable motivational differences. It is these differences which permit the abstraction of categories, whereas their similarities allow for the multi-faceted nature of integrated experience. Just as we may have several different motives vis á vis a particular action, so we might we also have multiple motives about how and why we modify our expressive behavior in some situations.

These three categories appear to show both similarities and differences in relation to positive vs. negative affects and in relation to prosocial vs. self-protective behavior. Cultural display rules and direct deception can modify the behavioral expression of both positive and negative affects. Personal display rules focus more often on negative affects. Cultural display rules are more frequently prosocially oriented insofar as their acquisition integrates the child into his or her culturally sanctioned emotional-communicative forms. Direct deception may also be for prosocial ends, but this appears to be less frequent among children. Personal display rules, virtually by definition, are self-protective, as are many instances of directly deceptive expressive behavior among children.

Finally, directly deceptive expressive displays illustrate how one can alter the report and command aspects of the first social-affective function of nonverbal behavior: an emotional display can be produced in a systematic or intentional way in order to make a particular communicative impact on the decoding observer. In the false fire alarm example above, the youngster may conceal the thrill at the commotion she or he has caused by substituting expressive behavior which reports an affective state of concern, bewilderment, or even fear. The command feature is that the youngster has no knowledge about the alarm as being false. Thus the child produces dissimulated expressive behavior which has a particular communicative impact on the observer. The youngster has also neatly avoided being caught, a definite advantage in most childish pranks.

Forms of Dissimulation

These categories of regulation of facial expression create four kinds of modification in the face. First, an individual may *minimize* the expression of his or her emotion. For example, one might choose in some situations to look mildly concerned when one actually feels quite worried. Second, one's feelings may be *exaggerated* in expression, e.g., sadness could be intensified to elicit sympathy. Third, *neutralization* of expression occurs when one's feeling is masked behind a neutral poker face. Fourth, *substitution* of expression occurs if one's real feeling is concealed by displaying another expression which corresponds to a different feeling; e.g., smiling is often used to conceal anxiety.

These four modifications affect the use of facial muscles. Ekman and Friesen (1975) suggest that with minimization and exaggeration the number of facial areas involved (e.g., forehead, mouth area) is varied, the duration of the expression may be lengthened or shortened, and the degree to which muscles are contracted may be altered. With neutralization the facial muscles may be relaxed, or they may be held tensely but without any obvious pattern of contraction. This latter option frequently creates a "wooden" quality to the facial expression. In substitution one must rely on one's memory to recreate the kinesthetic feedback necessary to adopt a facial expression that does not correspond to one's internal affect.

Ekman and Friesen (1975) contend that it is actually easier to substitute another expression than to adopt a neutral one (one's own emotion tends to leak through the poker face). They also cite Darwin for first noting that the smile is among the most common expressive substitutions because "the muscular movements required for smiling are most different from the muscular movements involved in the negative emotions" (p. 142). Our anatomy in this case provides us with a ready way out. However, there is currently no systematic research indicating a developmental sequence of acquisition of these four types of modification of affective expression. My hypothesis is that exaggeration may emerge first, e.g., when a toddler stubs a toe but howls as though she or he has surely broken her or his foot. Blurton Jones (1967) has also noted that children, ages 3 to 4 years, were likely to intensify their crying after falling and injuring themselves when they were aware of being observed as opposed to believing themselves to be unattended to. Minimization may follow next as preschoolers are often directly socialized to miniaturize their affective displays, both positive and negative. The former are often responded to by adults as boisterous, and the latter often invite reproach or invalidation, as mentioned earlier. As for the acquisition order of substitution and neutralization, they may emerge simultaneously, or a preference for one or the other may appear; both represent masking one's feeling. Some research evidence suggests that in our culture girls may be more likely to adopt smiling to mask their feelings (cf. Feldman et al., 1979; Saarni, Note 3). Popular stereotypic assumptions would suggest that the "stoic" poker face (neutralization) is more commonly associated with masculinity rather than with femininity. However, as noted above, there is no research to support these speculations.

Research on Display Rule Acquisition

There has been little systematic research on developmental processes in display rule acquisition (see Charlesworth & Kreutzer, 1973; Ekman et al., 1972; LaFrance & Mayo, 1978; Harper, Wiens, & Matarazzo, 1978). A number of studies exist that have examined children's explanations of incongruities between situation and expected expression, but these studies have not analyzed children's use of display rules for resolving those incongruities. In fact, many of the incongruities represent violations of cultural display rules (e.g., frowning at one's birthday party). One outcome of several of these studies is that older children are more likely to use some situational cues to describe the stimulus actor's real affect rather than to rely solely on facial expression (e.g., Burns & Cavey, 1957; Deutsch, 1974). This result implies that older children are aware that expressive behavior and emotion can be dissociated from one another.

My own research on children's use of display rules has examined (a) age and sex difference in the reasons for display rule usage, (b) children's personal and descriptive reasons for dissociating affect and expression in their own lives, and (c) observations of what children actually do when confronted with a mild interpersonal conflict in which an unexpected outcome occurs. Each of these studies will be briefly discussed.

Reasons for Display Rule Usage

In my first study on display rules (Saarni, 1979) children in grades one (mean age: 6.7 years), three (8.6 years), and five (10.7 years) responded to four interpersonal conflict situations presented in comic strip style but with photographs of real children. The four conflict situations were (a) a child boasting about his or her skating ability to another child and then falling down, (b) a child receiving a very disappointing birthday gift from someone who thought it would be appreciated, (c) a child being bullied by another child in front of an onlooker, and (d) a child setting off the school fire alarm and then being intercepted. In the final frame of each series the child's face was averted from the camera and could not be seen. Subjects had to select from a set of full-face portraits of the photographed child which facial expression was probably revealed; they also were asked to justify their choices.

Analysis of the data revealed, as expected, that display rule usage significantly increased with age. There were no significant sex differences. Of particular concern was the attempt to describe reasons for dissociation of affect and expression, and four descriptive uses were determined: (a) trouble-avoiding set (e.g., "If he shows he's scared, they'll beat him up for sure."); (b) maintenance of self-esteem (e.g., "He'd be pretty stupid to show he's hurt after he's been bragging how good he is."); (c) qualifying factors of a relationship (e.g., "You wouldn't want to hurt your aunt's feelings."); and (d) maintenance of norms (e.g., "It's impolite to show that you feel that way."). The results indicated that the most frequent reason given for dissimulation across all age groups was the trouble-avoiding set (43%), followed by preserving self-esteem (30%), qualifying factors of a relationship (19%), and norm maintenance (8%). Only the oldest children provided norm maintenance as a reason for dissimulating expressive behavior.

From my current perspective I would suggest that the trouble-avoiding set refers to direct deception in dissociation of affect and expression. Maintenance of self-esteem seems relevant to personal display rule usage, and norm maintenance appears related to cultural display rule usage. The descriptive use of qualifying factors of a relationship may include any of the three basic categories of dissociation of affect and expression and would require further probing into the motives for dissimulation to establish more clearly which particular category of dissociation was implicated.

Children's Personal Experiences

In a second study (Saarni, Note 3), the same subjects as in the above investigation were asked to discuss their personal experiences as to when and why they would *not* reveal their feelings and when and why they would. Only instances of neutralizing facial expression (poker face) and substitution of another expression were coded; minimization and exaggeration were omitted. Across all three age groups, children were able to cite instances in which they concealed their feelings and/or thought they had observed others do this (e.g., "My brother always tries to look important after he's done something stupid."). Age was a significant factor: the eight- and ten-year-old groups of children gave almost twice as many instances as the six-year-old subjects. There were again no significant sex differences. The results indicated that the most common reason (33%) for masking a variety of feelings by adopting a neutral facial expression was to avoid others' derisive teasing about an expression of vulnerability (e.g., "sissy," "cry-baby") or to avoid feeling embarrassed (the vulnerability barometer reveals its functioning when embarrassment makes its affective presence known).

The most common reason cited across all age groups for substituting another facial expression for one's real affective display was for playful or "pretend" purposes (70% among the six-year-olds). All three age groups also mentioned substitution as a way for getting attention, for making someone feel sorry for oneself, and to get help. The older children showed greater subtlety and variety in their suggestions for when one would want to substitute expressive behavior, such as to look sick when one actually felt upset, to fake anger in order to get a "righteous" revenge, to laugh to cover nervousness, to fake fear in order to stop a parental scolding, and so forth. Their considerably lower proportion of playful/pretend responses is also consistent with their greater variety of ideas for when substitution should be useful and/or appropriate.

Finally, children's responses about when it would be appropriate to show one's feelings were coded. Significant age differences were again obtained such that with increasing age children were able to cite more reasons or occasions for the appropriate expression of feelings (six-year-olds, 18% of the total; eight-year-olds, 35%; ten-year-olds, 46% of the total number generated). The emphasis on appropriateness is intentional here, for the youngest children seemed perplexed by the question posed, which was "Have you ever felt _____ (fill in with relevant affect term), but it didn't matter if anyone knew—like it was OK for them to see you feeling that way? Can you tell me about that time?" Granted that this was a leading question, but many of the youngest children simply replied, "No" or "I don't know," and probing was not productive.

Nine general categories of reasons were developed for when it was appropriate to show one's feelings, and in descending order of frequency they were: (a) if the feelings were very intense; (b) if one was sick, injured, or bleeding; (c) if one was with certain people such as parents or friends; (d) if special or unusual misfortunes occurred (e.g., being in a fire, falling off a building, dropping one's homework in a puddle, having one's lunch stolen at school, if one was threatened by really "bad" kids, etc); (e) if one was in a special setting or environment (such as in an amusement park, in a horror movie, alone watching TV, etc.); (f) if one was a young child; (g) if one was being scolded or had been caught doing something wrong; and finally, (h) one ten-year-old said if one had been unjustly accused one should show how one feels about it.

What the descriptive results of this study reveal is the common expectation of disapproval (e.g., derision) from others for revealing *un*regulated negative expressive behavior. The fact that the older children were much more likely to provide a variety of reasons and occasions for when it would be appropriate to show one's feelings suggests that they view expressive behavior as being indeed regulated: there are specific times and places for when feelings may be directly revealed in expressive behavior as well as when they should be inhibited.

Observation of Dissimulation

The third study to be reviewed here was strictly an observational one (Saarni, Note 3). A "pseudo-naturalistic" conflict situation was contrived, involving the experimenter acting as a market researcher assessing self-help academic workbooks for grade school children (three age groups, mean ages 6.9, 9.8, and 10.8 years). The children were individually videotaped while evaluating the difficulty level of a workbook, and for their effort they received candy, money, and juice. They returned a second time to evaluate another workbook and were again offered a gift, this time from a grab-bag. However, the grab bag consisted of drab, unimaginative baby toys, clearly inappropriate for this age group. The videotapes of the first session provided baseline data for the children receiving desirable rewards, against which expressive behavior in the second session could be compared.

Blurton Jones's (1971) criteria for describing children's facial expressions were simplified and reduced to facilitate reliability of scoring. In addition to facial behavior, vocalizations, changes in gaze direction (i.e., eye contact with the experimenter or the gift), several kinesic movements (e.g., head tilt, shoulder shrug), and attempts to leave the room abruptly were scored. The various categories of behavior were arbitrarily grouped into three dimensions of a simple sort: positive, negative, and transitional dimensions. The facial behaviors were assigned to the positive or negative dimensions by following Ekman and Friesen's (1975) analysis of facial behavior; added to the positive dimensions were "smiling eye contact with experimenter" and "enthusiastic thank-you." To the negative dimension were added "negative noise (e.g., snort, ugh)," "abrupt departure," "shoulder shrug," "omitted thank-you," and "gaze aversion from the experimenter." The transitional dimension consisted of the following behaviors: slight smile (open or closed lips), faint or mumbled thank-you, knit brows while smiling slightly, tongue movements, two or more gaze shifts between experimenter and gift, biting or teeth visible on lips, hand to face or head, head tilt, questioning vocalization, laughing/giggling, mouthing (opening and shutting mouth), and abrupt loss of smile.

The positive and transitional dimensions were of greater interest in scoring the children's behavior in that if the children, upon receiving the baby toy, showed more behaviors falling in the positive or transitional dimensions, it suggested that they were more likely dissimulating their negative feelings about receiving such an inappropriate reward. Of course, it was *inferred* that they felt negatively towards the baby toy; however, examination of the age trends within and between the two sessions provided evidence that this inference was probably correct. Multivariate analyses revealed that upon receiving the baby toy the oldest children gave significantly more positive responses than the youngest children, and the middle group gave significantly more transitional responses than the youngest children. This pattern of results in the second session suggested that the higher incidence of positive expressive behavior shown by the ten-year-old children may well have been "successful" substitution of positive behavior for feelings of disappointment. The greater frequency of transitional responses shown by the eight-year-olds may have represented only partially successful substitution of negative feelings. The youngest children (six-year-olds), in particular the boys, openly expressed their negativity at receiving the baby toy. Comparisons between the first and second sessions revealed significant differences in positive behaviors (decreased in second session), and in negative behaviors (increased in second session). Thus, the inappropriate toy did elicit significantly more negative and fewer positive expressive responses than did the candy and money across all three age groups.

Some of the transitional expressive behaviors appeared to be mildly anxious or uncertain behavior (e.g., frequent shifting of eye contact). For children still in the process of acquiring self-regulatory control over their affective-expressive behavior, showing such behaviors which appear to seek guidance from the target person or to ascertain the impression being made on the target person would be appropriate and adaptive. Mildly anxious behavior, such as the giggling that occasionally occurred, is also understandable as an expressive response to such a peculiar and unsuitable gift from an otherwise friendly (albeit unfamiliar) adult.

The sex differences obtained in the second session (girls showed significantly fewer negative expressive responses than boys) may be consistent with the pressures of sex-role socialization in North America

for girls to appear nice, pleasant, and agreeable, despite feeling otherwise (cf. Brooks-Gunn & Matthews, 1979). The youngest boys were by
far the most negative in both sessions, while the youngest girls did not
differ from the middle group (the oldest girls showed the least negative
behaviors and the most positive behaviors of all). Regulation of expressive behavior would appear to be an area in which sex-role socialization
differences would appear, yet in the preceding studies on verbalized
understanding of display rule usage there had been no notable sex
differences (Saarni, 1979, Note 2). This suggests that possibly there are
no sex differences in the understanding of display rule usage but that
the actual implementation of display rules may be more prevalent in
girls or is revealed by girls at an earlier age. There are undoubtedly
situational constraints here as well: boys may regulate their expressive
behavior more than do girls in different kinds of situations (e.g., where
they feel hurt or vulnerable but "should" not show it).

    Finally, the observational data obtained in this study suggest some
rich paths for further exploration of exactly how self-regulation affects
expressive behavior in a given situation. The fine-grained coding, allowed
by slow-motion and still-frame video playback, was also a methodological refinement which made more feasible careful study of the transitions
in affective reactions to various kinds of social interactions.

Conclusion

    In so far as the dissociation of emotional experience and expressive
behavior represents an aspect of self-regulation, the developmental
changes noted in this chapter may emerge and differentiate in ways
similar to that of the development in regulation of self control (e.g.,
Masters & Santrock, 1976; Schwarz, Note 4). Growth in cognitive
functions, social experience, and maturing muscle coordination are
certainly involved in the development of self-regulation in general. As
to more specific developmental time-lines for affect and expressive
behavior regulation, I think it is premature to conclude which of the
categories of dissociation discussed in this chapter emerges first or
subsequently differentiates into the other categories. However, I have
hypothesized in my current work that direct deception emerges first
and that personal display rule usage develops from it as a particular
strategy which is used with some consistency to facilitate the self's
avoidance of threat and vulnerability, these representing internal
disadvantages or discomforts to be avoided. For example, does a youngster initially want to avoid others' derision over his vulnerable expression,
and only later is his expressive inhibition felt as a stoic strength in the
face of adversity? Or, when a child is chastised for screaming tantrums
in restaurants, supermarkets, etc., and thus reproached for showing

his/her anger, does this later become transformed into a personal display rule of not revealing anger expressively or only in highly miniaturized forms in order to feel "in control" or to maintain a self-image of "niceness"? It is the consistency of application, over time, that gives the rule character to personal display rule usage.

Cultural display rule usage hypothetically would emerge last in that it expecially requires some cognitive appraisal of a *system* of norms for expressive behavior. Cultural display rule usage may rely on both direct deception and personal display rule usage for its acquisition. For example, a young boy may be told not to cry "because boys don't cry"; however, in the child's mind inhibiting his crying on future occasions may have more to do with avoiding a scolding or derision than with observing sex-typed social norms. In this example, the scolding/derision may provide not only an immediate and situational disadvantage but also stimulate the child's vulnerability barometer to signal threat to the child's self-acceptance or worth. With greater maturity the older boy may state that he holds back his tears "because he *should*," implying a propriety or social obligation, and by inference cultural display rule usage.

The report and command features of interpersonal transactions also reveal their regulatory impact on the self and on others in the three social-affective functions of nonverbal behavior. From a developmental perspective it appears as though we are virtually wired to regulate our interaction with others. Bretherton and Bates (1979) have reviewed the infancy communication literature and conclude that "the child begins in the first few days with built-in propensities to engage in interaction with conspecifics. These primitive tendencies insure that he will find himself firmly based within *regular and predictable interaction sequences, where he becomes aware of his own ability to influence the behavior and internal states of others*" (p. 97) (italics mine). Thus, children differentiate the content (i.e., report features) of their affective behavior and simultaneously extend and elaborate their communicative influence vis á vis others (i.e., command features). Likewise, their maturing self-regulatory capacity exerts a reciprocal influence on the report and command features of their internal communications; self-monitoring and self-evaluation are among the typical outcomes. The consequences for nonverbal expressive behavior are complex indeed: both intrapsychic and interpersonal affective and social transactions are mediated by what we display or withhold expressively, most notably in our faces.

Reference Notes

1. DePaulo, B., Irvine, A., Jordan, A. & Laser, P. *Age changes in detection of deception.* Paper presented at American Psychological Association, Montreal, September 1980.

2. Saarni, C. *When* Not *to show what you think you feel: Children's understanding of relations between emotional experience and expressive behavior.* Paper presented at Society for Research in Child Development, San Francisco, March 1979.
3. Saarni, C. *Observing children's use of display rules: Age and sex differences.* Paper presented at American Psychological Association, Montreal, September 1980.
4. Schwarz, C. J. *Measuring individual differences in self-control and self-regulation in early childhood.* Paper presented at Society for Research in Child Development, Boston, April 1981.

References

Bateson, G. *Steps to an ecology of mind.* New York: Ballentine Books, 1972.

Blurton Jones. N. Criteria for use in describing facial expressions of children. *Human Biology,* 1971, *43,* 365-413.

Blurton Jones, N. (Ed.). *Ethological studies of child behavior.* Cambridge, England: Cambridge University Press, 1972.

Breger, L. *From instinct to identity.* Englewood Cliffs, N.J.: Prentice-Hall, 1974.

Bretherton, I., & Bates, E. The emergence of intentional communication. In I. Uzgiris (Ed.), *New directions for child development* (Vol. 4). San Francisco: Jossey-Bass, 1979.

Brooks-Gunn, J. & Matthews, W. *He and she: How children develop their sex-role identity.* Englewood Cliffs, N.J.: Prentice-Hall, 1979.

Burns, N. & Cavey, L. Age differences in empathic ability among children. *Canadian Journal of Psychology,* 1957, *11,* 227-230.

Cappella, J. Mutual influence in expressive behavior: Adult-adult and infant-adult dyadic interaction. *Psychological Bulletin,* 1981, *89,* 101-132.

Charlesworth, W. & Kreutzer, M. Facial expressions of infants and children. In P. Ekman (Ed.), *Darwin and facial expression, a century of research in review.* New York: Academic Press, 1973.

Condry, J. & Condry, S. Sex differences: A study for the eye of the beholder. *Child Development,* 1976, *47,* 812-819.

Décarie, T. G. Affect development and cognition. In M. Lewis & L. Rosenblum (Eds.), *The development of affect.* New York: Plenum, 1978.

Deutsch, F. Female pre-schoolers' perceptions of affective responses and interpersonal behavior in video-taped episodes. *Developmental Psychology,* 1974, *10,* 733-740.

Eibl-Eibesfeldt, I. *Love and hate: The natural history of behavior patterns.* New York: Schocken Books, 1974.

Ekman, P. & Friesen, W. The repertoire of nonverbal behavior: Categories, origins, usage, and coding. *Semiotica,* 1969, *1,* 49-98.

Ekman, P. & Friesen, W. *Unmasking the face.* Englewood Cliffs, N.J.: Prentice-Hall, 1975.

Ekman, P., Friesen, W., & Ellsworth, P. *Emotion in the human face.* Elmsford, N.Y.: Pergamon Press, 1972.

146 Carolyn Saarni

Emde, R., Kligman, P., Reich, J., & Wade, T. Emotional expression in infancy: I. Initial studies of social signaling and an emergent model. In M. Lewis & L. Rosenblum (Eds.), *The development of affect.* New York: Plenum, 1978.

Feldman, R., Jenkins, L., & Popoola, O. Detection of deception in adults and children via facial expression. *Child Development,* 1979, *50,* 350-355.

Goffman, E. *The presentation of self in everyday life.* Garden City, N. Y. Doubleday, 1959.

Goffman, E. *Interaction ritual.* Garden City, N.Y.: Doubleday, 1967.

Goffman, E. *Frame analysis.* New York: Harper & Row, 1974.

Goffman, E. "Gender advertisements." *Studies in the Anthropology of Visual Communication,* 1976, *3* (2).

Grinder, J. & Bandler, R. *The structure of magic* (Vol. 2.) Palo Alto, CA: Science and Behavior Books, 1976.

Haley, J. *Strategies of psychotherapy.* New York: Grune and Stratton, 1963.

Harper, R., Wiens, A., & Matarazzo, J. *Nonverbal communication: The state of the art.* New York: Wiley, 1978.

Harris, P., Olthof, T., & Terwogt, M. Children's knowledge of emotion. *Journal of Child Psychology and Psychiatry,* in press.

Haviland, J. Looking smart: The relationship between affect and intelligence in infancy. In M. Lewis (Ed.), *Origins of intelligence.* New York: Plenum, 1976.

Hochschild, A. *Emotion work, feeling rules, and social structure. American Journal of Sociology,* 1979, *85,* 552-575.

Izard, C. *Human emotions.* New York: Plenum, 1977.

LaFrance, M. & Mayo, C. *Moving bodies: Nonverbal communication in social relationships.* Monterey, CA: Brooks/Cole, 1978.

Lazarus, R. S. The self-regulation of emotion. In L. Levi (Ed.), *Emotions: Their parameters and measurement.* New York: Raven Press, 1975.

Lewis, M. & Rosenblum, L. (Eds.). *The development of affect.* New York: Plenum, 1978.

Mahoney, M. Reflections on the cognitive-learning trend in psychotherapy. *American Psychologist,* 1977, *32,* 5-13.

Masters, J. C., & Santrock, M. W. Studies in the self-regulation of behavior: Effects of contingent cognitive and affective events. *Developmental Psychology,* 1976, *12* (4), 334-348.

Mehrabian, A. A semantic space for nonverbal bahavior. *Journal of Consulting and Clinical Psychology,* 1970, *35,* 248-257.

Mehrabian, A. *Nonverbal communication.* New York: Aldine-Atherton, 1972.

Meichenbaum, P. & Turk, P. The cognitive-behavioral management of anxiety, anger, and pain. In P. Davidson (Ed.), *The behavioral management of anxiety, depression, and pain.* New York: Brunner/Mazel, 1976.

Oster, H. Facial expressions in infancy. In M. Lewis & L. Rosenblum (Eds.), *Development of affect.* New York: Plenum, 1978.

Saarni, C. Children's understanding of display rules for expressive behavior. *Developmental Psychology,* 1979, *15,* 424-429.

Satir, V. *Conjoint family therapy.* Palo Alto, CA.: Science and Behavior Books, 1967.

Schwartz, G., Fair, P., Greenberg. P., Freedman, M., & Klerman, J. Facial electromyography in the assessment of emotion. *Psychophysiology,* 1974, *11,* 237.

Tomkins, S. *Affect, imagery, and consciousness* (Vol. 1). New York: Springer, 1962.

Tomkins, S. *Affect, imagery, and consciousness* (Vol. 2). New York: Springer, 1963.

Tomkins, S. Affect as amplification: Some modifications in theory. In P. Plutchik & H. Kellerman (Eds.), *Emotion: Theory, research, and experience* (Vol. 1). New York: Academic Press, 1980.

Watzlawick, P., Beavin, J., & Jackson, D. *Pragmatics of human communication: A study of interactional patterns, pathologies, and paradoxes.* New York: Norton, 1967.

Part Three
Cognitive Development and Encoding and Decoding Skill Approaches to Nonverbal Behavior

CHAPTER SIX

Age Changes in Deceiving and Detecting Deceit

Bella M. DePaulo and Audrey Jordan

Infants' and children's initial attempts to decipher the true nature of their interpersonal and physical worlds mark the beginning of a scientific enterprise that will last a lifetime. Such an awesome undertaking requires sophisticated privately-owned equipment (for example, developing cognitive structures and sensory capabilities) and dependable external sources of support (for example, the existence of discernible invariances in the real world). Another tremendously rich source of data consists of information that is conveyed by other people. Much of this information that is conveyed to infants and children is sensible and useful. For example, adults often try to convey to children the names of people and things, the meanings of words, and some notion of the currently acceptable standards of conduct and systems of values. On other occasions, however, adults tell children about verbally fluent bears and pigs; about wolves who dress up like grandmothers; black-clad women who travel by broomstick; and cows that jump over the moon. The child's world is punctuated with other types of verbal oddities as well. For example, when Junior smashes a priceless antique in his haste to escape to the great outdoors, his father remarks, "That's just great." Curiously, his father uttered the exact same words one day when Junior had picked up all of his toys.

Lies Told to Children

Fanciful stories, irony, and sarcasm are just a few examples of verbal communications that are not to be taken literally. Other such categories include jokes, metaphors, fantasies, playful exaggerations, and games of make-believe. Some—if not all—forms of nonliteral language present an interpretive challenge to the child (cf. Winner, Rosenstiel, & Gardner, 1976; Kotsonis, Note 2). It is not always immediately apparent that the literal meaning is not in fact the intended meaning. Further, even if the literal meaning does become suspect, it still may not be at all obvious to the child what meaning the speaker really did intend to convey.

Children's verbal environments include another important category of misleading literal meanings—the category of deceit. Some of the lies told to children are no less preposterous than fairy tales, cartoons, or television comedies. For example, children are often told that once a year, a fat man on a sled is flown through the air by a fleet of deer. Graver facts are usually described by less colorful lies ("Grandpa went on a long vacation.") or are dodged, denied, evaded, or cloaked by a veneer of silence. Many advertisements might also be classified as lies designed especially for children (e.g., "Wheaties make you big and strong."). Other kinds of untruths told to children are often regarded as innocuous or even beneficial. For example, an adult may tell a child that his or her scribbled blotch of blue really does look like a grasshopper (and quite a handsome one at that), or that the ball dribbled back to the pitcher was a great hit. Berko Gleason (1973) suggests that adults' exaggerated affective responses to children's unextraordinary life events are part of a "language of socialization" that serves to inform children of how they should feel rather than to convey accurately adult feelings. Finally, many deceptions that are not specifically child-oriented (e.g., self-presentational dissimulations; lies that adults tell to each other) are also part of the child's interpersonal world.

Direct deception differs from the nonliteral language forms in one extremely important way: the latter forms are intended to be interpreted nonliterally, whereas deception is purposefully designed to mislead. Thus, speakers communicating nonliteral messages fill their utterances with warnings of nonliteral intent (e.g., dripping with sarcasm). These clues often seem to be tone of voice cues, though facial expressions, gestures, and contextual cues can be important too. Deceptive speakers, on the other hand, usually try their best to mask the fact that deception is occurring, thereby seducing the unwitting listener into accepting the feigned meaning unquestioningly. This difference between deceptive communications and nonliteral language suggests that the ability to detect deception might develop even later than the ability accurately to interpret nonliteral language. Research on children's understanding of both message types is meager, and the two have never been directly compared.

Children's Evaluations of Deception

In order for children to distinguish truth from deceit, they must first realize that the phenomenon of deception exists, and they must also understand the defining features of deceit (a deceitful message is false and it is also intentionally misleading). Saarni's research (1979) suggests that school-age children are aware that something like deception exists, in that they realize that people's overt expressions do not always correspond to their internal feelings.

Piaget (1965) has investigated children's understanding of the defining characteristics of lies and their moral evaluations of different kinds of lies (e.g., what kinds of statements are "worse" or "naughtier" than others). His technique was to describe a brief scenario to the child and then ask the child if the protagonist had told a lie. Piaget might then do the same for a second story and ask the child to compare the naughtiness of the two key statements.

Young children, according to Piaget, tell lies in much the same spirit as they fantasize or play—that is, presumably with no intent to deceive. Curiously, some of their utterances call forth the wrath of their parents, and others do not. Similarly confusing things happen with single words: some are reacted to with indifference while others bring instant rebuke. To these five- to seven-year-olds (the youngest children Piaget questioned), the concept of deceit seemed to have no inherent rhyme or reason. A lie, to them, was simply a moral fault committed by means of language. While they may realize that many statements that are not true are lies, they also label unintentional errors and even "naughty words" as lies. The notion of intent is not at all salient to the six-year-old moral realist; instead, the six-year-old's moral evaluations are governed by judgments of objective responsibility. Thus, "a lie is a fault in so far as it is forbidden by God or adults" (p. 169). The more severe the punishment, the more naughty the lie is judged to have been. This basis for evaluating lies leads to the intriguing result that lies that fool other people (and therefore are not punished) are regarded as less naughty than transparent lies.

Eventually, naughty words drop out of the list of verbalizations labeled as lies, but for a time mistakes are still regarded as lies. This follows quite naturally from an objective assessment of lies as statements that are untrue. By this definition, a statement becomes more naughty as it deviates further from the truth. Thus, a child who claims to have seen a dog as big as a cow has told a very naughty lie since a cow is so much bigger than a dog could ever be. Similarly, a person who misjudges another person's age by eight years has told a worse lie than someone whose estimate is off by only four years. There is even some evidence that longer or more complicated stories are judged to be worse lies than simpler, more straightforward tales. These three examples deal with the content of the deception. However, the material consequences of the deceit are important, too. One pair of stories used to illustrate the importance of consequences involved a traveler asking for directions. In one scenario, a child intentionally gives the wrong directions, but the traveler finds his way nonetheless. In the other story, the child tries to give the right directions, but the traveler gets lost. Before the age of about eight or ten, children will judge the second child as naughtier than the first, since the objective outcome was more undesirable in the latter case.

By around the age of 10 or 11, children become sensitive to the importance of intent, and explicitly verbalize the adult definition of a lie ["any statement that is intentionally false" (Piaget, 1965, p. 145)]. At this age, lies are evaluated subjectively, in terms of their goals. Mistakes are no longer regarded as deceitful, and lies that do succeed in misleading others are regarded as more morally despicable than lies that are found out. Whereas younger children refrain from lying out of a sense of duty and respect for still another set of adult prohibitions that they do not completely understand, these pre-adolescents have learned from their interactions with each other that truthfulness is a necessary foundation for social reciprocity, and mutual respect and trust.

Piaget was careful to warn against too quick an extrapolation of his description of children's abstract or theoretical moral reasoning to the "practical" reasoning children might display in concrete situations. He hypothesized that children would show more sympathy and psychological insight (i.e., less moral realism) in their practical than in their theoretical thought. He also added that children's sensitivity to the importance of intentions should appear earlier with respect to their own untruths, compared to the falsehoods told by others. When the behavior of others is the object of judgment, the outward act (the statement that departs from the truth) is more salient to the child than the inner intent.

What implications might be drawn from Piaget's analysis about children's judgments of deception when only nonverbal cues are available? Perhaps at ages five to seven, children perceive negative nonverbals, such as sullen or surly facial expressions or sarcastic voice tones, as deceptive. Further, the more unpleasant the cue, the more "naughty" the communicator will be judged to be. Somewhat later, this negativity bias may wane, but children might judge more exaggerated dissimulations (whether positive or negative) as more deceptive than less theatrical displays. Finally, later still, perceivers may still infer some relationship between the exaggeration or intensity of a communication and the likelihood that deception is in fact occurring, but their moral evaluations of the deceptive act may become independent of those factors. That is, immorality will be judged primarily in terms of intent to deceive and not in terms of communicative style.

A study of adults' standards for evaluating the wrongness of lies demonstrated the importance of four key considerations: whether the liar would be helped or harmed by the lie and whether the person deceived would be helped or harmed (Lindskold & Walters, Note 3). Thus, adults do not perceive just one deceptive motive; rather, they distinguish among different types of deceptive intents and find some to be more morally reprehensible than others. This multiplicity of deceptive motives should be considered in future research on the development of children's judgments about deceit. It might be hypothesized, for example, that children will initially be most sensitive to deceiver outcomes when they are in the role of the deceiver, and to target outcomes when they are in the role of the recipient of the deceit. Finally, the Lindskold and Walters study (Note 3) suggests that factors such as the nature of the relationship between deceiver and deceived, and the number of persons affected by the lie, also enter into adults' moral evaluations of deceit. We would expect developmental changes to occur in the appreciation of these factors too.

Children's Detection of Deception from Facial Expressions

Aside from our own research which we will describe below, there have been only three studies of children's ability to detect deception. All three have examined children's detection of deceit from facial cues only.

In a study involving third graders (Feldman, Devin-Sheeham & Allen, 1978), students recruited to be tutors were instructed to praise their tutees for their performance on each of a series of problems, regardless of the true quality of the performance. In one condition, the tutees performed quite well, answering 90% of the problems correctly. Thus, in this condition, the tutors' praise was usually genuine. In the other condition, however, the tutee answered 90% of the problems incorrectly, and the tutors' praise was therefore insincere. Male and female third graders rated videotapes of the facial expressions of the tutors. Ratings were made on a six-point scale in response to the question, "How happy was the child you just looked at with his [or her] student?" Observers were able to distinguish between genuine and false praise, in that they rated the tutors of successful tutees as significantly happier with their students than the tutors of the unsuccessful tutees. Thus, this study showed that third graders were able to discern some differences between honest and dishonest communications. It cannot be assumed, however, that these children would have been able to relate the difference they perceived to a difference in deceptiveness. At least for adult lie detectors, the ability to identify senders' underlying affects appears to be independent of the ability to recognize the occurrence of deceit (DePaulo & Rosenthal, 1979b).

A subsequent study by Feldman and White (Note 1) directly assessed children's perceptions of deceptiveness. Both the liars and the lie detectors were five- to 13-year-old children. As encoders, the children tasted a good- and a bad-tasting drink, and either pretended to like both or to dislike both. As decoders, they rated videotapes of the facial expressions of half of the other children and indicated for each clip whether the child was being truthful or pretending. Overall, accuracy was only 51% (where 50% would be a chance level) and increased modestly and nonsignificantly ($r = .14$) with age. However, partialling out age, children's success at detecting deception did correlate significantly ($r = .34$) with their scores on Feffer's Role-Taking Task (Feffer, 1959). Feldman and White (Note 1) speculated that the skilled role-takers imagined the communicative situation from the deceiver's point of view, thus in essence providing themselves with contextual cues to facilitate their interpretive efforts. The inept role-takers, on the other hand, were hypothesized to be like decoders attempting to decipher nonverbal signals with little or no information about the situation in which the signals were generated.

A third study of children's deception detection skills involved first graders, fifth graders, and their parents (Morency & Krauss, this volume). The children watched a series of pleasant and unpleasant slides, and tried to "deceive" while viewing half of them. That is, they tried to convey the impression that the pleasant slides were unpleasant and that the unpleasant slides were pleasant. Videotapes were made of the children's facial expressions. The children and their parents then viewed these tapes, rating each clip for deceptiveness.

In this study, too, children's lie detection performance was unimpressive. The fifth graders' performance was no better than that of the first graders. Neither the first graders nor the fifth graders were able accurately to detect the deception of the fifth graders. They were able to spot the first graders' lies but only on the pleasant stimuli. Since the adults were able to detect the first graders' deception on both types of slides, and the fifth graders' deception when they were watching the pleasant stimuli, it appears that reliable cues to deceit were available but were not effectively utilized by the children. As in the two Feldman studies (Feldman et al., 1978; Feldman & White, Note 1), there were no significant sex differences in lie detection success.

Parental skills and attitudes have not yet been demonstrated to be powerful predictors of children's lie detection success. In the Morency and Krauss study (this volume), parents' lie detection scores were not significantly correlated with their children's scores. In an earlier study, Kraut and Price (1976) tested the hypothesis that parents' manipulative attitudes—their machiavellianism scores—might predict their children's lie detection success. They used a bluffing game in which each of a group of sixth graders rolled a die and then lied or told the truth about the outcome of the roll to another sixth grader who could see the first child, but not the roll of the die. Kraut and Price reported near-zero correlations between both mothers' and fathers' machiavellianism scores and their children's lie detection success. (They did not report the children's overall level of accuracy at detecting deceit).

One more finding from Morency and Krauss's study (this volume) merits special attention here: children's ability to detect deception when the senders were viewing pleasant slides was unrelated to their skill at detecting the deception that was communicated in response to the unpleasant slides. This finding suggests that some caution be used in regarding deception detection as a unitary skill, and the adult literature reinforces the need for that cautionary note. There, too, skills at detecting deception generated from pleasant vs. unpleasant stimuli have been shown to be uncorrelated (DePaulo & Rosenthal, 1979b). Also uncorrelated in the same study were the ability to detect deception and the ability to detect "leakage." Finally, several studies have reported nonsignificant correlations between skill at detecting women's lies and skill at detecting men's (DePaulo & Rosenthal, 1979b; Littlepage & Pineault, 1978).

In general, the few studies that have been reported do not offer a flattering view of the lie detection abilities of pre-adolescent children. Perhaps, though, these data in some ways present an unnecessarily dim picture of children's lie detection abilities. For example, children may do somewhat better at detecting deception when both vocal and verbal cues are available. It is already clear that this is true for adults (e.g., DePaulo, Zuckerman, & Rosenthal, 1980). Moreover, there is evidence to suggest that children may not be as far behind in their ability to understand vocal nonverbal cues as they are in their ability to understand facial expressions (Rosenthal, Hall, DiMatteo, Rogers, & Archer, 1979).

Probably more importantly, children may evidence more impressive lie detection skills when contextual cues as well as message cues are available to them, when the deceptive communications are truly interactive and extend over a longer time frame, when the deception detection task is a very involving one and one at which the children have had extensive practice, and when the deceivers are people who are familiar to the child judges (cf. Abramovitch, 1977; Abramovitch & Daly, 1979). While these conditions may seem to describe an extremely rare set of circumstances in the life of a pre-adolescent child, we argue below that they are characteristic of a fairly large number of popular games and sports.

In our own research program, we began by investigating children's ability to detect adults' deception from messages that included both verbal and nonverbal cues. That research will be described in the following section.

Adding Words: Children's Detection of Deception
from Verbal and Nonverbal Cues

Forewarned by the very low levels of deception detection accuracy reported for pre-adolescent decoders, we (DePaulo, Jordan, Irvine, & Laser, in press) focused our investigative efforts on somewhat older samples. Our youngest participants were approximately 11 years old, while our oldest ones were approximately 18 years old. Other evidence in addition to the low or nonexistent accuracy of pre-adolescents suggested to us that we look more closely at the adolescent years. First, visual cues tend to be uninformative or even misleading when used to convey deceit. It has been reported that children around the age of 12 begin to use a decoding strategy that is well-adapted to this differential informativeness of visual and vocal cues. When decoding discrepant and nondiscrepant messages, adolescents (compared to younger perceivers) pay relatively less attention to the visual cues and more attention to the vocal cues as the messages become more discrepant (Blanck & Rosenthal, this volume). This suggests that children may be learning effective lie detection skills during early adolescence.

There is also evidence that throughout adolescence, perceivers are continually acquiring a diversity of other skills, strategies, and experiences which should also facilitate their lie detection success. The experiential factors are the most obvious ones. With age, perceivers bring to the deception detection task more and more cultural, social, and interpersonal knowledge; this knowledge may help them to realize that certain affects, events, or experiences described by another person are unlikely to occur or unlikely to be described in the way that the person is describing them. With age, perceivers also accumulate more direct experience with deceptive communications; this, too, should facilitate their lie detection success. Research on the development of nonverbal decoding skills supports this suggestion; it shows that as children (particularly adolescents) are exposed to increasing amounts of nonverbal information, their accuracy at decoding that information increases, even in the absence of any performance feedback (DePaulo & Rosenthal, 1978).

There is also evidence that during adolescence, perceivers approach their interpersonal worlds in ways that should continuously increase their sensitivity to issues of sincerity and deceit. For example, adolescents (compared to younger perceivers) are more likely spontaneously to try to infer another's feelings, to explain the qualities they perceive in others, and to reconcile any apparent inconsistencies in other people's behaviors and traits (e.g., Flavell, 1977; Peevers & Secord, 1973).

Even if a perceiver has correctly inferred that another person's overt expression of feelings is dishonest, it is not always immediately apparent what the deceiver's true feelings are. The ability to identify the underlying affect that the deceiver is trying to hide is called "leakage" accuracy (Ekman & Friesen, 1969). Leakage accuracy is problematic because it requires that the perceiver discount the overtly expressed affect and infer an entirely different underlying affect that is much less salient. A Piagetian analysis would suggest that by early adolescence children should be able to do this (cf. Piaget, 1965). However, research with adult lie detectors suggests otherwise. When asked to identify senders' true affect, adults tend to report the affect that is overtly expressed rather than the underlying affect (Zuckerman, DePaulo, &

Rosenthal, 1981). If this strategy of reporting the overtly expressed affect is stable developmentally, then perceivers will be inaccurate leakage detectors at every age level. Further, if children are more overwhelmed by the overtly expressed affects than are adults, they might show even greater inaccuracy.

The subjects in our study were 176 children and adults from five age levels. Thirty-three of the participants were sixth graders, 38 were eighth graders, 29 were tenth graders, 33 were twelfth graders, and 43 were college students. The mean ages of the five samples were 11.5, 13.6, 15.0, 17.0, and 18.1 years, respectively.

All subjects were run in small groups. Within each group, subjects were randomly assigned to an audio or an audiovisual condition. Subjects assigned to the audiovisual condition sat facing the video monitor, while those assigned to the audio condition sat behind the monitor.

Videotaped stimulus materials were adapted from the Person Description Test developed by DePaulo and Rosenthal (1979b). The videotape showed four male and four female adults ("senders") each describing six people. Senders described (1) someone they liked, (2) someone they disliked, (3) someone they felt ambivalent about, and (4) someone they felt indifferent toward. (Ambivalence was defined for the senders as strong feelings of both liking and disliking, while indifference was defined as no particularly strong feelings of either liking or disliking.) For their other two descriptions, senders told two different kinds of lies: they described the person they liked, pretending to dislike him or her, and they described the person they disliked, pretending to like him or her. Two of the males and two of the females described males and the others described females. Senders were given one minute for each description and the middle 20 sec was recorded on the videotape. A 10-sec rating pause followed each description. Thus, the total length of the tape was 24 minutes. The eight senders gave their descriptions in different orders.

The experiment was described as a study of whether people can tell when others are lying and of how well they can understand the feelings of other people, by just listening to what they say or by listening to them and watching them. Subjects were then told about the six different kinds of descriptions that each sender would be making and were given a detailed description of the stimulus tape.

Subjects rated each description on 9-point scales of liking, dishonesty, and mixed feelings. (In order to control for potential differences in the use of the rating scales, each of the three sets of ratings was z-scored separately for each subject.) It was emphasized to the subjects that they should report the senders' true feelings and not the feelings that the senders were pretending to feel. Thus, if a sender was acting as if she or he liked the person being described but the subject thought the sender was lying, then the subject was to rate the sender as feeling *disliking* toward the person described.

Subjects' "dishonesty" and "mixed feelings" ratings of the deceptive and honest descriptions are shown in Table 6-1. Subjects' ability to detect deception (i.e., to perceive the dishonest messages as more deceptive than the honest messages) did not begin to exceed chance by a significant margin until the twelfth grade. Before perceivers can accurately label messages as lies, however, they must be able to discern some difference between truthful messages and deceptive messages. Subjects at all age levels were able to discriminate truth from deception along the liking dimension in that they perceived the deceptive messages as less evaluatively extreme than the honest messages (see Table 6-2). That is, they accurately perceived that senders feigning liking did not feel as much liking as senders honestly describing people whom they really did like, and they perceived that senders feigning disliking did not feel as much disliking as senders honestly describing disliked others. (A content analysis, based on the Peevers and Secord, 1973, scoring system, of the percentage of positive and negative verbalizations in each description, indicated that truthful messages really were more evaluatively extreme than deceptive messages.)

For the youngest subjects (sixth and eighth graders), the liking dimension was the only dimension along which they differentiated truth from deceit. Tenth graders also discriminated truth from deception by their liking ratings. Moreover, their judgments of "mixed feelings" also accurately distinguished deceptive messages from truthful messages in that they rated the deceptive speakers as expressing more mixed feelings than the truthful speakers (Table 6-1).

The differences between the younger adolescents and the older adolescents and adults were in (a) the number of dimensions along which they could accurately discriminate truth from deception and (b) their ability accurately to use the discriminations that they were able to

Table 6-1. "Dishonesty" and "Mixed Feelings" Ratings of the Deceptive and Honest Descriptions.[a]

	Type of Description		
Age Level	Deceptive[b]	Honest[c]	Accuracy[d]
Sixth grade	-.19 (.06)	.05 (.01)	-.24 (.05)
Eighth grade	.08 (-.03)	-.02 (-.09)	.10 (.06)
Tenth grade	.03 (.19)	-.01 (-.38)	.04 (.57)
Twelfth grade	.14 (.01)	-.09 (-.35)	.23 (.36)
College	.15 (-.03)	-.10 (-.55)	.25 (.52)

[a] Note: Ratings of "mixed feelings" are indicated in parentheses. The other entries are dishonesty ratings.
[b] Pretend to Like plus Pretend to Dislike.
[c] Like plus Dislike.
[d] Deceptive minus Honest.

make as a basis for inferring truthfulness or deceit. The sixth and eighth graders discriminated truth from deceit only along the liking dimension. The tenth graders also perceived the deceptive messages as conveying more mixed feelings than the truthful messages, but they still did not rate the dishonest messages as any more deceptive than the truthful messages. Only the twelfth graders and college students discriminated honesty from dishonesty along all three dimensions.

We have noted that subjects at all ages realized that the honest liking descriptions contained more liking than feigned liking descriptions and that the honest disliking descriptions contained more disliking than feigned disliking descriptions. Leakage accuracy, however, demands more than that. A perceiver who can see through to a deceiver's true, underlying affect would rate a deceiver who was pretending to dislike someone she or he actually did like as feeling more liking than a deceiver who was pretending to like someone who actually was disliked. We knew from previous research that adults do not show such incisive perceptions. Instead, they tend to take communications at face value, rating senders as feeling liking whenever they are saying positive things. We found that to be true in this study, also, for all five age levels (see columns 2 and 3 of Table 6-2).

Why is it that subjects' liking ratings corresponded so closely to the degree of overtly expressed liking when the speakers were lying? The more accurate strategy would have been to rate overt expressions of liking as very low on the liking scale, and overt expressions of disliking as very high on the liking scale, when the speakers were lying. One reason is that subjects were not told when the speakers were lying and when they were telling the truth. Moreover, as we have already shown, subjects were not remarkably accurate at determining when deception was occurring and when it was not. Further, even though subjects' perceptions of dishonesty were accurate some of the time, subjects could not have known for sure when their perceptions were or were not accurate. Once again, subjects had no basis for knowing with any certainty when they should or should not make their attributions of liking completely correspondent with the degree of liking overtly

Table 6-2. Liking Ratings of Each Type of Description.

	Type of Description			
Age Level	Like (Honest)	Pretend to Like (Deceptive)	Pretend to Dislike (Deceptive)	Dislike (Honest)
Sixth grade	.123	.034	−.070	−.291
Eighth grade	.297	.219	−.160	−.583
Tenth grade	.560	.310	−.330	−.693
Twelfth grade	.519	.444	−.376	−.832
College	.572	.401	−.309	−.712

expressed. Not knowing for sure when the speakers were lying and when they were telling the truth, subjects at every age level tended to conclude that the speakers actually felt about the same amount of liking that they were overtly expressing. This is probably the safest strategy in the face of uncertainty. Also, taking other people at their word is a more polite strategy than inferring an affect that is very different from the one that is overtly expressed.

It was not surprising to us that subjects at all age levels would make attributions of liking that were fairly consistent with the degree of liking that was overtly expressed. However, at first, it did surprise us very much to find that leakage accuracy scores actually decreased with age. Thus, older subjects (relative to younger ones) rated the faked expressions of liking (which concealed true disliking) higher on liking than the faked expressions of disliking (which covered up affects that actually were positive). We assumed that just the opposite would occur —that older subjects would be better at discerning the true, underlying affects since they are, presumably, more attuned to underlying intents and less influenced by more objective, but possibly irrelevant, criteria such as the degree of positivity that is overtly expressed. In fact, however, within this paradigm practically the only cues that subjects could use to decide whether or not to disregard the overtly expressed affects were cues in the message itself. For example, subjects could have gotten the impression that the expressed positivity really was not quite positive enough, and then decided that the affect the speaker really felt was disliking. Or, they could have come to suspect on the basis of other cues (e.g., speech hesitations, rate of speaking) that the overtly expressed message should not be believed. Apparently, subjects either were not able to make these kinds of judgments with any significant degree of accuracy, and/or, as discussed above, they may have made such judgments but had too little confidence in them to use them as a basis for doing anything so extreme as to infer an affect that was entirely different from the overtly expressed affect.

What strategy then is left to any of the subjects? They can simply assume that the affect expressed is the affect felt and report their perceptions accordingly. Older subjects can more strongly differentiate overt liking from overt disliking than can younger subjects. This is clear from the ratings of the two completely honest descriptions (see columns 1 and 4 of Table 6-2)—older subjects report a bigger difference in liking between the honest liking and honest disliking descriptions than do the younger subjects. In the case of these honest descriptions, the greater ability of the older subjects to distinguish overt expressions of liking from overt expressions of disliking leads them to a more accurate view of their interpersonal worlds. However, when senders' expressed affects and true affects do not correspond—i.e., when senders are lying—then older subjects' more pronounced differentiations between expressed liking and expressed disliking lead them (compared to younger subjects) even further astray from other people's true feelings.

The present findings add some interpretive clarity to earlier research. In the Feldman et al. (1978) study in which third grade subjects rated the facial expressions of tutors giving feedback to their students, subjects accurately rated the tutors as more pleased with their tutees when they had in fact done well than when the tutees had performed poorly. Thus, these third graders did distinguish deception from truth along a positivity dimension. Our results suggest that subjects may have simply reported the degree of positivity they perceived in the tutors' faces, without necessarily realizing that variations in positivity corresponded to variations in deceptiveness. If they had been asked to rate the deceptiveness of the tutors, they may not have been able to distinguish genuine praise from dissembled praise.

We would not like to suggest, on the basis of existing research, that people will never infer an affect or attitude that is very different from the one that is overtly expressed, or that they are never accurate when they do attempt to do so. What we do think that the available evidence indicates is that it is extremely difficult for perceivers to make such inferences on the basis of message cues alone, particularly when the deceivers are unknown strangers. When *will* perceivers draw such inferences? Perhaps they will do so when there are strong contextual cues (i.e., when the situation is one in which people might be motivated to express attitudes or affects that they do not really feel, for example, a job interview), or when other known facts about the sender cast doubt upon the veridicality of the sender's overt message. When such cues are available, we might find the developmental trend that we initially predicted—that people become better, with age, at seeing through to deceivers' underlying affects.

Apparently, visual cues were not at all useful to subjects in their attempts to detect deceit; deception accuracy was nearly identical in the audiovisual and audio-only conditions at every age level. The senders in this study, like others who have been studied previously, seem to have carefully controlled their facial expressions so as not to reveal the occurrence of lying. When the senders were not lying and simply wanted to convey their true feelings accurately, they were able to use their facial expressions to facilitate that goal too. Across all age levels, honest liking was more accurately discriminated from honest disliking when visual cues were available (audiovisual condition) than when they were not (audio-only condition).

As is clear from Table 6-1, the deceptiveness judgments of the sixth and eighth graders did not accurately correspond to the actual deceptiveness of the messages. However, these judgments were not random. Instead, they varied systematically with the one dimension that the youngest subjects could accurately understand, i.e., the positivity-negativity dimension. Younger subjects perceived the senders as rela- tively more deceptive when their descriptions were negative ("dislike" and "pretend to dislike" descriptions) than when they were positive ("like", "pretend to like"). With age, however, this tendency reversed, and the older subjects perceived the senders as relatively more dishonest when their descriptions were positive than when they were negative (see Table 6-3). The tendency of the younger subjects to perceive expressions of negative affect as deceptive is intriguingly similar to Piaget's observation (1965) that six-year-olds often label naughty words as lies. With our pre-adolescents, however, we suspect that they show this judgmental bias not because they do not understand what a lie is, but because of the rose-colored view of the world that adults often try to provide for children. These younger subjects perhaps are inhabitants of a social world in which adults refrain from making unflattering remarks about each other when children are around and tell children that the unkind things they have heard about others are simply untrue. The older subjects, on the other hand, are no longer protected from harshness in these ways, and further, have developed a closer acquain- tance with the norms of politeness that dictate the overt expressions of kindness even in the absence of equally fond feelings. Thus, the older subjects show a more cynical judgmental bias: if the overt message is kind, they are relatively more likely to see it as a lie than if it is harsh.

Lies That Children Tell

Non-literal (though not deceptive) forms of language such as similes, metaphors, and other figures of speech are generated spontaneously by children as young as three or four years old (cf. Gardner, Kircher, Win- ner, & Perkins, 1975). Children also learn to generate indirect rather than direct requests (e.g., "Could I have that toy?" rather than "Give me that toy.") (Bates, 1976). In generating these indirect directives, as

Table 6-3. Dishonesty Ratings of Descriptions in Which Liking or Disliking Was the Expressed Affect.

| | Expressed Affect | | |
| | Liking (Like plus | Disliking (Dislike plus | Liking minus |
Age Level	Pretend to Like)	Pretend to Dislike)	Disliking
Sixth grade	-.277	.131	-.408
Eighth grade	-.250	.312	-.562
Tenth grade	-.105	.129	-.234
Twelfth grade	.053	-.001	.054
College	.097	-.053	.150

in generating figures of speech, children are producing linguistic forms that are not necessarily intended to be taken literally. Clearly, children also embellish stories that are told to them and fabricate their own imaginative tales. A later linguistic achievement is the telling of jokes, puns, and riddles, which involves an appreciation of subtle syntactic and lexical ambiguity.

Verbal and nonverbal concoctions that really are intended to mislead (genuine lies) come in many varieties, not all of which should be expected to appear at the same point developmentally. Perhaps the earliest lies that children tell are those designed to escape imminent punishment. Lies generated to obtain a reward, in the absence of any obvious eliciting cue, probably appear later. Within this category, lies aimed at attaining material benefits (the candy bar promised to the child who performed the most good deeds) may predate deceits designed to secure more subtle social rewards. Among the latter are self-presentation lies; for example, exaggerating one's prior athletic or academic accomplishments in order to impress one's peers. Lies told to save or flaunt someone else's neck rather than one's own may appear later still. Within this grouping, loyalty lies (e.g., the teacher asks who broke the window and all of the culprit's friends remain quiet), probably predate truly altruistic lies (e.g., the teacher threatens to punish everyone unless the true villain is revealed; the culprit's friends remain quiet still, or perhaps even take the blame themselves).

If Piaget (1965) is correct in suggesting that children begin by telling lies in much the same way that they play or tell stories, then perhaps what appears to be the earliest occurrences of deceit are instead innocent instances of fantasy, with no intent to mislead. This ambiguity poses a problem to researchers who are interested in studying the onset and development of intentionally deceptive acts. Of greater interest to children, this ambiguity also poses a threat to their own well-being. If adults and peers do not recognize the innocence of these playful utterances, scoldings, ostracism, and other unsavory reactions might ensue. It seems reasonable to assume, then that children will eventually learn to "mark" their fanciful verbal musings as such. It is not yet known how or when this marking skill develops, but it is probably predated or facilitated by some of the same kinds of knowledge that contribute to children's ability to mislead intentionally. For example, skill at marking playful intent and skill at masking deceptive intent might both involve an awareness that speakers are held responsible for their verbal behaviors (and sometimes for their nonverbal behaviors) and that listeners usually assume some correspondence between what speakers say and what they truly feel or believe.

Research on children's deceit has stemmed from three very different kinds of perspectives. The earliest systematic investigation that we know of was a somewhat moralistic inquiry into "the nature of character." In their classic volume, *Studies of Deceit*, Hartshorne and May (1928) summarize dozens of studies of lying, stealing, and cheating (mostly the last) involving 11,000 children ranging in age from 8 to 16 years. Only two of the tests Hartshorne and May used in this research measured lying. One, considered to be a measure of "lying to escape disapproval," involved asking the children whether they had cheated on any of the previous tests. The other, described as a measure of "lying to win approval," was essentially a test of rare and unusual virtues (e.g., "Do you always smile when things go wrong?" "Do you usually pick up broken glass in the street?"). The authors assumed that while some of the children might in fact possess a few such virtues, only a "pious fraud" (Hartshorne & May, 1928, p. 102) could claim all 36. For our purposes, it will suffice to describe only the most striking finding to emerge from this program of research. Hartshorne and May never did find evidence for a "moral character" or "honest personality." Instead, their data strongly suggested that moral behavior is highly situationally specific.

Nearly half a century passed before the systematic study of children's deceit surfaced. This time, however, the research was described as an investigation of machiavellianism and political savvy, rather than of moral character and the effectiveness of religious training. Christie and Geis's 1970 volume ended not with a description of "experimental efforts to teach honesty" (Hartshorne & May, 1924, p. 368), but with an admission of "perverse admiration for the high machs' ability to outdo others in experimental situations" (Christie & Geis, 1970, p. 339). Times had changed.

Christie and Geis's (1970) research program was based on a self-report scale of machiavellian attitudes. High machs believe that other people are manipulable, and they seem to practice manipulative acts with an aura of emotional detachment. Among adults, low scorers distinguish themselves not by any morally grounded unwillingness to deceive, but rather by the ineptness of their deceptive attempts. Among children, too, it appears that high and low machs practice deception in notably different ways.

Three studies of children's deceptive abilities grew out of the Machiavellianism research. Two of these (Kraut & Price, 1976; Nachamie, Note 4) involved a "bluffing game" in which children roll dice and win candy if they are successful at detecting deceit (recognizing the other child's bluffs). In the third study (Braginsky, 1970a, b), the experimenter, presenting herself as a representative of a cracker company, gave children a taste of a cracker that had been dipped in a quinine solution. She then offered the children a nickel for every cracker they could convince an unsuspecting peer to eat.

Results across the two paradigms were inconsistent with respect to the relationship between parents' and children's machiavellianism scores, and also between parents' machiavellianism and children's success at deceiving others. In Kraut and Price's study (1976), children's own machiavellianism scores did not predict their manipulative success. However, in Braginsky's paradigm (Braginsky, 1970a, b), which allowed for much more variability in the design and implementation of deceptive techniques, high and low mach children differed markedly. First, high machs were more successful than lows: they convinced their peers to eat many more of the quinine-dipped delicacies. Second, high machs engaged in more of all sorts of manipulative behaviors (omissive lies, commissive lies, bribery, two-sided arguments, blaming the experimenter) than did low machs, although the difference was significant only for omissive lies. Finally, the high machs sounded like little angels. Judges who listened to tape-recordings of the transactions rated the high machs as sounding more innocent, honest, calm, and comfortable than the low machs. The judges also thought that the high machs used more effective arguments and were more likely to be successful in a sales position than the low machs.

Little girl machs told different kinds of lies than little boy machs. High mach girls more often told omissive lies (they withheld information and evaded questions), while high mach boys more often told commissive lies (they distorted information). In each case, the strategy was apparently appropriate: frequency of omissive lies predicted manipulative success for girls but not for boys, while the reverse was true for commissive lies. These results are intriguingly similar to those reported for adult liars: women, more so than men, make comments that are less evaluatively extreme and more neutral (more evasive and noncommittal) when they are lying, compared to when they are telling the truth (DePaulo, Rosenthal, Rosenkrantz, & Green, Note 1).

Lie-Telling Skills

De Villiers and de Villiers (1978), in discussing children's progressive mastery of the intricacies of discourse, describe a process of decreasing dependence on context in the understanding and production of language. They suggest that the "ultimate achievement" in this developmental trend is the ability to lie successfully.

The ability to transcend coolly the compelling cues in an immediate context is a skill that many beginning liars clearly do not have. For example, many budding checkers champions exude exuberance upon spotting the development of a much longed-for double-jump; of course, unless the partner is equally naive in the ways of deceit, the jump is soon destroyed by the anticipatory ebullience that it created.

Astute liars must not only realize when contextual cues should be defied; they also need to have the necessary control over their own mechanisms of verbal and nonverbal production to defy successfully. The checkers champ, for example, might decide to feign a feeling of disappointment in order to convince the opponent that his or her move was about to dethrone the champ. To do this well, the champ will need muscular control (cf. Ekman, Roper, & Hager, 1980) and also some knowledge of what disappointment should look like. In short, the deceiver must be able deliberately to encode disappointment. An awareness of what one's own attempts to appear disappointed look or sound like to the opponent might also be useful.

Effective liars might be expected to fine-tune their messages to the characteristics of their listeners. Also, as the message is communicated, they will monitor the listener's responses for signs of skepticism and then modify the message accordingly. These sophisticated maneuverings presuppose the realizations that one's verbal and nonverbal behaviors are ambiguous stimuli that are often of interest to others, and that one can control such behaviors in order to affect the inferences that are drawn from them.

As children master those skills and others, they should become increasingly effective liars: this developmental prediction is perhaps the most obvious one. It would also be unsurprising to find an increase, with age, in the flexibility of deceit. That is, children perhaps begin by mastering certain fairly rigid deceptive routines within certain contexts; subsequently, they may learn a variety of deceptive techniques, which become increasingly adapted to the characteristics of their listeners.

There may also be developmental trends in the specific deceptive strategies that are mastered and utilized. In attempts to conceal a particular emotion, for instance, one might attempt to simulate a very different emotion. In this dissimulation, the liar might attempt to convey a very natural expression of the emotion or a very exaggerated or intensified display. Or, instead of feigning a different emotion, the liar might simply try to present a neutral expression (cf. Ekman & Friesen, 1969). More verbally oriented strategies of deceiving include denial, distortion, evasiveness, nonresponsiveness, making things up, introducing irrelevancies, and omitting important information. Denial may be the most cognitively simple of these strategies and thus may appear rather early developmentally. The order of development of the other strategies is best left to empirical testing.

Finally, there may also be important developmental changes in the affects and attitudes that become associated with deceit, with resulting changes in the verbal and nonverbal behaviors that occur during deception. For example, one of the earliest affects that might accompany deceit is a fear of getting caught. This would be consistent with Piaget's (1965) suggestion that children initially do not understand adults' moral bases for evaluating lies and know only that certain verbalizations are forbidden. Later, as the interpersonal foundations of truthfulness become meaningful, lying may begin to be accompanied by affects such as guilt or shame or evaluation apprehension. These affects may increase as children more strongly internalize moral standards regarding deceit. Thus, perhaps children's developing role-taking skills, muscular control, metalinguistic sophistication, and other abilities that augment their deceptive success are counteracted in part by an increase in emotionality about the moral and interpersonal ramifications of deceit.

Where do children learn and practice their skills at deceiving and also at detecting deceit? There are many contexts, but here we will discuss just one. We propose that child's play, in many of its manifestations, functions as a training ground for the development and refinement of deceptive abilities. Probably every major category of play—for example, card games, board games, party games, and sports—includes numerous specific games that involve deceit. Many of these are popular games that fill countless childhood hours. For example, some sports, such as football and basketball, involve faking a pass or a throw in one direction but then actually tossing the ball in a different direction. This involves intricate coordination on the part of the ball-handler, as well as sophisticated decoding strategies on the part of the defensive players. Card games that teach deceit include Old Maid and children's versions of poker. These games provide ample opportunity to practice concealment and dissimulation of both positive and negative affects. Board games such as checkers and party games such as "buttoney-button" (in which children try to determine who *really* has the button) train nonverbal skills especially. Other, more complicated games, such as diplomatic or war-type simulations, sharpen children's skills at verbal deceit. Other games and ritual activities do not involve deception per se, but do allow for practice in the control of nonverbal behaviors (e.g., staring contests) and in the control of emotions (e.g., "the dozens").

It can be argued that most of these games differ in several important ways from other more serious situations involving deceit (e.g., lying to friends, parents, or other authority figures in nongame contexts). First, deception in children's games is sanctioned deceit, generated under the implicit presumptions that it is all in fun and no one will be hurt. While feelings of guilt, shame, or evaluation apprehension may still remain, these affects are probably relatively less important than the joy of fooling others. Second, these games are usually played with friends. The targets of deceptive attempts are probably varied in nongame settings. Third, participants in games involving deceit usually realize that deception is likely to occur. This is different from many real life situations, in which it may never occur to the interactants to entertain the possibility that deception might be taking place. Finally, in most games, the probable object or content of the deceit is also usually known. For example, in Old Maid, dissimulations clearly will be centered around the location of the Old Maid card. In everyday interactions, on the other hand, virtually any entity could provide grist for the mill of deceit.

Two entirely different conclusions might be drawn from this set of features which distinguishes game-type deceptions from other deceptions. One is that the two types of deceit are entirely different, such that the skills and strategies mastered in the game-type settings will be irrelevant in other types of settings. The other conclusion is that these special features, rather than rendering irrelevant to other settings the skills learned in game contexts, instead serve to facilitate the development and refinement of such skills, which can be used in other contexts as well. We favor the latter.

If one were to design a program to teach deceptive skills, one might in fact incorporate many of the special features that characterize game-type deceits. For example, one might like one's trainees to practice their developing skills guiltlessly, or perhaps even gleefully. One might also try to hold many factors constant, while teaching a small number of key skills. In a communication task, it might help to have some familiarity with the other participants' expressive styles; this requirement is met quite adequately by involving friends as co-trainees. Finally, in a training program the phenomenon of interest is highly salient, and the examples of that phenomenon that are to be mastered at any given point in the program are held to a reasonable number. So, too, in games involving deceit, deception is often highly salient and the range of possible contents of the deceit is not unmanageably large. Thus, while it may be true, as Piaget (1965) has claimed, that children learn from their interactions with their peers moral and interpersonal reasons for not lying, we would like to propose that children also learn and practice with their peers the skills necessary to tell lies, should they decide to do so.

The suggestion that children might be learning deceptive skills in game situations that are then used in other contexts implies an assumption of skill-generality, which is quite different from the specificity hypothesis advanced in our discussion of the detecting of deceit. While we believe that different types of lie-telling tasks involve very different skills, there is some evidence to suggest that lie-telling skills may be more general than lie detection skills. This evidence comes primarily from studies that involved a single deception task, in which different measures of lie telling and lie detecting were gathered (DePaulo & Rosenthal, 1979b; Kraut, 1978). Also suggestive is the finding reported by Christie and Geis (1970) that children who had extensive experience with board games performed better at the die-rolling bluff game than children who had not played board games as frequently. More definitive evidence would come from studies involving multiple, diverse deceptive tasks. To address developmental concerns, these studies must be conducted across numerous age levels. Evidence from nonverbal decoding studies (DePaulo & Rosenthal, 1979a) and other very different developmental domains (cf. Werner, 1957) strongly suggests that skills will become more highly differentiated with age.

Children's Use of Nonverbal Cues in Deceiving: Previous Research

Like the research on children's detection of deception, most studies of children's skills and strategies in deceiving have focused on the use of visual nonverbal cues—usually facial cues and sometimes body cues. Morency and Krauss's study (this volume) involved first and fifth graders who watched pleasant and unpleasant slides and pretended to be watching just the opposite type of slide on half of the trials. Parents and peers then rated the deceptiveness of each trial. Fifth graders fooled their peers on both types of trials. First graders fooled their peers only when viewing the unpleasant slides; when viewing the pleasant slides, their peers were able accurately to determine when they were lying and when they were telling the truth. The child liars were not quite so successful at deceiving the parent judges: parents could detect the first graders' deception on both the pleasant and the unpleasant slides, and they could detect the fifth graders' deception when they were viewing the pleasant slides.

According to Ekman and Friesen's theory of leakage and deception (1969), senders should be more able and more motivated to control facial cues than body cues. This is because senders receive more fine-grained internal feedback from their facial musculature than from their body movements, because they receive more external feedback about their facial expressions than about their body movements (e.g., people tend to comment on each other's facial expressions), and because the face has a better sending capacity than the body (i.e., it can send more different kinds of messages, more quickly). One might expect that, with age, children would become relatively more adept at controlling their facial expressions, compared to their body movements and postures. Feldman and White (1980) tested this hypothesis with children ranging in age from 5- to 12-years-old. The children sampled good- and bad-tasting drinks and for half of the trials tried to convince the experimenter that the good drink actually tasted bad or vice versa. One camera recorded subjects' facial expressions while another simultaneously recorded their body movements from the neck down. Undergraduate observers then judged the degree of deceptiveness of each clip. For girls, the results were exactly as predicted: with age, their facial expressions become less and less revealing of deception while their body communication becomes more transparent. Unexpectedly, the opposite pattern tended to occur for boys: their deceptiveness becomes more and more obvious, with age, to observers who viewed their faces, while their bodily expressed deceit tended to become somewhat better concealed. Although Feldman and White (1980) entertained numerous hypotheses to account for these results (socialization differences, differences in the amount of guilt experienced by boys vs. girls; differences in the judges' ability to understand face and body cues of girls vs. boys), all await empirical testing.

In the Morency and Krauss (this volume) and Feldman and White (1980) studies, judges rated the deceptiveness of the senders. In most other studies, judges rated the senders' affects or attitudes. These latter studies are particularly informative with regard to the strategies used by children at various ages in their attempts to deceive. Based on the literature, three strategies seem particularly important. The first strategy is perhaps no strategy at all. Its occurrence is indexed by a pattern of readability or leakage—when senders are pretending to feel a certain affect, their true affect "leaks" out, and the judges are not fooled. For example, a child pretending to like a bad-tasting drink would be accurately perceived as liking the drink less than when she or he was actually sampling a good-tasting drink. A second strategy involves a naturalistic reproduction of the simulated affect. When utilized successfully, the sender would be perceived as liking the drink just as much when only pretending to like it as when the sender actually did like the drink. The last strategy might be called exaggeration, augmentation, or "hamming." When "hams" pretend to like a bad-tasting drink, they are perceived as liking the drink even more when they actually do like it.

Feldman, Jenkins, and Popoola (1979) used a drink-tasting paradigm in which children sipped good- and bad-tasting drinks but always tried to convince the experimenter that the drink tasted good. Undergraduate observers rated how much the child *really* liked each drink. The results were clear and straightforward. The deception attempts of the youngest subjects were readily apparent to observers—that is, the first graders leaked. The seventh-graders' strategy was naturalistic reproduction—they appeared just as pleased when the drinks tasted bad as when they tasted good. The oldest subjects (college students) were hams —they appeared to like the bad-tasting drink even more than the good-tasting drinks. An earlier aforementioned Feldman study involving third graders (Feldman et al., 1978) also showed that very young grade school liars leaked their true affects. The subjects, acting as tutors for other children who were performing well or poorly, were instructed to give uniformly positive and encouraging feedback, regardless of the actual quality of the tutee's performance. Other third graders, when judging the videotapes of the tutors' facial expressions, could tell that the tutors were less pleased with their student when the student had failed than when he or she had performed well. Feldman and his colleagues also pinpointed some of the particular behaviors that varied systematically under conditions of truth vs. deceit: when lying (i.e., when the tutors actually were *dis*pleased with their tutees), tutors smiled less, showed more mouth displeasure, and paused more than when telling the truth.

Allen and Atkinson (1978) used a different paradigm with slightly older subjects. Fourth and fifth graders listened to easy or difficult lessons, and tried to "trick" a teacher into believing that they completely understood the difficult lesson or did not understand at all the very easy lesson. Undergraduate observers, who were not informed that the children were sometimes lying, rated the degree to which the children seemed to understand each lesson. These fourth and fifth graders succeeded in fooling the observers, who rated them as understanding the lesson more when they were feigning comprehension than when they were feigning noncomprehension. However, since there were no conditions in which subjects deliberately tried to convey their actual degree of understanding, it is not clear whether these subjects were using a naturalistic reproduction strategy or a hamming strategy.

Earlier we described some of the skills that might be involved in successful deceiving. Other findings reported in studies of children's deception are relevant to some of those speculations. For example, we suggested that successful liars need to resist compelling cues in the immediate environment. Consistent with this suggestion, Morency and Krauss (this volume) found that first graders who were especially good encoders of spontaneous expressions (i.e., children who are naturally very responsive facially) were especially poor at masking their deception (when viewing unpleasant stimuli). We also suggested that effective deceivers are people who should be able to encode various affects out-of-context. Morency and Krauss's findings were again supportive: children who were particularly adept at deliberately producing particular nonverbal expressions tended to be successful deceivers (when viewing pleasant stimuli).

We have argued that skill at deceiving presupposes an awareness of the interpersonal consequences of one's nonverbal (and verbal) behavior (e.g., that senders are held responsible for many of their expressive behaviors, that such behaviors are interpreted by others and influence others). Senders who are aware of the interpersonal implications of nonverbal behaviors and who can effectively control their nonverbal expressions might regulate their facial expressions differently when their communications can be seen and heard, compared to when they can only be heard. Two of Feldman's studies provided data relevant to this formulation. In his tutoring simulation (Feldman et al., 1978), tutors either faced their tutees or were seated facing away from their tutees. In this study there were no differences in the third graders' communications across the two conditions. In the drink-tasting study involving first graders, seventh graders, and college students (Feldman et al., 1979), subjects described their reactions to the drinks either to the experimenter (public condition) or to a tape recorder (private condition). In this study, judges' ratings differentiated truth from deceit more strongly in the public than in the private condition. Also, subjects (particularly the females) appeared more pleased overall in public than in private. However, none of these effects increased (or decreased) with age. To clarify these findings, future research designs should allow for the independent assessment of children's motivation to monitor their nonverbal behaviors and their ability to do so. Also, children should be given ample opportunity to implement innovative communicative strategies. In the tutoring study, for example in which tutors simply said "good" in response to their tutee's answers, there was less room for creative regulation of facial expressions than in the drink-tasting study, in which the deceivers answered a number of different questions about each drink. Finally, future investigations should measure children's communicative behaviors across all channels. Perhaps children cannot communicate different messages in different channels; if this is true, then affects that are expressed vocally will also be expressed facially, even if no one is present to observe the facial expressions. Or, perhaps communicative effort comes in finite, fixed amounts for children; thus, if they try hard to control their vocal communications, their facial expressions will be left unguarded. Feldman and White's (1980) finding that successful facial deception co-occurs with unsuccessful bodily concealment (and vice versa) is consistent with this latter formulation.

Personal and Interpersonal Consequences of Skill at Deceit

At this point we feel we should acknowledge that we may have offended certain readers by our somewhat cavalier attitude toward children and deception. In discussing children's mendacity and their uncovering of others' falsehoods we have primarily used the language of "abilities" and "skills" rather than of "morals," "virtues," or "interpersonal respect and trust." At times, we may even seem to have implied that good liars and lie detectors should be commended for their talents. The question we face now is, "Should we apologize?"

There are many ways to approach such a difficult question. One could, for example, consider whether the practice of deceit erodes the moral fabric of a society. We will leave those kinds of questions to the philosophers (see, for example, Bok, 1980, and Scheibe, 1980). Instead, we will assume a psychological and empirical perspective and ask, "What are the personal and interpersonal consequences of detecting lies and telling lies?"

We will tackle the detection question first. Let us assume that most of the time when people tell lies, they would prefer that their insincerity *not* be discovered. Observers who are skilled at detecting deceit may suffer worse interpersonal consequences than those who are not blessed with this particular talent; for example, they may have fewer friends and feel less satisfied with the relationships that they do have.

Suggestive evidence supportive of this point of view comes from a series of studies of sex differences in the use of a "politeness" strategy in nonverbal communication (Rosenthal & DePaulo, 1979a, b). The premise of the politeness research was that different sources of nonverbal cues or kinds of cues (e.g., face, body, and tone of voice cues; discrepant cues) vary in leakiness (e.g., the degree to which they reveal affects that senders might be trying to hide). The major finding of this research program was a sex difference in the accuracy with which these various cues were decoded. While females tend to surpass men in their accuracy at understanding nonverbally communicated affects, their decoding advantage decreases as the cues become more leaky. Also, in decoding messages in which several different cues communicate conflicting emotions, females (more than males) trust the more overt and less leaky cues. It is as if females are politely refraining from reading just those cues that the senders would prefer to remain unnoticed. In the DePaulo et al. (in press) study described earlier, for example, females were relatively better than males at differentiating *honest* liking from *honest* disliking; in detecting deception, however, the females were not at all superior to the males. Further, there is evidence from a study involving purely nonverbal decoding tasks that this sex difference in politeness increases with age (Blanck, Rosenthal, Snodgrass, DePaulo, & Zuckerman, 1981).

More relevant to the present discussion is the evidence suggesting that there are social costs to reading unintended messages. In a sample of high school students, both males and females who were especially skilled at reading covert cues were rated by their teachers as less popular and less socially sensitive than other students who showed the politeness pattern of superiority at reading overt (nonleaky) cues. This result was slightly more characteristic of the females than the males. For a sample of college students (though not for the high school sample), similar findings were obtained based on self-ratings; that is, students who were especially skilled at reading unintended messages felt less satisfied with the quality of their interpersonal relationships (Rosenthal & DePaulo, 1979a, b).

The available evidence thus suggests that skill at uncovering deceit is at least in some sense not such a good thing. For one thing, it might cause social friction. A more naive approach to decoding deceit—namely, taking messages at face value—may have its advantages. This unsuspecting approach may in some circumstances be the easiest, quickest, and safest way to deal with the many complex and multileveled affective messages that people sometimes convey. Seeing only what you are supposed to see might be simpler not only cognitively but also emotionally. People who begin to doubt external appearances are first of all going to experience more uncertainty. They may also feel guilt about their suspiciousness and lack of trust; and finally, they might find out something about another person's feelings toward them that they might be much happier not knowing (cf. DePaulo, 1981).

However, we do not deny that there are circumstances under which perceivers are much better off deciphering the truth; for example, when the communicator might act in a way that will be harmful, insulting, or damaging, and knowledge of the communicator's true feelings can be used to prevent the harmful actions. We also believe that in certain professions, such as psychiatry and medicine, sensitivity to true, but covered-up, feelings might be especially beneficial.

Can we make a similar case that skill at deceiving is most often (though not always) socially hazardous? We think that predictions are less straightforward for this issue. (Also, there are less relevant data.) Consider, for example, the tale of the emperor's new clothes. This typifies the folklore of children as occasionally unselfconsciously and brutally honest. Children are sometimes especially notable not for the lies that they do tell, but for those that they do not tell. When children are young and cute enough, this forthrightness is usually excused as innocent or even adorable. However, when children get old enough to be accountable for courtesy, parents and other authority figures begin to regard such frankness as socially embarrassing. At this point, it is costly for children *not* to tell lies.

Other kinds of lies are rewarded by peers rather than parents. For example, in delinquent gangs, children who can con a police officer earn status, prestige, and the adoration of their fellow members. For this young conniver to reap such rewards, it is important not only that the lie be told, but that it be told well (convincingly). This is true for many categories of deceit, i.e., the interpersonal consequences depend upon whether the lie is discovered.

The likely interpersonal ramifications of deceit might be conceptualized in terms of Linkskold and Walters' (Note 3) multiple classification of deceptive intents. Deceivers who are caught lying probably suffer negative interpersonal consequences if they intended to harm the target of the lie or if they were attempting to benefit themselves by their deceit. More positive social outcomes might accrue to the liar who was trying to help the target, particularly if the lie involved some possibility of risk or harm to the liar. Even in these instances, however, the consequences may not be entirely positive. The target of the lie might resent any dishonesty, even well-intended white lies or misrepresentations. Too, the recipient of a helpful lie might experience other negative affects that sometimes accompany the receipt of aid, such as an aversive state of indebtedness (cf. Fisher, DePaulo, & Nadler, 1981; Greenberg, 1980).

In keeping with our discussion of the personal and interpersonal correlates of skill at detecting deceit, it is possible that skill at deceiving others carries different implications for females than for males. The one relevant empirical finding is consistent with this hypothesis: in Braginsky's (1970a) study in which children were offered a nickel for each bitter cracker they could convince a peer to consume, the children who felt most uncomfortable after the interaction were the successful girls and the unsuccessful boys.

Summary

Research on children's ability to detect lies and to deceive is meager. From the handful of studies that have been reported, the following conclusions can be drawn. (1) Studies involving only facial expressions as stimuli suggest that prior to adolescence, children's ability to distinguish deception from truth along the dimension of deceptiveness hovers near chance. Accuracy is somewhat better for the decoding of particularly revealing targets (e.g., first-graders) and for judges who are especially skilled at role-taking. (2) In a study in which older subjects were given access to both verbal and nonverbal cues, subjects at every age level (sixth graders, eighth graders, tenth graders, twelfth graders, and college students) perceived feigned expressions of liking as less positive than sincere expressions of liking, and feigned expressions of disliking as less negative than the honest expressions of disliking. The three oldest groups also discriminated truth from deception by their "mixed feelings" ratings—they perceived the speakers as having more mixed feelings when they were lying than when they were telling the truth. However, only the twelfth graders and college students perceived the dishonest messages as more deceptive than the honest messages. There were also systematic changes, with age, in the kinds of messages that subjects perceived as deceptive. At the younger age levels, subjects judged expressions of negative affect as more deceptive than expressions of positive affect; however, among the older subjects, this trend reversed and subjects judged expressions of positive affect to be relatively more deceptive than expressions of negative affect. (3) First graders, it appears, cannot tell a lie. When they attempt to do so, their underlying affect leaks out, and the fact that they are lying is obvious to their parents and sometimes even to their peers. Third graders have trouble, too, in much the same way—their true feelings leak. There seems to be notable improvement by fourth or fifth grade. These children can fool their peers and adult strangers, and sometimes they can even fool their parents. Between the ages of 5 and 12, girls become increasingly adept at masking their deception facially (though their body movements become more revealing). The reverse trend tends to occur for boys. Seventh graders succeed at deceiving by using a strategy of trying to convey the feigned affect with the same degree of intensity as when it naturally occurs under conditions of truth. College students are also facile deceivers, an outcome they achieve by "hamming" (exaggerating the dissimulated affect.)[1]

It was speculated that children learn and practice many of their deceptive abilities through their participation in card games, board games, party games, and sports. It was also suggested that there may be numerous interpersonal contexts in which it is socially beneficial to be a good liar but a poor lie detector.

Acknowledgment. Preparation of this chapter was supported by grants from the University of Virginia Research Council and the National Institute of Mental Health to the first author. The second author was supported by a National Science Foundation fellowship.

Reference Notes

1. Feldman, R. S. & White, J. B. Children's decoding ability and role-taking skills. In C. J. Patterson (Chair), *Perspectives on the development of nonverbal behavior*. Symposium presented at the meeting of the Society for Research in Child Development, Boston, April 1981.
2. Kotsonis, M. *Children's interpretations of conversationally-implied meanings*. Unpublished doctoral dissertation, University of Virginia, 1980.
3. Linkskold, S. & Walters, P. S. *Utilitarian standards for the acceptance of lying*. Unpublished manuscript. Ohio University, 1981.
4. Nachamie, S. *Machiavellianism in children: The children's Mach scale and the bluffing game*. Unpublished doctoral dissertation, Columbia University, 1969. (Cited in Christie & Geis, 1970).

References

Abramovitch, R. Children's recognition of situational aspects of facial expressions. *Child Development*, 1977, *48*, 459-463.

Abramovitch, R. & Daly, E. M. Inferring attributes of a situation from the facial expressions of peers. *Child Development*, 1979, *50*, 586-589.

Allen, V. L. & Atkinson, M. L. Encoding of nonverbal behavior by high-achieving and low-achieving children. *Journal of Educational Psychology*, 1978, *70*, 298-305.

Bates, E. *Language and context: The acquisition of pragmatics*. New York: Academic Press, 1976.

---

[1] The one exception to these findings comes from a drink-tasting study involving Korean first graders, seventh graders, and college students (Feldman, 1979). In this study, only the seventh grade females leaked. The males used a hamming strategy at every age level, and the strategy became more exaggerated with age. Female first graders also used hamming, while the college students used the natural reproduction strategy. While the details of the findings are in need of further explication, one general conclusion appears to be that the Korean subjects were better able to control their facial expressions than were the American subjects.

Berko Gleason, J. Code-switching in children's language. In T. E. Moore (Ed.), *Cognitive development and the acquisition of language*. New York: Academic Press, 1973.

Blanck, P. D., Rosenthal, R., Snodgrass, S. E., DePaulo, B. M., & Zuckerman, M. Sex differences in eavesdropping on nonverbal cues: Developmental changes. *Journal of Personality and Social Psychology*, 1981, *41*, 391-396.

Bok, S. On lying. *Berkshire Review*, 1980, *15*, 7-14.

Braginsky, D. D. Machiavellianism and manipulative interpersonal behavior in children. *Journal of Experimental Social Psychology*, 1970, *6*, 77-99. (a)

Braginsky, D. D. Parent-child correlates of machiavellianism and manipulative behavior. *Psychological Reports*, 1970, *27*, 927-932. (b)

Christie, R. & Geis, F. L. *Studies in machiavellianism*. New York: Academic Press, 1970.

DePaulo, B. M. Success at detecting deception: Liability or skill? *Annals of the New York Academy of Sciences*, 1981, *364*, 245-255.

DePaulo, B. M., Jordan, A., Irvine, A., & Laser, P. S. Age changes in the detection of deception. *Child Development*, 1982, *53*, in press.

DePaulo, B. M. & Rosenthal, R. Age changes in nonverbal decoding as a function of increasing amounts of information. *Journal of Experimental Child Psychology*, 1978, *26*, 280-287.

DePaulo, B. M. & Rosenthal, R. Age changes in nonverbal decoding skills: Evidence for increasing differentiation. *Merrill-Palmer Quarterly*, 1979, *25*, 145-150. (a)

DePaulo, B. M. & Rosenthal, R. Telling lies. *Journal of Personality and Social Psychology*, 1979, *37*, 1713-1722. (b)

DePaulo, B. M., Rosenthal, R., Rosenkrantz, J., & Green, C. R. Actual and perceived cues to deception: A closer look at speech. *Basic and Applied Social Psychology*, in press.

DePaulo, B. M., Zuckerman, M., & Rosenthal, R. Detecting deception: Modality effects. In L. Wheeler (Ed.), *The review of personality and social psychology*. Beverly Hills, CA: Sage, 1980.

deVilliers, J. G. & deVilliers, P. A. *Language acquisition*. Cambridge, MA: Harvard University Press, 1978.

Ekman, P. & Friesen, W. V. Nonverbal leakage and clues to deception. *Psychiatry*, 1969, *32*, 88-105.

Ekman, P., Roper, G., & Hager, J. C. Deliberate facial movement. *Child Development*, 1980, *51*, 886-891.

Feffer, M. H. The cognitive implications of role-taking behavior. *Journal of Personality*, 1959, *27*, 152-268.

Feldman, R. S. Nonverbal disclosure of deception in urban Korean adults and children. *Journal of Cross-Cultural Psychology*, 1979, *10*, 73-83.

Feldman, R. S., Devin-Sheehan, L., & Allen, V. L. Nonverbal cues as indicators of verbal dissembling. *American Educational Research Journal*, 1978, *15*, 217-231.

Feldman, R. S., Jenkins, L., & Popoola, O. Detection of deception in adults and children via facial expressions. *Child Development*, 1979, *50*, 350-355.

Feldman, R. S. & White, J. B. Detecting deception in children. *Journal of Communication*, 1980, *30*, 121-129.

Fisher, J. D., DePaulo, B. M., & Nadler, A. Extending altruism beyond the altruistic act: The mixed effects of aid on the help recipient. In J. R. Rushton & R. M. Sorrentino (Eds.), *Altruism and helping behavior*. Hillsdale, NJ; Erlbaum, 1981.

Flavell, J. H. *Cognitive development*. Englewood Cliffs, NJ: Prentice-Hall, 1977.

Gardner, H., Kircher, M., Winner, E., & Perkins, D. Children's metaphoric productions and preferences. *Journal of Child Psychology*, 1975, *2*, 125-141.

Greenberg, M. S. A theory of indebtedness. In K. J. Gergen, M. S. Greenberg, & R. H. Willis (Eds.), *Social exchange*. New York: Plenum, 1980.

Hartshorne, H. & May, M. A. *Studies in deceit*. New York: Macmillan, 1928.

Kraut, R. E. Verbal and nonverbal cues in the perception of lying. *Journal of Personality and Social Psychology*, 1978, *36*, 380-391.

Kraut, R. E. Humans as lie-detectors: Some second thoughts. *Journal of Communication*, 1980, *30*, 209-216.

Kraut, R. E. & Price, J. D. Machiavellianism in parents and their children. *Journal of Personality and Social Psychology*, 1976, *33*, 782-786.

Littlepage, G. E. & Pineault, T. Verbal, facial and paralinguistic cues to the detection of truth and lying. *Personality and Social Psychology Bulletin*, 1978, *4*, 461-464.

Peevers, B. H. & Secord, P. F. Developmental changes in attribution of descriptive concepts to persons. *Journal of Personality and Social Psychology*, 1973, *27*, 120-128.

Piaget, J. *The moral judgment of the child*. New York: The Free Press, 1965.

Rosenthal, R. & DePaulo, B. M. Sex differences in accommodation in nonverbal communication. In R. Rosenthal (Ed.), *Skill in nonverbal communication*. Cambridge, MA: Oelgeschlager, Gunn & Hain, 1979. (a)

Rosenthal, R. & DePaulo, B. M. Sex differences in eavesdropping on nonverbal cues. *Journal of Personality and Social Psychology*, 1979, *37*, 273-285. (b)

Rosenthal, R., Hall, J. A., DiMatteo, M. R., Rogers, P. L., & Archer, D. *Sensitivity to nonverbal communication: The PONS test*. Baltimore, MD: The Johns Hopkins University Press, 1979.

Saarni, C. Children's understanding of display rules. *Developmental Psychology*, 1979, *15*, 424-429.

Scheibe, K. E. In defense of lying: On the moral neutrality of misrepresentation. *Berkshire Review*, 1980, *15*, 15-24.

Werner, H. The concept of development from a comparative and organismic point of view. In D. B. Harris (Ed.), *The concept of development*. Minneapolis: University of Minnesota Press, 1957.

Winner, E., Rosenstiel, A., & Gardner, H. The development of metaphoric understanding. *Developmental Psychology*, 1976, *12*, 287-297.

Zuckerman, M., DePaulo, B. M., & Rosenthal, R. Verbal and nonverbal communication of deception. In L. Berkowitz (Ed.), *Advances in experimental social psychology* (Vol. 14). New York: Academic Press, 1981.

CHAPTER SEVEN

Children's Nonverbal Encoding and Decoding of Affect

Nancy Lee Morency and Robert M. Krauss

The expression (encoding) and perception (decoding) of affect play critical roles in the individual's social and emotional development. For example, the ability to recognize the emotional state of others is an important component of social competence. Similarly, the ability to control one's own emotional expressiveness has important consequences for social development.

It is useful to distinguish between two types of affective encoding skills and their decoding counterparts: (1) *Spontaneous encoding*, in which an affective expression is elicited by some stimulus in the absence of any specific communicative intent. The complimentary decoding skill, *spontaneous decoding*, consists of the ability to recognize others' spontaneously encoded affects. (2) *Communicative encoding*, in which an affective expression is simulated for the purpose of communicating something about one's purported emotional state. *Communicative decoding* consists of the ability to identify such expressions.

It needs to be stressed that these two sorts of encoding and decoding are "ideal types." The expressions seen in everyday life are, for the most part, mixtures of the two. Nevertheless the distinction is useful because it draws our attention to the possibility that quite different sets of competencies may be involved in each. It seems generally to be assumed that emotional expressiveness involves a unitary underlying competency—that someone who is particularly expressive spontaneously ought also to be an unusually skillful simulator. But it is equally plausible to suppose that the individual who is high in spontaneous expressiveness will be just average or, conceivably, less good than average at simulating expressions. Parallel assumptions are made about the two corresponding decoding skills.

These distinctions become especially important when one considers deceptive affective communication. In such situations, an encoder attempts to convey that she/he is experiencing an emotion that is not actually genuinely felt. The decoder's task in such situations is to distinguish between expressed emotions that are genuinely felt and those that are simulated. As Ekman and Friesen have pointed out, "Most deceptive situations not only dictate the need to conceal one item of information but also to require the substitution of a false message" (Ekman & Friesen, 1969, p. 135). Thus affective deception often requires the supression of a spontaneously elicited affect and, simultaneously, the simulation of the affect one wishes to convey.

Although deception (which we define as communication intended to create in another a belief that the communicator regards as untrue) usually tends to be thought of as evidence of flawed character, more careful analysis reveals this to be an overly-simplistic view (Bok, 1979). Certainly some types of deceit are maliciously intended and can have a corrosive effect on interpersonal relations. Nevertheless, other sorts of deception seem to derive from precisely the opposite motivation and have a positive effect. Indeed, one can argue (as does Goffman, 1959) that affective deception is necessary to the maintenance of the social order. We often find ourselves required to feign delight and supress revulsion, to act confidently when we are fearful, to mute our expression of joy in triumph, and so forth. Consider the situation of an American with conventional eating habits who is invited to the home of a Japanese friend. On being offered an exotic delicacy such as raw octopus, politeness conventions and regard for a host's feelings might require the guest to dissimulate—or, to put it bluntly, to deceive. And note that in order to accomplish this deception successfully he must do two things: he must attempt to conceal expression of the revulsion that he feels; and, at the same time and to the extent he is capable of so doing, he ought to simulate an expression of a positive affect—if not unalloyed joy then at least pleasant anticipation. And while acts of this sort involve deception in a very real sense, it is difficult to imagine that the world would be better off without them.

While the literature on the encoding and decoding of affective expression is vast (see Harper et al., 1978, for a review), few studies have examined the relations among different encoding and/or decoding abilities. Of those that have, only a handful have used children as subjects. Levy (1964) found positive relationships between adults' vocal encoding and decoding of communicative expressions. Zuckerman, Lipets, Koivumaki and Rosenthal (1975) found a significant positive correlation for adults between the accuracy with which an individual's posed (i.e., communicative) facial expression could be identified and that individual's ability to identify the posed expressions of others. While the results of these studies indicate that good encoders are also good decoders, two other studies suggest that the opposite is true. Lanzetta and Kleck (1970) and Cunningham (1977) found significant negative correlations between spontaneous encoding and decoding. The

Cunningham study additionally found a negative correlation between the ability to encode and decode communicative expressions. Not surprisingly, other studies have reported zero-order correlations between communicative encoding and decoding (Osgood, 1966; Zaidel & Mehrabian, 1969). The studies cited employed a wide variety of procedures and it is possible that some of the conflicting findings are attributable to this, but it must be said that our knowledge on the relationship of encoding and decoding abilities is far from certain.

Fewer investigations have examined the relationship between spontaneous and communicative encoding or spontaneous and communicative decoding, but the findings appear to be more consistent. Zuckerman, DeFrank, Hall and Rosenthal (1976) found significant positive correlations between both the two encoding abilities and the two decoding abilities. While the design of the Zuckerman et al. (1976) study would have permitted the examination of encoding-decoding relationships for spontaneous and communicative expressions separately, these data are not reported; the correlation between combined (spontaneous plus communicative) encoding and decoding was found to be nonsignificant. It will be recalled that Cunningham (1977), on the basis of separate analyses, found significant negative correlations for the two types of encoding-decoding.

Given the sparseness of the adult literature in this area, it is not surprising that even less is known about the relations among these skills in children. Only a very few studies have addressed the question, and the methodology employed in some makes their results difficult to interpret. For example, Odom and Lemond (1972) and Hamilton (1973) attempted to ascertain the relationship between encoding and decoding skills, comparing kindergarteners and fifth graders in the former case and nursery school, second graders, and fifth graders in the latter. Both studies report that the development of productive capacities (encoding) lags behind receptive capacities (decoding), but since in neither study was encoding accuracy directly measured, the conclusion rests on shaky empirical grounds. A study by Buck (1975) compared spontaneous and communicative encoding in nursery school students and found them to be positively correlated. However, as with the two studies cited above, an indirect measure of encoding ability was employed (judges' ratings of an expression's appropriateness rather than the actual accuracy with which the expression could be identified), and it is not clear how the relationship should be interpreted. Alper (Note 1) examined spontaneous encoding and decoding in nursery school children and found the relation to be negative. (For a more detailed examination of this literature see Morency, Note 2). Finally, Daly, Abramovitch and Pliner (1981) examined the relationship between children's spontaneous decoding ability and their mother's spontaneous encoding and decoding abilities. Mothers who were good encoders tended to have children who were good decoders, but no relation was found between the decoding abilities of mothers and their children.

Over the last decade or so, the study of deceptive affective encoding and decoding has become a burgeoning research area (for reviews see Zuckerman, DePaulo, & Rosenthal, in press; Kraut, 1980). Yet, while there is good theoretical reason to believe that the encoding and decoding of affect and the encoding and decoding of deception are related phenomena, virtually no research has examined this relationship directly. Ekman and Friesen (1969) have suggested that some people are more effective deceivers than others—for example, those whose vocations require skill in communicating emotion. According to these authors, such people have a heightened awareness of the effect of their nonverbal behaviors on others and thus tend to make more convincing liars. Mehrabian (1971) has suggested that people who are skilled in interpersonal relations tend to be better at controlling their emotions and, as a result, are better at deception. While these conjectures seem plausible, they are presently unsupported by empirical evidence. Generally speaking, children's abilities both to deceive and to detect deception appear to increase with age (Feldman, Devin-Sheehan & Allen, 1978; Feldman, Jenkins, & Popoola, 1979; Feldman & White, 1980; DePaulo, Jordan, Irvine & Lasser, 1981).

The nature of the relationships among the various sorts of nonverbal encoding and decoding skills discussed above bears importantly upon the structure of the skills which underlie what has been termed "communication competence" (Krauss & Glucksberg, 1969). While we presently have available a fair amount of data on the encoding and decoding of nonverbal information, there is a serious lack of plausible explanatory models. To draw an analogy with a closely related area, for verbal communication we not only know a good deal about the development of children's performance capabilities (e.g., Glucksberg, Krauss, & Higgins, 1975), we also know a fair amount about the structure of the skills that underlie these capabilities at different ages. In the case of nonverbal communication, we are in a far less fortunate position. The present study is an attempt to fill in some of the gaps in our knowledge, by examining the relationships among different encoding and decoding skills in a cross-sectional developmental design. More specifically, among the questions that motivated our research were the following.

1. How does the ability of children to encode and decode various sorts of nonverbal information vary with their age?
2. In what ways are the different types of encoding skills related, and do these relationships vary with age? (Similarly for decoding skills.)
3. What are the relationships between encoding and decoding skills, and do these vary with age?
4. To what extent are children's encoding and decoding skills related to the decoding skills of their parents?
5. Are parents better able to decode the nonverbal communications

of their own children, compared to those of a randomly selected child?

Experimental Methodology and Findings

Our study was run in three phases: an *encoding* phase, a *child's decoding* phase, and a *parent's decoding* phase. In each phase, subjects performed three different tasks. The three phases, and the sequence of tasks within phases, are illustrated schematically in Figure 7-1.

In phase one, subjects (first and fifth grade students drawn from two public schools in northern New York state) viewed and rated the pleasantness of 10 affect-inducing slides while their facial expressions were covertly videotaped. The procedure is virtually identical to that employed by Buck (1975) and his colleagues. Next, subjects were video-

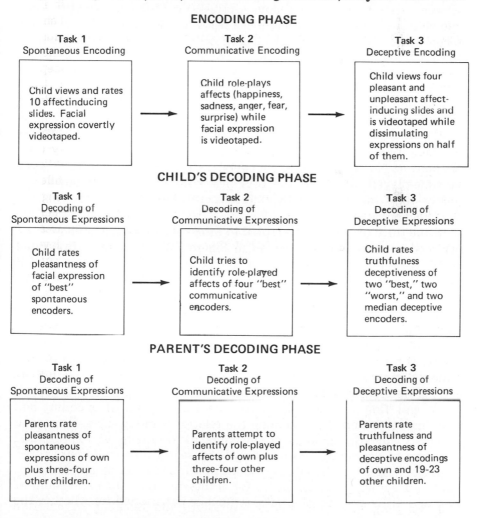

Figure 7-1. Three Experimental Phases.

taped while role-playing five primary affects (happiness, sadness, surprise, fear, and anger). Finally, each subject was shown four pleasant and four unpleasant affect-inducing slides similar to those used in the first task and instructed to dissimulate expressively on half of them—that is, to appear as though two of the pleasant slides were unpleasant and conversely for two of the unpleasant slides.

In the second phase of the study, we attempted to assess the decoding abilities of our subjects, We determined the two best spontaneous encoders in the first and fifth grades, the two best communicative encoders in each of the two grades, and the best, worst, and the median deceptive encoders in each grade of one of the two schools from which subjects were drawn. Selection was based on the accuracy achieved by a panel of undergraduate judges who viewed the videotapes and rated the pleasantness of the spontaneous expressions, tried to identify each role-played expression, and rated the truthfulness-deceptiveness of each deceptive encoding. These selected encodings were then edited onto a master videotape for use in the decoding phase of the experiment.

In the decoding phase, a total of 44 first graders and 40 fifth graders, approximately evenly divided between females and males, all of whom had participated in the first phase, attempted to decode the encodings on the master tape. These children were drawn from the second school, to eliminate any possible effects of familiarity. As is indicated in Figure 7-1, they first rated the pleasantness-unpleasantness of the expressions of the four best spontaneous encoders; next they attempted to identify the role-played affects of the four best communicative encoders; and finally they rated the truthfulness-deceptiveness of the six selected deceptive encoders.

In the third phase, we attempted to assess the decoding ability of our subjects' parents. As in indicated in Figure 7-1, the parents first rated the pleasantness-unpleasantness of the spontaneous expressions of their own child, plus those of three or four of their child's classmates. Next they attempted to identify the role-played expressions of their own and three or four other children. Finally, they rated the truthfulness-deceptiveness and also the pleasantness-unpleasantness of the deceptive encodings of their own child plus those of all of his or her same-sexed classmates. A total of 13 fathers and 33 mothers participated. Because preliminary analyses revealed no differences in accuracy between fathers and mothers, their judgments are combined in the results to be reported.

We will first present results for the three types of encoding and decoding skills and then examine the relations among them. How good are first and fifth graders as encoders of spontaneous expressions? One way of answering this question is by seeing how well their expressions can be decoded by adults who are presumably competent decoders. Table 7-1 shows accuracy scores for adults decoding the expressions of first and fifth graders; the data is further partitioned by whether the

Table 7-1. Mean Accuracy Scores of Children's Encoding of Spontaneous Expressions.

Decoder	Encoder	
	First Grade	Fifth Grade
Own Parents	0.18	0.41
Other Parents	0.28	0.39

decoder is decoding the expressions of his or her own child or those of another child. The accuracy scores are product-moment correlations computed between the child's pleasantness rating of an affect-inducing slide and the judge's rating of the child's facial expression. While the average magnitude of these values is small, overall they depart significantly from a zero-order correlation. We can conclude that the spontaneous expressions of both first and fifth graders can be decoded better than chance accuracy, although fifth graders are significantly better encoders than first graders. Interestingly, children are not reliably better encoders of spontaneous expressions for their own parents, compared to a randomly selected parent.

How well can these same children *decode* spontaneous expressions? Table 7-2 displays mean accuracy scores of first and fifth graders decoding the expressions of other first and fifth grade encoders. While these correlations overall depart significantly from zero, it is clear that both first and fifth graders have considerable difficulty decoding the expressions of first graders, despite the fact that the encodings they saw were selected as particularly good ones. The performance of fifth grade decoders is marginally superior to that of first graders. Both first and fifth graders are considerably better able to decode the spontaneous expressions of fifth grade encoders.

In comparison, first and fifth graders are substantially better both as encoders and as decoders of communicative or role-played expressions. Table 7-3 displays the number of correct identifications out of five made by parents of the encoders, as compared to other parents. The results depart significantly from a guessing probability of 20%. Note again that fifth graders overall are better encoders than first graders. However, in contrast to the findings for spontaneous expressions, chil-

Table 7-2. Mean Accuracy Scores of Children's Decoding of Spontaneous Expressions.

Decoder	Encoder	
	First Grade	Fifth Grade
First Grade	0.12	0.66
Fifth Grade	0.17	0.80

Table 7-3. Mean Number of Correct Identifications of Children's Encoding of Communicative Expressions.

	Encoder	
Decoder	First Grade	Fifth Grade
Own Parents	2.80	3.38
Other Parents	2.54	3.05

dren's communicative expressions are more accurately decoded by their own parents than by other parents. Children's decoding of selected communicative expressions was also quite good. Table 7-4 displays the results for first and fifth grader decoders. In all conditions, performance is significantly more accurate than chance, but the difference in performance between first and fifth grade decoders is not.

Our data on the encoding and decoding of deception required two different sorts of analyses. The first type of analysis employed a "detection index" as the dependent variable. In general, such indexes are calculated by taking the sum of the truthfulness ratings given to truthful (nondeceptive) stimulus segments and subtracting from it the sum of the truthfulness ratings given to deceptive segments. In a rough way, this index taps the observer's ability to discriminate between truthful and deceptive instances. An index was calculated for each parent through a two-step process. First, individual indexes were calculated for each child viewed by a particular parent. Second, the individual indexes were averaged to provide an overall detection index for that parent. Separate indexes were calculated for deception on pleasant and unpleasant stimuli. Thus, the index for pleasant (PL) deception was determined by taking the truthfulness rating made by a parent when the child was telling the truth about a pleasant stimulus and subtacting from it the truthfulness rating when the child was lying about a pleasant stimulus. Likewise, the index for unpleasant (UNPL) deception was formed by taking the parent's truthfulness rating when the child was telling the truth about an unpleasant stimulus and subtracting from it the truthfulness rating when the child was lying about an unpleasant stimulus. For both PL and UNPL deception, it was possible for the detection index (which we will refer to as the T-L score) to range from +4 to -4. A positive score

Table 7-4. Mean Number of Correct Identifications of Children's Decoding of Communicative Expressions.

	Encoder	
Decoder	First Grade	Fifth Grade
First Grade	3.07	3.98
Fifth Grade	3.08	4.31

indicates accurate discrimination of truth and lie, a negative score indicates that the rater has been deceived, and a score of zero indicates no discrimination of truthful and deceptive instances.

The second type of analysis employed the method of signal detection theory. Like the detection index, this technique allows one to examine subjects' ability to discriminate truthful from deceptive instances. But in addition, it allows one to distinguish response bias from sensitivity (Green & Swets, 1966). The measure of sensitivity is d', which is derived from receiver operating characteristic (ROC) curves. In the present study, ROC curves were formed by pooling parents' truthfulness ratings for each of the five points along the rating scale on the truthfulness measure. Similarly, ROC curves were formed by pooling parents' ratings on the 5-point pleasantness measure. Accurate discrimination was indicated by positive d' values, reverse discrimination by negative d' values, and no discrimination by d' values close to zero.

Table 7-5 presents adults' mean T-L scores both for the detection of pleasant stimuli and unpleasant stimuli. T-tests were used to determine whether the adults' T-L scores were significantly greater than zero. Adults were able to decode deception (that is, to discriminate truthful from deceptive expressions) of both first and fifth graders significantly better than chance when the deception involved stimuli that were pleasant. For unpleasant stimuli, adults could detect the deceptions of first but not fifth graders. In general, parents were better than other adults at detecting their child's deception.

A signal detection analysis allowed us to examine these data in a somewhat different way. Figure 7-2 shows the ROC curves for adults' ratings on the pleasantness measure; separate curves indicate ratings made when the children were telling the truth and lying. The d' values indicate that adults were able to discriminate pleasantness from unpleasantness but that they could not discriminate dissimulations. Thus, if a

Table 7-5. Mean T-L Scores and Significance Levels for Children's Encoding of Deception.

Decoder	Encoder	
	First Grade	Fifth Grade
PL Stimulus		
Own Parents	+0.750*	+0.541
Other Parents	+0.178*	+0.359***
UNPL Stimulus		
Own Parents	−0.500	+0.351
Other Parents	+0.243**	+0.027

*$p < .05$
**$p < .01$
***$p < .001$

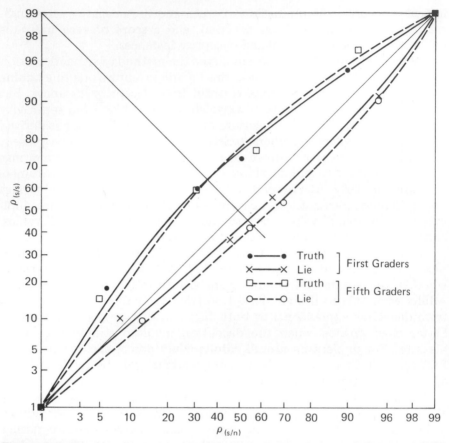

Figure 7-2. Receiver Operating Characteristic (ROC) Curves of First and Fifth Graders Parents' Ratings on the Pleasantness Measure.

child acted as though an unpleasant stimulus was pleasant, adults tended to rate the facial expression as pleasant; if the child pretended that a pleasant stimulus was unpleasant, adults rated the expression as unpleasant. In other words, both first and fifth graders were able to simulate appropriate facial expressions of emotion during deception.

For truthfulness ratings, ROC curves are shown separately for adults' ratings of first grade children (Figure 7-3) and for adults' ratings of fifth grade children (Figure 7-4). The ROC curves indicated that when viewing first graders, adults were able to discriminate lying from truth when deception concerned either pleasant or unpleasant stimuli. On the other hand, the ROC curves indicated that when viewing fifth graders, adults were able to discriminate lying from truth only when deception concerned reactions to pleasant stimuli. These findings are identical to those based on the detection index and confirm that the adults' responses represent true discrimination and are not a result of response bias.

Findings for children's detection of deception are shown in Table 7-6.

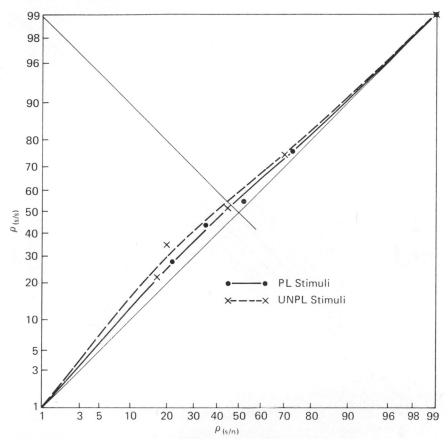

Figure 7-3. Receiver Operating Characteristic (ROC) Curves of First Graders Parents' Ratings on the Truthfulness Measure.

Mean T-L scores were calculated for children in the same way as was done for adults. Both first and fifth graders were able to detect deception of first graders on pleasant stimuli. However, neither group did better than chance with first graders on unpleasant stimuli or with fifth graders on either type of stimulus.

As concerns relations among different encoding and decoding skills, we examined five different classes of relations: (1) among parents' decoding skills, (2) among children's decoding skills, (3) among children's encoding skills, (4) between children's encoding and decoding skills, and (5) between parents' decoding skills and their children's encoding and decoding skills. Given the number of correlations we examined, one would ordinarily be concerned about the frequency of alpha errors—that is, false positives. To our disappointment, this was not a serious problem in our data: we found depressingly few significant correlations among the different categories of encoding and decoding skills, and those that we did find, with only a few exceptions, can

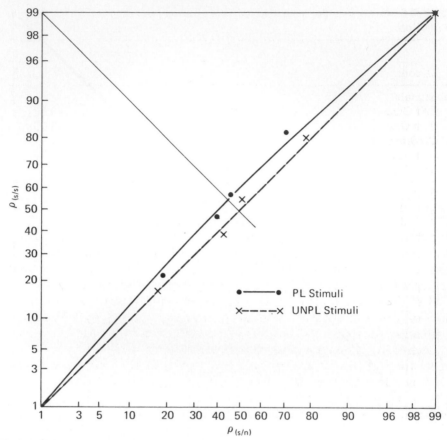

Figure 7-4. Receiver Operating Characteristic (ROC) Curves of Fifth Graders Parents' Ratings on the Truthfulness Measure.

be dismissed as uninteresting and probably unreliable. To be more specific, we found no relationships among parents' decoding scores: parents who were good decoders of spontaneous expressions were not especially good at decoding communicative expressions or deception, and so on. The same is fairly true (with exceptions to be noted below) for children, both within and across the different kinds of encoding an decoding. Nor were there sensible patterns of relations among a parent's decoding skills and the offspring's encoding or decoding abilities. Most striking was a failure to find a relation between children's scores for decoding deception on positive and negative stimuli, something we have always assumed to be a unitary ability.

The one interesting, and we think reliable, intertask relation we did find concerns the correlates of first-graders' deceptive skills. Children who were good encoders of spontaneous expressions (that is, who were spontaneously responsive facially) were poor deceivers on unpleasant stimuli; in contrast, children who were good encoders of communicative

Table 7-6. Mean T-L Scores and Significance Levels for Children's Decoding of Deception.

Decoder	Encoder	
	First Grade	Fifth Grade
PL Stimulus		
First Grade	+0.43*	-0.08
Fifth Grade	+0.81***	-0.03
UNPL Stimulus		
First Grade	-0.28	+0.07
Fifth Grade	-0.21	-0.07

*$p < .05$
**$p < .01$
***$p < .001$

expressions (that is, good at simulating expressions) tended to be good deceivers on pleasant stimuli. These relations were not found for fifth graders. Taken together with the finding that fifth graders' (but not first graders') deceptions on unpleasant stimuli are undetectable by adults, these results make sense. An important aspect of the socialization of nonverbal behavior involves teaching a child to supress the expression of negative affect. "Don't make a face when you are served spinach" and "Don't appear disappointed when your aunt gives you socks for Christmas" are typical of the sorts of admonitions a young child is likely to hear. It makes sense to suppose that the youngster who is unusually expressive will have more difficulty mastering this skill than one who is normally pokerfaced.

Implications

What can be concluded from these results? To begin with, we have shown that children in our two age groups can perform the sorts of encoding and, except for deception, decoding that our experimental tasks require. Generally speaking, it is clear that the older children are superior to their younger schoolmates—which in fact supports the theory that communication skills develop with age (see Glucksberg, Krauss, & Higgins, 1975, for a detailed review of this research).

In considering the development of communication skills, it is frequently assumed that older children are less egocentric and thus better able to take the role perspective of someone else (Flavell, Botkin, Fry, Wright, & Jarvis, 1968). By "taking the role of the other," they learn to view themselves as they appear to others, thereby making it possible for them to predict the effect their behavior will have on others. Thus in communicating their nonverbal behaviors, older children are more sensitive to the possible impact of these behaviors. Hence, they tend to express and perceive facial expressions more accurately and effectively than younger children.

However, it is not clear that this notion applies equally to spontaneous and communicative facial expressions of emotions. For communicative encoding, an emotional expression is simulated for the purpose of communicating one's purported affective state. Because individuals intend to communicate this affective state to others, they try to predict which of their nonverbal behaviors will convey this intention most effectively. For spontaneous encoding, an emotional expression is elicited by an affective stimulus in the absence of any specific communicative intent. Because there is no intent to communicate, individuals are not necessarily taking the role perspective of others into consideration when performing such behaviors. Therefore, it is not apparent that older children should be more spontaneously communicative than younger children simply because they tend to be less egocentric. While the ability to take the role perspective of others is certainly an important component of successful communication, the greater control that older children have over their nonverbal behaviors is also a critical factor. It may be that their superior control makes both their spontaneous and communicative expressions more informative than those of younger children.

Given the assumption that older children have greater control over their nonverbal behaviors than younger children, one would expect the older children to be more effective in their ability to deceive affectively. Because affective deception requires that the encoder suppress her/his spontaneous affect and at the same time simulate the appropriate affect, a successful encoder must be able to control both spontaneous and communicative facial expressions of affect. For unpleasant deception, the encoder must be able to suppress a spontaneous reaction of unpleasantness and at the same time simulate a pleasant response. On the other hand, the encoder of pleasant deception must suppress a spontaneously pleasant reaction while simulating an unpleasant one.

Feldman, Jenkins, and Popoola (1979), who examined unpleasant deception in first graders, seventh graders, and college students, found that seventh grade children and college students were able to deceive adults successfully while first grade children were not. Thus, the findings of Feldman et al. (1979) provide support for the assumption of an increase in the control of nonverbal behaviors with an increase in age.

The present study, which examined both pleasant and unpleasant deception, provides additional support for this assumption. For unpleasant deception, it was found that adults could detect first graders' deceptive facial expressions but not those of fifth graders. For pleasant deception, however, it was found that adults could detect both first and fifth graders' deceptive facial expressions. From a developmental viewpoint, then, it appears that children's abilities to control their deceptive expressions on pleasant stimuli lags behind their abilities to control deceptive expressions on unpleasant stimuli.

Several explanations are possible. One is that children learn earlier to simulate pleasant facial expressions compared to unpleasant ones. This explanation seems reasonable when we examine the conventions of politeness which seem to more often require children to simulate a pleasant affect than an unpleasant one. For example, it is not difficult to think of situations where children are expected to appear happy when they are really unhappy; but circumstances in which they are required to appear sad when they are actually happy (e.g., when a child consoles a friend for losing a contest he or she secretly hoped the friend would lose) seem rare.

Upon closer examination, it may not be the case that younger children are less able to simulate the appropriate expressions. In fact, the signal detection analysis of parents, ratings on the pleasantness measure revealed that both first and fifth graders were able to simulate the appropriate facial expressions for both pleasant and unpleasant deception. It may be that the lag is due to children learning earlier to *suppress* unpleasant facial expressions, compared to pleasant ones. That is, it actually might be the case that the disappointed young child who received socks for Christmas has an easier time hiding his or her disappointment from the aunt than does the young child who must hide his or her glee from the friend who lost the contest. The older child apparently is able to suppress both equally well.

Finally, it should be noted that another possible explanation for the lag exists, albeit a far less interesting one. We have been making the assumption of the equipotentiality of positive and negative stimuli. In other words, we have been assuming that the degree of pleasantness experienced by subjects in reaction to positive stimuli is equal to the degree of unpleasantness experienced by subjects in response to negative stimuli. It may be the case that this assumption is false. If so, the lag may simply be due to the fact that for our subjects the pleasant stimuli were more pleasant than the unpleasant ones were unpleasant. When examining children's pleasantness ratings of the deception slides, it was found that first graders' average departure from the midpoint was 1.89, while their average departure for unpleasant slides was 1.38. It was found that fifth graders' average departure from midpoint for pleasant slides was 1.56, while their average departure for unpleasant slides was 1.48. Unfortunately, it is difficult to determine what these extremity ratings actually mean since they are confounded by the two presentation conditions (truth and lie) in which ratings were made. Hence, children's ratings simply may reflect their differential ratings of pleasantness in response to stimuli viewed in the truth condition compared to the lie condition.

In considering the development of children's communication skills, mention should be made of the lack of sex differences found for the encoding and decoding of spontaneous and communicative expressions of emotions. These findings are consistent with those of earlier developmental studies (Buck, 1975; Gates, 1923; Gitter, Mostofsky, & Quincy, 1971; Hamilton, 1973) which report no sex differences in children's abilities to express and perceive facial expressions of emotions. In general, the lack of sex differences for children is surprising in view of adult studies which do report sex differences. Typically, studies with adult subjects have found that females are better decoders than males (Cunningham, 1977; Zaidel & Mehrabian, 1969; Zuckerman et al., 1975). For encoding, findings are less consistent. Thompson and Meltzer (1964) found females to be significantly better encoders than males, while Zaidel and Mehrabian (1969) found males significantly better than females. Zuckerman et al. (1975) and Zuckerman et al. (1976) found no differences between adult males and females in their ability to encode facial expressions of affect. The fact that developmental studies do not report sex differences suggests that the differences that do exist are learned, although they are not yet apparent in first and fifth grade children.

One question addressed in the present study is the role of parents in their children's acquisition encoding and decoding skills. One would expect that parents play a significant role in the development of their children's affective encoding and decoding skills, both by serving as models for encoding of communicative expressions and through the necessity of decoding the children's expressions.

Daly, Abramovitch, and Pliner (1981) who found a positive relationship between a mother's encoding ability and her child's decoding ability for spontaneous expressions, suggest a direct role on the part of mothers. They propose that mothers who are good encoders provide a good source of nonverbal information which enables their children to become skilled decoders, whereas mothers who are poor encoders provide a poor source of information for their children who, as a result, become less adept at decoding.

The present study did not examine the relationship between parents' encoding abilities and their children's decoding abilities. Rather, it examined the complementary relationship between a parent's decoding ability and his or her child's encoding ability. The present study also examined the relationship between a parent's decoding ability and his or her child's own decoding ability. It was proposed that positive relationships would be found for parents' decoding abilities and their children's encoding abilities. Similar to the Daly et al. study (1981), it was expected that parents who were good decoders would provide an accurate source of feedback which would aid their children in becoming good encoders. Likewise, parents who were poor decoders would provide a less accurate source of nonverbal feedback, making it less likely that their children would be able to develop the skills necessary to become good encoders.

However, the positive and significant relationships expected between parents' decoding abilities and their children's encoding abilities were not found. As stated earlier, no sensible patterns of relations could be found among a parent's skill and the offspring's skills. While it is probably the case that parents do play a role in the development of their children's encoding and decoding skills, it seems that this role is not as straighforward as one might expect.

The failure to find consistent relationships between the different sorts of performances is troubling. Let us acknowledge that there is more than one way not to find a correlation between two variables: one can use unreliable measures, employ a small sample, and so forth. In addition to being aesthetically unsatisfying, null results are intrinsically inconclusive. Yet our sample size was large relative to most studies done is this area, including some that have found the sorts of relationships which we did not find. The tasks we used were essentially the same as those used by others, and our subjects' performance on the various tasks generally exceeded chance levels.

Future Work

Perhaps it is most reasonable to conclude that there is a great deal that remains to be learned about the component skills that combine to produce competence in nonverbal communication. Indeed, it may turn out to be the case that the notion of a general competence is not particularly useful, as some have suggested in research with adults. For example, Levy (1964) posits the existence of a "general communication factor" within individuals to express and perceive nonverbal affect. Along the same lines, Zuckerman et al. (1976) argue that the ability to encode posed and spontaneous expressions involves the same set of nonverbal skills. Because the same set of skills is involved, decoding the two types of expressions should be positively related within individuals because it, too, involves the decoding of these same cues.

While such abilities may be positively related in adults, such relations may not yet be developed in children. It is not unlikely that children's nonverbal behaviors will become more consistent as they gain increasing control over these behaviors with age. Yet the point should be made that, in general, the present study provides no demonstrable evidence that there exists within individuals a general competence to encode and decode facial expressions of emotion.

Acknowledgment. This chapter is based on a doctoral dissertation submitted by the senior author to Columbia University. The research received support from Bell Laboratories, Murray Hill, N.J. Some of these data were presented as part of the symposium, "Developmental Aspects of Nonverbal Behavior," at the 1980 meetings of the American Psychological Association held in Montreal, Canada.

Reference Notes

1. Alper, S. *Nonverbal receiving ability in preschoolchildren*. Unpublished master's thesis, University of Connecticut, 1977.
2. Morency, N. L. *Nonverbal encoding and decoding of affect by first and fifth graders*. Unpublished doctoral dissertation, Columbia University, 1980.

References

Bok, S. *Lying: Moral choice in public and private life*. New York: Pantheon, 1978.
Buck, R. Nonverbal communication of affect in children. *Journal of Personality and Social Psychology*, 1975, *31*, 644-653.
Cunningham, M. R. Personality and the structure of the nonverbal communication of emotion. *Journal of Personality*, 1977, *45*, 564-584.
Daly, E. M., Abramovitch, R., & Pliner P. The relationship between mothers' encoding and their children's decoding of facial expressions of emotion. *Child Development*, 1981.
Ekman, P., and Friesen, W. V. Nonverbal leakage and clues to deception. *Psychiatry*, 1969, *32*, 88-106.
Feldman, R. J., Devin-Sheehan, L., & Allen, V. L. Nonverbal cues as indicators of verbal dissembling. *American Educational Research Journal*, 1978, *15*, 217-231.
Feldman, R. S. Jenkins, L., & Popoola, O. Detection of deception in adults and children via facial expressions. *Child Development*, 1979, *50*, 350-355.
Flavell, J. H., Botkin, R. T., Fry, C. L., Wright, J. W., & Jarvis, P. W. *The development of role-taking and communication skills in children*. New York: Wiley, 1968.
Gates, G. S. An experimental study of the growth of social perception. *Journal of Educational Psychology*, 1923, *14*, 449-462.
Gitter, A. G., Mostofsky, D. I., & Quincy, A. J. Race and sex differences in the child's perception of emotion. *Child Development*, 1971, *42*, 2071-2075.
Glucksberg, S., Krauss, R. M., & Higgins, E. T. The development of referential communication skills. In F. O. Horowitz (Ed.), *Review of child development research*, (Vol. 4). Chicago: University of Chicago Press, 1975.
Goffman, E. *The presentation of self in everyday life*. New York: Doubleday Anchor Books, 1959.
Green, D. M. & Swets, J. A. *Signal detection theory and psychophysics*. New York: Wiley, 1966.
Hamilton, M. L. Imitative behavior and expressive ability in facial expression of emotion. *Developmental Psychology*, 1973, *8*, 138.
Harper, R. G., Weins, A. N., & Matarazzo, J. D. *Nonverbal behavior: The state of the art*. New York: Wiley, 1978.
Krauss, R. M. & Glucksberg, S. The development of communication: Competence as a function of age. *Child Development*, 1969, *40*, 255-266.
Kraut, R. E. Humans as lie detectors: Some second thoughts. *Journal of Communication*, 1980, *30*, 209-216.
Lanzetta, J. T. & Kleck, R. S. Encoding and decoding of nonverbal affect in humans. *Journal of Personality and Social Psychology*, 1970, *16*, 12-19.
Levy, P. K. The ability to express and perceive vocal communication of feelings. In J. R. Davitz (Ed.), *The communication of emotional meaning*. New York: McGraw-Hill, 1964.

Mehrabian, A. Nonverbal betrayal of feeling. *Journal of Experimental Research in Personality*, 1971, *5*, 64-73.

Odom, R. D. & Lemond, C. M. Developmental differences in the perception and production of facial expressions. *Child Development*, 1972, *43*, 359-369.

Osgood, C. E. Dimensionality of the semantic space for communication via facial expression. *Scandinavian Journal of Psychology*, 1966, *7*, 1-30.

Thompson, D. F. & Meltzer, L. Communication of emotional intent by facial expression. *Journal of Abnormal and Social Psychology*, 1964, *68*, 129-135.

Zaidel, S. F. & Mehrabian, A. The ability to communicate and infer positive and negative attitudes facially and vocally. *Journal of Experimental Research in Personality*, 1969, *3*, 233-241.

Zuckerman, M., DeFrank, R. S., Hall, J. A., & Rosenthal, R. Encoding and decoding spontaneous and posed facial expressions. *Journal of Personality and Social Psychology*, 1976, *34*, 966-978.

Zuckerman, M., DePaulo, B. M., & Rosenthal, R. Verbal and nonverbal communication of deception. In L. Berkowitz (Ed.), *Advances in experimental social psychology* (Vol. 14). New York: Academic Press, in press.

Zuckerman, M., Lipets, M. S., Koivumaki, J. H., & Rosenthal, R. Encoding and decoding nonverbal cues of emotion. *Journal of Personality and Social Psychology*, 1975, *32*, 1068-1076.

Part Four

Discrepant Communication
Approaches to Nonverbal Behavior

Developing Strategies for Decoding "Leaky" Messages: On Learning How and When to Decode Discrepant and Consistent Social Communications

Peter D. Blanck and Robert Rosenthal

Introduction

Perhaps W. C. Fields' intense dislike of children stemmed from his experience that children were unable to appreciate his sarcastic and lampooning humor. After all, a comedian is only as funny as the strength of his audience's response. By definition, sarcastic humor expresses meaning contrary to what might be expected in a particular context. Similarly, feelings of ambivalence and attempts at deception also might lead senders, or comedians, to express different messages or affects in different verbal and nonverbal channels. This chapter is concerned with how and when children learn to interpret and understand these discrepancies among social messages, channels, or affects. In everyday life, children's and adults' interpretations, weighing, and "trusting" of these discrepant or "inconsistent" social messages certainly have implications for the development of satisfying interpersonal relations in general, to say nothing of the appreciation of sardonic comedians in particular.

In the past decade, several researchers have begun systematically to examine developmental changes in nonverbal decoding styles and skills in response to discrepant and consistent multichannel communications (for a review see DePaulo & Rosenthal, 1979a). A great deal of research has also been directed toward studying children's emotional responses to these inconsistent or discrepant social communications (e.g., Bugental, Love, Kaswan, & April, 1971). In this chapter we first summarize past research on how children learn to decode discrepant social messages. Next, we consider developmental changes in learning when to decode or interpret specific discrepant and consistent social messages. Finally, data collected by means of a new instrument, the Measure of Verbal and Nonverbal Sensitivity (MOVANS) Test, which was designed to provide a standardized instrument for the assessment of developmental changes in sensitivity to discrepant and consistent social messages in the verbal and nonverbal channels, will be discussed.

Learning How to Decode Discrepant Social Messages

In this section we summarize past research on how children learn to decode and interpret discrepant social messages as they grow older.

Infancy to Five Years Old

How and when do children learn to detect and decode discrepant events? Between seven and twelve months of age profound changes are taking place, some of which may indirectly enhance the infant's capacity to detect discrepant events. To name a few, during this period the infant shows (1) increased attentiveness to discrepant representations of a human's face (Kagan, Kearsley, & Zelazo, 1979), (2) increased non-reflexive inhibition in reaching for novel objects (Parry, 1973), (3) the beginnings of stranger and separation anxiety (Ainsworth, Bell, & Stayton, 1974), and the "universal fears" (Ekman, 1973), which may result from new and unfamiliar people and situations, (4) the growth of memorial competencies (Kagan, Kearsley, & Zelazo, 1979), and (5) some prelinguistic capacity for mapping elements from different sensory modalities that are judged by adults to be metaphorically similar (Ruff & Kohler, 1978; Wagner, Winner, Cicchetti, & Gardner, Note 8).

Perhaps the detection of discrepant events is determined not only by experience but also by these maturational developments in the young child. It is probably only when these maturational requirements are met (i.e., perhaps beginning at around eight months of age) that the infant can both interpret discrepant affect and apply its meaning to a social context. For example, it is not known whether infants are capable of "reweighting" nonverbal channels as the channels are perceived as discrepant, so as to gain more information about an encoder's true affect. If a young child or infant perceives a discrepancy between the mother's face and voice channels (e.g., the mother is smiling but is speaking in a very sad tone of voice), does the child give more weight to the affective quality of the voice because the voice is a less "controllable" channel? Recent evidence, based on over sixty studies with adults (Rosenthal & DePaulo, 1979a, b), has supported this hypothesis that the voice is indeed a less controllable or more "leaky" source of affect. However, we do not know if these affective weighting processes are learned through socialization, are innate to the young child, or both. An affective weighting process of this sort would certainly assist young children in detecting an encoder's true emotions and might be biologically adaptive.

There have been very few studies examining discrepant social communications in preschool children between the ages of one and five years of age. In an interesting series of studies, Volkmar, Hoder, and Siegel (1980) and Volkmar and Siegel (1979; this volume) presented discrepant and consistent communicative messages in the visual and auditory modalities, asking children either to approach an experimenter or to stay away. Children's responses to the requests that were discrepant across channels (e.g., a warm tone of voice saying "come here," but cold facial expressions indicating "stay away") were more variable, while all children approached when the experimenter was unambiguously inviting them to approach with positive affect displayed in one or both of the visual or auditory modalities. These results demonstrated that very young children are sensitive to, and wary of, these naturally presented multichannel discrepant social messages.

A more interesting result of the above series of studies bear on the relative impact, or weighting, of the visual and auditory channels when the information presented in these channels is discrepant. Consistent with the decoding strategy discussed earlier, the results showed that as the modalities became discrepant, children's responses tended to be more dictated by the auditory channel than by the visual channel. Evidently, children as young as one year of age are capable of differentially weighing or interpreting verbal and nonverbal discrepant social messages so as to gain information about an encoder's true affect.

Five to Sixteen Years Old

The results of studies with older children between the ages of 5 and 16 years of age which have examined skills and styles (e.g., weighting processes) in response to discrepant multichannel messages have provided evidence for increases with age in the detection and interpretation of discrepant social messages. Bugental, Kaswan, and Love (1970) employing pairings of discrepant verbal, video, and audio messages found that "joking" (e.g., sarcastic) messages (negative tone affect paired with positive video affect) were interpreted more negatively by children than by adults. These results suggested that these joking messages were not appreciated by and/or were more disturbing to young children relative to adults because of the differential weight children seemed to place on the negative audio portion of the message. This result, to be sure, would have further added to W. C. Fields' contempt for children.

Zuckerman, Blanck, DePaulo, and Rosenthal (1980) examined developmental changes in skill and style at decoding discrepant and nondiscrepant nonverbal cues. In this study children between the ages of 9 and 15 were administered the Nonverbal Discrepancy Test (DePaulo, Rosenthal, Eisenstat, Rogers, & Finkelstein, 1978), a standardized test for assessing individual differences in skill at recognizing inconsistences in nonverbal communications and differences in style in the weighting of video and audio cues when these channels present discrepant affects. This weighting strategy, style, preference, or bias, termed video primacy (DePaulo et al., 1978) suggests that in certain situations, adults are more influenced by video cues—particularly facial expressions—than by audio cues, a result emerging whether the video and audio components of a message are consistent or discrepant. Specifically, research has shown that judgments of consistent multiple-channel video plus audio cues were more similar to judgments of single-channel video cues than to judgments of single-channel audio cues (Berman, Shulman, & Marwit, 1976; Levitt, 1964; Rosenthal, 1966). Similarly, judgments of inconsistent or discrepant multiple-channel video plus audio cues were more in line with the video than with the audio component of the message (Bugental et al., 1970; DePaulo et al., 1978; Mehrabian & Ferris, 1967).

The results of Zuckerman et al.'s (1980) developmental examination of video primacy and discrepancy decoding accuracy showed that video primacy increased when face was contrasted with voice, but not when body was contrasted with voice. This pattern of results was consistent with the finding of greater overall increase in decoding accuracy for facial, relative to body, cues. It seems that the face develops into a major communication channel, relative to both the voice and the body.

In line with earlier findings (e.g., DePaulo & Rosenthal, 1979b), the results of the Zuckerman et al. (1980) study also indicated that sensitivity to consistent nonverbal communications is less differentiated at younger ages. That is, the differences in sensitivity to different affects and channels are less emphasized than they are at an older age. The increase in sensitivity to facial cues with age suggests that in comparison to older children, youngsters are relatively more influenced by less controllable channels, such as the body and the voice, and less influenced by more controllable channels, such as the face, thus paralleling the results reported by Rosenthal, Hall, DiMatteo, Rogers, and Archer (1979) and the results of children's responses to joking messages described by Bugental's earlier research.

Finally, turning to a consideration of extremely discrepant nonverbal messages, the results of the Zuckerman study (1980) showed some indication that relative to young children, older children treated these extremely discrepant nonverbal messages with greater caution. Specifically, whereas children below the age of 12 showed greater video primacy when the video and audio messages were extremely discrepant, children older than 12 did not show this pattern. As previously mentioned, DePaulo et al. (1978) speculated that people perceive extremely discrepant messages as indicative of deception or sarcasm and therefore may attend relatively more to the audio cues. It might be expected that this pattern would be emphasized more for older children. It appears that older children have developed some degree of distrust toward facial expressions when the expressions are accompanied by extremely discrepant vocal cues. Thus, it appears that as children grow older they put more weight on facial expressions under ordinary conditions of communication but put less weight on facial expressions under conditions of great channel discrepancy.

A recent study by Blanck, Rosenthal, Snodgrass, DePaulo, and Zuckerman (1982) examined longitudinal and cross-sectional age effects on accuracy of decoding discrepant nonverbal cues and video primacy. DePaulo and Rosenthal (1978) had shown that increases in nonverbal accuracy with increasing amounts of information were more pronounced for older than for younger children. They suggested that increasing efficiency with age in the utilization of information in nonverbal decoding tasks might be attributable to a growing information processing capacity, and this increase might be moderated by the amount or type of information that is available. Indeed, Case (1972) and Pascual-Leone (1970) have suggested that information processing capacity increases with age and can account for the growth of many cognitive-developmental skills.

In line with these suggestions concerning the growth of nonverbal accuracy with increasing amounts of information, Blanck et al.'s (1982) study found that increases in age, examined both longitudinally and cross-sectionally, were associated with increases in ability to decode nonverbal cues. More interestingly, the advantages of age were especially great for the decoding of discrepant nonverbal cues which involve interpreting complicated mixed channel messages. That is, relative to younger children, older children benefited more from the effects of retesting in terms of accuracy at decoding discrepant cues. It appears that abilities to decode discrepant, as opposed to consistent messages, do not develop at the same rate.

Another question of interest concerned longitudinal and cross-sectional changes in differential attentiveness to, or reliance on, various channels of nonverbal cues (e.g., video primacy). It was found that there was a tendency for all children to show less video primacy after retesting, and relative to younger children, older children displayed less body primacy (body compared to tone) after retesting. These results suggest that with practice, and as nonverbal cues become more discrepant, children display a tendency to rely more heavily on less controllable channels (i.e., tone) to gain information about an encoder's true affect. This effect of retesting and/or practice is greater for older than for younger children.

Finally, the Blanck et al. (1982) study replicated cross-sectionally the results of Zuckerman et al.'s (1980) study showing that relative to younger children, older children treat extremely discrepant messages with some caution. That is, older children, it appears, have developed some degree of distrust toward facial expressions when the expressions are accompanied by discrepant vocal cues, and retesting does not seem to affect this result differentially for the older or the younger children.

College Students and Adults

The findings obtained in examining children's sensitivity at interpreting and weighing discrepant communications parallel results obtained with adult subjects. In an early study on the decoding of inconsistent communications, Mehrabian and Wiener (1967) showed that overall, when the attitude communicated by the verbal content contradicted, or was discrepant with, the attitude communicated by a negative tone of voice, the effects of tone on inferred attitudes were stronger than the effects of verbal content. These findings support the results obtained with children showing that as social messages are perceived by decoders as discrepant, or inconsistent, more weight is given to less controllable channels to aid in inferring the true attitudes or affects of the sender.

In another more recent study with junior high school, high school, and college students, DePaulo et al. (1978) and DePaulo and Rosenthal (1979b), examined changes in modality (video) primary as a function of the degree of discrepancy of the channels comprising the multichannel message. The results showed that subjects attended relatively more to, or weighed more heavily in their judgments, the audio modality when the messages were very discrepant as compared to when the messages were only slightly discrepant. DePaulo and Rosenthal (1979b) suggest that as the channels comprising a multichannel communication become more and more discrepant, or inconsistent, adults and children tend to weight the affective meaning of the audio component of the message more heavily, relative to the video component. In support of this suggestion, recent evidence on the vocal characteristics of deceptive messages have shown that vocal cues differ in truthful and deceptive messages (Kraut, 1978; Krauss, Geller, & Olsen, Note 6).

Summary

Research has shown that children and adults are sensitive to inconsistencies in social messages. When individuals perceive these discrepancies in a message, they tend to rely more heavily on less controllable (more leaky) channels which are perceived to express the true underlying meaning of the message. This decoding strategy seems to be more characteristic of older, compared to younger, children. Interestingly, older children also benefit more from retesting and/or practice in terms of accuracy at detecting discrepant messages and, perhaps through socialization, have learned to be more cautious at decoding these discrepant communications.

Learning When to Decode Discrepant Social Messages

In this section we address the question of how children learn when to decode social messages. That is, we consider developmental changes in how children learn when it is socially appropriate to decode and interpret certain social messages.

A great deal of research has been directed toward studying the development of nonverbal skills in children (for reviews see Charlesworth & Kreutzer, 1973; DePaulo & Rosenthal, 1982), while, as we have suggested, relatively fewer studies have examined age changes in ability at decoding discrepant verbal and nonverbal messages. This section will consider the recently accumulating evidence suggesting that developmental changes in ability at decoding and interpreting verbal and nonverbal messages, particularly discrepant messages, is likely to be affected by socialization variables to which the growing child is exposed.

Learning When Not to Eavesdrop on Nonverbal Cues

Recently, the finding that females are superior to males in understanding nonverbal cues (Hall, 1978, 1979; Rosenthal et al., 1979) has been importantly qualified (Rosenthal & DePaulo, 1979a, b). Although females are in fact very much superior to males in decoding overt and intentionally communicated cues (such as cues from the face, which is a very controllable channel), they are less superior, or not superior at all, at decoding more covert, leaky, unintended, or inconsistent communications (such as cues from the body or the tone of voice). When different types of nonverbal cues were arranged from most controllable to least controllable (most leaky), women showed a systematic decrease in their superiority over men in going from the less to the more leaky channels. Rosenthal and DePaulo (1979a, b) suggested that these results might show that women were more polite or accommodating in their decoding of nonverbal cues. That is, perhaps women refrain from decoding effectively the less controllable cues of the encoder. The operation of this kind of politeness mechanism would be consistent with traditional sex role socialization standards.

The plausibility of the Rosenthal and DePaulo (1979a, b) hypothesis is strengthened by (a) the well-documented result that females are interpersonally more polite than men (LaFrance & Carmen, 1980; LaFrance & Mayo, 1978; Thorne & Henley, 1975; Weitz, 1976), and (b) the evidence suggesting that social relationships may suffer when people are especially skillful at decoding nonverbal messages that they were not intended to receive (Rosenthal et al., 1979; Rosenthal & DePaulo, 1979a, b; Zuckerman, Note 9). If it is in fact disruptive to smooth interpersonal functioning for a participant to "know too much" about the state of the other, then we would expect females to show relatively less advantage over men in decoding nonverbal cues when those cues are under less control of the sender and more likely to be inconsistent or unintended. Evidence based on over sixty studies supports these predictions (Rosenthal & DePaulo, 1979a, b).

A recent investigation by Blanck, Rosenthal, Snodgrass, DePaulo, & Zuckerman (1981) examined the developmental acquisition of females' nonverbal accommodation both cross-sectionally and longitudinally. We wanted to know whether women's greater social civility, which is evident in their decoding skills, is leashed through socialization. In other words, we wanted to know whether women have learned through socialization that there may be social hazards in being "too good" at decoding certain nonverbal cues.

The results of our cross-sectional analysis showed that as age increased, females lost significantly more and more of their advantage for the more leaky, or more covert, channels while they gained more and more of their advantage for the less leaky channels. The results of the longitudinal one year analysis supported those of the cross-sectional analysis. Specifically, during the year, women lost more and more of their advantage in the more leaky channels. These results suggest, consistent with a learning (i.e., socialization) interpretation, that as females grow older, they may become more nonverbally accommodating. Further, the findings suggest that females may learn through experience (e.g., from retesting, practice, and/or through maturation) that there may be social hazards in being "too good" at the decoding of leaked, discrepant, or unintended nonverbal cues. These developmental changes in females' nonverbal accommodation may be guided, in part, by the increase with age of females' awareness of traditional sex role standards. Evidently, as females grow older, they learn when it is socially appropriate to decode certain nonverbal communications.

Teaching People How to "Eavesdrop" on Nonverbal Cues

In another study, Blanck and Rosenthal (Note 1) examined the effects of practice in nonverbal sensitivity on responses to video (face and body) nonverbal cues. We administered two short versions of a standardized test of nonverbal decoding skill to the Harvard University Varsity and Junior Varsity Men's basketball teams during the course of the season. The two measures were designed to test (a) decoding accuracy of facial and body cues for two-second exposure clips of twenty everyday life situations, and (b) decoding accuracy of facial and body cues for very brief exposure times for these same situations (median length = 250 ms.).

Consistent with a learning interpretation and earlier experimental findings, we thought that practice in decoding nonverbal messages even without any feedback on the accuracy of one's interpretation, would improve nonverbal decoding skills (Blanck et al., 1981, 1982; Blanck, Zuckerman, DePaulo, & Rosenthal, 1980; Blanck & Rosenthal, Note 2; Rosenthal et al., 1979). In addition, the benefits of training might be different for easier, more controllable nonverbal cues (i.e., the normal exposure length) vs. more difficult, less controllable (more leaky) nonverbal cues (i.e., the brief exposure length).

We also explored the relationship between nonverbal decoding skills and basketball ability, particularly defensive basketball ability which may rely on an acute sensitivity to body cues. Specifically, in line with our predictions concerning the effects of socialization on ability to decode discrepant or leaky social communications, we wanted to know whether individuals who were relatively good at decoding nonverbal cues when those cues were under less control of the sender (i.e., body relative to facial cues), and more likely to be unintended than intended cues, were better basketball players.

In other words, if it is in fact disruptive to basketball abilities to pay too much attention to, or weigh too heavily, the more controllable nonverbal channels (i.e., the face), then we would expect better basketball players to show relatively more advantage over less expert basketball players in decoding these leaky messages (see also Blanck, Rosenthal, Snodgrass, DePaulo, & Zuckerman, 1981; Ekman & Friesen, 1969, 1974; Rosenthal & DePaulo, 1979a, b). Perhaps, as any basketball coach might suggest, better defensive players are less likely to be deceived or "faked out" because, instead of watching the opponent's face, these players are more attentive to the opponent's less controllable and less deceptive body cues (for reviews of modality effects in the detection of deception see DePaulo, Zuckerman, & Rosenthal, 1980; Zuckerman, DePaulo, & Rosenthal, 1981).

Consistent with the results of earlier findings (e.g., Rosenthal et al., 1979), practice with these test materials increased all participants' sensitivity to nonverbal stimuli. More interestingly, practice tended to affect decoding ability differently on the two nonverbal measures. Specifically, there was a tendency for practice to be associated with increased decoding accuracy on the relatively easier nonverbal measure (i.e., the normal exposure length), but to be associated with relatively decreased decoding accuracy on the more difficult nonverbal test (i.e., the brief exposure length). These results, obtained over a relatively short interval of several weeks, parallel the results mentioned earlier that suggest that individuals may learn from practice and/or socialization over longer periods of time (e.g., several years) that there may be social hazards to being too good at the decoding of more socially embarrassing, inconsistent, or more leaky nonverbal cues (Blanck et al., 1981).

These results may appear to contradict those of Zuckerman et al. (1980) described earlier, which showed that older children treated extremely discrepant nonverbal messages with greater caution than younger children. However, those results were obtained with children between the ages of 9 and 15, while these results were obtained with college age students. In addition, the Zuckerman et al. (1980) study with children dealt with the variable of video primacy while the Blanck and Rosenthal (Note 1) study with college students dealt with the variable of accuracy.

In line with our suggestion concerning the socialization of sensitivity to certain nonverbal cues, although the varsity and the junior varsity teams did not differ with respect to their overall level of decoding ability, the varsity was more accurate at decoding body cues, while the junior varsity team was more accurate at decoding facial cues. These results suggest that basketball skill is related to nonverbal decoding accuracy of the body. This relationship may be especially marked for defensive basketball skills which require sensitivity to body cues. This differential result for the two teams may be related to selection, socialization, and/or other learning factors which make better basketball players become more attentive to body cues, or alternatively, make more accurate decoders of the body become better basketball players, or both. At this point we can only speculate about these alternative directions of causality.

Summary

This section has examined the effects of sex and age on the development of skills and styles of decoding nonverbal communications. Our purpose has been to stimulate inquiry into how abilities of interpreting social messages may be influenced by childhood socialization. We know relatively little about how children learn to interpret social messages, and even less about when they feel it appropriate to employ these abilities. It remains for future research to examine the types of socialization variables that increase or decrease skills and styles in interpeting social messages.

Measuring the Development of Sensitivity to Discrepant and Consistent Verbal and Nonverbal Social Messages: The MOVANS Test

Overview

As we have suggested, several researchers have begun systematically to examine developmental changes in nonverbal decoding skills and styles in response to discrepant and consistent multichannel communications. However, this line of research has investigated accuracy in decoding discrepant and consistent auditory and visual *nonverbal* cues almost exclusively (Friedman, 1978, 1979). The verbal modality, on the other hand, has been relatively de-emphasized in studying these intermodality discrepancies and consistencies. This de-emphasis is surprising given that most theorizing about discrepant communications that we have reviewed in this paper has emphasized the discrepancy between verbal and nonverbal modalities (e.g., Bateson, Jackson, Haley, & Weakland, 1956). In addition, discrepancy between verbal and nonverbal channels would seem more obvious and easier to detect than discrepancy between two nonverbal channels. Perhaps it is also of greater social consequence (Goffman, 1974). Accordingly, a new instrument, the Measure of Verbal and Nonverbal Sensitivity (MOVANS) Test, was designed to provide a standardized instrument for the assessment of sensitivity to discrepant and consistent messages in the verbal and nonverbal channels (Blanck & Rosenthal, Note 3).

The MOVANS Test was broadly conceived to investigate verbal and nonverbal decoding styles and skills in the processing discrepant and consistent multichannel communications. Three types of variables can be examined: (1) decoding accuracy, or subject's ability to identify the degree of positivity and dominance in verbal, face, body, and tone of voice cues; (2) discrepancy accuracy, or subject's ability to recognize the degree of discrepancy between paired multichannel messages; and (3) modality primacy, or the extent to which subjects weigh, or are influenced by, perceptual information from the verbal, face, body, or tone modalities when the channels comprising the multichannel message conflict (DePaulo et al., 1978; Posner, Nissen, & Klein, 1976). The theoretical rationale for each of these variables will be briefly discussed.

Decoding Accuracy

In everyday life most affects are communicated by the sender in several channels simultaneously. It seems safe to say that generally senders communicate the same affect in each channel (for a review see Rosenthal et al., 1979). These affects are perceived by decoders as "consistent" messages (DePaulo et al., 1978). In fact, a great deal of research has been directed toward studying the perception of consistent single and multichannel nonverbal (face, body, and tone) messages (for reviews see Argyle, 1969; DePaulo & Rosenthal, 1982; Izard, 1971; Scherer, 1982). Unfortunately, as Friedman (1978) points out, in many cases the particular nonverbal cues employed limit the generalizability of these results to the real world. For example, few studies have examined different affective dimensions in different channels. The present instrument was designed in part to help foster our knowledge of the ability to decode consistent social messages which are systematically varied on independent affective dimensions.

Discrepancy Accuracy

Our second general interest, and the focus of this chapter, was in examining the ability to decode discrepant multichannel messages. While more and more researchers have begun carefully to examine the importance of and reactions to inconsistent or discrepant multichannel messages, few studies have experimentally manipulated the degree of discrepancy between the verbal and nonverbal channels which comprise a multichannel communication.

Friedman (1979) has extended the findings of earlier studies in this area (e.g., Bugental, Kaswan, & Love, 1970) by demonstrating the unique effects of verbal and nonverbal cue combinations when the channels comprising a multichannel communication are discrepant. In this study, decoders rated the degree of positivity and dominance of photographs of facial expressions of emotion paired with sentences of varying affective meaning. Perceived sincerity, or consistency, of the communicated message was found to be a function of the consistency of positivity but not dominance cues. These results suggest that different affective dimensions are interpeted differently by decoders when channel combinations are discrepant. Apparently, overall channel integrations effects may be both a function of the degree of discrepancy of the channels comprising the message, as well as a function of the affective dimension expressed in each separate channel (Friedman, 1979).

The findings reported by Friedman (1979) were based on the study of still facial expressions paired with affective sentences. The present research attempts to extend these findings to "real time" emotional expression because of the growing evidence that important information which is communicated in ongoing affect displays may not be captured in still affect displays (McLeod, Rosenthal, Blanck, & Snodgrass, Note 7). In addition, the present study investigates the decoding of discrepant messages using pairings of verbal, visual, and vocal inputs in order to address the question of how "discrepancy decoding ability" varies as a function of the type of channel pairings presented (Ekman & Friesen, 1969).

Modality Primacy

Our next interest was in further examining variations in the modality primacy which we have already discussed in earlier sections. The addition of verbal information, however, has not been previously assessed. We were also interested in the extent to which this modality primacy (verbal/video; verbal/audio; or video/audio) was influenced by the degree of discrepancy between the components of the multichannel message. As we have already mentioned, the possibility of discrepancy among channels raises the question of which channels individuals trust more, or weigh more heavily, in their judgments. We have seen that as nonverbal cues become more and more discrepant, both children and adults show a decrease in video primacy. The present study extends this "leakage decoding strategy" to include verbal cues.

The naturally co-occurring channels that were specifically examined in our extended leakage hierarchy were (1) the verbal transcript, perhaps the most informative and controllable of all channels; (2) the face, which has been shown to be the most informative and controllable non-verbal channel (e.g., Ekman & Friesen, 1969; Izard, 1971; Rosenthal et al., 1979; Zuckerman, Larrance, Spiegel, & Klorman, Note 10); (3) the body, which is more likely than the face to give off or leak deception or discrepant cues (Ekman & Friesen, 1969, 1974); (4) tone of voice, which has been shown to be an additional source of nonverbal leakage or deception cues (e.g., Ekman, Friesen, & Scherer, 1976; Streeter, Krauss, Geller, Olsen, & Apple, 1977; Zuckerman, DeFrank, Hall, Larrance, & Rosenthal, 1979; or for a review see DePaulo, Zucker-man, & Rosenthal, 1980), and may leak one's true feelings about oneself (e.g., Bugental, Caporael, & Schennum, 1980; Bugental, Henker, & Whalen, 1976; Bugental & Love, 1975; Holzman & Rousey, 1966) or about others (Weitz, 1972); and (5) discrepancies among verbal, video, and audio channels which are also difficult to control and are additional sources of leakage (e.g., Blanck et al., 1981, 1982; DePaulo et al., 1978; Zuckerman et al., 1980).

Utility of the MOVANS

The present research extends the findings of previous studies on discrepant and consistent multichannel communications in several ways:

1. The verbal, visual, and auditory stimuli are presented in real time 2-second videotaped segments, as in Mehrabian and Ferris's (1967) and DePaulo et al.'s (1978) studies. As in DePaulo's research, the auditory stimuli are 2-second segments that are altered in various ways so that only tone of voice can be distinguished. However, un-like earlier studies on inconsistent communications, the stimuli are naturally occurring channel discrepancies in the sender's message.
2. The verbal channel has been systematically included in this new test of inconsistent communications, and unlike earlier studies (e.g., Bugental et al., 1970; Friedman, 1979), the verbal stimuli are presented in conjunction with videotaped "real time" segments. In addition, unlike earlier research which varied channel discrepancies on one affective dimension (e.g., Bugental et al., 1970; Mehrabian & Ferris, 1967), all the stimuli were varied on two different affec-tive dimensions as in DePaulo et al.'s (1978), Friedman's (1979), and Rosenthal et al.'s (1979) earlier research.
3. Finally, unlike earlier research, the leakage hierarchy (Blanck et al., 1981, 1982; Ekman & Friesen, 1969; Rosenthal & DePaulo, 1979a, b) has been systematically extended to include verbal, visual, and auditory stimuli. As described earlier, the verbal cues are predicted to be the most controllable, or least leaky, while the face, then body, and finally auditory cues are thought to be less controllable, or more leaky. The various channel pairings in the MOVANS can therefore be characterized by the degree of discrep-

ancy, on a dimension of leakiness, of the channels comprising the paired channel message.

Test Construction and Materials

The MOVANS Test was developed from the Profile of Nonverbal Sensitivity (PONS) test (Rosenthal et al., 1979). The PONS test is a film consisting of 220 2-second audio and/or visual nonverbal stimuli. In each segment, a 24-year-old female portrays 1 of 20 different emotional situations, such as "criticizing someone for being late" or "talking to a lost child." The 20 situations are categorized with reference to four different types of affect, each created by the crossing of two affective dimensions: positivity-negativity and dominance-submissiveness. These categorizations were determined by ratings of two independent samples of judges (Rosenthal et al., 1979). The items for the MOVANS Test were developed from the videotaped and audiotaped enactments of these everyday life situations and the transcripts (verbal content) of these enactments.

The 220 PONS items consist of a random ordering of these 20 situations, each represented in 11 different channels of nonverbal communication. Three channels are pure video channels: face only, body only (neck to knees), and face plus body (figure). Two channels are pure audio channels: "content filtered" (CF) (Rogers, Scherer, & Rosenthal, 1971) and randomized spliced (RS) (Scherer, 1971). In both of these channels, verbal messages are rendered incomprehensible. CF preserves sequence and rhythm (RS does not); RS saves pitch and intensity. The other six channels are mixed channels consisting of all audiovisual combinations of the two audio with the three video channels. In the MOVANS, the verbal content (transcript) was recorded for each message and displayed in the visual mode (e.g., on film).

The nine channel pairings in the new MOVANS Test are displayed on the top line of Table 8-1. The categorization of the individual channels for the eight situations from the PONS into the two types of multichannel messages (i.e., high discrepancy and low discrepancy) was determined by the ratings of three independent samples of judges ($N = 56$).[1]

For each of the nine channel pairings, the differences between the judges' mean ratings on the positivity and dominance dimension were computed, after correction was made for the overall effect of item and the overall effect of channel (i.e., employing the residuals). Discrepant multichannel messages were defined as the three pairings which were

---

[1] Each judge ($N = 56$: 27 males and 29 females) rated all the verbal, video, and audio channels for their degree of positivity and dominance in one of three counterbalanced sequence conditions: (1) verbal, video, audio channels, (2) video, audio, verbal channels, and (3) audio, verbal, video channels. Approximately the same number of male and female judges were employed in each condition.

Table 8-1. The 54 MOVANS Scenes Arranged in Their Channel Combinations.

	Face-Body	Face-CF[a]	Face-RS[b]	Verbal-Face	Body-CF[a]	Body-RS[b]	Verbal-Body	Verbal-CF[a]	Verbal-RS[b]
High Discrepancy (number of scenes)	3	3	3	3	3	3	3	3	3
Low Discrepancy (number of scenes)	3	3	3	3	3	3	3	3	3
Total Number of Scenes	6	6	6	6	6	6	6	6	6
Weights for differences in leakiness of the individual channels comprising the multichannel message	1	3	2	1	2	1	2	4	3
Final contrast weights for the leakage hierarchy	-10	8	-1	-10	-1	-10	-1	17	8

Initial Weights for Determining the Differences in Leakiness
of the Channels Comprising the Nine Multichannel Messages

Raw Weight	Channel
5	Verbal (most controllable)
4	Face
3	Body
2	RS[b]
1	CF[a] (most leaky)

[a] CF = content filtered speech
[b] RS = randomized spliced speech

found as most different on the positivity and dominance dimensions, and consistent multichannel messages were defined as the three channel pairings which were found least different on the positivity and dominance dimensions. Thus, a 54-item test was created (6 scenes [3 high and 3 low in discrepancy] × 9 different channel combinations). Every test item then consisted of a simultaneous pairing of some combination of verbal, facial, body, RS, or CF channels for the nine combinations.

Validation of the MOVANS

The validation of the MOVANS required that channel pairings whose elements had been rated very differently by judges rating them in isolation (N = 56) would also be rated as substantially more discrepant than the channel pairings whose elements had been rated less differently by these same judges. In line with the predictions of our extended leakage hierarchy, the validation of the MOVANS Test further required that when the nine verbal and nonverbal channel combinations were arranged from those with the greatest differences in leakiness of the channels comprising the multichannel message to those with the least differences, people would show a systematic decrease in their accuracy at decoding discrepancies between the two presented modalities.

Subjects were 20 Harvard University students (13 females and 7 males), and the MOVANS Test was administered in one group session. Subjects rated the degree of discrepancy of each multichannel scene in the MOVANS on a 9-point rating scale: not discrepant (1), discrepant (9). In order to assess the degree to which our validity requirements were met, a three-way mixed design analysis of variance (ANOVA) was performed. The between-subjects factor was sex of subject, and the two within-subject factors were discrepancy of the scene (high/low) and type of channel pairing (Face-Body/Face-CF/Face-RS/Verbal-Face/ Body-CF/Body-RS/Verbal-Body/Verbal-CF/Verbal-RS).

As suggested earlier, the validation of the MOVANS Test required that the channel pairings whose elements had been rated very differently by judges rating them in isolation would also be rated as substantially more discrepant than the channel pairings judged to be less discrepant by the judges rating the paired multichannel messages. The results were moderately consistent with our validity requirements with d = .58 ($t(20)$ = 1.22, $p \cong$ .12).[2]

The validation of the extended leakage hierarchy required that people would show a systematic increase in their accuracy at decoding discrepancies between the two presented modalities as the differences

---

[2] The d is an estimate of the size of the effect, expressed in standard deviation units (Cohen, 1977). Cohen considers a d of 0.20 to be a small effect, 0.50 a moderate effect, and 0.80 a large effect. The obtained d of .58 is equivalent to an r of .28.

in leakiness of the individual channels comprising the multichannel message increased. The final contrast weights and the initial weights for determining the differences in leakiness of the channels comprising the nine multichannel messages are displayed in the bottom of Table 8-1. The theoretical rationale for determining the differences in leakiness of the individual channels comprising the multichannel pairings has already been discussed (for further discussions see Blanck et al., 1981). Ekman, Friesen, and Scherer (1976) and Rosenthal and DePaulo's (1979a, b) results based on evidence of over sixty studies, have provided good support for the construct validity of this general ordering of the five measures.

As predicted, when the nine verbal and nonverbal channel combinations were arranged from the greatest differences in leakiness of the channels comprising the multichannel message to the least differences, we found a systematic decrease in accuracy at decoding discrepancies between the two presented modalities (linear contrast for modality $\times$ discrepancy, $F(1, 144) = 5.65$, $t = 2.38$, $p < .01$, one-tailed, $d = .40$). Overall, these results suggest that as the paired channels become systematically more discrepant on the dimension of leakiness, decoders become increasingly aware of discrepancies between the two presented modalities.

Developmental Changes in MOVANS Test Performance: Preliminary Findings

This series of studies examined the effects of age on accuracy and style of decoding discrepant and consistent messages in verbal and nonverbal channels. Subjects were 220 children (140 males and 80 females) between the ages of 10 and 17.

Materials and Instructions

Sensitivity to discrepant and consistent verbal and nonverbal cues was measured by the MOVANS Test. The MOVANS was administered in group sessions and the experimenter explained to the subjects that they were going to see a series of film clips showing pairings of verbal (transcripts), face, body, and audio segments. The subjects were told that sometimes they would get very similar impressions from the two presented channels, but other times the impressions from the two presented channels would be different. After each of the 54 scenes, subjects were required to indicate, in the form of three judgments, their overall impression based on the two presented channels. Specifically, they judged each scene on two dimensions (positive-negative and dominant-submissive) and also judged the extent to which they thought the emotions expressed in the channel pairings were discrepant.

Dependent Variables and Data Analysis

Subjects' ratings of the scenes in the MOVANS Test yield accuracy scores, discrepancy scores, and modality primacy scores. Thus, three sets of scores for the nine channel pairings are generated (two sets for accuracy and one for primacy). The two types of accuracy scores are accuracy of decoding consistent affect and accuracy of decoding discrepancies between emotions expressed in the different channels paired.

People who are accurate at decoding affect should rate the channel pairings whose elements had been rated as very positive by the judges rating them in isolation as more positive than the scenes that were rated by the judges in isolation as very negative. People who are accurate at decoding affect should similarly rate the channel pairings whose elements had been rated as very dominant by the judges rating them in isolation as more dominant than the scenes which were rated by the judges in isolation as very submissive. Hence, total accuracy at decoding affect was defined as the mean of these positivity and dominance accuracy scores. As in DePaulo et al.'s (1978) Nonverbal Discrepancy Test, positive accuracy, dominance accuracy, and total accuracy scores for each channel pairings were computed for the *consistent items only* and, therefore, were completely independent of the modality primacy scores which were computed only for the inconsistent items.

Accuracy of decoding discrepancy reflects subjects' ability to recognize the degree of discrepancy between the channels comprising the multichannel message. Specifically, subjects who are accurate at judging discrepancies between the channels comprising the multichannel message should rate as more discrepant the scenes that were defined by our group of judges rating scenes in isolation as most different (on both the positive and dominance dimensions). Accuracy of decoding discrepancy for each of the nine channel pairings was computed by subtracting the mean of the subject's ratings for the three consistent scenes from the mean of the subject's ratings for the three discrepant scenes for a specific channel pairing. In this formula, as in the other accuracy formulas, the expected value under the null hypothesis of no accuracy is zero.

Leakage hierarchy accuracy, a particular type of discrepancy accuracy, reflects subjects' ability to recognize the degree of discrepancy between channel pairings which vary in their level of leakiness (refer to Table 8-1 for these contrast weights).

Accurate judges of leakage, those who are better able to take advantage of the differences in level of leakiness of the paired channels, should rate the scenes that are further apart on the leakage hierarchy as more discrepant than the scenes that are closer together. Thus, this type of accuracy was computed from subjects' discrepancy ratings (1 = not discrepant, 9 = discrepant) according to the following formula: mean of (1) (mean of the scenes discrepant by one level of leakiness $\times$ -3), (2) (mean of the scenes discrepant by two levels of leakiness $\times$ -1), (3) (mean of the scenes discrepant by three levels of leakiness $\times$ 1), and (4) (mean of scenes discrepant by four levels of leakiness $\times$ 3). Higher scores reflect a higher accuracy at decoding discrepancy as a function of the level of discrepancy of the leakiness of the channels that were combined.

Finally, modality primacy scores reflect the extent to which subjects were influenced by each of the channels comprising the multichannel message.

> Modality primacy scores were computed for the *discrepant items only*. A subject who is more influenced by, for example, the verbal channel than the CF channel (in the Verbal-CF message) should rate as more positively the scenes in which the verbal channel was actually rated as more positive by the judges rating the scenes in isolation, than the scenes in which the verbal channel was actually rated as more negative by this same sample of judges. This same process is repeated for both channels of the paired channel message and the difference between these scores computed. The modality primacy scores for dominance for each of the nine channel pairings were computed in the same manner. Total modality primacy scores for each of the nine channel pairings was defined as the mean of positivity and dominancy primacy. Thus, as in both accuracy scores, there were primacy scores for each of the nine channel pairings and on the two emotional dimensions (positivity and dominance). Higher scores reflect more influence by the channel listed first in each of the nine channel pairings in Table 8-1. It should be noted again that for both primacy and accuracy in decoding affect, the expected value under the null hypothesis of no primacy and/or no accuracy is zero, and individual differences in the use of rating scales (e.g., the tendency to rate scenes as extremely positive or as extremely negative) *have no effect* on this expected value.

Accuracy at decoding affect and discrepancy, and modality primacy, were examined in unweighted means analyses of variance in which group (youngest males/middle-aged males/oldest males/middle-aged females/oldest females) was the between-subjects factor, and channel combinations (Face-Body/Face-CF/Face-RS/Verbal-Face/Body-CF/Body-RS/Verbal-Body/Verbal-CF/Verbal-RS), the within-subjects factor (repeated measures).[3] For both accuracy scores and primacy scores, main effects and/or interactions involving age were further examined in linear contrasts. The contrast weights are specified when applicable.

Age Changes in Accuracy of Decoding Affect and Discrepancy

Prior to presenting the results due to age, it should be noted that the overall mean accuracy score ($\bar{x}$ = 1.84) differed significantly from zero ($t(215)$ = 2.56, $p < .01$, d = .35), indicating that overall accuracy of decoding verbal and nonverbal cues was better than chance.

---

[3] Subjects in this study were divided into five comparison groups. The groups were (1) males less than 12 years old; N = 40, (2) males 12-13 years old; N = 53, (3) males 14 or older; N = 47, (4) females 11-13 years old (there were only three 11 year old females); N = 57, and (5) females 14 or older; N = 23. The groups were divided in this manner in order to maximize the N's per cell which were too low to have age and sex fully crossed at all age levels.

Consistent with earlier findings (e.g., Blanck et al., 1982), the results showed that although older children performed better than younger children at the decoding of consistent verbal and nonverbal cues (F [1, 202] = 3.11, t = 1.76, p < .05, one-tailed, d = .25), older children were even more effective than younger children at verbal-nonverbal discrepancy accuracy which involves making sense of complicated mixed channel message (F [1, 215] = 11.74, t = 3.42, p < .001, one-tailed, d = .47).

When we examined age differences in decoding accuracy of consistent and discrepant messages which (1) contained a verbal component as one of its channels, as compared to, (2) those that consisted solely of nonverbal stimuli, it became apparent that abilities to decode different channels do not develop at the same rate. Specifically, older children were relatively superior to younger children at decoding both consistent and discrepant *nonverbal* messages (F [1, 215] = 3.51, t = 1.87, p < .05, one-tailed, d = .26, for consistent messages; F [1, 215] = 3.93, t = 1.98, p < .05, one-tailed, d = .27, for discrepant messages). However, older children were clearly superior to younger children at decoding discrepant *verbal* messages (F [1, 215] = 8.39, t = 2.90, p < .0025, one-tailed, d = .40) as opposed to consistent verbal messages (F [1, 215] = 1.25, t = 1.12, d = .16). This pattern of results suggests that older children are better than younger children at most nonverbal decoding tasks (e.g., decoding consistent and discrepant nonverbal cues). However, the advantages of age are especially great for the decoding of discrepant verbal messages.

Learning When Not to Eavesdrop on Verbal and Nonverbal Cues

Blanck et al. (1981) showed that as females grow older, they become more nonverbally accommodating and perhaps learn when it is appropriate to decode certain nonverbal messages. The developmental aspects of verbal and nonverbal accommodation, however, has not yet been previously assessed.

Consistent with our earlier suggestions concerning the developmental acquisition of females' nonverbal accommodation, it was predicted and found that with age, males became more accurate at decoding discrepancy as a function of the level of discrepancy of the leakiness of the paired multichannel messages, while females became less accurate at this leakage decoding strategy (linear contrast of sex by age: F [1, 215] = 7.29, t = 2.70, p < .005, one-tailed, d = .37). In other words, as males got older they were more able to take advantage of the differences in level of leakiness of the paired channels and thus rated the scenes that were further apart on the leakage hierarchy as more discrepant than the scenes that were closer together. Females, on the other hand, showed a systematic decrease in leakage decoding accuracy as they became older. These results might suggest that women, relative to men, tend to grow more polite or accommodating in their decoding of both verbal and nonverbal messages.

Age Changes in Modality Primacy

Zuckerman et al.'s (1980) developmental examination of video primacy showed that video primacy increased with age, especially when the face was contrasted with the voice. Employing new stimulus materials (e.g., the MOVANS Test), the present investigation replicated the results of Zuckerman et al.'s (1980) study showing that as children grew older, they were more influenced by video cues, as opposed to audio cues (linear contrast for age: $F[1, 215] = 4.37$, $t = 2.09$, $p < .025$, one-tailed, $d = .28$).

Interestingly, with age, there was also a tendency for all children to show more video primacy over verbal *and* nonverbal audio cues (linear contrast for age: $F[1, 215] = 2.58$, $t = 1.60$, $p < .07$, one-tailed, $d = .22$). It seems that as children grow older, video cues (especially facial cues) develop into a major communication source, relative to both verbal and nonverbal audio cues.

Elsewhere, we have speculated about the cognitive processes underlying increases in video primacy with age (Zuckerman et al., 1980). We can not determine from the present investigation and earlier data (i.e., Zuckerman et al., 1980) whether older children actually attend less to the voice and verbal cues than to video (e.g., face and body) cues, or that they attend equally to both but weigh the video information more heavily. We have speculated about a two-stage model; that is, as children grow older they first attach smaller weights to leaky channels (e.g., voice and emotionally charged verbal statements) but eventually learn to pay less attention to them. Perhaps people learn that it does not make sense to acquire information that is not going to be used. This question remains a challenge for future research.

Summary

In this section, we have provided data from a new instrument, the Measure of Verbal and Nonverbal Sensitivity (MOVANS) Test, concerning developmental changes in sensitivity to discrepant and consistent social messages in the verbal and nonverbal channels. Although older children were more effective than younger children at decoding consistent messages, they were even more effective at organizing and interpreting discrepant verbal and nonverbal cues which involve making sense of complicated mixed channel messages. The advantages of age were especially great for the decoding of discrepant verbal messages.

In addition, consistent with earlier findings, as females became older they became more verbally *and* nonverbally accommodating. The results suggested that as females grow older, they may learn when it is socially appropriate to decode certain verbal and nonverbal communications.

Finally, employing a new instrument, the present investigation replicated the presently accumulating body of evidence suggesting that as children grow older, video cues, relative to verbal and voice cues, become a major source of information for decoding a sender's true affect.

Conclusion

In this chapter we first summarized past research on how children learn to decode discrepant and consistent social messages. It seems that both children and adults are sensitive to inconsistencies in social messages. When individuals perceive these discrepancies in a message, they tend to rely more heavily on less controllable (more leaky) channels which are perceived to express the true underlying meaning of the message. This decoding strategy seems to be more characteristic of older, relative to younger, children.

We next considered developmental changes in how children learn when it is socially appropriate to decode and interpret certain social messages. Our purpose was to suggest that abilities of interpreting social messages may be influenced by childhood socialization (Blanck & Rosenthal, Note 4). We saw, for example, that as females grow older, they seem to learn when it is socially appropriate to decode certain social messages, or become more socially accommodating.

Finally, we provided data from a new instrument, the Measure of Verbal and Nonverbal Sensitivity (MOVANS) Test, for the assessment of developmental changes in sensitivity to discrepant and consistent social messages in verbal and nonverbal channels. Older children were more effective than younger children at decoding complicating mixed channel messages. In addition, consistent with findings discussed earlier, as females became older, they became more verbally and nonverbally accommodating. Finally, as all children became older, video cues, relative to verbal and voice cues, became a major source of information for decoding a sender's true affect.

In conclusion, this chapter has examined how and when children learn to interpret and understand discrepancies among social messages in verbal and nonverbal channels. It does seem that young children do develop certain standard expectations for social interaction and communication. Consequently, when these expectations are violated (i.e., the communicative message is discrepant or inconsistent) shared meanings are lost, distorted, or misinterpreted. Young children seem sensitive to these violations and their awareness of this possible discrepancy among social messages, channels, or affects, has raised the question of which cues or channels children learn to "trust" more, or weigh more heavily in their judgments. The social and cognitive processes by which children learn to trust or weigh these incoming discrepant communications may influence the development of satisfying interpersonal relationships with others. For example, the effects of discrepant social messages on the development of psychopathology in children has been hypothesized (i.e., the double-bind hypothesis: Bateson, Jackson, Haley, & Weakland, 1956; Haley, 1959). Furthermore, children who have experienced prolonged exposure to these discrepant and inconsistent verbal and nonverbal messages tend to show more aggressive and anxious behaviors relative to children who have been exposed to more consistent messages (Bugental & Love, 1975; Hall & Levine, 1976). Finally, the growing literature on developmental changes in the detection of deception and lying (DePaulo, Jordan, Irvine, & Laser, Note 5) may demonstrate children's sensitivity and susceptibility to these discordant messages relative to adults' skill at decoding these messages. Examinations of this sort may some day help children (and adults) to a greater appreciation of W. C. Fields. More generally, this line of research may some day aid children and adults to a more effective and competent interpretation of the communication in our social world.

Acknowledgment. Our research reported in this chapter was in part supported by the National Science Foundation. We thank Albert and Bertha Blanck, Bella M. DePaulo, Robert S. Feldman, Fred R. Volkmar, and Miron Zuckerman for their comments on an earlier version of this chapter. Judith A. Hall and Wendy J. Kislik assisted in the development of the MOVANS Test. This chapter is dedicated to all the children and staff at Camp Wah-Nee who generously participated in our research program on the development of nonverbal sensitivity. In particular, we thank Mike and Ellie Gordon, and Dave Stricker and Mark "Tranz" Transport, who are still growing up with us at camp.

Reference Notes

1. Blanck, P. D. & Rosenthal, R. Training and practice in nonverbal sensitivity and athletic team performance. Presentation at the meeting of the New England Psychological Association Convention, Boston 1980. Manuscript submitted for review, 1982.
2. Blanck, P. D. & Rosenthal, R. Nonverbal styles and skills in best-friend relationships. Presentation at the meeting of the New England Psychological Association Convention, Brandeis, 1981.
3. Blanck, P. D. & Rosenthal, R. *Measuring sensitivity to verbal and nonverbal discrepant and consistent multichannel messages: The MOVANS Test.* Paper presented at the meeting of the Eastern Psychological Association Convention, New York, 1981.
4. Blanck, P. D. & Rosenthal, R. *Masculinity, femininity, and the nonverbal decoding skill of children.* Manuscript, Harvard University, 1981.

5. DePaulo, B. M., Jordan, A., Irvine, A., & Laser, P. S. *Age changes in detection of deception.* Manuscript submitted for review, 1981.
6. Krauss, R. M., Geller, V., & Olsen, C. *Modalities and cues in the detection of deception.* Paper presented at the meeting of the American Psychological Association, Washington, D.C., 1976.
7. McLeod, P. L., Rosenthal, R., Blanck, P. D., & Snodgrass, S. E. *Micromomentary movement and the decoding of face and body cues.* Paper presented at the meeting of the American Psychological Association Convention, Montreal, 1980.
8. Wagner, S., Winner, E., Cicchetti, D., & Gardner, H. *Metaphorical matching in human infants.* Paper presented at the meeting of the Eastern Psychological Association Convention, Philadelphia 1979.
9. Zuckerman, M. Personal communication, 1981.
10. Zuckerman, M., Larrance, D. T., Spiegel, N. H., & Klorman, R. *The controllable face and the leaky voice: A comparison between two nonverbal channels.* Manuscript submitted for review, 1981.

References

Ainsworth, M. D. S., Bell, S. M., & Stayton, D. J. Infant-mother attachment and social development: Socialization as a product of reciprocal responsiveness to signals. In M. P. M. Richards (Ed.), *The integration of a child into a social world.* Cambridge, England: Cambridge University Press, 1974.

Argyle, M. *Social interaction.* Chicago: Aldine, 1969.

Bateson, G., Jackson, D., Haley, J., & Weakland, J. Toward a theory of schizophrenia. *Behavioral Science,* 1956, *1*, 251-264.

Berman, H. J., Shulman, A. D., & Marwit, S. J. Comparison of multidimensional decoding of affect from audio, video, and audiovideo recordings. *Sociometry,* 1976, *39*, 83-89.

Blanck, P. D., Rosenthal, R., Snodgrass, S. E., DePaulo, B. M., & Zuckerman, M. Longitudinal and cross-sectional age effects in nonverbal decoding skills and style. *Developmental Psychology,* 1982, *18*, 491-498.

Blanck, P. D., Rosenthal, R., Snodgrass, S. E., DePaulo, B. M., & Zuckerman, M. Longitudinal and cross-sectional age effects in nonverbal decoding skills and style. *Developmental Psychology,* in press.

Blanck, P. D., Zuckerman, M., DePaulo, B. M., & Rosenthal, R. Sibling resemblances in nonverbal skill and style. *Journal of Nonverbal Behavior,* 1980, *4,* 219-226.

Bugental, D. B., Caporael, L., & Shennum, W. A. Experimentally-produced child uncontrollability: Effects on the potency of adult communication patterns. *Child Development,* 1980, *51*, 520-528.

Bugental, D. B., Henker, B., & Whalen, C. K. Attributional antecedents of verbal and vocal assertiveness. *Journal of Personality and Social Psychology,* 1976, *34*, 405-411.

Bugental, D., Kaswan, J. W., & Love, L. R. Perception of contradictory meanings conveyed by verbal and nonverbal channels. *Journal of Personality and Social Psychology,* 1970, *16*, 647-655.

Bugental, D. B. & Love, L. Nonassertive expressions of parental approval and disapproval and its relationship to child disturbance. *Child Development,* 1975, *46*, 747-752.

Bugental, D. E., Love, L. R., Kaswan, J. W., & April, C. Verbal-nonverbal conflict in parental messages to normal and disturbed children. *Journal of Abnormal Psychology*, 1971, 77, 6-10.

Case, R. Validation of a neo-Piagetian mental capacity construct. *Journal of Experimental Child Psychology*, 1972, 14, 287-302.

Charlesworth, W. R. & Kreutzer, M. A. Facial expressions of infants and children. In P. Ekman (Ed.), *Darwin and facial expression*. New York: Academic Press, 1973.

Cohen, J. *Statistical power analysis for the behavioral sciences* (Rev. ed.). New York: Academic Press, 1977.

DePaulo, B. M. & Rosenthal, R. Age changes in nonverbal decoding as a function of increasing amounts of information. *Journal of Experimental Child Psychology*, 1978, 26, 280-287.

DePaulo, B. M. & Rosenthal, R. Age changes in nonverbal decoding skills: Evidence for increasing differentiation. *Merrill-Palmer Quarterly*, 1979, 25, 145-150. (a)

DePaulo, B. M. & Rosenthal, R. Ambivalence, discrepancy, and decpetion in non-verbal communication. In R. Rosenthal (Ed.), *Skill in nonverbal communication*. Cambridge, MA: Oelgeschlager, Gunn, & Hain, 1979. (b)

DePaulo, B. M. & Rosenthal, R. Measuring the development of nonverbal sensitivity. In P. B. Read & C. Izard (Eds.), *Measuring emotions in infants and children*. New York: Cambridge University Press, 1982.

DePaulo, B. M., Rosenthal, R., Eisenstat, R. A., Rogers, P. L., & Finkelstein, S. Decoding discrepant nonverbal cues. *Journal of Personality and Social Psychology*, 1978, 36, 313-323.

DePaulo, B. M., Zuckerman, M., & Rosenthal, R. Detecting deception: Modality effects. In L. Wheeler (Ed.), *The review of personality and social psychology*. New York: Sage, 1980.

Ekman, P. Cross-cultural studies of facial expression. In P. Ekman (Ed.), *Darwin and facial expression*. New York: Academic Press, 1973.

Ekman, P. & Friesen, W. V. Nonverbal leakage and clues to deception. *Psychiatry*, 1969, 32, 88-106.

Ekman, P. & Friesen, W. V. Detecting deception from the face or body. *Journal of Personality and Social Psychology*, 1974, 29, 288-298.

Ekman, P., Friesen, W. V., & Scherer, K. R. Body movement and voice pitch in deceptive interaction. *Semiotica*, 1976, 16, 23-37.

Friedman, H. S. The relative strength of verbal versus nonverbal cues. *Personality and Social Psychology Bulletin*, 1978, 4, 147-150.

Friedman, H. S. The interactive effects of facial expressions of emotion and verbal messages on perceptions of affective meaning. *Journal of Personality and Social Psychology*, 1979, 15, 433-469.

Goffman, E. *Frame analysis*. New York: Harper & Row, 1974.

Haley, J. An interactional description of schizophrenia. *Psychiatry*, 1959, 22, 321-332.

Hall, J. A. Gender effects in decoding nonverbal cues. *Psychological Bulletin*, 1978, 68, 807-816.

Hall, J. A. Gender, gender roles, and nonverbal communication skills. In R. Rosenthal (Ed.), *Skill in nonverbal communication: Individual differences*. Cambridge, MA: Oelgeschlager, Gunn, & Hain, 1979.

Hall, J. A. & Levine, S. Affect and verbal-nonverbal discrepancy in schizophrenic and non-schizophrenic family communication. *British Journal of Psychiatry*, 1980, *137*, 78-92.

Holzman, P. S. & Rousey, C. The voice as percept. *Journal of Personality and Social Psychology*, 1966, *4*, 78-86.

Izard, C. D. *The face of emotion*. New York: Appleton-Century-Crofts, 1971.

Kagan, J., Kearsley, R. B., & Zelazo, P. R. *Infancy: Its place in human development*. Cambridge: Harvard University Press, 1979.

Kraut, R. E. Verbal and nonverbal cues in the perception of lying. *Journal of Personality and Social Psychology*, 1978, *36*, 380-391.

LaFrance, M. & Carmen, B. The nonverbal display of psychological androgyny. *Journal of Personality and Social Psychology*, 1980, *38*, 36-49.

LaFrance, M. & Mayo, C. *Moving bodies: Nonverbal communication in social relationships*. Monterey, CA: Brooks/Cole, 1978.

Levitt, E. A. The relationship between abilities to express emotional meanings vocally and facially. In R. R. Davitz (Ed.), *The communication of emotional meaning*. New York: McGraw-Hill, 1964.

Mehrabian, A., & Ferris, S. R. Inference of attitudes from nonverbal communication in two channels. *Journal of Consulting Psychology*, 1967, *81*, 248-252.

Mehrabian, A., & Wiener, M. Decoding of inconsistent communication. *Journal of Personality and Social Psychology*, 1967, *6*, 109-114.

Parry, M. H. Infant wariness and stimulus discrepancy. *Journal of Experimental Child Psychology*, 1973, *16*, 377-387.

Pascual-Leone, J. A mathematical model for the transition rule in Piaget's developmental stages. *Acta Psychologica*, 1970, *32*, 301-345.

Posner, M. I., Nissen, M. J., & Klein, R. M. Visual dominance: An information-processing account of its origins and significance. *Psychological Review*, 1976, *83*, 157-171.

Rogers, P. L., Scherer, K. R., & Rosenthal, R. Content-filtering human speech. *Behavioral Research Methods and Instrumentation*, 1971, *3*, 16-18.

Rosenthal, R. *Experimenter effects in behavioral research*. New York: Appleton-Century-Crofts, 1966.

Rosenthal, R. & DePaulo, B. M. Sex differences in eavesdropping on nonverbal cues. *Journal of Personality and Social Psychology*, 1979, *37*, 273-285. (a)

Rosenthal, R. & DePaulo, B. M. Sex differences in accommodation in nonverbal communication. In R. Rosenthal (Ed.), *Skill in nonverbal communication*. Cambridge, MA: Oelgeschlager, Gunn, & Hain, 1979. (b)

Rosenthal, R., Hall, J. A., DiMatteo, M. R., Rogers, P. L., & Archer, D. *Sensitivity to nonverbal communication: The PONS test*. Baltimore, MD: The Johns Hopkins University Press, 1979.

Ruff, H. A. & Kohler, C. J. Tactual-visual transfer in six-month-old infants. *Infant Behavior and Development*, 1978, *1*, 259-264.

Scherer, K. R. Randomized-splicing: A note on a simple technique for masking speech content. *Journal of Experimental Research in Personality*, 1971, *5*, 155-159.

Scherer, K. R. Assessment of vocal expression. In P. B. Read & C. Izard (Eds.), *Measuring emotions in infants and children*. New York: Cambridge University Press, 1982.

Streeter, L. A., Krauss, R. M., Geller, V., Olson, C., & Apple, W. Pitch changes during attempted deception. *Journal of Personality and Social Psychology*, 1977, *35*, 345-350.

Thorne, B. & Henley, N. (Eds.). *Language and sex differences and dominance.* Rowley, MA: Newbury House, 1975.

Volkmar, F. R., Hoder, E. L., & Siegel, A. E. Discrepant social communications. *Developmental Psychology*, 1980, *16*, 495-505.

Volkmar, F. R. & Siegel, A. E. Young children's responses to discrepant social communication. *Journal of Child Psychology and Psychiatry*, 1979, *20*, 139-149.

Weitz, S. Attitude voice and behavior: A repressed affect model of interracial interaction. *Journal of Personality and Social Psychology*, 1972, *24*, 14-21.

Weitz, S. Sex differences in nonverbal communication. *Sex Roles*, 1976, *2*, 175-184.

Zuckerman, M., Blanck, P. D., DePaulo, B. M., & Rosenthal, R. Developmental changes in decoding discrepant and nondiscrepant nonverbal cues. *Developmental Psychology*, 1980, *16*, 220-228.

Zuckerman, M., DeFrank, R. S., Hall, J. A., Larrance, D. T., & Rosenthal, R. Facial and vocal cues of deception and honesty. *Journal of Experimental Social Psychology*, 1979, *15*, 378-396.

CHAPTER NINE

Responses to Consistent and Discrepant Social Communications

Fred R. Volkmar and Alberta E. Siegel

A naive assertion about human communication is that it consists of words. A more sophisticated statement recognizes that extralexical aspects of communication, including gestures, posture, facial expression, tone of voice, dress, and timing of speech, also convey meaning. In human social interaction information, typically, is conveyed redundantly so that a speaker's facial expressions, gestures, tone of voice, postures, and words are mutually consistent, augmenting and reinforcing each other. For purposes of analysis the various communication components may be grouped into "channels" which are defined as sets of communication components which convey information and which are emitted and responded to in a systematic manner (Wiener & Mehrabian, 1968). Although the delineation of any set of component behaviors as belonging to the same communication channel is somewhat arbitrary, it can be justified pragmatically and empirically (Wiener, Devoe, Rubinow, & Geller, 1972).

Any sensory system is capable of receiving information, and a broad classification of nonverbal communications into the several sensory channels on which information is received, e.g., olfactory, auditory, visual, has been proposed (Poyatos, 1974, cited in Harper, Wiens, & Matarazzo, 1978). In practice the visual and auditory channels appear to convey the most information in human social communications (Hinde, 1974).

There are noteworthy differences in the nature of the information conveyed on each channel. Lexical aspects of speech are highly specific and differentiated; words are spoken in intermittent episodes separated by pauses. Dress and other physical attributes are persistent over the course of an interaction and are less specific than words. Posture, gestures, tone of voice, and facial expressions are typically more lasting than single words but like the lexical content of the communication they succeed each other as the transaction unfolds.

There is a large research literature supporting the notion that adults selectively attend to different channels for different kinds of information. Thus an adult may rely of the lexical content of a communication for "objective meaning" while simultaneously evaluating the speaker's attitude and the state of the interpersonal relationship by noting facial expression, gestures, and tone of voice (see Wiener et al., 1972, for a discussion).

It is unclear whether the concept of communication channels is useful in understanding the communication abilities of young children. Even during the school years there are developmental changes in the ability to interpret information on a single channel, e.g., facial expression (Mayo and LaFrance, 1978). Facial cues are relatively ineffective indicators of communication failure with older children compared to auditory cues (Peterson, Danner, & Flavell, 1972). It is conceivable that for the very young child a total and coherent *Gestalt* is required, i.e., that the child must both see and hear the information to comprehend it. Alternatively, it may be the case that a single channel of communication dominates the young child's interpretation of communications. The young child may not be able to "decenter" from one channel of information in order to simultaneously evaluate another one (Piaget, 1963; see DePaulo & Rosenthal, 1978, for a discussion). This idea receives some support from experimental studies of intersensory integration (Birch & Lefford, 1963).

Various strategies may be used to understand how children (and adults) integrate the various communication channels to derive meaning. Information may be presented on only one communication channel, and the responses of subjects to this information may be compared to their responses when the information is supported by the content of other channels of communication. Alternatively, messages may contain discrepant or mutually contradictory information on the communication channels and subjects' responses may be interpreted in accordance with which components of the communication are used to derive meaning.

Various investigators have studied the response of adults to discrepant communications. Mehrabian and Wiener (1967) communicated positive, neutral, and negative attitudes in both lexical and vocal components of messages to adult subjects. While subjects made reliable observations about the speaker's attitudes based on either lexical or vocal stimuli, the variability in inferences about the speaker's attitude was based mainly on variations in tone. Mehrabian & Ferris (1967) varied facial expression and tone independently, pairing them with a neutral word. For their adult subjects, the speaker's inferred attitude was a linear function of a combination of both components, with facial expression weighted more heavily in the judgment. This result is consistent with Levitt's (1964), who reported that the facial channel contributes more to decoding than the vocal channel. Solomon & Yaeger (1969b) asked adult subjects for judgments of objective meaning as well as speaker's attitude. While intonation dominated judgments of attitude, lexical content dominated judgments of objective meaning. Bugental et al. (1970a) and DePaulo and Rosenthal (1978) report that adults give greater weight to the visual channel in the resolution of conflicting messages. In sum, the research literature with adults suggests that objective meaning is derived by adults from a speaker's words, while interpretations of the speaker's attitude and emotionality are based on the speaker's non-lexical communications, especially facial expression and tone of voice.

The research literature with children is sparser than the literature with adults. Many of the studies with children have been performed by Bugental and her colleagues. Using both videotaped stimuli and video-recorded observations of naturally occurring communications in a clinic waiting room, Bugental has documented the "literal mindedness" of children. For example, unfriendly words spoken by a person with a friendly facial expression are interpreted negatively by children, whereas adults find them humorous (Bugental, Kaswan, Love, & Fox, 1970b; Bugental, 1974). Parents who observed videotapes of their interaction with their children were surprised to discover that joking messages are interpreted as ridicule by the child (Bugental, 1970). Both lexical and vocal aspects of statements were important to the perception of both adults and children but the visual aspect of the statement was more important to adults than to children (Bugental, Kaswan, & Love, 1970a). Younger children gave less weight to facial expressions than did older children. The relative dominance of nonverbal over verbal cues increases with age, presumably reflecting increasing competence in interpreting nonverbal communications (Bugental, Kaswan, Love, & Fox, 1970b). Discrepant messages from women were perceived more negatively than those from men (Bugental, Love & Gianetto, 1971).

Content and intonation, both independently and in interaction, have been reported to have significant effects on the perceived meaning of reinforcers. In a study of 96 fourth grade boys, Solomon & Yaeger (1969a) found that lexical content was a more important determiner of the meaning of a social reinforcer than was intonation. This effect was weakened if aspects of meaning shifted from cognitive to affective. Indifferent vocal intonation attenuated the effect of positive and negative lexical content more than did contradictory intonation. Subsequently, Solomon and Ali (1972) conducted a developmental study of perception of verbal reinforcers. They found that lexical content was the most important determinant of reinforcer effectiveness, but with increasing age there was a clear trend for children to rely more on other aspects of the communication. Young adult subjects were more likely to rely on vocal intonation to judge affective meaning than they were to rely on lexical content.

Social class differences have been reported in children's interpretation of social reinforcement for task performance. For example, correctness reinforcers are more effective than praise for children from middle class families, while praise reinforcers are more effective with children from lower class families (Zigler & Kanzer, 1962). Tonal inflection has been reported to be a more important cue for lower class children than for those from the middle class, who respond to lexical content with or without tonal inflection (Brooks, Brandt, & Wiener, 1969).

The range of methods suitable for studying social communication with children is considerably narrower than the wide diversity of methods employed in the study of social communications with adults. Methods which rely heavily on the subject's literacy have commonly been employed with adults, especially college students. They are of questionable usefulness with children until at least the second decade of life, and typically therefore questionnaires and rating scales are abjured by developmentalists. Methods which rely on the subject's verbal skills and large receptive vocabulary, such as interviews, may well have some use with 7- or 8-year-olds but are not readily applicable to a 1-, 2-, or 3-year-old. Researchers with very young children have relied on measures like changes in skin conductance (Buck, 1977) or adult ratings of videotapes of children observing emotionally loaded scenes (Buck, 1975). Direct observations of child responses are the predominant method. An example is observation of children's motor responses in social reinforcement tasks (Brooks et al., 1969).

In many studies of adults' and children's understanding of communicative transactions, the subject is put in the position of an observer or bystander, a third party in a two-party exchange. He is asked to assess what is going on between two persons, rather than between another person and himself. Videotapes or photographs may be used to show the communicative acts to the subject. Their use achieves standardization of stimuli.

We choose, instead, to have the child subject's role to be participant rather than observer. We do not ask children to predict a response, nor to observe and rate a response, nor to describe a response. Rather, we ask the child to make a response. The child subject becomes a party in the two-party transaction. The loss of standardization which occurs when each subject is involved with a live communicator for research purposes is more than offset by the gains entailed. Fewer cues are needed to make such a transaction explicit (Jancovic, Devoe, & Wiener, 1975), and the direct approach has ecological validity. In their everyday lives, young children are never asked to rate or rank communicative acts, and probably they are rarely asked to describe them; but they are routinely expected to participate in communicative exchanges, to respond to communications directed by others to them. In our studies, the adult experimenter asks the child to approach and asks the child to stay away. Such requests are common in children's lives. The children's wide experience with them lends increased interest to their responses to discrepant and contradictory messages with this content.

Because the message communicator in our studies, the experimenter, is an unfamiliar adult whose task of conveying single-channel and also discrepant messages to the child entails behaving very strangely indeed at times, the child's mother is present throughout the experimental session (Ainsworth, Blehar, Waters, & Wall, 1978; Rheingold, 1969). We recognize the risk that she may interpret the communications to the child or otherwise guide his or her response, perhaps even very subtly, although of course we ask her not to do so. Her presence is reassuring to the child in the presence of the strange adult. Discrepancy from the familiar may produce responses in young children ranging from surprise and interest to wariness, fear, and overt distress (Bronson, 1972). The presence of the mother is intended to minimize the child's discomfort. Seated in a chair next to the child's, the mother provides the child with a secure base from which he or she can range.

Because our subjects are very young, we study discrepancies that are pronounced, emphatic, and prolonged, rather than subtle and fleeting. To adults, the prolonged messages seem wooden. Youngsters find them acceptable and seek meaning from them, participating in our experiments soberly and in a task-oriented way.

Two Experiments

Subjects

For our experiments, we recruited children whose parents are among the graduate students and young professionals in the Stanford University area. We required that the subject be between 12- and 42-months old, able to walk unassisted, and come from a home in which English is the first language. Essentially, all children were from middle-class families of modest economic status, mostly highly educated. The experiment was explained to the mother in the child's presence and the mother signed informed consent papers prior to participation.

The experimenter took the mother and child to the playroom, which measured 10 × 13 feet (3.05 × 3.96 m). Its floor was marked off in a 2 ft × 2 ft matrix (0.61 × 0.61 m) consisting of 31 squares. The only furniture in the room was an adult-size chair for the mother in one corner, in a position which prevented her watching herself or her child in the one-way mirror at the opposite end of the room. A child-size chair was next to hers. At the opposite end of the room was a low stool for the experimenter. When he was seated, his back was to the wall containing the one-way mirror. A small mirror on the wall opposite him (above the child's head on the wall behind the child) permitted observers to monitor the experimenter's facial expressions. A built-in cabinet along the wall to the experimenter's left had some doll furniture atop it, as well as a wooden doll house; these toys gave the child something moderately interesting to do during the initial brief observation period and also later provided an alternative to interacting with the experimenter.

The experimenter devoted his initial minutes with the child and mother to make sure that they were both at ease in the room and with him. Ordinarily, he would chat with the mother while the child, after first eyeing him warily and remaining distant from him, would eventually approach him and initiate an interaction, e.g., by offering him a toy or by pointing to an object of shared interest. Once this initiation had occurred, the experimenter felt confident that the experimental routines could be launched.

Reminding the mother to remain seated in her chair throughout the session, the experimenter left the room, saying "I'll be back soon." The dyad was observed for one minute in his absence, for baseline information. This procedure allowed the child to explore the room and to accommodate to it.

The experimenter returned carrying a large balloon which he placed on the floor in front of the low stool he occupied. He asked the child to be seated in the child's own low chair and then signaled to the observers behind him that the trials would begin.

On each trial, if the child approached to within one foot of the adult, he was allowed to detach a plastic self-adhesive flower sticker from a sheet of stickers and place it on the balloon. The balloon thus served as attraction for the child and as a source of joint activity between experimenter and child.

Trials

Four different messages were used in Study 1 (Volkmar & Siegel, 1979), plus a totally positive message at the conclusion of the trials. Forty children and their mothers participated, each dyad in its own scheduled session.

The same four messages were used in Study 2; a totally positive message was given at the start of the trials as well as at their conclusion, and two new messages were added for the 32 subjects (Volkmar, Hoder, & Siegel, 1980).

Each individual message was a request to the child either to approach the experimenter or to stay away from him. The principal dependent measure was whether or not the child did approach to within one foot. In Study 1, we allowed 60 seconds for the child to reach this criterion. During that time interval, the experimenter would repeat his spoken message, either "come here" or "stay away," at short intervals. We learned that if a child were going to approach the experimenter, the child would do so within 45 seconds. So in Study 2 we allowed 45 seconds for the child to reach criterion. Shortening the trial length made the procedure seem less arbitrary and artificial. If the child had interpreted a given trial's message to mean that he was to stay away and therefore remained seated, it was somewhat clumsy for the trial to run on, with the experimenter continuing the message. (Some older children commented on this by replying to the continuing message by averring, "I *am*" or "I'm *doing* it.")

Two males in their mid-twenties alternated in the role of experimenter in the two studies, acting as an observer in one instance and as experimenter in the other. Both rehearsed the various messages over many hours, critiquing each other's performances and seeking standardization of messages across the two experiments.

We use the labels A and B for the nondiscrepant positive trials, the labels C and D for the discrepant trials, and E and F for the nondiscrepant negative trials (used in Study 2 but not in Study 1). These labels do not indicate the order of trials in the experiment. The order of trials was systematically counterbalanced across subjects, to control for possible sequence effects. For details, consult Volkmar & Siegel (1979) and Volkmar, Hoder, & Siegel (1980). In neither experiment did sequence of messages prove to have a systematic influence on the results.

In all trials, gestural and facial messages were displayed continuously throughout. Spoken messages were emitted at the rate of about one word per second, with a two-second pause between repetitions. Figure 9-1 shows a summary of the trials in Study 1, and Figure 9-2 shows comparable information for Study 2.

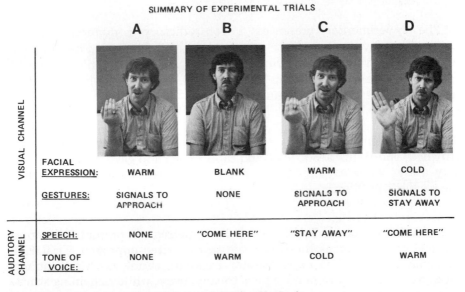

Figure 9-1. Summary of Experimental Trials—Study 1.

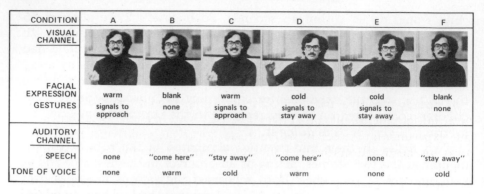

CONDITION	A	B	C	D	E	F
VISUAL CHANNEL						
FACIAL EXPRESSION	warm	blank	warm	cold	cold	blank
GESTURES	signals to approach	none	signals to approach	signals to stay away	signals to stay away	none
AUDITORY CHANNEL						
SPEECH	none	"come here"	"stay away"	"come here"	none	"stay away"
TONE OF VOICE	none	warm	cold	warm	none	cold

Figure 9-2. Summary of Experimental Trials—Study 2.

Trial A

The experimenter smiled broadly, beckoned the child with his hand, and nodded his head affirmatively. He did not speak. Our "shorthand" for this trial is +/0, meaning positive on the visual channel and neutral on the auditory channel.

Trial B

The experimenter maintained a blank face and avoided head movements or manual gestures, while inviting the child to approach in a warm, pleasant tone of voice: "Come here, come here (child's name)." Our shorthand for Trial B is 0/+, meaning neutral on the visual channel and positive on the auditory. Trial B is the complement of Trial A.

Trial C

The experimenter presented a contradictory communication by smiling broadly, beckoning to the child with his hand, and nodding his head affirmatively, while saying "Stay away, stay away (child's name)" in a cold tone of voice. This is a +/- trial, positive on the visual and negative on the auditory channel.

Trial D

The complement of Trial C is a -/+ trial. On Trial D, the experimenter frowned, shook his head, looked disapproving, and gave hand signals to stay away, while saying "Come here, come here (child's name)" in a pleasant tone of voice.

Trial E

On Trial E, as on Trials A and B, a message is presented on one channel only. Whereas those two messages invited approach, Trial E is a stay-away trial. The experimenter frowned, shook his head, looked disapproving, and gave hand signals to stay away, while remaining wordless and silent. This is a -/0 trial.

Trial F

This trial is a 0/– trial, complementing Trial E. The experimenter is expressionless and gestureless, while saying to the child coldly "Stay away, stay away (child's name)."

A totally positive trial concluded the experiment in Study 1 and both initiated and concluded it in Study 2. In such a trial, denoted +/+, the experimenter smiles broadly, beckons to the child with his hand, nods his head affirmatively, and says warmly "Come here, come here (child's name)."

For ethical reasons and because of the personal preferences of the experimenters, we did not have –/– trial. In such an instance, the adult would tell the child to stay away in a cold tone of voice and would also have a negative facial expression, give hand signals to stay away, etc. There seems little doubt that we would see few or no children approach in response to such an unambiguous statement, but there was some fear on our part that such a negative message would "spread" in its effects to adjacent trials or might even disrupt the experiment. We also did not have a 0/0 trial. Such an event might be indistinguishable from between-trial or "at rest" behavior of the experimenter.

The final +/+ trial served several functions. It provided each child with a positive experience at the end of his participation. It demonstrated that the experimental messages had not "turned him off" so thoroughly that he would not come over to the experimenter even when unambiguously invited to do so.

We introduced the +/+ trial as the initial trial in Study 2, in order to use it to screen out children who were so shy and wary they would not respond directly to any message. Only children who approached the experimenter in response to it were retained for the research, and there were three who were dropped because of their failure to do so.

On Trials A, B, E, and F, the child received a consistent message on one channel and very little information on the other. If the child responded appropriately, we could say that the child understands the message even though it comes to him on a single channel.

For example, a child who approaches on Trial A and remains seated on Trial E can be said to understand social communication even when it reaches him or her only over the visual channel. Similarly, a child who approaches on Trial B and remains seated on Trial F is demonstrating that he or she understands speech even when it is not embellished with gestures, postures, or facial expressions.

In Trials C and D, the two channels convey mutually contradictory requests. The child's response may convey something about the relative prepotence of each channel. The child who remains seated on Trial C and who approaches the experimenter on Trial D is essentially relying on the auditory channel for the "definitive" or "operative" instruction, and is discounting or minimizing the information on the other channel. The reverse holds for a child who approaches on Trial C and remains seated on Trial D—such a child is "tuned into" facial expressions and gestures to the extent of discounting contradictory auditory information.

Measures

We collected many measures of the children's behavior during the experimental trials in Study 1, including a "map" of each child's timed movements in the room during each trial and a dictated account of his behavior. We recorded each child's time to criterion on each trial as clocked by two observers independently with stop watches. In Study 2 we also videotaped most sessions. Our simple measures of behavior in time and space proved to be highly intercorrelated. In the end, we placed most reliance simply on whether or not the child did approach the experimenter on each trial, i.e., "reached criterion."

Results

Cochran's Q test provides an overall test for differences among the frequencies with which the children reached criterion on the different trials.

In Study 1, of the 40 children, the number reaching criterion ranged from 7 (on Trial C) to 27 (on Trial B). According to Cochran's test, the frequencies differ significantly for the four trials: $Q = 38.59$, $df = 3$, $p < .001$.

In Study 2, of the 32 children, the number reaching criterion ranged from 4 (on Trial E) to 24 (on both Trials A and B). The frequencies differ significantly for the six trials: $Q = 64.75$, $df = 5$, $p < .001$.

Comparison and interpretation of the results of the two studies is facilitated by converting the frequencies to percentages. The results appear in Table 9-1. In general, the children in Study 2 approached the experimenter somewhat more frequently than those in Study 1. This is probably because of our use of an initial totally positive trial in Study 2, which served as a warm up or habituation trial.

What is more noteworthy is that if the percentages are arrayed from high to low, as is done in Table 9-1, the rank occupied by each message is the same in the two separate experiments. Children approach routinely when the message is positive on both channels. The majority do the same when the message is positive on one channel while neutral on the other (Trials B and A). They are least likely to approach when the message is negative on one channel and neutral on the other (Trials E and F). The results for the discrepant or mutually-contradictory messages (Trials C and D) are intermediate.

The strength of the results in Table 9-1 led us to investigate whether there might be even stronger regularities in the observations, i.e.,

Table 9-1. Percentage of Children Reaching Criterion on Each Trial.

Trial	Visual Channel	Auditory Channel	Percentage of Subjects who Approached the Experimenter	
			Study 1	Study 2
Initial	+	+	na	100
Final	+	+	100	100
B	0	+	68	75
A	+	0	60	75
D	–	+	52	59
C	+	–	18	34
F	0	–	na	28
E	–	0	na	13

whether they scaled. The data appear in Tables 9-2 and 9-3, separately for the two studies.

Entries in the body of Tables 9-2 and 9-3 indicate whether a child approached the experimenter (x) or stayed away from him (o) on each trial.

In Study 1, there were 13 children who did not approach the experimenter on any of the trials except the final totally positive trial. These subjects (2, 4, 8, ... 36) are represented by the top 12 rows in Table 9-2. In Study 2, there were only four such abstainers (2, 14, 20, and 23) and they appear in the top four rows of Table 9-3.

In the first study, 6 children approached the experimenter on every trial. Their results are represented by the bottom six rows in Table 9-2. There were two such children in the second study, and their results appear at the bottom of Table 9-3.

Arrayed in the tables between these extremes are the children who reached criterion on some but not all trials. We arranged the rows in each table so that those who approached the least are near the top of the table and those who approached the most are near the bottom. We sought a steplike representation of the data whereby no o would be under the steps while most of the x's would be. This representation is achieved by arraying the rows in the order shown in Tables 9-2 and 9-3.

Table 9-2 shows that of the 40 children in Study 1 there are only 4 whose data are not described totally by the steps. They are cases 23, 35, 40 and 17. In three of these cases, one x is out of order and in the fourth case two x's are out of order. (See the column near the right of the table.)

Table 9-3 shows that in the second study there were 9 children whose results are not entirely described by the steplike function. This larger proportion is not surprising, for the number of items to be scaled is half again as large as in Study 1. All of those children in Table 9-3 represented by a 0 in the column labelled "Number of X's Out of Order

Table 9-2. Observations on Whether Child Does (x) or Does Not (o) Approach the Experimenter on Each Trial, Study 1.[a]

Child's Case Number	Child's Age in Months	Child's Gender	Visual Auditory	C + −	D − +	A + 0	B 0 +	FI + +	No. of Xs Out of Order in Row	Child's Sequence of Trials[b]
2	17	f		o	o	o	o	x	0	1
4	23	f		o	o	o	o	x	0	3
8	19	f		o	o	o	o	x	0	1
9	14	f		o	o	o	o	x	0	1
16	12	m		o	o	o	o	x	0	2
19	41	f		o	o	o	o	x	0	1
22	19	m		o	o	o	o	x	0	2
24	27	m		o	o	o	o	x	0	2
25	15	m		o	o	o	o	x	0	3
27	18	m		o	o	o	o	x	0	1
34	31	f		o	o	o	o	x	0	4
36	13	m		o	o	o	o	x	0	4
23	17	f		o	o	x	o	x	1	3
6	24	m		o	o	o	x	x	0	4
35	25	f		o	x	o	x	x	1	1
40	42	f		o	x	o	x	x	1	2
17	20	f		x	x	o	x	x	2	3
1	42	f		o	o	x	x	x	0	1
10	21	f		o	o	x	x	x	0	4
14	24	f		o	o	x	x	x	0	1
30	41	f		o	o	x	x	x	0	3
37	40	m		o	o	x	x	x	0	2
5	26	m		o	x	x	x	x	0	4
7	27	m		o	x	x	x	x	0	2
13	36	f		o	x	x	x	x	0	4
20	25	f		o	x	x	x	x	0	3
21	42	f		o	x	x	x	x	0	4
28	31	f		o	x	x	x	x	0	1
29	30	m		o	x	x	x	x	0	4
31	31	f		o	x	x	x	x	0	1
32	40	m		o	x	x	x	x	0	3
33	33	f		o	x	x	x	x	0	2
38	34	m		o	x	x	x	x	0	3
39	21	f		o	x	x	x	x	0	3
3	30	m		x	x	x	x	x	0	3
11	30	f		x	x	x	x	x	0	2
12	23	m		x	x	x	x	x	0	4
15	12	m		x	x	x	x	x	0	4
18	14	f		x	x	x	x	x	0	2
26	31	f		x	x	x	x	x	0	2

Percentage approaching experimenter: 18 52 60 68 100

[a] Symbols used for visual and auditory channels over the five trials are: − = stay away, 0 = neutral or silent. and + = come here.
[b] Trial sequences are: 1 = ACBD, 2 = ADBC, 3 = BCAD, and 4 = BDCA.

in Row" are the 23 for whom the stairway perfectly represents their responses to the messages.

The existence of this stairway structure in each set of observations suggests that the messages constitute a unidimensional and cumulative ordinal scale, i.e., a Guttman scale. The order of the messages in that scale is the one appearing at the top of Tables 9-2 and 9-3 and is the same as the rank order in Table 9-1:

$$E < F < C < D < A < B < FI$$

At the risk of being repetitious, we must stress that this scale is not a priori. It emerged from inspection of the children's responses. There was no other way to array the messages that would yield such a clear cumulative structure in either set of observations.

When evaluated by scalogram analysis, the data in both Tables 9-2 and 9-3 meet the criteria for a Guttman scale. Table 9-2 has a coefficient of reproducibility of .96, which represents a 22% improvement over the minimum marginal reproducibility (.74). Table 9-3 has a coefficient of reproducibility of .91, which represents a 15% improvement over the minimum marginal reproducibility (.76). The coefficients of scalability are .85 for Table 9-2 and .62 for Table 9-3, both values that are above the stated minimum level for a Guttman scale.

Before discussing the meaning of the scale, we should consider other sources of contribution to the results in addition to the character of the messages.

We designed the studies so that sequences were counterbalanced with treatments and therefore sequence effects could be assessed independently. The detailed analyses of sequence effects appears in Volkmar & Siegel (1979, p. 7) and in Volkmar, Hoder, & Siegel (1980, p. 502). In brief, they are not significant. The order of trials does not affect the results significantly nor account for them.

The same is true of sex differences. The detailed discussions of sex of subject in Volkmar and Siegel (1978, pp. 8-9) and in Volkmar, Hoder, and Siegel (1980, p. 502) support the conclusion that there are no systematic sex differences in the results. Readers may reassure themselves on this point by examining the third column in Tables 9-2 and 9-3 and noting that males and females are interspersed more or less randomly in those columns.

Age differences are somewhat more perplexing. In general, of course, older children within this age range move more quickly: they leave their chairs more directly, enter more squares in the room, and reach criterion more rapidly (Volkmar & Siegel, 1979, p. 8). These results are clearer on those trials on which most children eventually approach the experimenter, Trials A and B. On those trials on which most children do not, age differences in performance time are minimal.

Table 9-3. Observations on Whether Child Does (x) or Does Not (o) Approach the Experimenter on Each Trial, Study 2.[a]

Child's Case Number	Child's Age in Months	Child's Gender		Child's Behavior on Each of Eight Trials								No. of X's Out of Order in Row	Child's Sequence of Trials[b]	Child's Rank
				E	F	C	D	A	B	IN	FI			
			Visual	−	0	+	−	+	0	+	+			
			Auditory	0	−	−	+	0	+	+	+			
2	17	m		o	o	o	o	o	o	x	x	0	7	2.5
14	16	m		o	o	o	o	o	o	x	x	0	3	2.5
20	19	m		o	o	o	o	o	o	x	x	0	8	2.5
23	14	m		o	o	o	o	o	o	x	x	0	1	2.5
4	36	m		o	o	o	o	x	o	x	x	1	8	6
15	28	m		o	o	o	o	x	o	x	x	1	1	6
16	28	m		o	o	o	o	x	o	x	x	1	5	6
19	36	f		o	o	o	x	x	o	x	x	2	6	8
5	16	m		o	o	o	o	x	x	x	x	0	2	9.5
8	42	m		o	o	o	o	x	x	x	x	0	6	9.5
9	16	m		o	o	x	o	x	x	x	x	1	8	11.5
29	28	m		o	o	x	o	x	x	x	x	1	8	11.5
10	16	f		o	o	o	x	x	x	x	x	0	5	13.5
11	13	f		o	o	o	x	x	x	x	x	0	3	13.5
12	24	f		o	x	o	x	x	x	x	x	1	1	15
3	18	f		x	x	o	o	x	x	x	x	2	4	16
17	21	m		o	o	x	x	x	x	x	x	0	7	19
22	27	f		o	o	x	x	x	x	x	x	0	4	19
27	27	m		o	o	x	x	x	x	x	x	0	7	19
31	24	m		o	o	x	x	x	x	x	x	0	1	19
13	25	f		o	o	x	x	x	x	x	x	0	5	19
1	37	m		x	o	x	x	x	x	x	x	1	7	22
18	20	m		o	x	x	x	x	x	x	x	0	5	23.5

25	24	m	o	o	x	x	x	x	x	x	0	3	23.5
7	14	m	o	x	x	x	x	x	x	x	0	6	27.5
21	14	m	o	x	x	x	x	x	x	x	0	2	27.5
24	38	m	o	x	x	x	x	x	x	x	0	2	27.5
26	34	m	o	x	x	x	x	x	x	x	0	3	27.5
28	15	f	o	x	x	x	x	x	x	x	0	4	27.5
32	30	m	o	x	x	x	x	x	x	x	0	2	27.5
6	19	f	x	x	x	x	x	x	x	x	0	6	31.5
30	39	m	x	x	x	x	x	x	x	x	0	4	31.5

[a]Symbols used for visual and auditory channels over the eight trials are: − = stay away, 0 = neutral or silent, and + = come here.
[b]Trial sequences are: 1 = AFCEBD, 2 = BECFAD, 3 = EBCFAD, 4 = FACBED, 5 = AFDEBC, 6 = BEDFAC, 7 = EBDAFC, and 8 = FADBEC.

The child's age in months appears in the second column of Table 9-2 for the subjects in Study 1 and in the comparable column of Table 9-3 for the subjects in Study 2. We can correlate those ages with the child's rank on the scale (see the right-hand column of Table 9-3). For Study 1, this correlation is $r_s = .30$. For Study 2, the correlation is $r_s = .16$.

The messages used in Studies 1 and 2 appear in the left-hand column of Table 9-4. The next two columns indicate whether each message's respective auditory and visual components are negative (– = stay away), neutral (0 = silent or expressionless), or positive (+ = come here).

The messages are arrayed in the order which emerges from the results in Tables 9-2 and 9-3. Those results are summarized, as a heuristic, in Table 9-4.

When the reader scans the patterns of +'s, 0's, and –'s, the first thing to be noticed is that the +'s are clustered at the top and the –'s are clustered at the bottom. This property of the scale reflects the simple observation that in each study more children approached in response to messages with positive components than to messages with negative components.

In fact, any message containing a – falls below all messages containing no –. Thus, the top four messages are

+	+
+	+
0	+
+	0

and none of these contains any –. Then the bottom four messages are

–	+
+	–
0	–
–	0

and all of these messages contain a – component.

The messages which elicit approach behavior universally are, not surprisingly, the totally positive messages. They fall at the top of the scale: +/+, +/+.

Table 9-4. Summary of Results of Studies 1 and 2.

Message	Visual	Auditory	Results
FI	+	+	Study 1 C ⟨ D ⟨ A ⟨ B ⟨ FI
IN	+	+	
B	0	+	Study 2 E ⟨ F ⟨ C ⟨ D ⟨ A ⟨ B ⟨ IN ⟨ FI
A	+	0	
D	–	+	
C	+	–	
F	0	–	
E	–	0	

The next two messages on the scale are those which are positive in one component and neutral in the other: B, 0/+ and A, +/0. What is interesting about these complements is that the message that is positive on the *auditory* channel attracts more approach behavior.

The same result is reflected by the relative positions of the next two messages, D (-/+) and C (+/-). In both Study 1 and Study 2, message D elicited much more approach behavior than its complement message C. These are the discrepant social communications, totally contradictory between channels. In the face of these outright contradictions, the children in Study 1 and those in Study 2 voted with their feet to respond to the *auditory* component of the message. This is perhaps the most striking comparison in these studies.

Messages with only 0 and - components essentially contain no invitation to approach at all. All the messages that rank higher on the scale are + in at least one channel. But messages F and E are not, and they fall at the bottom of the scale: F, 0/- and E, -/0. Given our other findings about the prepotence of the auditory message in two complementary messages, we are surprised to find that between messages E and F apparently the visual channel dominates. This is a reverse of our general finding.

Our general finding may be seen by examining the pattern of "valences" in the visual column and in the auditory column in Table 9-4. The reader will see that the array of +'s, 0's, and -'s is somewhat more orderly in the latter. This greater orderliness reflects the prepotence of the auditory message in influencing the children's behavior.

An Experiment with Adults

A Stanford undergraduate student who assisted us with Studies 1 and 2 wondered how adults would behave in response to the messages. For his honors thesis, he conducted an experiment modelled on Study 2 but using university students as subjects and experimenters (Crooks, Note 1). His 32 subjects averaged 21 years of age and included equal numbers of males and females. Half were assigned to a male experimenter, half to a female experimenter.

Several modifications of the protocol were introduced to make it usable with students. They were told the experiment replicated one with 2-year-olds to see how adults would respond in a communication situation devised originally for very young children. Trial length was shortened. No balloon was used. The third person in the room was a "referee" and timekeeper, not the mother. The experimenter said "stay seated" rather then "stay away." The implicit reason for approaching the experimenter was to pick up a block from the experimenter's table and hand it to the referee. It was not required that a subject respond appropriately to the initial and final +/+ messages in order to be included in the data analysis.

About four-fifths of the university students approached the experimenter is response to messages IN, FI, A, and B. Only about one-fourth
did so in response to messages C and D, the discrepant messages. Almost
none did so in response to messages E and F.

The scale yielded by the students' responses is

$$E \langle F \langle D \langle C \langle B \langle A$$

but the regularities in the students' data are not as impressive as those
in the children's data (Tables 9-2 and 9-3). It is worth mentioning that
this scale is in accord with various reports of research with adults show-
in that the visual message dominates the auditory for adults. The reader
will note that in Crooks' study, $E < F$, and $D < C$, and $B < A$.

As observers for all three studies, we felt that the comparability of
this one to the earlier two may have been compromised by differences
in the implicit attitudes of the subjects. The university students did not
appear uniformly to believe that the experiment was to compare their
responses to children's. Instead they apparently suspected some sort of
deception. Furthermore, the fact that the experimenter and the referee
were age peers of the subjects appeared to introduce a fun-and-games
and sometimes flirtatious tone to the encounter, however earnestly the
experimenter and referee maintained seriousness and decorum. Our
experience with this study left us more aware of the difficulties to be
encountered in comparing very young children's behavior in a laboratory
situation with that of adults.

Having counterbalanced sequence of trials across subjects as well as
sex of subject against sex of experimenter, Crooks analyzed his data for
effects other than those of the messages. With several measures, he
found occasional isolated effects but the overall pattern of his results
was the same as the pattern with children: message (trial) effects are
major and prepotent, sequence effects are nonexistent, and sex of subject effects are minor and scattered. He did not find effects of sex of
experimenter.

The principal difference between his results with adults and the
results with children is that the visual component of the message seems
to be more significant than the auditory for adults, whereas the auditory
component dominates the visual for children.

Discussion

From the results of our two studies, we conclude that most very
young children can respond appropriately to an invitation to approach
or stay away when that invitation reaches them on a single channel,
either visual or auditory. Apparently an overall gestalt of communication

acts redundant across channels is not essential to conveying a simple message to children older than one year, however helpful it may be. Our third conclusion is that when the content of the visual channel and the auditory channel are contradictory, the information on the auditory channel guides the responses of most children. Trials C and D yield the relevant data, and the findings on both those trials are in the same direction for both studies. Indications from Crooks' study are that the opposite is true for adults.

The emergence of the Guttman scales from our two independent sets of data appears to suggest that a common underlying strategy was employed cognitively by the children in evaluating these messages. This strategy appears to involve the perception and interpretation of information across the two channels (rather than discounting or denial), and a tendency to rely on the auditory rather than the visual channel when the total "value" of the messages thus integrated would otherwise be the same.

Given the cognitive orderliness of the behavior across subjects, we think that the individual differences on the scale are social, reflecting different propensities to approach a strange experimenter holding an attractive balloon. We have no basis for judging the basis of those individual differences except that our evidence would not support the suspicion that they are developmental. Within the age range represented by our subjects, we did not find any pronounced trend for older children to be friendlier or more or less wary.

Because infants younger than one year lack the motor skills to approach an experimenter readily, we have not succeeded in extending our studies to a younger age group. Our pilot efforts to do so have left us with the impression that infants in the final quarter of the first year do attend to the messages but do not act on them predictably or promptly.

As for children older than those we studied, we believe the same messages could usefully be employed with children up to age four or so, but with older children our task and messages will increasingly impress them as trivial, silly, and uninvolving. This belief has no direct empirical verification in our research.

Even more obvious than the need to extend our findings about age is the need to extend our investigations to different tasks. All to date have used the "come here" and "stay away" messages. We are now collecting pilot data on different tasks. Our format is to give the child verbal instructions while simultaneously modeling behavior that is opposite to that instructed.

Our studies have some implications for understanding compliance and negativism in young children. Our results suggest that children are most compliant with requests that are totally consistent across communication channels, e.g., our +/+ requests. The age group we studied is widely thought to be oppositional and negativistic. We suggest that it is important to distinguish true oppositional behavior—willful failure to comply with a request—from noncompliance arising from the child's inability to respond appropriately to requests that are either incomplete or mutually contradictory. Requests expressed merely verbally without supporting information in the tone of voice and in facial expressions and gestures are less apt to elicit compliance. The young child's apparent ability to interpret both the auditory and the visual channel, which we confirmed in our studies, could mislead parents and other caregivers to assume that presenting information on one channel is sufficient or even optimal for the child at any given time. This error in adult judgment could account for some of the negativism of the 2-year-old.

Volkmar and Cohen (1982) have analyzed autistic children's responses to verbal and nonverbal requests by an adult for verbal and nonverbal responses from the child. They identified a hierarchy of "negativistic" responses. With autistic youngsters, known to be intellectually retarded, verbal requests for nonverbal responses from the child were most apt to elicit compliance. Verbal requests for verbal responses were least likely to elicit compliance. This result also supports the suggestion that the child's current level of verbal and nonverbal skills, both receptive and expressive, needs to be considered before any behavior is labelled simply negativistic.

Humor and sarcasm are undoubtedly prominent among the discrepant communications young children encounter in everyday life. The literature on children's appreciation of humor appears to be scanty and to center on school-age children (Prentice & Fathman, 1975). It has been reported (Bugental, Kaswan, & Love, 1970a) that while adults often perceive discrepant messages as humorous, children perceive them as criticism. Joking messages, which combine a friendly tone of voice with critical lexical content, are seen as humorous and friendly by adults but as unfriendly and critical by children. This is yet another example of the child's literal-mindedness.

In our studies, only an occasional child perceived humorous aspects of our discrepant communication. Often their mothers, but not the children, laughed when first attending to them. The more common response of the children to discrepant communications was to be wary, perplexed, and hesitant. Even those who approached the experimenter in response to such messages did so diffidently and cautiously.

In their well known, "double-bind" hypothesis about the genesis of schizophrenia, Bateson, Jackson, Haley, and Weakland, (1956) proposed a relation between discrepancy in parental communications to children and the subsequent development of psychopathology in the children. They suggested that the parents of schizophrenics characteristically produce discrepant communications directed to the child. The recipient of these communications, unable to resolve the discrepancies, was consequently placed in the position of producing such communications himself. This attractive hypothesis stimulated a variety of empirical studies but in the end has resisted empirical testing (Schuam, 1967).

While studies of families with a "disturbed" child—and perhaps we should use quotation marks for *child* as well, for often the offspring has grown up by the time the research is conducted—have not supported the distinctiveness of double-bind communications to such families, they have indicated some relations between patterns of communication and psychopathology. For example, Beakel and Mehrabian (1969) did find an association between the negativity of parental communications and the degree of disturbance exhibited by their adolescents. What they did not uncover is a relation between psychopathology in the offspring and incongruity in parental communication. Bugental, Love, Kaswan, and April (1971) found higher frequencies of communication inconsistency among the mothers of children who demonstrated emotional or behavioral disturbances than among mothers of "normal" control children. A more recent study (Bugental & Love, 1975) confirmed that mothers of disturbed children, in comparison with mothers of normal children, are less assertive and definite in their vocal tone when expressing either approval or disapproval. Our series of studies is not designed to bear directly on the existence of double-bind communications in families nor on the possible relations between discrepant parental communications and child disturbance. Our work does suggest, however, that young children do respond with exquisite sensitivity to discrepancies in communications.

Most writers who consider the mass appeal of television center on its visual component. In fact, it is common to speak of television as a visual medium. One is led to question this by the observation that infants, widely thought to be especially attuned to visual inputs, attend to television only sporadically. Our research leads us to think that the appeal of television to very young children is that it is a redundant medium, with both visual and auditory components. Children attend steadily to television after age one or two, and their attention time increases rapidly between the second and third birthdays. Anderson's (Levin & Anderson, 1976) laboratory studies of television watching have shown that "children begin purposive, systematic television viewing between 2 and 3 years of age," an appraisal that appears also in independent parental reports. Although attention to television can be assessed most readily by observing the child's viewing or nonviewing, the fact is that auditory cues seem to predominate in children's determining whether to watch or not (Anderson, Lorch, Field, & Sanders, 1981), a finding that has emerged independently in the Kansas studies (Rice, Houston, & Wright, 1980). Among the cues which recruit children's visual attention to television are women's voices, children's voices, auditory changes, peculiar voices, sound effects, laughter, and applause. Cues that terminate TV viewing and inhibit further looks include extended zooms and pans, animals, and still pictures (Collins, 1982, p. 8).

The notion that young children benefit from, and might even require, redundant inputs over the auditory and visual channels is suggested by the enthusiasm young children display for television—it occupies more hours in their day than any activity except sleep—and their difficulties in using the telephone (a single channel medium), their boredom with silent films (another single channel medium), and their apathy towards opera (a multichannel entertainment form in which the auditory component is complex and sophisticated).

Summary

In typical social interactions information is conveyed redundantly over the visual and auditory channels, i.e., a speaker's facial expressions and gestures are generally consistent with tone of voice and lexical content of speech. Adults selectively attend to the different channels of communication for different sorts of information; adults may, for example, rely on lexical content for "objective" meaning and extralexical content for evaluation of a speaker's attitude. Several distinct lines of research suggest the importance of both auditory and visual information to the young child. The precise strategies used by young children in deriving meaning from social communications and the relative salience of visual and auditory information in young children's judgments regarding such communications were investigated in two studies employing a total of 72 young children, ages 12 to 42 months as subjects. Children were observed individually in the presence of their mothers. Messages were delivered by male experimenters and varied systematically between the auditory and visual channels. Some messages consisted of either a visual or auditory instruction to approach or stay away from the experimenter. Other messages were discrepant in that an approach message on one channel was contradicted by a simultaneous "stay away" message on the other channel. Order of presentation was counterbalanced across subjects. When the experimenter unambiguously invited the child to approach, all children did so in response to the consistent information on both the visual and auditory channels. When the request was emitted on only one channel, about three fourths of the subjects conformed to the request. When the message was discrepant across communication channels, children more often conformed to the auditory rather than to the visual message. Responses to the messages were observed to form a cumulative, ordinal scale which suggested that a common underlying strategy was employed by the subjects in interpreting the communications. An experiment with adults using similar messages suggests that the visual component of such communication is relatively more significant than it is in the case for young children.

Acknowledgments. The Boys Town Center for the Study of Youth Development at Stanford provided financial support for this research, as did National Institute of Mental Health Training Grant MH11028-12. Initial versions of the two studies reported here were read at the annual meeting of the American Psychological Association, Washington, DC, in September 1976, and at the biennial meeting of the Society for Research in Child Development in New Orleans, Louisiana, March 1977. We are grateful to E. Lawrence Hoder, Betty Anne Shoaff, Gary W. Crooks, and Robert A. Bailey who assisted in observation and videotaping. We thank Helena E. Kraemer and Samuel J. Messick for statistical advice and Harriet L. Rheingold for several useful discussions with us. Figure 9-1 is adapted with permission from "Young children's responses to discrepant social communications," by F. R. Volkmar & A. E. Siegel, *Journal of Child Psychology and Psychiatry*, 1979, *20*, pp. 139-149, copyright Pergamon Press. Figure 9-2 and Table 9-2 and 9-3 are adapted with permission from "Discrepant social communications," by F. R. Volkmar, E. L. Hoder, & A. E. Siegel, *Developmental Psychology*, 1980, *16*, pp. 495-505, 1980, copyright American Psychological Association.

Reference Note

1. Crooks, G. Adult responses to discrepant social communication. Undergraduate Honors Thesis, Program in Human Biology, Stanford University, 1977.

References

Ainsworth, M. D. S., Blehar, M. C., Waters, E., & Wall, S. *Patterns of attachment: A psychological study of the strange situation.* Hillsdale, NJ.: Erlbaum, 1978.

Anderson, D. R., Lorch, E. P., Field, D. E., & Sanders, J. The effects of TV program comprehensibility on preschool children's visual attention to television. *Child Development*, 1981, *52*, 151-157.

Bateson, G., Jackson, D. D., Haley, J., & Weakland, J. Toward a theory of schizophrenia. *Behavioral Science*, 1956, *1*, 241-264.

Beakel, N. G., & Mehrabian, A. Inconsistent communications and psychopathology. *Journal of Abnormal Psychology*, 1969, *74*, 126-130.

Birch, H. G. & Lefford, A. Intersensory development in children. *Mongraphs of the Society for Research in Child Development*, 1963, *28* (2, Whole No. 89).

Bronson, G. W. Infants' reactions to unfamiliar persons and novel objects. *Monographs of the Society for Research in Child Development*, 1972, *37* (3, Whole No. 148).

Brooks, R., Brandt, L., & Wiener, M. Differential response to two communication channels: Socioeconomic class differences in response to verbal reinforcers communicated with and without tonal inflection. *Child Development*, 1969, *40*, 453-470.

Buck, R. Nonverbal communication of affect in children. *Journal of Personality and Social Psychology*, 1975 *31*, 644-653.

Buck, R. Nonverbal communication of affect in preschool children: Relationships with personality and skin conductance. *Journal of Personality and Social Psychology*, 1977, *35*, 225-236.

Bugental, D. C. Interpretations of naturally occurring discrepancies between words and intonation, modes of inconsistency resolution. *Journal of Personality and Social Psychology*, 1974, *30*, 125-133.

Bugental, E. E., Kaswan, J. W., & Love, L. R. Perception of contradictory meanings conveyed by verbal and nonverbal channels. *Journal of Personality and Social Psychology*, 1970, *16*, 647-655. (a)

Bugental, D. E., Kaswan, J. W., Love, L. R., & Fox, M. N. Child versus adult perception of evaluative messages in verbal, vocal, and visual channels. *Developmental Psychology*, 1970, *2*, 367-375. (b)

Bugental, D. E. Love, L. R. Kaswan, J. W., & April, C. Verbal-nonverbal conflict in parental messages to normal and disturbed children. *Journal of Abnormal Psychology*, 1971, *77*, 6-10.

Bugental, D. E., Love, L. R., & Gianetto, R. M Perfidious feminine faces. *Journal of Personality and Social Psychology*, 1971, *17*, 314-318.

Bugental, D. B., & Love, L. Nonassertive expression of parental approval and disapproval and its relationship to child disturbance. *Child Development*, 1975, *46*, 747-752.

Collins, W. A. Cognitive processing aspects of TV viewing. In D. Pearl (Ed.), *Television and Behavior: Ten years of Scientific Progress*, NIMH, Washington, DC, 1982.

DePaulo, B. M. & Rosenthal, R. Age changes in nonverbal decoding as a function of increasing amounts of information. *Journal of Experimental Child Psychology*, 1978, *26*, 280-287.

Harper, R. G., Wiens, A. W., & Matarazzo, J. D. *Nonverbal communication: The state of the art.* New York: Wiley, 1978.

Hinde, R. A. *Biological bases of human social behavior.* New York: McGraw-Hill, 1974.

Jancovic, M., Devoe, S., & Wiener, M. Age-related changes in hand and arm movements as nonverbal communication: Some conceptualizations and an empirical exploration. *Child Development*, 1975, *46*, 922-928.

Levin, S. R. & Anderson, D. R. The development of attention. *Journal of Communication*, 1976, *26*, 126-135.

Levitt, E. A. The relationship between abilities to express emotional meanings vocally and facially. In J. R. Davitz (Ed.), *The communication of emotional meaning.* New York: McGraw-Hill, 1964.

Mayo, C. & LaFrance, M. On the acquisition of nonverbal communication: A review. *Merrill-Palmer Quarterly*, 1978, *24*, 213-228.

Mehrabian, A. & Ferris, S. R. Inference of attitudes from nonverbal communication. *Journal of Consulting Psychology*, 1967, *31*, 248-252.

Mehrabian, A. & Wiener, M. Decoding of inconsistent communications. *Journal of Personality and Social Psychology*, 1967, *6*, 109-114.

Peterson, C. L., Danner, F. W., & Flavell, J. H. Developmental changes in children's response to three indications of communicative failure. *Child Development*, 1972, *43*, 1463-1468.

Piaget, J. *The origins of intelligence in children.* New York: Norton, 1963.

Prentice, N. M. & Fathman, R. E. Joking riddles: A developmental index of children's humor. *Developmental Psychology*, 1975, *11*, 210-216.

Rheingold, H. L. The effect of a strange environment on the behavior of infants. In B. M. Foss (Ed.), *Determinants of infant behavior* (Vol. 4). London: Metheun, 1969.

Rice, M. L., Houston, A. C., & Wright, J. C. The forms and codes of television: Effects on children's attention, comprehension and social behavior. In D. Pearl, (Ed.), *Television and behavior: Ten years of scientific progress*, NIMH, Washington, DC, 1982.

Schuam, A. I. The double-bind hypothesis a decade later. *Psychological Bulletin*, 1967, *68*, 409-416.

Solomon, D., & Ali, F. A. Age trends in the perception of verbal reinforcers. *Developmental Psychology*, 1972, 7, 288-243.

Solomon, D. & Yaeger, J. Determinants of boys' perceptions of verbal reinforcers. *Developmental Psychology*, 1969, *1*, 637-645. (a)

Solomon, D. & Yaeger, J. Effects of content and intonation on perceptions of verbal reinforcers. *Perceptual and Motor Skills*, 1969, *28*, 319-327. (b)

Volkmar, F. R. & Cohen, D. J. A hierarchical analysis of patterns of noncompliance in autistic and behavior disturbed children. *Journal of Autism and Developmental Disorders*, 1982, *12*, 35-42.

Volkmar, F. R., Hoder, E. L., & Siegel, A. E. Discrepant social communications. *Developmental Psychology*, 1980, *16*, 495-505.

Volkmar, F. R. & Siegel, A. E. Young children's responses to discrepant social communications. *Journal of Child Psychology and Psychiatry*, 1979, *20*, 139-149.

Wiener, M. & Mehrabian, A. *Language within language*. New York: Appleton, Century, Croft, 1968.

Weiner, M., Devoe, S., Rubinow, S., & Geller, J. Nonverbal behavior and nonverbal communication. *Psychological Review*, 1972, *79*, 185-214.

Zigler, E. & Kanzer, P. The effectiveness of two classes of reinforcers on the performance of middle-class and lower-class children. *Journal of Personality*, 1962, *30*, 157-163.

Part Five
Personality Development and Individual Difference Approaches to Nonverbal Behavior

CHAPTER TEN

Social Skills and Nonverbal Behavior

Robert S. Feldman, John B. White, and Debra Lobato

Introduction

Social skills are an important aspect of individual difference among children. Variously conceived of as "social competence," "impression management," or "interpersonal competence," social skills generally refer to the complex set of behavioral and cognitive skills that are used to direct and facilitate social behavior (Eisler & Frederiksen, 1980). Implicit in the concept of social skills is the notion that social behavior is comprised of both verbal and nonverbal skills.

In this chapter, the use and control of nonverbal behavior is viewed as a specific social skill that can be employed during social interaction. Although nonverbal behavior has a number of functions, including its use as a replacement for verbal behavior or to augment and support speech (Argyle, 1976), we will concentrate on its role in the maintenance and facilitation of social interaction. Our primary assumption is that nonverbal behavioral abilities are related to other sorts of social skills and that individuals who show a particular level of competence in their nonverbal encoding and decoding abilities will show a concomitant degree of success in other related social skills. We also hypothesize that there are individual differences in nonverbal behavioral skills that exist independently of age per se.

Research in Children's Social Skills

During recent years, there has been a good deal of research on the development of social skills in children. The research issues have included the identification and assessment of the component skills of social behavior (e.g., Herson & Bellack, 1977; Hartup, Glazer, & Charlesworth, 1967), the design and implementation of strategies that remediate existing social deficits (e.g., O'Connor, 1972; Whitman, Mercurio, & Caponigri, 1970), and development of strategies that prevent potential future problems. Much of the impetus for this research has been provided by evidence of the relation between social skills in childhood and later interpersonal adjustment in adulthood (cf. VanHasselt, Herson, White-hill, & Bellack, 1979; Combs & Slaby, 1977). Specifically, children and adolescents who have had poor social relationships with their peers later demonstrate a greater rate of delinquency (Roff, Sells, & Golden, 1972), bad-conduct discharges from military service (Roff, 1961), and adult mental health problems (Cowen, Pederson, Babigan, Izzo, & Trost, 1973).

Although work in children's social skills has acknowledged the importance of both verbal and nonverbal abilities, most researchers have emphasized the verbal components of social skills. Yet, a good deal of research on nonverbal behavior has indicated that the nonverbal communication channels can be more influential than the verbal channels, at least in the communication of affective states (e.g., Mehrabian & Wiener, 1967; Watson, 1972). Indeed, some work has demonstrated that there is a relationship between nonverbal behavior and certain personality and behavioral traits potentially related to social skills.

Buck has presented evidence that the ability of preschoolers (1975, 1977) and undergraduates (Buck, Miller, & Caul, 1974) to nonverbally communicate affect to others is related to certain personality variables. In preschoolers, accurate "sending" ability positively correlated with having friends, high activity level, and measures of extraversion and hostility expression; and negatively correlated with measures of cooperation, emotional control and solitary play. Undergraduates who were categorized as "internalizers" (associated with greater introversion and sensitization) exhibited poorer ability than "externalizers" in nonverbally communicating their affective state to others.

Christensen, Farina, and Boudreau (1980) have suggested that sensitivity to the nonverbal cues of others is an important component of general social competence. Using the Greengrass-Jain Scale of social competency, 30 undergraduate women were divided into equal groups of high social competence and low social competence. Using standard interview questions, the subjects were instructed to interview confederates and to change the interview topic if it seemed to produce discomfort for the other person. Low-competence women persisted longer with interview topics that produced nonverbal signs of discomfort in the partner. After the interviews, these women accurately reported when their partners began to exhibit signs of distress, but they had continued with the interview because the distresssed reaction did not seem warranted. Christensen et al. concluded that the unskilled women based their judgments on situational, rather than on interpersonal factors, tending to act according to how they felt others should behave, rather than on their actual behavior.

Although prior research is suggestive of a relationship between nonverbal behavior and social competence, most earlier work has been limited primarily to adult or preschool populations. Because of the important changes that occur during middle childhood and adolescence in social abilities, these periods are of particular interest. Accordingly, we designed two studies to examine the relationships between social skills and nonverbal behavior in subjects ranging in age from five to eighteen years. In our first work, we looked at a particular social skill, that of role-taking ability, and its relationship to nonverbal behavior. Our later research used a more global behavioral measure of social skills to determine the correspondence between subjects' nonverbal encoding and decoding abilities and their level of social competence.

Children's Encoding and Decoding Ability
and Role-Taking Skills

The method we used to investigate nonverbal encoding and decoding ability in our initial work was to examine children's skill in encoding and decoding deceptive communications. From an encoding perspective, we reasoned that the degree of nonverbal revelation of verbal deception is an indicant of encoding ability. Thus, nonverbal encoding skill is related to the degree to which a person masks from observers true, underlying feelings, and the fact that he or she is being verbally deceptive. This approach offers the advantage of relatively high ecological validity. Subjects who are attempting to deceive an interactant are involved in an ongoing social interaction and must decide what nonverbal cues are appropriate throughout the course of the interaction in order to successfully conceal their true feelings. Similarly, the detection of another's deception can be considered an important measure of skill in the use of nonverbal behavior during social interaction and, thus, we used this as a measure of decoding ability.

Encoding

Our research began by considering the question of how children develop the ability to be verbally deceptive effectively. One basic hypothesis of the research was that the ability to use and control nonverbal behavior is a developmental skill. This hypothesis was based on a number of types of evidence. As children develop, they grow both in cognitive ability (Piaget & Inhelder, 1969) and fine muscular control (Charlesworth & Kreutzer, 1973). Furthermore, as children gain more awareness of the social ecology and become less egocentric, they develop the skill to put themselves in the position of an observer and see the situation from an observer's point of view. Flavell and his associates have referred to this ability, in reference to verbal communication skills, as "taking the role of the other" (Flavell, Botkin, Fry, Wright, & Jarvis, 1968).

Role-taking skills would seem to be particularly critical in developing control over nonverbal behavior during social interaction. Role-taking theory assumes that the skill to be an effective interactant in social situations rests partially upon the ability to take the "other" (the interactant) into account. The individual must not only possess a set of attributes or performance skills in a given situation, but he must also be aware of the nature of the impact that various alternative behaviors will have upon the other. Thus, an individual must have a sensitivity towards the presence of an interactant.

Research by Flavell and others (e.g., Feffer, 1959; Selman & Byrne, 1974; Urberg & Docherty, 1976) has shown a clear developmental sequence in role-taking ability. Preschool children appear to have relatively little knowledge that there can be variation in perspective from that of their own view. Sensitivity grows throughout middle childhood, however, and by the time the individual reaches adolescence, he or she is much more successful in taking the role of the other into account. It should be noted, however, that even adults vary in their role-taking ability.

The development of role-taking skills would appear to be related to the ability to manage nonverbal behavior while being deceptive. In order to be deceptive successfully, individuals must possess not only the skill to control their behavior, but must also be aware that such nonverbal behavior may have an effect upon others. Relating this to the role-taking literature, one would expect role-taking ability to influence one's ability to control nonverbal behavior while being deceptive, and, thus, skill in controlling nonverbal behavior would show a developmental progression. More specifically, it seems reasonable to expect an increase, concomitant with the growth of role-taking skills, in the ability to encode and control nonverbal behavior. Indeed, role-taking ability could be a better predictor of nonverbal encoding skill than age per se.

Although theoretically compelling, the notion that there are changes in the use and control of nonverbal behavior during childhood has received little direct, or even indirect, empirical support. Most of the research relating to the development of nonverbal behavior in children has attempted to show how a particular emotional state is displayed differentially at various age levels. Spawned primarily by Darwin's (1872/1965) view that there is a phylogenetic continuity of facial expressions for specific emotion-evoking situations, the nature of this research is exemplified by the observations of Spitz (1963), who has outlined a progression of nonverbal encoding during the first year of life and how it relates to infants' emotions. Overall, there is now a reasonably large body of research on the development of nonverbal behavior as it relates to the expression of emotions.

In contrast, very little research has looked at the developmental process with respect to the management of nonverbal behavior. There is some indirect evidence, from a study of a role-playing nature by Odom and Lemond (1972), that increasing age leads to more proficiency in the control and use of nonverbal behavior. Odom and Lemond (1972) asked children in kindergarten and fifth grade to encode poses presenting eight emotions. There was a clear developmental trend: the older subjects were more successful in producing the appropriate expressions (as determined by adult raters), which suggest that the older children had greater proficiency in the encoding of their nonverbal behavior. However, few studies have directly investigated the nature of the changes that occur in the ability to spontaneously manage nonverbal behavior.

Decoding

We also considered the development of children's ability to successfully interpret others' nonverbal cues. It is clear that social interaction is often guided by the interpretation of nonverbal cues that are not consciously communicated. Effective interpersonal relationships demand the interpretation of subtle nonverbal cues that are transmitted without the intention of the sender (and even may be responded to without the awareness of the receiver). It is often insufficient to respond to others simply on the basis of what is intentionally being conveyed. Successful social interaction also depends on the ability to go beyond what is being communicated verbally, by making inferences about the underlying feelings and motivations of others on the basis of nonverbal cues. Numerous studies have supported the notion that the interpretation of nonverbal behavior is important in successful social interaction by demonstrating that individuals who are proficient at decoding nonverbal cues also tend to be more effective in their interpersonal relationships (Hall, Rosenthal, Archer, DiMatteo, & Rogers, 1978; Rosenthal, Hall, Archer, DiMatteo, & Rogers, 1979; Rosenthal, Hall, DiMatteo, Rogers, & Archer, 1979).

There have been only a handful of experiments conducted examining children's skill at decoding nonverbal cues, and only one of these has looked at decoding of dissembled affect. Most existing studies have either been directed at the emergence of nonverbal decoding skills in infancy (for a review, see Charlesworth & Kreutzer, 1973), or at decoding ability of preschool children (Dashiell, 1927; Gates, 1923; Honkavaara, 1961; Izard, 1971; Zuckerman & Przewuzman, 1979). The most relevant study was carried out by DePaulo and Jordan (this volume) who compared the ability of sixth, eighth, tenth, twelfth graders, and college students in detecting deception and found increases in ability with age. However, the stimulus persons being decoded were adults; to date, no studies have examined decoding of verbal deception of other children *by* children during middle childhood.

The preceding theory and research suggest that, as with encoding, one crucial variable related to the development of the ability to accurately interpret the nonverbal behavior of others is role-taking skill. A child's ability to take the perspective of others would appear to be important in developing the ability to make inferences on the basis of others' nonverbal communication. By understanding the way others perceive a situation in which they are involved, an observer should be relatively accurate in interpreting the nonverbal behavior that is a reaction to that situation. On the other hand, an inability to imagine the way others will react in various situations will tend to make nonverbal cues difficult to comprehend accurately. Thus, the situation of an observer who is deficient in the ability to take the perspective of an other may be seen as analogous to the case in which an observer is asked to make a judgment about another's nonverbal behavior, but who is not given information regarding the context in which the nonverbal cues are emitted. The interpretation of nonverbal behavior under such circumstances will tend to be idiosyncratic and probably will depend on the individual's guess about the type of situation that evoked the nonverbal cues. The observer's understanding of the stimulus situation is important because identical nonverbal cues that are believed to have been elicited in different contexts will have different implications concerning the underlying feelings and motivations of the person being judged. Theoretically, the individual who is adept at taking the perspective of others will have a better understanding of the context in which nonverbal cues are emitted, and consequently, will have greater insight when interpreting the nonverbal behavior of others.

Overview

In our first study, subjects participated as both encoders and decoders. Children's ability to effectively manage their nonverbal behavior was assessed by our leading them to be deceptive verbally. Then, adult observers viewed silent videotapes of the children and indicated whether they thought the children were lying or telling the truth. The children's ability to accurately interpret the nonverbal cues of others was measured by putting the children in the role of observers attempting to assess the truthfulness of other children on the basis of the same silent videotapes. To test the hypothesis of a relationship between nonverbal behavioral skills and role-taking, the children's role-taking ability was determined using an objective measure.

Method and Procedure

The children who acted as nonverbal encoders ranged in age from 5 to 12 years, with approximately equal numbers at each year. There were 32 males and 29 females, and each child was individually observed. The children were administered a variant of Feffer's Role-taking Task, a measure of role-taking skill (Feffer, 1959). The task consisted of showing subjects a picture containing three individuals and having them tell a story about the picture as a whole. Subjects were then asked to pretend that they were one of the people in the picture and to describe what was happening to them in the story and how they would feel. This same procedure was then carried out for each of the other figures in the story. Each subject was asked to do this for two different pictures.

The subjects' responses were coded by two scorers according to criteria described by Feffer (1959). Basically, scoring consists of assessing subjects' ability to take the perspective of others as indicated by changes in description of characters from the initial story. The scoring also takes into account the level of sophistication of the description of the actors.

Following completion of the role-taking measure, the children were led to be both verbally truthful and verbally deceptive in order to assess their skill at nonverbal encoding. In addition, the type of deception was manipulated by instructing half of the children to pretend to enjoy a negative experience, while the other children were asked to pretend to dislike a positive experience.

The children were told that the purpose of the experiment was to sample two drinks and attempt to convince an interviewer that both drinks either tasted good (positive verbalization condition) or that both drinks tasted bad (negative verbalization condition), regardless of how the drinks actually tasted. The children were told that they should pretend to like (or dislike) both drinks in order to "fool" the interviewer in a game-like situation. It was explained that they would taste each drink and then respond to a set of questions concerning how much they enjoyed the drinks.

Each child participated in both the truth and deception conditions. All children were given a sweetened grape drink mixed according to directions and an identical drink mixed without sugar. The children who were told to answer the questions as if they enjoyed both drinks (positive verbalization condition) were, therefore, lying after tasting the unsweetened drink and telling the truth after tasting the sweetened drink. Conversely, those who were asked to pretend that both drinks tasted bad (negative verbalization condition) were being truthful when talking about the unsweetened drink and deceptive while discussing the sweetened drink. The children tasted each beverage immediately before being asked the questions about the drink. The order in which the drinks were sampled was random, as was the assignment to either verbal-ization condition.

During each of the two interviews, a camera (which could be seen by the subjects) recorded the face and neck of the child. Fifteen-second silent segments of each child's responses while being truthful and decep-tive were then transcribed from the original tapes onto a new tape, in a random order. A total of 61 children participated in the nonverbal encoding task; therefore, the new tape consisted of 122 videotape seg-ments. Each segment showed a child responding to the same questions from the interviewer.

Twelve untrained male and female college-age observers viewed the silent videotape clips. Observers judged each segment on a forced-choice scale labeled "truthful" or "pretending" after having the procedure involved in making the videotapes described to them.

Decoding Procedure

The children who served as stimulus persons (encoders) were recon-tacted approximately six months after the initial study was conducted and were asked to participate as decoders in the second phase of the study. A total of 22 males and 17 females who were in the previous experiment agreed to serve as decoders. Due to the tedious nature of the judging process, each subject was shown only half of the samples, with the restriction that subjects did not view themselves on the tape. The subjects viewed the samples in two settings in order to minimize fatigue. The conditions under which the videotapes were made were reiterated to the subjects and they were asked to choose whether the stimulus person in each segment was being "truthful" or "pretending" on a forced-choice scale.

Results

Encoding

Nonverbal encoding scores were derived for each subject in the experiment. The encoding measure was a deception ability score, which consisted of the percentage of all observers who identified as being truthful a stimulus child who was actually being deceptive. Thus, the percentage correct across all observers of a particular child was deter-mined. Higher scores indicate more incorrect responses and more suc-cess at being deceptive on the part of the child.

The basic hypothesis of the study suggested that role-taking ability would be positively related to skill in managing one's nonverbal cues. Because the subjects' role-taking ability was significantly correlated with age ($r = .39$), partial correlations, removing the effects of age, were employed. There were no significant differences between types of lie (positive verbalization or negative verbalization), and, therefore, all analyses were carried out collapsing across the variable.

The partial correlation coefficients between role-taking ability and nonverbal encoding scores are reported in Table 10-1. The analysis of the entire group of subjects, collapsed across sex, confirmed the hypothesis that role-taking ability is positively related to skill in controlling one's nonverbal behavior. The partial correlation coefficient between role-taking ability and nonverbal encoding score indicated a moderate positive relationship, $r = .28$, $p < .05$, one-tailed. Therefore, children who were better able to take the perspective of others were also better able to avoid detection while being verbally deceptive.

A similar pattern of results was obtained for the sample of female subjects, although the correlation coefficient was of greater magnitude. As predicted, the partial correlation between role-taking ability and deception score was positive, $r = .43$, $p < .05$, one-tailed. Thus, higher role-taking abilities were associated with more success in controlling one's nonverbal behavior.

In contrast to the results of the total sample and those based on the female subjects, the hypothesized relationship between role-taking and nonverbal encoding ability was not confirmed for the sample of male subjects. Role-taking ability was only weakly associated with nonverbal encoding ability, $r = .20$, $p =$ n.s. However, the apparent difference between male and female partial correlations failed to reach statistical significance.

Correlations were also carried out between age and encoding ability. Surprisingly, age was not significantly related to encoding ability for males, females, or the entire sample.

Decoding

Decoding ability was measured by a deception detection score which was determined by the percentage of deceptive film segments that a child was able to correctly identify as "pretending." Higher scores indicated greater ability to identify other children who are dissembling.

The partial correlation coefficients between role-taking ability and nonverbal decoding scores are also presented in Table 10-1. The partial correlation, based on the entire sample, between role-taking ability and

Table 10-1. Relationship Between Nonverbal Skill and Role-Taking Ability (with Age of Subject Partialled out).

	Encoding	Decoding
Total Sample's Role-Taking	.278*	.343*
Female's Role-Taking	.425*	.579**
Male's Role-Taking	.204	.166

*$p < .05$
**$p < .01$

nonverbal decoding was also positive and statistically significant, $r = .34$, $p < .05$, one-tailed. Thus, subjects with higher role-taking scores were more adept at interpreting the nonverbal cues emitted by others. Results based on the female sample of subjects also indicated that success at detecting instances of deception in others is positively related to role-taking ability, $r = .58$, $p < .01$, one-tailed. As in the case of the encoding data, the male sample of subjects did not exhibit a statistically significant relationship between role-taking ability and the interpretation of nonverbal behavior, $r = .17$, $p = $ n.s. However, the difference between the partial correlations based on the male and female samples failed to reach statistical significance. There was also no significant relationship between age and decoding ability for males, females, or the total sample.

Encoding-Decoding Relationship

We also calculated correlations between subjects' encoding and decoding scores to assess the relationship between the ability to control nonverbal communication and skill in interpreting others' nonverbal cues. Data based on the entire sample of subjects did not yield a statistically significant relationship between encoding and decoding scores, $r = .18$, $p = $ n.s. However, analysis of the data based on the female sample of subjects indicates a positive correlation between encoding and decoding abilities, $r = .42$, $p < .05$, one-tailed. The male sample of subjects demonstrated a zero-order correlation between encoding and decoding scores, $r = .08$, $p = $ n.s.

Implications

The results of our first study clearly suggest the importance of cognitive role-taking ability in both the interpretation of others' nonverbal behavior and in avoiding detection while being verbally deceptive. The results of the sample of female subjects indicate a clear relationship between role-taking ability and successful detection of deception by other children. In addition, the awareness that one's nonverbal behavior during social interaction has an impact on the perception of others appears to be an important factor influencing the ability to control nonverbal cues. Girls who were better able to take the perspective of others in the role-taking task were also more effective at controlling their nonverbal behavior. These results are congruent with those of Shennum and Bugental (this volume), who found a relationship between perspective-taking ability and expression control.

Given the relationship between role-taking and both encoding and decoding ability, it is not surprising that encoding ability is positively related to nonverbal decoding ability. Furthermore, the relationship between nonverbal communication skills and role-taking ability are considerably stronger than the correlations between nonverbal abilities and age. This latter result implies that taking the perspective of others may be of more importance in the development of nonverbal communication skills than other cognitive abilities that are closely related to age (for example, intellectual ability).

The hypothesized relationship between role-taking and nonverbal skills failed to reach statistical significance for the male sample of subjects. This result suggests that other factors may play a strong role in the development of boys' nonverbal communication skills. A large body of research has demonstrated that women tend to be generally more proficient in nonverbal communication skills than men (see Hall, 1978, for a review of the literature). Women's superiority in nonverbal communication is generally attributed to the role that women in our culture traditionally play, which tends to emphasize abilities relevant to successful interpersonal relationships. The results of the present study suggest the possibility that cultural values may tend to inhibit the development of nonverbal communication skills in some males, despite the fact that they possess the requisite cognitive abilities. In contrast, cultural expectations may encourage females to develop nonverbal communication skills to their full potential.

The hypothesized relationship between role-taking ability and nonverbal communication assumes that skill in taking the perspective of others is causally related to the effective interpretation and control of nonverbal cues. As in any correlational study, however, it is impossible to unequivocally demonstrate a direct cause and effect relationship. Role-taking ability is obviously related to numerous aspects of cognitive processing in a highly complex manner. It is conceivable that some other type of cognitive ability, which is highly correlated with role-taking skill, is responsible for the observed relationship. However, the results of the present study show a nonsignificant correlation between age and both nonverbal encoding and decoding scores despite the fact that age and role-taking scores were highly correlated. This result suggests that role-taking is an important factor in determining the ability to interpret and control nonverbal cues. Cognitive skills of all types presumably increase with age, and, thus, statistical procedures that control for the effects of age would be expected to control for the effects of other cognitive factors.

Nevertheless, the possibility that other factors are responsible for the observed relationship cannot be ruled out. For instance, one specific alternative explanation for the present findings is that some general ability may influence both role-taking scores and the ability to avoid detection. For instance, children who are more skillful socially may be able to construct a story from various perspectives more easily, as well as being more successful in their nonverbal communication.

A similar argument may be put forth concerning children's ability to make discriminations. It is possible that children who possess a high general ability to differentiate stimuli are better at discriminating between perspectives in the role-taking task and are also more proficient in distinguishing nonverbal cues that are associated with deception from those associated with truthfulness. Thus, skill in discrimination may be an underlying determinant of both role-taking scores and nonverbal decoding scores.

The experimental paradigm that was employed in the present study provides a particularly stringent test of the hypothesized relationship between role-taking ability and successful detection of others' verbal decepetion. Because all subjects who participated as decoders had previously acted as stimulus persons, they were obviously familiar with the conditions under which the deceptive verbal behavior was elicited. Although a number of months passed between participation in the two phases of the experiment, there still was likely some recollection of the initial stimulus situation. Such memories probably were reinforced by the experimenter in the decoding phase, who reminded subjects of the nature of their earlier participation. This suggests that the advantage that the most proficient role-takers held over less proficient role-takers in placing themselves in the role of the stimulus persons may not have been as great as it would have been in a situation in which all the decoders had not participated first as stimulus persons. Thus, it is possible that the correlation between role-taking and accuracy in decoding could have been attenuated by the nature of the procedure that was employed.

Encoding and Decoding in Normal and
Emotionally Disturbed Adolescents

The results of our previous study show quite clearly that there is a relationship between individual's role-taking skills and their encoding and decoding abilities, at least for females. However, role-taking skills are but one of a complex of various social skills that might have been investigated, although clearly the ability to take the role of the other is a crucial skill associated with successful social interaction. In our next study, we examined adolescents' social skills in terms of ratings on a set of 17 specific competencies (such as "is considerate of peers' needs," "initiates contact and conversation with others," and—scored negatively—"is shy and withdrawn"). After dividing subjects into high and low social skills group, we examined their nonverbal encoding and decoding abilities. We also looked at two different populations of subjects which we expected to differ considerably in level of social skills. A group of residents of an institution for the socially and emotionally disturbed were compared to a group of their noninstitutionalized, well-adjusted peers.

We predicted that adolescents labeled emotionally disturbed would be less accurate than "normal" adolescents in their ability to nonverbally express their own affective states as well as to interpret the affective state of others using nonverbal cues. Moreover, following the same logic, we expected that even within the normal and emotionally disturbed samples, those subjects with better behavioral social skills would be more proficient in encoding and decoding than those with less adept social skills.

To test these hypotheses, normal and emotionally disturbed subjects were shown a series of scenes designed to evoke emotions that were positive, negative, or neutral in character. The subjects' nonverbal behavior while watching the scenes was rated by observers to determine their degree of encoding ability. To test decoding skills, subjects were shown the nonverbal behavior of a group of persons exposed to the same emotion-evoking scenes, and they were asked to decode the meaning of these persons' nonverbal behavior. It should be noted that although this procedure for determining skill in nonverbal encoding and decoding is methodologically quite different from that employed in our earlier study, we assumed that conceptually it provided a correlated measure of nonverbal skills.

Method and Procedures

We used two groups of subjects, one from an institution for the emotionally disturbed and the other from a normal suburban high school. The subjects in the emotionally disturbed sample were 12 male adolescents ranging in age from 13 to 16 years. To assess the general social skills level of each of these subjects, we had two teachers or therapists familiar with the behavior of each subject fill out a rating scale which listed 17 social skills. These ratings were used to find a general level of social skill functioning for each subject. The subjects were then divided into groups of high and low social skills using a median split.

The normal sample consisted of the group of 12 adolescents matched in age to the subjects in the disturbed sample. These subjects had no history of psychopathology or institutionalization. Once again, to get a general measure of social competence, subjects in this group were rated on a behavioral social skills measure by at least two teachers and counselors familiar with them. The scale was analogous to the measure for the disturbed sample and, except for minor changes in wording, tapped the same skills. Subjects in this group were divided into high and low social skills groups. Thus, our experimental design was a 2×2 factorial with two population levels (emotionally disturbed or normal) and two social skills levels.

Using Buck's (1975) methodology of eliciting emotional reactions, we employed a series of three, two-minute stimulus videotapes which were designed to evoke positive, neutral, or negative emotional experiences. The positive tape was a sequence from a television comedy series; the negative tape was taken from a film depicting the effects of the bombing of Hiroshima; and the neutral tape presented views of a bucolic pastoral scene. Pilot testing and experimental results showed that both the normal and emotionally disturbed subjects rated the affective content of the three tapes appropriately.

To test subject's encoding ability, each subject was asked to watch the three two-minute stimulus tapes (with order counterbalanced within subjects). After viewing each tape, subjects were asked to rate their affective experience on a 5-point scale that ranged from very unpleasant to very pleasant. Videotapes of the stimulus persons viewing each of the three stimulus tapes were made. Ten-second samples were then placed in random order on a new master tape which was shown to a group of college undergraduates, who rated the facial expressions of the subjects using the same 5-point scale that the subjects had completed earlier.

Subjects also participated in the decoding phase of the experiment. They were told that they would be viewing silent videotapes of a set of stimulus persons who were watching a television set and, on the basis of the appearance of the individual they were seeing, should try to determine how pleased the person was feeling. The stimulus persons that were viewed by each of the subjects were a group of ten university-age students who had watched the same three videotapes that had been used in the encoding portion of the experiment. After viewing each videotape, the stimulus persons had been asked to rate how pleased they felt using the same scale that the subjects used in their ratings.

Both the encoding and decoding data were analyzed in terms of the degree of correspondence between the subject's ratings of the tapes and the observer's ratings. In the case of the encoding data, a set of correlations between observer ratings and subject ratings was found for each of the four encoding groups (high and low social skilled, emotionally disturbed and high and low social skilled normals), and these correlations were then entered into a 2 (population) × 2 (level of social skill) analysis of variance. For the decoding data a correlation coefficient was calculated between each subject's judgments and each stimulus person's ratings. These correlations were then entered into an analogous analysis of variance.

Results and Discussion

Encoding

The analysis of variance revealed strong effects both for population and level of social skill. Examination of the means showed that, as predicted, the concordance between the ratings of the emotionally disturbed subjects and the observers was significantly less than with the normal subjects (mean $r = .24$, emotionally disturbed, vs. mean $r = .32$, normal population). Thus, there is clear evidence that the normal subjects were better encoders than the emotionally disturbed subjects. However, even the mean correlation for the emotionally disturbed group was still marginally greater than chance, indicating that subjects in both groups could generally encode successfully—although with varying degrees of success.

There was also a general effect for levels of social skills. The correlations between subject and observer ratings were generally stronger for subjects high in social skill (mean $r = .34$) than for subjects low in social skill (mean $r = .22$). Thus, level of social skill was clearly related to encoding ability. Once again, though, encoding for both the high and low social skills group was better than chance, indicating that even subjects relatively poor in social skills were able to encode at above-chance levels.

Decoding

The analysis of the decoding data showed only one major result. The emotionally disturbed group tended to be significantly less accurate (mean $r = .48$) than the normal group (mean $r = .66$), as predicted. Thus, it appears that the emotionally disturbed group was less successful in using nonverbal behavior to make inferences about the affective experience of the stimulus persons than were the normal persons. Still, even members of the emotionally disturbed group were able to decode the stimulus persons' nonverbal behavior at levels greater than chance. No differences were found according to level of social skills of the subjects. Thus, both high and low skill persons within the normal and emotionally disturbed groups were comparable in their decoding success.

Implications

It is clear from our results that the general level of our subjects' social competence was related to skill in the successful production and interpretation of nonverbal behavior. Subjects who were rated by adults familiar with their behavior as being generally more successful than their peers in their social interactions tended to encode nonverbally in a way that was easier for observers to discern. Likewise, subjects institutionalized for emotional disturbance were less readily decoded than a group of noninstitutionalized peers.

The results of the decoding portion of the study are congruent with the encoding data, although in this case level of social skill does not emerge as a significant factor. What is important is whether the individuals have been labeled as normal or emotionally disturbed; members of the normal group decoded at significantly higher levels than the members of the emotionally disturbed group.

It is important to note that there was significant communication accuracy in both normal and emotionally disturbed groups in both high and low social skills groups, even though there were relative differences between the various groups. Thus, despite deficits in general social skills, subjects still were able to successfully encode and decode. It also bears noting that we have been rather cavalier in describing "success" in decoding and encoding. This is a rather imprecise term, because it suggests more volition on the part of individuals than the Buck paradigm allows (for a fuller discussion, see Buck's chapter, this volume). We have operationalized "success" as a high degree of correspondence between the rated emotional experience of an individual exposed to an emotion-evoking stimulus and a judge's ratings of what that person was experiencing. Because the stimulus persons are in what they consider to be a private situation, we are unable to assess their ability at producing various emotional states that they desire to communicate to others. (Conversely, we are also unable to tell the degree to which they would be able to withhold emotional information that may be a cue to their actual emotional state, something we could tell from our first study.) It is clear, then, that our data are applicable to a rather finite set of circumstances, and it is imperative that future research assess the relationship between social skills and nonverbal behavior in a variety of alternate settings.

Summary and Conclusions

Taken together, the results of these two studies indicate a clear relationship between individuals' social skills and their successful use and interpretation of nonverbal behavior. In the first study, we found that the specific, but crucial, skill of taking the role of the other was related both to encoding and decoding ability. Because role-taking is one of the crucial developments in the growth of social cognition and the ability to interact with others effectively, we view this relationship as an important one. Indeed, knowledge of the nature of the relationship between the encoding and decoding of nonverbal behavior and role-taking skills is intrinsic to an understanding of how social cognition develops generally and how children learn effective impression management techniques. Despite a large body of research examining how verbal language is modified to meet the demands and characteristics of the listener (e.g., Glucksberg, Krauss, & Higgens, 1974), there is little analogous research on the ways in which children learn to modify their nonverbal behavior. The present research is a beginning toward understanding how nonverbal behavior develops as part of self-presentational strategies.

The results of the second study speak to a different, but related set of social skills. Rather than examining a unidimensional ability such as role-taking, we looked at social skills in terms of a set of behaviors that are indicative of good social interaction. We also examined two populations (normals and emotionally disturbed) who would be expected to differ in their level of general social interactional skills. Our results were congruent with the studies examining role-taking abilities: There was a clear relationship between individual differences in social skills and population membership, and nonverbal behavioral skills.

Unfortunately, the tantalizing question of the direction of causality is left unanswered by our studies. It is plausible to assume that skill in the use of nonverbal behavior is a result of such abilities as general social competence. But it is also reasonable to posit the opposite sequences: that skill in the use of nonverbal behavior affects the adeptness of general social skills. (Indeed, we cannot rule out the possibility that some third, unmeasured variable is bringing about changes simultaneously in both social skills and nonverbal behavior.) Future research must be directed towards this question in order to fully explain the role of nonverbal behavior in children's social interaction.

References

Argyle, M. *The psychology of interpersonal behavior*. London: Penguin Books, 1972.

Argyle, M. Social skills theory. In V. L. Allen (Ed.), *Children as teachers: Theory and research on tutoring*. New York: Academic Press, 1976.

Buck, R. Nonverbal communication of affect in children. *Journal of Personality and Social Psychology*, 1975, *31*, 644-653.

Buck, R. Nonverbal communication of affect in preschool children: Relationships with personality and skin conductance. *Journal of Personality and Social Psychology*, 1977, *35*, 225-236.

Buck, R., Miller, R. E., & Caul, W. F. Sex, personality, and physiological variables in the communication of emotion via facial expression. *Journal of Personality and Social Psychology*, 1974, *30*, 587-596.

Charlesworth, W. R. & Kreutzer, M. A. Facial expressions of infants and children. In P. Ekman (Ed.), *Darwin and facial expression*. New York: Academic Press, 1973.

Christensen, D., Farina, A., & Boudreau, L. Sensitivity to nonverbal cues as a function of social competence. *Journal of Nonverbal Behavior*, 1980, *4*, 146-156.

Combs, M. L. & Slaby, D. A. Social skills training with children. In B. B. Lahey & A. E. Kazdin (Eds.), *Advances in clinical child psychology* (Vol. 1). New York: Plenum, 1977.

Cowen, E. L., Pederson, A., Babigan, H., Izzo, L. D., & Trost, M. D. Long-term followup of early-detected vulnerable children. *Journal of Consulting and Clinical Psychology*, 1973, *41*, 438-446.

Darwin, C. *The expression of the emotions in man and animals.* Chicago: The University of Chicago Press, 1965. (Originally published, 1872)

Dashiell, J. F. A new method of measuring reactions for facial expressions of emotion. *Psychological Bulletin*, 1927, *24*, 174-175.

Eisler, R. M. & Frederiksen, L. W. *Perfecting social skills.* New York: Plenum Press, 1980.

Feffer, M. H. The cognitive implications of role-taking behavior. *Journal of Personality*, 1959, *27*, 152-268.

Flavell, J. H., Botkin, P. T., Fry, C. K., Wright, J. C., & Jarvis, P. T. *The development of role-taking and communication skills in children.* New York: John Wiley, 1968.

Gates, G. S. An experimental study of the growth of social perception. *Journal of Educational Psychology*, 1923, *14*, 449-461.

Glucksberg, S., Krauss, R., & Higgens, E. T. The development of referential communication skills. In F. D. Horowitz (Ed.), *Review of child development research.* Vol. IV. New York: Russell Sage Foundation, 1975. Pp. 205-345.

Hall, J. A. Gender effects in decoding nonverbal cues. *Psychological Bulletin*, 1978, *85*, 845-857.

Hall, J. A., Rosenthal, R., Archer, D., DiMatteo, M. R., & Rogers, P. L. The profile of nonverbal sensitivity. In P. McReynolds (Ed.), *Advances in psychological assessment* (Vol. 4). San Francisco: Jossey-Bass, 1978.

Hartup, W., Glazer, J., & Charlesworth, R. Peer reinforcement and sociometric status. *Child Development*, 1967, *38*, 1017-1024.

Herson, M. & Bellack, A. S. Assessment of social skills. In A. R. Ciminero, K. S. Calhouse, & H. E. Adams (Eds.), *Handbook of behavioral assessment.* New York: Wiley, 1977.

Honkavaara, S. The psychology of expression. *British Journal of Psychological Monograph Supplements*, 1961, *32*, 1-96.

Izard, C. E. *The face of emotion.* New York: Appleton-Century-Crofts, 1971.

Mehrabian, A. & Wiener, M. Decoding of inconsistent communication. *Journal of Personality and Social Psychology*, 1967, *6*, 109-114.

O'Connor, R. D. Relative efficacy of modeling, shaping, and the combined procedures for modification of social withdrawal. *Journal of Abnormal Psychology*, 1972, *79*, 327-334.

Odom, R. D. & Lemond, C. M. Developmental differences in the perception and production of facial expressions. *Child Development*, 1972, *43*, 359-369.

Piaget, J. & Inhelder, B. *The psychology of the child.* New York: Basic Books, Inc., 1969.

Roff, M. Childhood social interactions and young adult bad conduct. *Journal of Abnormal Social Psychology*, 1961, *63*, 333-337.

Roff, M., Sells, B., & Golden, M. *Social adjustment and personality development in children.* Minneapolis: University of Minnesota Press, 1972.

Rosenthal, R., Hall, J. A., Archer, D., DiMatteo, M. R., & Rogers, P. L. The PONS test: Measuring sensitivity to nonverbal cues. In S. Weitz (Ed.), *Nonverbal communication* (Rev. ed.). New York: Oxford University Press, 1979.

Rosenthal, R., Hall, J. A., DiMatteo, M. R., Rogers, P. L., & Archer, D. *Sensitivity to nonverbal communication: The PONS test.* Baltimore: The Johns Hopkins University Press, 1979.

Selman, R. L. & Byrne, D. F. A structural-developmental analysis of levels of role-taking in middle childhood. *Child Development*, 1974, *45*, 803-806.

Spitz, R. A. Ontogenesis: The proleptic function of emotion. In P. H. Knapp (Ed.), *Expression of the emotions in man.* New York: International University Press, 1963.

Urberg, K. A. & Docherty, E. M. Development of role-taking skills in young children. *Developmental Psychology*, 1976, *12*, 198-203.

VanHasselt, V. B., Herson, M., Whitehill, M. D., & Bellack, A. S. Social skill assessment and training for children: An evaluative review. *Behavioral Research and Therapy*, 1979, *17*, 413-437.

Watson, S. G. Judgements of emotions from facial and contextual cue combinations. *Journal of Personality and Social Psychology*, 1972, *24*, 334-342.

Whitman, T., Mercurio, J. R., & Caponigri, V. Development of social responses in two severely retraded children. *Journal of Applied Behavior Analysis*, 1970, *3*, 133-138.

Zuckerman, M. & Przewuzman, S. J. Decoding and encoding facial expressions in preschool-age children. *Journal of Environmental Psychology and Nonverbal Behavior*, 1979, *3*, 147-163.

CHAPTER ELEVEN

Individual Differences in the Expressivity of Neonates and Young Infants

Tiffany Field

Individuals may differ in the production and discrimination of facial expressions as early as birth. These differences may relate to other individual characteristics such as temperament, autonomic reactivity, and social responsivity. In this chapter I will briefly review research by others and by our group on individual differences in expressivity at the neonatal stage and during early infancy.

Evidence for Early Individual Differences

Several decades ago Jones (1930, 1935) studied the overt emotional expressions and electrodermal responses of infants and preschool children to stimuli such as a live rat, buzzers, and bells. He noted consistent patterns of overt expressivity and autonomic reactivity which he labelled "externalizer," "internalizer," and "generalizer" (Jones, 1950). Externalizers were overtly expressive with very infrequent galvanic responses, internalizers were the opposite, and generalizers were both overtly and internally responsive. Jones (1960) suggested that infants were extraverted by nature, but during early and later childhood children increasingly control or inhibit their overt expressions, and electrodermal responding increases. Inhibition of overt expressions, Jones claimed, resulted from disapproval and punishment.

More recently, Buck and his colleagues have provided supportive data for the externalizer-internalizer distinction among preschool children and adults (Buck, 1975, 1977; Buck, Miller, & Caul, 1974; Buck, Savin, Miller, & Caul, 1972). Their method of recording expressivity is a slide-viewing paradigm in which pleasant and unpleasant slides are viewed by subjects whose facial expressions are simultaneously videotaped. Judges then guess the types of slides that were viewed by viewing videotapes of the subjects' facial expressions. Buck and his colleagues have generally reported large individual differences in the accuracy of expressions among adults and children, with some people being very expressive and others being impossible to accurately judge. Sex differences were also noted, with females tending to display more accurately guessed expressions and showing less autonomic reactivity starting sometime around the preschool years. In addition, relationships were noted between sending accuracy and psychometric measures of extraversion and between sending accuracy and teachers' ratings of extraversion and self-esteem on Buck's Affect Expression Rating Scale among preschool children (Buck, 1975, 1977). Sending accuracy and the ability to pose emotional expressions were also related among preschool children (Buck, 1975, 1977). Although a more tentative finding among children than adults, relationships have also been reported between sending accuracy and receiving or guessing accuracy (Zuckerman, Lipets, Koivumaki, & Rosenthal, 1975). Finally, negative relationships were noted between sending accuracy and physiological responses with those persons who tended to display easily guessed expressions showing smaller physiological responses (skin conductance or heart rate) (Buck, 1977; Buck, et al., 1972, 1974).

Similarly, in a series of studies with adults Eysenck (1967) noted that facially expressive adults show low level physiological responses. In addition, they rate themselves as more extraverted, have higher thresholds to stimulation, and are more difficult to condition. By contrast, introverted adults are less expressive facially, have lower thresholds to stimulation, show considerable physiological responsivity to stimulation, and are more readily conditioned. Eysenck (1967) suggested that introverts have a lower threshold to activation of the ascending reticular activating system (ARAS) and therefore are more readily conditioned or sensitive to socialization influences. During socialization, overt responses are inhibited and thus the negative relationship between overt expression and electrodermal responding develops in the introverted person. The lower thresholds of the ARAS, and the propensity to introversion, however, is seen as an innate process by Eysenck (1967). The internalizing/externalizing mode of expressivity may be present from birth and merely reinforced or attenuated by socialization experiences.

Gray (1972) modified Eysenck's theory, suggesting that the critical differences between introverts and extraverts is their susceptibility to punishment (not conditioning). He proposed that the locus of physiological activity is the hippocampus and the septal area which acts as a pacemaker for the hippocampal theta rhythm. According to this model, greater amounts of theta activity would indicate greater susceptibility to the inhibitory effects of punishment and/or introversion. Although a number of models have been advanced (cf. Buck, 1979), the underlying physiological mechanisms for the individual differences observed in externalizer/internalizer characteristics remain unclear.

dictive of adult typology (Nebylitsyn, 1972)" (pp. 365-366). Thus, by chance those who have reported successful conditioning of young infants may have recruited high-magnitude orienters or internalizers while those who were unable to show conditioning may have had a preponderance of low-magnitude orienters or externalizers in their sample.

Similarly, individual differences in orienting responses and heart rate variability have been demonstrated for 6- to 24-month-old infants by Hutt and Hutt (1967). Dividing the infants at the median to form high heart rate variability and low variability subgroups, Hutt and Hutt found that the magnitude of orienting decelerations to novel stimuli such as a stranger and a novel toy was greater for the high variability group. The high variability group also showed a shorter duration of visual fixation on the stranger. The authors interpreted this gaze avoidance as a negative affective state of high arousal. In addition, very high rank order correlations were reported for heart rate variability between 6 and 12 months and between 12 and 24 months supporting Lacey's (1967) original suggestion that heart rate variability is a temperamental or consitutional characteristic of the individual.

Finally, in a study by Coll (Note 2) 21 and 22-month-old infants were divided on the basis of inhibited/uninhibited responsivity to novel stimulation. As had been reported previously by Kagan and colleagues (Kagan, Kearsley, & Zelazo, 1978), inhibited infants showed less variable and higher heart rates than uninhibited infants, another finding of individual differences among young infants that is consistent with an externalizer/internalizer dimension.

Thus, the very few infant studies that have reported individual differences have somewhat consistently suggested differences on measures comprising the externalizer/internalizer or extraverted/introverted typology, i.e., expressivity, autonomic reactivity, thresholds and conditionability. Unfortunately, all of these measures were not included in any one study. In the following studies at the neonatal and early infancy stages, we collected data on a number of the measures included in the externalizer/internalizer typology by Jones (1960), Eysenck (1967), and Buck (1979). Unfortunately, one or two of the measures are occasionally missing because we only became aware of the externalizer/internalizer model and literature after the completion of these studies when we were searching for possible interpretations of the data.

A Study on Neonatal Differences in Facial Expressivity

This study (Field, Woodson, Greenberg, & Cohen, 1982) was designed to observe the production and discrimination of facial expressions by neonates. Thresholds to stimulation and physiological activity were recorded to determine the extent to which neonates' physiological reactivity was related to facial expressiveness. We considered that since the cataloging of adult expressions had recently been adapted for infants (Oster, 1978), the facial expressions of neonates could be more systematically investigated at this time. Oster and Ekman (1978), using a fine-grained measurement system, have confirmed that all but one of the discrete facial muscle actions visible in the adult can be identified and finely discriminated in newborns. Given these data and the anecdotal evidence for various neonatal facial expressions offered by Watson (1919) and Wolff (1963), we anticipated finding some of the basic facial expressions in neonates. Our questions were: (1) do infants spontaneously emit any of the basic eight facial expressions or can these be elicited? (2) can infants discriminate these facial expressions? and (3) is there evidence for a relationship among facial expressiveness, stimulus thresholds, and physiological responsivity in neonates?

We observed the following behaviors in 74 sleeping neonates: sleep state, activity level, facial expressions, and heart rate. A series of five pin-pricks was then administered as in the Brazelton Neonatal Behavior Assessment Scale (Brazelton, 1973) to determine the sleeping neonates' threshold to tactile stimuli. The neonates' cry sounds were recorded; latency to cry and cry duration were measured. A series of buzzer tones were then presented and the infants' thresholds for the auditory stimulation were calculated and cardiac responses to these were concurrently monitored. These were followed by an administration of the Brazelton Scale while we continuously filmed the neonates' facial expressions. Finally, the neonates' discrimination between three facial expressions (happy, sad, and surprised) were assessed during a trials-to-criterion habituation procedure.

The auditory threshold assessment involved presenting a series of four buzzer tones varying in intensity from 80-110 db (the hypothesized range in which orienting and defensive responses might be elicited). These were presented for 1½ sec periods with an interstimulus interval of 20 seconds.

Filming of the facial expressions during Brazelton items was done with a zoom lens focused on the neonate's face so that judges might observe facial expressions without stimulus or situation cues. The babies' faces were filmed during the following stimulus presentations: (1) orienting stimuli; face alone, voice alone, face and voice, inanimate auditory (rattle to each side of face), inanimate visual (red ball tracked across field of vision); and (2) the 20 Brazelton reflex maneuvers. The infant's expressions were then coded, using a catalog of eight basic emotions (happy, sad, fearful, interested, surprised, ashamed, angry, or disgusted), by research assistants trained on photographs of children modelling those expressions.

Preliminary analyses of the facial expressions produced during the Brazelton examination revealed that several expressions occurred at greater than chance frequencies to specific stimuli. The face and voice orientation stimulus and the first animate and inanimate auditory orientation stimuli produced an interested expression. The second animate and inanimate auditory orientation stimuli presented to the opposite side of the head from the initial presentation, and the tonic neck deviation reflex maneuver elicited surprised expressions in the neonates. Sad or pre-cry grimaces were elicited by the tonic neck reflex. Elicitation of the Moro reflex produced fearful facial expressions. Disgusted faces were elicited during the insertion of a (soapy tasting) finger when evaluating the sucking reflex. Ashamed and angry facial expressions were not observed. While happy expressions (smiles) occurred with moderate frequency during sleep, these were rarely observed during awake states except occasionally during the elicitation of rooting.

Neonates' ability to discriminate among happy, sad, and surprised expressions modeled by the examiner was assessed using a trials-to-criterion habituation procedure. Although there are no published studies on discrimination of facial expressions by neonates, we hypothesized that they would be capable of discriminating facial expressions since (1) neonates can discriminate scrambled from regular faces (Goren, Sarty, & Wu, 1975), (2) neonates can imitate facial movements such as tongue protrusion and mouth widening (Meltzoff & Moore, 1977), and (3) slightly older infants (3-months-old) can discriminate happy from surprised faces using a trials-to-criterion habituation paradigm (Young-Browne, Rosenfeld, & Horowitz, 1977).

For the faces habituation procedure, the model held the neonate in an upright position with the newborn's face located approximately 10 inches from her face. The neonate's visual fixation on the adult's face and the neonate's facial movement patterns were recorded by an observer who stood behind the model in order to see the infant's face but to remain unaware of the expression being modelled. Split-screen videotaping of the neonates' and model's faces provided checks on the reliability of coding by observer and face presentation by model. With practice the model was able to reliably "fix" the same expressions with very minimal variability across trials and subjects.

To sustain alertness and elicit the neonate's visual fixations on the model's face, the model provided vestibular stimulation (two deep knee bends) and auditory stimulation (two tongue clicks) prior to each trial. The model then fixed one of these expressions on her face: a happy, sad, or surprised expression. Three series of trials or one series for each face was presented in a counter-balanced Greco-Latin square order to control for state change effects. Face 1 was sustained in a fixed position until the infant looked away from the model's face, at which time the model re-elicited the neonate's visual fixation with vestibular and auditory stimulation. Face 1 trials were repeated until the neonate looked at that face for less than two seconds. Face 2 and Face 3 trials were then presented using the same trials-to-criterion habituation procedure (see Figure 11-1 for modelled faces).

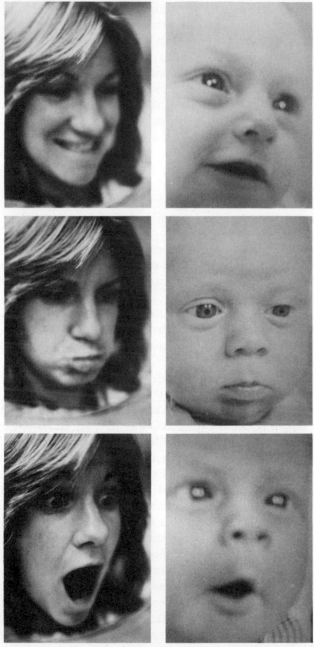

Figure 11-1. Sample photographs of model's happy, sad, and surprised expressions and infant's corresponding expressions.

The observer coded on a paper grid for each trial the following: (1) total time per trial; (2) predominant target and pattern of neonatal visual fixation per trial on the model's eyes, mouth, or alternately on

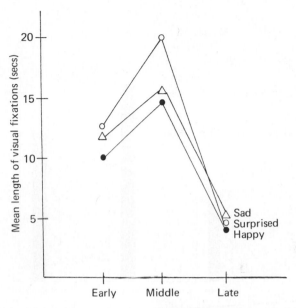

Figure 11-2. Mean length (in seconds) of visual fixations on facial expressions averaged over early, middle, and late trials.

the eyes and mouth; (3) the presence of specific mouth movements of the neonate, including widening of the lips (as in a happy face), tight and somewhat protruded lips (pouting or sad face), wide opening of the mouth (as in a surprised face), or tongue protrusion; (4) presence or absence of eye widening (as in a surprise face); (5) presence of relaxed or furrowed brow (as in happy or sad face, respectively); and (6) observer's guess as to which expression was being modelled.

There were no significant effects of order or trials or type of facial expression in the habituation-dishabituation procedure. Visual fixations significantly decreased from the middle to late trials (M decrease = 11.5 secs) and significantly increased from the late trials of the facial expression to the early trials of the subsequent expression (M = 8.5 secs). Thus, the visual habituation and dishabituation of the face stimuli suggest that neonates can discriminate at least these three basic facial expressions (see Figure 11-2).

Figure 11-3 illustrates selective fixations and looking patterns for different features of the different faces. The neonate visually fixated the mouth region and alternately looked at the mouth and eye regions for a greater proportion of the trials than the eye region, irrespective of the facial expression being modelled. The neonate's alternating fixations on the mouth and the eye region occurred during a greater proportion of the surprise expression trials than for the other facial expressions. Fixations on the mouth region occurred for a greater proportion of trials

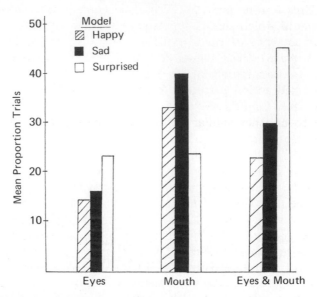

Figure 11-3. Mean proportion of trials during which the predominant pattern of visual fixations occurred in the region of the eyes, mouth, or alternately on the eyes and mouth as a function of the expression modelled. Proportions do not total 100 because a predominant pattern did not occur for approximately 17% of trials.

during happy and sad than surprised expressions. The model's surprise expression features salient eye and mouth positions (both widened), while the happy and sad expressions are characterized primarily by salient mouth positions, widening of the lips for the happy expression and tightened, protruding lips for the sad expression (see Figure 11-1). These differential visual fixation patterns suggest that the neonate can perceive distinctive features of these facial expressions, i.e., the mouth in the case of the happy and sad faces, and both the mouth and eyes in the case of the surprised expression.

Figure 11-4 depicts the proportion of trials on which differential mouth movements were observed during the different face trials. Because of the problem posed by different baseline frequencies, the distributions of each behavior were analyzed separately across the different expressions modelled. There were no differences in the proportion of trials that tongue protrusion occurred as a function of different facial expressions. However, widened eyes and wide mouth opening occurred for a greater proportion of surprise than other face trials. Lip widening occurred more frequently during happy face trials, and tightened mouth/protruding lips and furrowed brow occurred more frequently during sad expression trials. Comparison of the occurrence of these facial movements across the expressions for which these movements would not be expected (omitting the imitative expressions movements corresponding to the modelled expressions) yielded no significant differences. This finding provides additional support that the neonate's facial movements which simulate those of the model are attributable to imitation. An analysis of early, middle, and late trials data for these expressions revealed that a greater proportion of these expressions occurred during the middle trials, suggesting that these were not arousal responses or fixed action patterns. As Meltzoff and Moore (1977) have suggested, if each infant's response to one expression is compared to his response to another similar expression demonstrated by the same adult at the same distance from the infant and under the same conditions, then if differential imitation occurs, it cannot be attributed to a mere arousal of activity by a human face.

Analyses of the observer's guesses included only those data for each subject's first series of trials. The chance probability of correctly guessing the facial expression would be 33%. The surprise facial expressions were correctly guessed 76% of the trials, at a significantly greater than chance level. Surprise expressions were correctly guessed more often than happy expressions (58%) or sad expressions (59%). However, the happy and sad expressions were also correctly guessed at significantly greater than chance levels. The surprise expression shows two salient features in two regions (eyes and mouth). When the infant reproduces

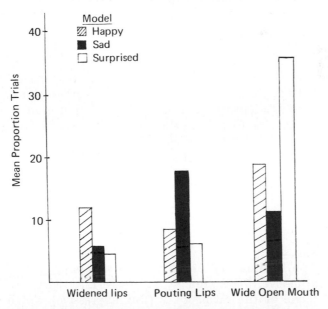

Figure 11-4. Mean proportion of trials during which different neonatal mouth movements occurred as a function of facial expression modelled. Mouth movements include widened lips (as in happy expression), pouting lips (sad), and wide open mouth (surprised). Proportions do not total 100 because these discrete movements occurred predominantly during the middle trials (approximately 39% of the trials).

both of these features, the probability of an accurate guess by the observer is increased.

These results, then, suggest that the neonate is capable of discriminating at least these three different facial expressions. Ensuring that the infant was in an alert stage and using a trials-to-criterion habituation procedure so that each infant could process the information at his or her own pace may have facilitated the demonstration of facial discriminations.

The imitative expressions provide support for the data previously reported by Meltzoff and Moore (1977) on imitative gestures by 12 to 21-day-old infants. These authors suggested three potential underlying mechanisms including shaping of the response by the model, an innate releasing mechanism, and the neonate's capacity to integrate visual and proprioceptive information. Consistent with their conclusions (Meltzoff & Moore, 1977), the videotapes of the model's behaviors suggest that shaping or reinforcing of the neonate's responses did not occur. Although fixing a face is not easy and may produce some muscle movement, there were no discernible movements on the model's face. That these imitations might be based on an innate releasing mechanism or fixed action pattern is also unlikely given the organization and lack of stereotypy of the infants' differential responses to these three different facial expressions. Instead, we favor the view of Meltzoff and Moore (1977) that there is an innate ability to compare the sensory information of a visually perceived expression (as evidenced in this study by their ability to discriminate the facial expressions) with the proprioceptive feedback of the motor movements involved in matching that expression (as manifested by their differential responses to the facial expression). In any case, the imitation of facial expressions by neonates may be viewed as adaptive inasmuch as it may elicit more nurturing and responsive behaviors from parents, their responsivity being facilitated by infant imitative behaviors (Field, 1979).

Of greater interest here perhaps are the individual differences that emerged in this study. First, there were very few sex differences. The boys showed a more immediate cry response to the pinpricks, and their mean looking time was shorter for the happy face trials. In addition, they showed less scanning-type visual fixations, but only during the happy face trials.

Infant expressivity was rated by the observer during the course of the face imitation/habituation procedure on a 5-point Likert-type scale (1 = not expressive, 5 = extremely expressive). A division of the infants was then made at the rating of 2 (low expressive) which by chance yielded a median split of the sample with half of the infants ($N = 37$) having received ratings of 1 or 2 and half receiving ratings of 3 or greater.

Analyses of differences between the low and high expressive groups yielded the following: (1) high expressive infants received more optimal

Brazelton interactive, state organization, and response to stress scores, (2) low expressive infants had a higher mean heart rate but lower heart rate variability during sleep, (3) low expressive infants had a longer mean latency to crying during the pinprick procedure, (4) high expressive infants looked longer during the later trials of the series of faces, (5) high expressive infants showed more scanning-like visual fixations during the surprised face trials, (6) high expressive infants' facial expressions were guessed accurately a greater proportion of the time, and (7) high expressive infants showed more frequent imitative expressions, e.g., more frequent widened lips during happy face trials, more frequent furrowed brows and protruded lips during sad expressions, and more eye and mouth widening during surprised expressions.

These data suggest that the high expressive infants were more socially responsive during the Brazelton interaction items and were more modulated or less irritable in their responses to stimulation and particularly to stressful stimulation during the Brazelton scale. While the Brazelton scale data would suggest that the high expressive infants were less aroused, showing higher sensory thresholds and less intense responses to stimulation, analyses of responses on specific items of the Brazelton require a larger sample.

During sleep the high expressive infants showed a lower mean heart rate but greater heart rate variability than the low expressive infants. Coll (Note 1) similarly found that infants who were uninhibited in their behavior had lower resting mean heart rate but greater heart rate variability. Similarly, during auditory stimulation trials, the high expressive infants showed lower mean heart rate but greater heart rate variability. Unfortunately, because of concerns about movement artifacts, neither our group nor Coll (Note 1) collected heart rate data during the actual procedure for which the expressive or uninhibited behaviors were collected (in our case, the face habituation trials). These kind of data would more directly address the hypothesized negative relationship between facial expressivity and autonomic reactivity. Another problem which will require further study is the relationship between electrodermal responding (the autonomic measure most frequently used in the externalizer/internalizer studies) and heart rate measures (mean heart rate and heart rate variability).

The longer looking at the face stimuli during the late trials suggests that the high expressive infants less readily habituated to the face stimuli, a finding that is somewhat similar to Eysenck's (1967) data on extraverted adults who were less readily conditioned. Finally, the greater incidence of correctly guessed facial expressions and imitative expressions by the high expressive group suggests that the expressive neonates were not indiscriminately expressive but displayed specific facial movements which simulated those of the model.

Thus, there are significant individual differences between high and low expressive infants in their attentiveness, responsivity to social stimulation, autonomic reactivity, and sending accuracy soon after birth. Although these data are also suggestive of an externalizer/internalizer typology (Buck, 1975; Jones, 1950), or the extraverted/introverted distinction proposed by Eysenck (1967) with expressive infants being less reactive autonomically, having higher thresholds and being less readily habituated to the face stimuli, these relationships are tenuous. More precise measurement of sensory thresholds and the habituation process and simultaneous measurement of autonomic and overt behaviors during the faces procedure would provide a more direct assessment of the externalizer/internalizer question.

A Study on Differences in Expressivity Among Young Infants

This study (Stoller & Field, 1982) like the neonatal study, was not designed to investigate individual differences in expressivity or the externalizer/internalizer model. But the data that emerged from this study are illustrative of early individual differences in expressivity, the mode of expressivity, or the externalizer/internalizer typology. The purpose of this study was to test an affect model formulated by Sroufe and Waters (1976) and tested earlier by Fogel and colleagues (Fogel, Diamond, Langhorst, & Demos, 1981) in the context of an early mother-infant interaction situation.

A model of infant emotion developed by Sroufe and his colleagues (Sroufe, 1979; Sroufe & Waters, 1976) postulates an association between emotional expressions and tension release. Increasing tension occurs with the infant's increasing attention to a stimulus and an effort to process stimulus content. At this point, the infant can assimilate the event and experience a pleasurable decrease in tension characterized by smiling and laughter (Sroufe, Waters, & Matas, 1974; Tomkins, 1962).

Fogel and his colleagues (1981) assessed Sroufe's tension release model utilizing a still-face paradigm (an interaction situation during which the mother becomes still-faced). They recorded mother-infant face-to-face interactions using the following procedure: The mother and her infant participated in a natural face-to-face interaction. The mother then left the infant alone. When she returned, she assumed the still-face posture following either the infant's first look or the infant's first smile. Another natural face-to-face interaction followed the still-face condition.

Each infant was randomly assigned to one of two groups prior to the session. In the first group, the experimenter signaled the mother to begin the still-face as soon as the infant first looked at her and in the second group, after the infant's first smile. Fogel et al. (1981) postulated that the infant's first look at the mother would be accompanied by increasing tension whereas the infant's first smile would represent decreasing tension. Their findings confirmed that when the still-face was presented following the infant's first look, significantly more gaze averting and distress behavior occurred than when the still-face followed the first smile. These findings suggest that the first look group may have been experiencing increasing tension and the first smile group decreasing tension.

In our attempt to replicate this study (Stoller & Field, 1982) we added an additional control group, a late look group of infants whose mothers were asked to go still-face on a second or third occasion that the infant looked at her. In addition, we recorded heart rate during the entire procedure as an independent measure of tension or arousal. Although there were trends in our behavioral data which partially replicated the findings of Fogel et al. (1981) and lent support to theirs and the Sroufe et al. (1976) models, our heart rate data did not suggest that the first or late look groups were more aroused physiologically than the first smile group either at the onset of the mother's still-face or during the first 10 seconds of the still-face. Although the heart rate curves suggested that heart rate was slowly accelerating for the first look group at the onset of the still-face and decelerating for the first smile group at the onset of the still-face (in accord with the Fogel et al., 1981, and Sroufe et al., 1976, models), heart rate was also decelerating for the late look group. The cardiac change in this group is contrary to the prediction of the model, and none of these shifts in heart rate at the onset of the still-face were significant either within groups or between groups.

There are several possible interpretations of these data. First, the literature suggests that both looking (Graham & Clifton, 1966) and smiling (Provost & Decarie, 1979) behaviors are accompanied by cardiac decelerations. Thus, cardiac deceleration in the late look and the first smile groups is not necessarily inconsistent. Cardiac acceleration in the first look group may represent increasing arousal or may be the effect of antagonistic action on the heart of both looking and movement, with the motor activity contributing to an acceleration.

Secondly, the cardiac change may lag behind the behavior. However, by two seconds post onset of the still-face, the two groups who were showing a deceleration just prior to the onset (the first smile and late look infants) evidenced acceleration, and the first look infants, who were experiencing a cardiac acceleration at the onset were, by two seconds post onset, showing a deceleration. Thus, shifts in the direction of heart rate were parallel for the first smile and late look groups (contrary to the prediction of the model). By second four, all three groups showed a deceleration and by second seven an acceleration. A behavioral interpretation of these parallel, directional changes in heart rate may be that all three groups experienced a "what's happening?" orienting response, followed by an aversive response to the still-face mother.

However, the behaviors occurring at the time of the acceleration were somewhat different across groups.

The first smile group showed distress brow and motor activity, the first look group motor activity and gazing away, and the late look group distress brow, motor activity, and crying. Despite the distress brow and crying behavior of the late look group, the heart rate of the late look group showed no significant change. Thus, the late look group appeared to be expressing distress primarily in its behavior with only minimal change in heart rate. This is surprising inasmuch as distress brow contributed a signficant amount to the variance on heart rate, suggesting that distress brow behavior is typically associated with an increase in cardiac activity. The late look group infants showed distress brow during every second of the still face, and this was observed among several of the infants in that group. While the first smile group also showed distress brow for almost all of this period, fewer numbers showed distress brow than in the late look group. Fewer infants of the first look group showed distress brow and for fewer seconds. Just as the late look group was showing distress primarily in their behavior, the first look group appeared to manifest their distress primarily in cardiac activity. The first smile group, on the contrary, appeared to manifest their distress in both distress brow behavior and cardiac activity.

Because a significant amount of the heart rate variance was explained by distress brow, the absence of significant cardiac change in that group which was showing the greatest incidence of distress brow (late look) is surprising. It could be that different types of infants were pre-assigned to groups by using the behavior criterion of first look, first smile, and late look, netting a self-selection confound. These infants may correspond to those described by Jones (1960) or to the three types of adults described by Eysenck (1967), i.e., the internalizers, externalizers, and generalizers. A possible interpretation of the distress brow/cardiac activity relationship in these data is that the infants assigned to our first look group were internalizer types (lesser incidence of distress brow but significant cardiac change), our late look infants were externalizers (greater incidence distress brow but minimal cardiac reactivity), and our first smile infants were generalizers (moderate incidence of distress brow and significant cardiac reactivity). Thus, the late look group may not have shown the physiological change predicted by the Sroufe et al. (1967) and Fogel et al. (1981) models simply because they were less reactive physiologically.

While these data, then, do not provide strong support for the models of Sroufe et al. (1967) and Fogel et al. (1981), they do not refute them either. Rather they suggest that there may be individual differences in the degree to which distress responses are evidenced behaviorally and/or physiologically. The procedure used here for assignment of infants to conditions based on their behaviors may have inadvertently confounded the assignment of the behavioral/cardiac relationship in response to stress. Nonetheless, the complexity of the relationships noted highlights the importance of investigating individual differences in the behavioral and physiological components of infants' affective responses to changes in their mothers' behaviors.

The Significance of Detecting Early Individual Differences in Expressivity

According to Eysenck (1967) approximately 60% of adults are generalizers or both overtly expressive and internally reactive, 20% are externalizers, and 20% internalizers. Although he speculates that individual differences in expressivity are innate, the evidence from our studies is only weakly supportive. Clearly, a more direct investigation of that typology and a longitudinal study from the neonatal stage to at least the preschool years is needed to trace the origins and development of individual differences in expressivity.

Our data, however, do underscore the importance of detecting early individual differences in expressivity. Expressive neonates begin life with the advantage of being socially responsive, as evidenced by superior Brazelton interactive scores which, in turn, contributes to better interactions with their parents. At the preschool stage more expressive children are more popular (Buck, 1975; Field & Walden, 1982) and experience more positive social interactions with their peers (Field, Note 2). Children's sending accuracy or expressivity at this stage is a factor that highly correlates with friendship selection; friends tend to select each other in part by the extent to which they match each other on the degree of expressivity (Field, Note 2). In addition to experiencing less difficulty interacting with people, externalizers may experience less physiological arousal and less stress-related disease. While speculative, these possibilities highlight the need for more intensive and longitudinal research on individual differences in expressivity. The data we have reviewed suggest that these differences may first occur as early as birth.

Acknowledgments. I would like to thank the mothers and infants for their participation, and Debra Cohen, Reena Greenberg, Sherilyn Stoller, and Robert Woodson for their assistance in conducting these studies. This investigation was supported by a Research Scientist Development Award, #1 K02 MH003311-01, from the ADAMHA awarding institute, NIMH, and by grants from the National Foundation-March of Dimes and the Administration for Children, Youth and Families.

Reference Notes

1. Coll, C. G. Psychophysiological correlates of a tendency toward inhibition in infants. Paper presented at the Biennial Meeting of the Society for Research in Child Development, Boston, April 1981.
2. Field, T. *Individual differences in friendship patterns.* Unpublished manuscript. University of Miami, 1981.
3. Fitzgerald, H. E. & Brackbill, Y. *Stimulus-response organization, state and conditionability in young infants.* Paper presented at the biennial meetings of the Society for Research in Child Development, Philadelphia, 1973.

References

Birns, B., Barten, S., & Bridges, W. H. Individual differences in temperamental characteristics of infants. *Transactions, New York Academy of Sciences*, 1969.

Brazelton, T. B. *Neonatal behavioral assessment scale* Philadelphia: J. B. Lippincott Co., 1973.

Buck, R. Nonverbal communication of affect in children. *Journal of Personality and Social Psychology*, 1975, *31*, 4, 644-653.

Buck, R. Nonverbal communication of affect in preschool children: Relationships with personality and skin conductance. *Journal of Personality and Social Psychology*, 1977, *35*, 225-236.

Buck, R. Individual differences in nonverbal sending accuracy and electrodermal responding. The externalizing-internalizing dimension. In R. Rosenthal (Ed.), *Skill in nonverbal communication: Individual differences.* Cambridge, MA: Oelgeschlager, Gunn & Hain, 1979.

Buck, R., Miller, R., & Caul, W. Sex, personality, and physiological variables in the communication of affect via facial expression. *Journal of Personality and Social Psychology*, 1974, *30*, 4, 587-596.

Buck, R., Savin, V. J., Miller, R. E., & Caul, W. F. Communication of affect through facial expression in humans. *Journal of Personality and Social Psychology*, 1972, *23*, 362-371.

Campos, J., Emde, R., Gaensbauer, T., & Henderson, C. Cardiac and behavioral interrelationships in the reactions of infants to strangers. *Developmental Psychology*, 1975, *11*, 589-601.

Eysenck, H. J. *The biological basis of personality.* Springfield, IL: Charles C. Thomas, 1967.

Field, T. Games parents play with normal and high-risk infants. *Child Psychiatry and Human Development*, 1979, *10*, 41-48.

Field, T. & Walden, T. Production and perception of facial expressions in infancy and early childhood. In H. Reese & L. Lipsitt (Eds.), *Advances in child development* (Vol. 16). New York: Academic Press, 1982.

Field, T., Woodson, R., Greenberg, R., & Cohen, D. Discrimination and imitation of facial expressions by neonates. *Science*, 1982, in press.

Fogel, A., Diamond, G. R., Langhorst, B. H., & Demos, V. Affective and cognitive aspects of the two-month old's participation in face-to-face interaction with its mother. In E. Tronick (Ed.), *Joint regulation of behavior.* Cambridge, England: Cambridge University Press, 1981.

Goren, C. C., Sarty, M., & Wu, P. Y. K. Visual following and pattern discrimination of face-like stimuli by newborn infants. *Pediatrics*, 1975, *56*, 544-549.

Graham, F. K. & Clifton, R. K. Heart rate change as a component of the orienting response. *Psychological Bulletin*, 1966, *65*, 305-320.

Gray, J. A. The psychophysiological nature of introversion-extraversion: A modification of Eysenck's theory. In V. D. Nebylitsyn & J. A. Gray (Eds.). *Biobehavioral bases of individual behavior*. New York: Academic Press, 1972.

Hutt, C. & Hutt, S. J. Heart rate variability: The adaptive consequences of individual differences and state changes. *Human Behaviors and Adaptation*, 1967.

Ingram, E. & Fitzgerald, H. E. Individual differences in infant orienting and autonomic conditioning. *Developmental Psychobiology*, 1974, *7*, 359-367.

Jones, H. E. The galvanic skin reflex as related to overt emotional expression. *Child Development*, 1930, *1*, 106-110.

Jones, H. E. The galvanic skin reflex as related to overt emotional expression. *American Journal of Psychology*, 1935, *47*, 241-251.

Jones, H. E. The study of patterns of emotional expression. In M. Reyment (Ed.), *Feelings and emotions*. New York: McGraw-Hill, 1950.

Jones, H. E. The longitudinal method in the study of personality. In I. Iscoe & H. W. Stevenson (Eds.), *Personality development in children*. Chicago: University of Chicago Press, 1960.

Kagan, J., Kearsley, R. B., & Zelazo, P. R. *Infancy: Its place in human development*. Cambridge, MA: Harvard University Press, 1978.

Lacey, J. I. Somatic response patterning and stress: Some revisions of activation theory. In M. H. Appley & R. Trumbull (Eds.), *Psychological stress: Issues in research*. New York: Appleton-Century-Crofts, 1967.

Lewis, M., Brooks, J., & Haviland, J. Hearts and faces: A study in the measurement of emotion. In M. Lewis & L. A. Rosenblum (Eds.), *The development of affect* (Vol. 1). New York: Plenum Press, 1978.

Meltzoff, A. N. & Moore, M. K. Imitation of facial and manual gestures by human neonates. *Science*, 1977, *198*, 75-78.

Nebylitsyn, V. D. *Basic properties of the nervous system in man*. New York: Plenum, 1972.

Oster, H. Facial expression and affect development. In M. Lewis & L. Rosenblum (Eds.), *The development of affect* (Vol. 1). New York: Plenum Press, 1978.

Oster, H. & Ekman, P. Facial behavior in child development. In *Minnesota Symposium on Child Psychology* (Vol. 11). Minneapolis: University of Minnesota Press, 1978.

Provost, A. M. & Gouin-Decarie, T. Heart rate reactivity of 9- and 12-month-old infants showing specific emotions in natural settings. *International Journal of Behavior Development*, 1979, *2*, 109-120.

Sroufe, L. A. Socioemotional development. In J. D. Osofsky (Ed.), *Handbook of infant development*. New York: John Wiley & Sons, 1979.

Sroufe, L. A. & Waters, E. The ontogenesis of smiling and laughter: A perspective on the organization of development in infancy. *Psychological Review*, 1976, *83*, 173-189.

Sroufe, L. A., Waters, E., & Matas, L. Contextual determinants of infant affective response. In M. Lewis & L. Rosenblum (Eds.), *The origins of behavior, Vol. 2: Fear*. New York: Wiley, 1974.

Stoller, S. & Field, T. Alteration of mother and infant behavior and heart rate during a still-face perturbation of face-to-face interaction. In T. Field & A. Fogel (Eds.), *Emotion and interactions*. New York: Lawrence Erlbaum Associates, 1982.

Tomkins, S. S. *Affect, imagery, consciousness* Vol. 2: *The positive affects.* New York: Springer, 1962.

Tomkins, S. S. & McCarter, R. What and where are the primary affects? Some evidence for a theory. *Perceptual and Motor Skills*, 1964, *18*, 119-158.

Waters, E., Matas, L., & Sroufe, L. A. Infants' reactions to an approaching stranger: Description validation, and functional significance of wariness. *Child Development*, 1975, *46*, 348-356.

Watson, J. B. *Psychology from the standpoint of a behaviorist.* Philadelphia: Lippincott, 1919.

Wolff, P. H. Observations on the early development of smiling. In B. Foss (Ed.), *Determinants of infant behavior.* New York: Wiley, 1963.

Young-Brown, G., Rosenfeld, H. M., & Horowitz, F. D. Infant discrimination of facial expressions. *Child Development*, 1977, *48*, 555-562.

Zuckerman, M., Lipets, M., Koivumaki, J., & Rosenthal, R. Encoding and decoding nonverbal cues of emotion. *Journal of Personality and Social Psychology*, 1975, *32*, 1068-1076.

Author Index

Subject Index